THE AUTOMOBILE IN AMERICA

The American Heritage History of

THE AUTOMOBILE IN AMERICA

by Stephen W. Sears

Published by American Heritage Publishing Co., Inc., New York
Book Trade Distribution by Simon and Schuster, Inc., New York

We are grateful for permission to quote from these copyrighted works:
—page 22: *Horseless Carriage Days,* by Hiram Percy Maxim. Copyright 1936, 1937 by Harper & Brothers. Reprinted by permission of the publisher.
—page 40: *Brownstone Front,* by Guy Gilpatric. Copyright 1934 by Dodd, Mead & Company. Reprinted by permission of the publisher.
—page 62: "Racing with Lozier: A Memoir," by Ralph Mulford, in *Automobile Quarterly,* Vol. 7, No. 4 (1969). Copyright © 1969 by Automobile Quarterly, Inc. Reprinted by permission of the publisher.
—pages 102 and 147: "Farewell, My Lovely!" by Lee Strout White (a collaboration between E. B. White and Richard L. Strout). Originally in *The New Yorker.* © 1936, 1964 The New Yorker Magazine, Inc.
—page 120: *Forty Years on Main Street,* by William Allen White. Copyright 1937 by William Allen White. Reprinted by permission of Holt, Rinehart & Winston.
—page 139: *Henry Ford: An Interpretation,* by Samuel S. Marquis. Copyright 1923 by Little, Brown and Company. Reprinted by permission of the publisher.
—page 169: *Life of an American Workman,* by Walter P. Chrysler. Copyright 1937, 1950 by Walter P. Chrysler, Jr., and published by Dodd, Mead & Company. Reprinted by permission of Walter P. Chrysler, Jr.
—page 270: Reprinted by permission from *Time,* The Weekly Newsmagazine (February 9, 1942); Copyright Time Inc. 1942.
—page 278: *The Best Years, 1945–1950,* by Joseph C. Goulden. Copyright © 1976 by Joseph C. Goulden and published by Atheneum. Reprinted by permission of the publisher.
—page 303: "Halfway to the Moon on Wheels," by R.L. Heilbroner in *Petroleum Today* (Spring, 1960). Copyright © 1960 by *Petroleum Today.* Reprinted by permission of the publisher.
—page 306: "Naming the Edsel," by David Wallace, in *Automobile Quarterly,* Vol. 13, No. 2 (1975). Copyright © 1975 by Automobile Quarterly, Inc. Reprinted by permission of the publisher.
—page 314: *Unsafe at Any Speed,* by Ralph Nader. Copyright © 1965 by Grossman Publishers. Reprinted by permission of The Viking Press, Inc.
—page 331: *The Road and the Car in American Life,* by John B. Rae. Copyright © 1971 by The Massachusetts Institute of Technology. Reprinted by permission of The Massachusetts Institute of Technology Press.
—page 324: *The New York Times,* May 15, 1977. © 1977 by The New York Times Company. Reprinted by permission.

AMERICAN HERITAGE BOOKS
EDITOR-IN-CHIEF Ezra Bowen

THE AMERICAN HERITAGE HISTORY OF
THE AUTOMOBILE IN AMERICA
AUTHOR/EDITOR Stephen W. Sears
ART DIRECTOR Murray Belsky
ASSOCIATE ART DIRECTOR Marion Flynn Logan
PICTURE EDITORS Douglas Tunstell, Myra M. Mangan
COPY EDITOR Helen C. Dunn

AMERICAN HERITAGE PUBLISHING CO., INC.
CHAIRMAN OF THE BOARD Samuel P. Reed
PRESIDENT AND PUBLISHER Rhett Austell
EDITORIAL ART DIRECTOR Murray Belsky

Library of Congress Cataloging in Publication Data: p. 352
ISBN: 0-8281-0200-7 (regular)
    0-8281-0201-5 (de luxe)

Book Trade Distribution by Simon and Schuster, Inc.
ISBN: 0-671-22986-9 (regular)
    0-671-22987-7 (de luxe)

Ernst Haas took the photograph on the title pages from the driver's seat of a vintage Model T on a backwoods road in Tennessee in 1962. The picture of the patriotically decorated Cole on page 6 was taken by Floyd Gunnison in Canandaigua, New York, in 1916; it is from the International Museum of Photography, George Eastman House.

For Kathryn and Jeffrey, and for Sally

CONTENTS

INTRODUCTION

In 1978 the American automobile industry celebrates three significant milestones: the seventy-fifth anniversary of the founding of the Ford Motor Company, the seventieth anniversary of the founding of General Motors, and the seventieth anniversary of the birth of the most famous motorcar of them all, Henry Ford's ubiquitous Model T. These seminal events, occurring in the opening decade of the century, touched off a revolution of sufficient force to change the face of the nation and to alter radically the fundamental living patterns of its citizens. No other single instrument of twentieth-century technology has affected more lives more profoundly in more ways than the automobile. It became, writes historian Daniel J. Boorstin, "a providential instrument for a people with much space and little time"; within an astonishingly short period, it had "diffused and leveled and stirred and homogenized a continent-civilization."

The Automobile in America is a detailed chronicle, in text and in more than 350 illustrations, of this momentous revolution. It is a synthesis of concurrent themes. It narrates the history of the machines themselves, from the earliest struggling efforts to achieve practical self-propulsion to the latest efforts to achieve energy-efficient vehicles. At the same time, it records the parallel tale of the rise of the automobile industry to its position as a bellwether of the national economy, and of the remarkable cast of characters who created and nourished this industrial empire. Finally, these pages recount the many complexities of the automobile culture, which has become so deeply embedded in the American social fabric that as a people we can neither recall nor face a life without cars.

Virtually every aspect of the automotive phenomenon in the United States has been documented pictorially, and the photographs, drawings, paintings, prints, illustrations, and memorabilia accompanying the narrative have been drawn from a wide variety of archival sources and private collections across the country. Many of these pictures reflect the enthusiasm with which Americans adapted themselves to the auto over the past seven decades; indeed, commentators have termed the infatuation a love affair.

Supposedly the ardor has cooled in the face of the often stark realities of today's car culture. Two decades ago Bernard de Voto observed that "the implications of the automobile have always outrun our ability to understand them. The necessities it has created have multiplied faster than we have kept up with them." The observation remains valid. Understanding is needed now more than ever, for as John B. Rae, the dean of automotive historians, points out, "the American automobile has become a way of life, and whatever happens to it must profoundly affect the economy and the whole culture of the United States."

—Stephen W. Sears

1
HORSELESS CARRIAGES

In the year 1889 Charles E. Duryea, a twenty-seven-year-old bicycle manufacturer in Peoria, Illinois, read with mounting excitement an article in *Scientific American* describing the experimental work of a Karl Benz of Mannheim, Germany. Herr Benz had built a road carriage that actually ran under its own power. It was propelled, the magazine reported, by an internal-combustion engine of the type first devised by a fellow German, Nicolaus Otto. For several years Charles Duryea had been thinking along these very lines. Although he had never seen such a machine, the article invigorated his dream of building a "horseless carriage" of his own.

The following year he commissioned the Ames Manufacturing Company near Springfield, Massachusetts, to build his newly designed Sylph bicycle and moved there to supervise production. With him went his twenty-year-old brother Frank, a journeyman toolmaker, who took a job with Ames. In his spare time Charles continued to formulate his automotive theories, reading, planning, sketching, testing his ideas against Frank's practical experience as a skilled machinist. Early in 1892 he decided it was time to translate theories into practice. He

needed two commodities, technical skill and money. He found the first by hiring his brother Frank, persuading him to leave Ames for a ten per cent increase in salary. The money he obtained from a local man, Erwin F. Markham, who agreed to put up $1,000 to finance "mechanically-propelled road vehicles, and in otherwise developing said invention" in return for a share of any profits. Charles promptly bought a second-hand ladies' phaeton for $70 and rented the second floor of a Springfield machine shop for working space.

By summer the two brothers had reworked the buggy chassis and assembled the running gear for their vehicle. Charles's ideas for a gasoline engine proved mostly theoretical, however, and they had to resort to trial-and-error experimentation. In their first trial they sprayed gasoline into the single cylinder with a perfume atomizer while spinning the flywheel, but the engine would not fire. Late in September Charles had to move back to Peoria to oversee his bicycle ventures, leaving Frank to complete the horseless carriage—if he could.

Frank was now wholeheartedly caught up in the project, but he was

In 1888 Lucius D. Copeland demonstrated the latest in road vehicles, bringing his steam tricycle (opposite) to the front door of the Smithsonian Institution. His passenger is Frances Benjamin Johnston, a noted Washington photographer. Sixteen years later the automobile was all the rage, and the comic weekly *Life* predicted that come the millennium horses would be reduced—literally—to carriage dogs.

stricken with typhoid fever and not until January, 1893, did he recover sufficiently to resume work. Trial-and-error modifications continued. He finally coaxed the engine into life, but it ran poorly. "I have tho't over yr engine and am still trying to find out if it will run . . . ," Frank wrote his brother in Peoria; "it looks some as tho it might give trouble." He had in fact already begun a complete redesign. He talked Markham into investing more money by agreeing to work without salary.

Through the summer months he made good progress on the revamped engine, writing Charles, "I have got the carriage almost ready for the road. . . ; will take it off somewhere so that no one will see us have the fun." On September 16 the Springfield *Evening Union* reported that "a new motor carriage, which, if the preliminary tests prove successful, as expected, will revolutionize the mode of travel on highways, and do away with the horse . . . , is being made in this city." Three days later the motor carriage was finished. It was brought down from the machine shop's second floor and concealed behind the building. After dark, hitched behind a horse, it was pulled unnoticed through Springfield to a barn on the edge of town owned by Howard Bemis, Markham's brother-in-law.

The next morning, September 20, 1893, the machine was rolled out into Spruce Street. With Duryea were Markham, Bemis, and Rudy Mac-

Phee, a young *Evening Union* reporter. Frank climbed onto the seat, fiddled with the controls, grasped the steering tiller, and signaled the three men to start pushing. After fifty feet the engine exploded into life. Trailing clouds of exhaust smoke, the carriage rattled ahead under its own power for two hundred feet before stalling against an earthen curb. So far as he knew, twenty-three-year-old J. Frank Duryea had driven the first American-built gasoline vehicle.

Even as he celebrated his triumph, Frank realized that he must correct serious weaknesses, particularly in the drive train, if he was to have a practical vehicle. Over the next four months changes were made and new trials held. "Residents of the vicinity of Florence Street flocked to the windows yesterday afternoon astonished to see gliding by in the roadway a common top carriage with no shafts and no horse attached," reporter MacPhee wrote after one of these trials. "This vehicle is operated by gasoline and is the invention of Mr. Edwin Markham and J. F. Duryea." By January, 1894, Frank concluded that he had reached the end of profitable experimentation with this first machine. Markham had by now lost heart in the venture, but the determined Frank was able to locate a new backer, Henry W. Clapp, to finance a second vehicle—one intended to be the pilot model for commercial production.

The new "motor wagon" and its two-

cylinder engine proved sturdy and reliable. "Everybody pleased with wagon," Frank wrote his brother in April, 1895. "She takes Pearl Street and Maple Street in second speed six or seven miles an hour anyway. . . . She will run anything that can be found in the road." And on June 10, in what can be considered the American automotive industry's first business report, he wrote in excitement, "Clapp is getting actual orders every day. An order received this A.M. says book me for two carriages to be delivered at earliest possible date. . . ."

The Duryea brothers did not build the first self-propelled road vehicle in the United States—and perhaps not even the first one powered by a gasoline engine. Yet their record of makeshift and trial and error is perfectly typical of what was happening in hundreds of sheds and barns and machine shops across the land. The time was ripe. Man's dream of a vehicle that would run under its own power on the "common roads" was an old one, and given the advanced state of machine technology and the favorable climate for innovation in late-nineteenth-century America, the appearance of the automobile was inevitable. It was, in fact, overdue. More than a century of experimentation, in the Old World and the New, was on the record.

Despite highly vocal proponents of treadmills, sails, springs, kites, and clockwork, it was a certainty that the world's first true road

The first self-propelled vehicles in Europe and America were massively constructed to support the large, heavy steam engines and boilers of the period. Frenchman Nicholas-Joseph Cugnot's artillery tractor (left), dating from 1770–71, featured a forward-mounted boiler and front-wheel drive. Oliver Evans's huge amphibious dredge (right) was first exhibited publicly in Philadelphia in 1805. Although it is inaccurate in details (e.g., the belt drive), this nineteenth-century view at least suggests the bulk of the unwieldy machine.

machines would be driven by steam. Steam engines of the Newcomen type were powering the nascent Industrial Revolution by the early eighteenth century, and late in the 1760's Scotsman James Watt's invention of a condenser to recycle the steam made the "fire engine" an eminently practical device. In 1769, the year Watt applied for a patent on his improved engine, a French military engineer named Nicholas-Joseph Cugnot won a royal commission to develop a steam tractor for pulling artillery. Cugnot's first model was demonstrated the next year and showed sufficient promise that a second machine was authorized. Built at the Paris Arsenal, it was a hulking three-wheeler with a twin-cylinder engine and boiler mounted ahead of the single front driving wheel. Cugnot's tractor never received an official government trial — his patron, the Duc de Choiseul, minister of war, had fallen out of favor with Louis XV — but in informal tests in 1771 on the arsenal grounds it proved able to haul up to five tons at a snail's pace for fifteen minutes before fuel and water needed replenishment. During these trials it reportedly knocked down a stone wall, achieving two firsts: the world's first self-propelled road vehicle, and the first to have an accident.

In 1801 in Cornwall, across the Channel, Richard Trevithick made a trial run in a crude road steamer nicknamed "Captain Dick's Puffer," carrying some half-dozen passengers clinging to the rear platform along with the engineer. His "London Carriage," built the next year, was more sophisticated, rumbling along Oxford Street and the Tottenham Court Road on its ten-foot driving wheels at 10 miles per hour. Unable to find financial backing to develop the London Carriage further, Trevithick turned his attention elsewhere. In 1804 he built the world's first rail locomotive.

Dozens of promoters of steam road carriages and omnibuses soon appeared on the British scene, producing elaborate prospectuses and handsome colored prints and even some quite workable machines, but all of them encountering bitter opposition from turnpike companies and others with vested interests in horse-drawn transport. Exhorbitant tolls and the railroads' corner on risk capital had crippled the infant road-carriage business by 1840. The 1865 Locomotives and Highways Act killed it. The so-called Red Flag Act set speed limits of 2 mph in urban areas and 4 mph on open roads and required a crewman to walk ahead of the vehicle swinging a red warning flag by day and a lantern by night. The act, somewhat modified, remained on the books until 1896.

In the United States the landscape was also littered with broken dreams. Even before the Revolution, a pattern developed that would be repeated time and again over the next century. Oliver Evans spoke for countless future automotive experimenters when he described his quandary in 1772: "I . . . declared that I could make steam waggons, and endeavoured to communicate my ideas to others; but, however practicable the thing appeared to me, my object only excited the ridicule of those to whom it was known."

Oliver Evans is a major figure in the history of American technology. Not only was he the first to build a self-propelled vehicle and the first to devise a high-pressure steam engine in this country, but he also laid important groundwork for mechanized mass production. In the mid-1780's he assembled a water-powered mill for turning farmers' grain into barreled flour which was so completely automated that workmen were needed only to put on the barrel heads. The grain, explains Siegfried Giedion in *Mechanization Takes Command,* "made its way . . . through all the floors [of the mill] from bottom to top and top to bottom, much as the automobile bodies in Henry Ford's plant of 1914. . . . At a stroke, and without forerunner in this field, Oliver Evans achieved what was to become the pivot of later mechanization."

In 1801 Evans demonstrated a powerful high-pressure steam engine of his own design in Philadelphia, and three years later he petitioned a local turnpike company to finance his scheme for putting steam freight wagons into service. He was turned down. He saw a chance to make his case when the Philadelphia Board of

The prints below depict steam carriages that plied English roads in the 1820's and 1830's. The coaches constructed by John Squire and Francis Macerone (upper left) and by F. Hills (upper right) carried firemen to stoke their boilers. Goldsworthy Gurney chose a tractor-type configuration (bottom). The world's first road-machine fatalities were recorded in Scotland in 1834 when the boiler of John Scott Russell's steamer burst and five died; the mishap is pictured at right.

BIBLIOTHÈQUE NATIONALE SERVICE PHOTOGRAPHIQUE; SCIENCE MUSEUM, LONDON (ABOVE RIGHT)

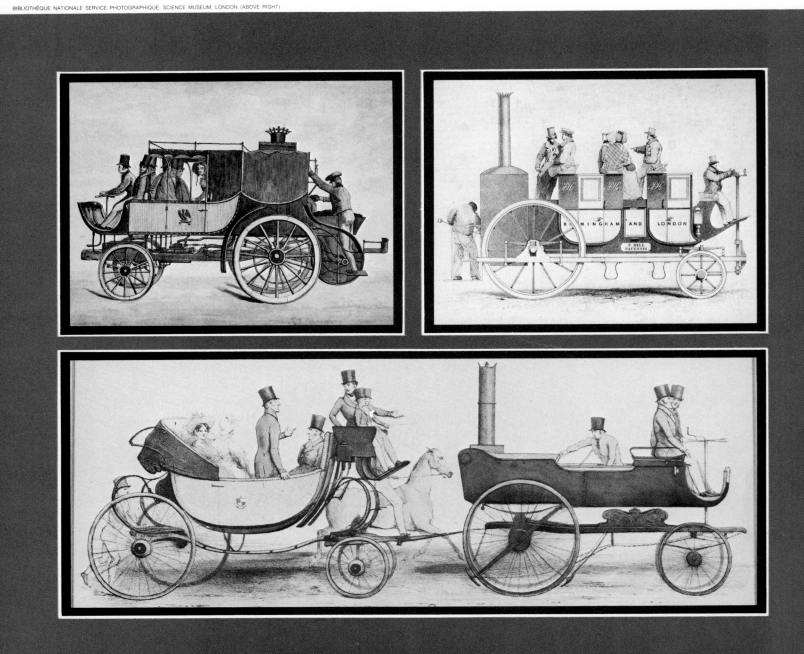

Health commissioned him to build a dredger to clean up the city's waterfront. He called his machine the Orukter Amphibolos (amphibious digger), but it was in fact an adaptation of the "steam waggon" he had vowed to build thirty-three years before. The Orukter was a twenty-ton "boat" mounted on four wooden wheels. A high-pressure engine was geared to the driving wheels through a cogwheel on the axle to produce motion, Evans claimed, "forward or backwards at pleasure, and enable the engineer to turn his carriage on a small space of ground."

Early in July, 1805, Evans made a successful trial run, and on July 13 he announced several days of public demonstrations, during which he drove his Juggernaut around the Philadelphia waterworks on Center Square and up Market Street at speeds of 3 or 4 mph. He insisted that such a steam wagon, with a full load of freight, could perform more efficiently than any horse-drawn wagon. A few days later the Orukter rumbled down to the waterfront and began dredging. How efficient a dredger it was is not stated; but in any event it never became the prototype for a fleet of steam wagons. Like Trevithick before him and many after him, Evans could not raise the capital to finance his venture, and the Orukter Amphibolos disappeared from history.

In the decades following Evans's experiments there was rapid advance in steam technology for railroad and marine use. Progress in steam-driven road transport, however, was decidedly erratic. Newspaper accounts of 1826 credit Thomas Blanchard of Springfield, Massachusetts, with building a steam carriage that "could run forward and backwards, steer properly and climb hills"; and in this period two Philadelphia brothers named Johnson allegedly made a trial run in an Evans-type machine. Further verification is lacking in both cases. In 1829 one William T. James may have operated a steamer on the streets of New York. Several attempts to organize steam-carriage companies produced only optimistic prospectuses. Like their English counterparts, American promoters of such enterprises found that investors preferred to put their risk capital into such "sure things" as railroads, canals, and steamships.

Most steam engines of the mid-nineteenth century were so heavy and bulky that highway steamers were often termed "road locomotives." In 1857 New Yorker Richard Dudgeon exhibited an omnibus resembling a scaled-down railroad locomotive, complete with iron-tired wheels; his later model, built in 1866, is probably America's oldest surviving powered road vehicle. There was a flurry of interest in self-propelled steam fire engines, but it took them so long to raise steam that they found little immediate use. The ultimate in road-locomotive development was the massive steam tractor, which was used in some numbers on western farmlands in the post-Civil War years.

If any evidence was needed that this approach to steam power for personal transport was a dead end, it was found in the contest sponsored by the Wisconsin state legislature in 1878 to develop "a cheap and practical substitute for use of horses and other animals on the highway and farm." There were only two entries in the two-hundred-mile race, both steamers. The *Oshkosh* weighed nearly five tons, the *Green Bay* more than seven. When the *Green Bay* broke through a road culvert the *Oshkosh* was an easy victor, but the legislature concluded that this was hardly a "cheap and practical" replacement for the horse and awarded the winner only half of the $10,000 prize.

There were, however, exceptions to the road-locomotive approach. In automotive history steamers would have their day in the sun, due in some measure to Sylvester H. Roper and his flamboyant agent and promoter, "Professor" W. W. Austen. *Scientific American* reported in 1863 that Roper, of Roxbury, Massachusetts, had built a steam carriage that weighed only 650 pounds, carried two people, and could reach 25 mph. Roper's little coal-fired high-pressure engine, reported the magazine, moved the machine "with as much ease as if drawn by a horse." He went on to build other carriages, which, thanks to Austen, were the first American self-propelled vehicles to capture widespread public attention. The self-styled professor sold the Spalding & Rogers circus on the idea of making Roper's "Family Steam Carriage for Common Roads" a featured attraction of its show, handbills proclaiming the vehicle exquisite in design and more docile than any horse: "It halts instantly, turns deviously, or proceeds at funeral pace. . . ." In New York Austen charged a quarter admission to "The Greatest Mechanical Exhibition in the World," and at county fairs all across the eastern states he promoted match races with trotters, winning most of the challenges. Roper seems to have made no effort to exploit this publicity by producing steamers commercially, and in the 1890's both he and Austen were killed in trials of his machines.

The 1870's and 1880's saw a burst of experimentation with steamers utilizing light boilers and high-pressure engines. Among the many Americans working to develop a truly practical steam road vehicle, two in particular should be cited. In the mid-1880's Lucius D. Copeland of Phoenix in Arizona Territory assembled an elegant little three-wheeler with a brightly polished boiler and a fringed top that featured automatic regulation of both the burner and the boiler water level. He organized the Moto-Cycle Manufacturing Company of Philadelphia, but it soon went broke. Copeland complained that people

would pay no more than $500 for a motor vehicle, at which price, he wrote, "there would be little profit."

In the same period James H. Bullard of Springfield, Massachusetts, went further in simplifying and automating a light steam power plant. Instead of solid fuel Bullard used kerosene, with a wick-type pilot light and a device to atomize the fuel to produce a clean hot flame. He achieved rapid build-up of steam pressure with a "fire tube" boiler—tubing inside the boiler multiplied the heating surface to generate steam more quickly than, in effect, simply heating the water on the teakettle principle—and devised a control to fire the burner automatically when steam pressure fell below a certain point. Bullard was content to secure patents on his improvements and turned his attention elsewhere.

In the meantime, another source of automotive power—electricity—was attracting attention. The electric motor had been invented in 1830 by Joseph Henry, a brilliant scientist and the first secretary of the Smithsonian Institution. Henry concluded that the inefficient galvanic battery of the period rendered his little motor a mere "philosophical toy." An untutored Vermont blacksmith, Thomas Davenport, patented his own electric motor in 1837 and spent a lifetime trying to improve the breed, but Henry's judgment was prophetic. Until batteries were radically improved, the future of the electric-powered vehicle was dim indeed.

It was almost half a century before the rechargeable storage battery was developed to the point of becoming a practical power source, although the weight of these early lead-acid batteries remained a handicap in automotive use. The first really successful American electric car was built in 1890 by William Morrison, an inventor from Des Moines, Iowa, and a rousing success it was. A big six-passenger wagon, it carried ranks of batteries under the seats. Morrison once drove his machine thirteen hours without a recharge at an average speed of 14 mph, a performance remarkable for *any* type of road vehicle in the 1890's. When it appeared on the streets of Chicago in 1892 it caused a sensation. The *Western Electrician*, which not surprisingly gave the story good coverage, reported: "Ever since its arrival the sight of a well loaded carriage moving along the streets at a spanking pace with no horses in front and apparently with nothing on board to give it motion, was a sight that has been too much even for the wide-awake Chicagoan. . . . So great has been the curiosity that the owner when passing through the business section has had to appeal to the police to aid him in clearing the way."

The Morrison carriage was acquired by Harold Sturges of the American Battery Company of Chicago, who proceeded to publicize it (and his company's batteries) at public gatherings, including the World's Columbian Exposition in Chicago,

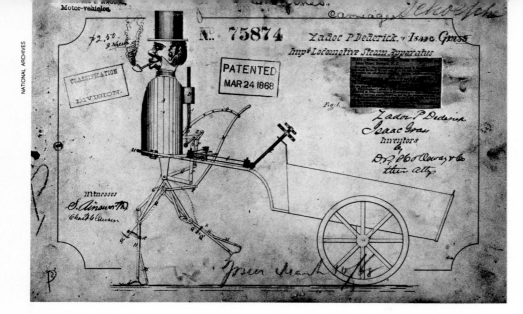

During the nineteenth century American inventors sought patents on self-propelled road machines of every imaginable sort. This antic contrivance, which might best be described as a steam-driven mechanical jinrikisha, was the joint brainstorm of Zadoc P. Dederick and Isaac Grass, from Newark, New Jersey, who said that the welter of pivots and cranks and connecting rods would produce "alternately-stepping motion." Astonishingly, they were awarded a patent.

with a flair which rivaled that of the redoubtable Professor Austen. Thousands saw and were impressed by the silent, smooth-running machine, giving the electric car the impetus to challenge steam and gasoline power.

Steam and electric power plants had in common the drawback of an external power source—the steam engine's boiler, the electric motor's batteries. The concept of a compact, self-contained "explosion engine" operating on the principle of internal combustion was easily arrived at by logic but not easily achieved in practice.

The first recorded American experiment in internal combustion was that of New Hampshirite Samuel Morey, who was granted a patent in 1826 and apparently built a working model. Within the cylinder of Morey's "gas or vapor engine" combustion was produced "by firing [with an electric spark] an explosive mixture of atmospheric air and vapor from common proof spirits, mixed with a small portion of turpentine." Barring "unforeseen difficulties," Morey predicted "the greatest improvement which has been made for many years, particularly in its application to locomotive engines." The "unforeseen difficulties" must have materialized, for nothing more was heard of the Morey engine.

Internal-combustion experimenters naturally enough made use of readily available steam-engine technology, in some cases simply adapting

steam engines to their own purposes. In the mid-1840's New Yorker Stuart Perry patented one such engine, powered by a turpentine-and-air mixture pumped into the cylinder and exploded by a live-flame igniter. Like a steam engine, it was double-acting: combustion alternated at either end of the piston, driving it back and forth within the cylinder. Another American pioneer of note was Dr. Alfred Drake of Philadelphia, who climaxed two decades of internal-combustion experiments by displaying an "explosive gas engine" at New York's Crystal Palace exhibition hall in 1857.

Étienne Lenoir, a Belgian living in Paris, was the first to achieve any commercial success with the internal-combustion principle. In 1860 he patented an engine not unlike Perry's: a double-acting two-cycle steam-engine conversion that burned a mixture of air and coal gas (the common illuminating gas of the period). French engineering journals, *Scientific American* reported, boasted that "the age of steam is ended—Watt and Fulton will soon be forgotten." Several hundred Lenoir engines were sold, but in fact it was a noisy, inefficient power plant and its success was brief.

The Perry, Drake, and Lenoir internal-combustion designs were all stationary engines, conceived as economical substitutes for steam power in small-scale applications—breweries, machine shops, pumping stations—where the power demand

was neither great nor continuous. They weighed as much as one ton per horsepower and were tied to fixed fuel sources such as municipal illuminating gas. In 1872 Boston engineer George B. Brayton took out a patent on a two-cycle combustion engine that was distinctive in two respects. For one thing, its fuel was "a distillate of kerosene called gasoline"; for another, it was single-acting: combustion acted on only one face of the piston. The carburetor was a felt "wick" saturated with gasoline, which was vaporized for admission to the cylinder by a jet of compressed air. Experiments made with the Brayton engine to power streetcars and omnibuses were inconclusive, but at the 1876 Centennial Exposition in Philadelphia it successfully operated pumps for an aquarium.

The "Brayton Ready Motor," as it was advertised, was not a notable commercial success, but while on exhibit in Philadelphia it caught the eye of one George B. Selden, a patent attorney and amateur inventor from Rochester, New York. Selden watched it thumping steadily along and made an imaginative mental leap. He envisioned it as the power plant for a road vehicle that would use liquid hydrocarbon fuel, be steerable, and have a means of engaging the driving wheels. Selden applied for a patent on his "road engine" idea in 1879 but did not build a prototype vehicle. He would later re-enter automotive history as a figure to be reckoned with.

Suddenly, with astonishing speed, a road vehicle powered by internal combustion became a practical reality. That all the essential steps were taken in Europe rather than the United States is something of a historical puzzle. America in the closing decades of the century was certainly not short of the necessary technological resources or the engineering know-how to solve the problem. Part of the answer is probably money: most risk capital in those decades was being channeled into the conquest of the continent and the exploitation of its resources. But the primary reason may be that the *logic* of road transport was earlier and more clearly visualized in Europe. The European highway system was unexcelled, and experimenters with self-propelled vehicles could easily envision road travel between major cities. Such travel could not be so easily imagined in the United States. Not only were the distances greater, but road building in this country was, and always had been, a local undertaking for local needs, and the rapid growth of railroads in the post-Civil War period removed the incentive for national or state-wide highway systems. Country roads, remarked a contributor to *The Nation*, were no better in the 1890's than they had been in John Smith's Virginia. Another commentator charged that American roads were "inferior to those of any civilized country."

For these or whatever reasons, Eu-ropeans took the lead. The crucial first step was made by the German Nicolaus Otto, a traveling salesman for a wholesale grocery firm and a man with a strong bent for things mechanical. Otto set out to improve on Lenoir's design and in 1876, after much experimentation, produced an eminently workable engine.

His was a four-step internal-combustion process, the key step being his innovation of compressing the explosive fuel mixture to produce truly efficient power. What became known as the "Otto cycle" could be achieved with two or four strokes of the piston; Otto settled on four strokes as the most practicable. On its first inward stroke, toward the crankshaft, the piston created a vacuum within the cylinder that drew in the combustible charge (Otto used a mixture of air and illuminating gas). The outward second stroke compressed the charge. At the peak of compression a jet of flame ignited the mixture, driving the piston inward. The outward fourth stroke exhausted the spent gases of combustion from the cylinder, and the cycle was ready to repeat—intake, compression, power, exhaust. A heavy flywheel carried the engine smoothly through the non-power strokes, and a steam-engine sliding valve was modified to admit the charge and exhaust the spent gases. It was soon evident that Otto's design was sound—and highly adaptable.

After the "Silent Otto" (an extrava-

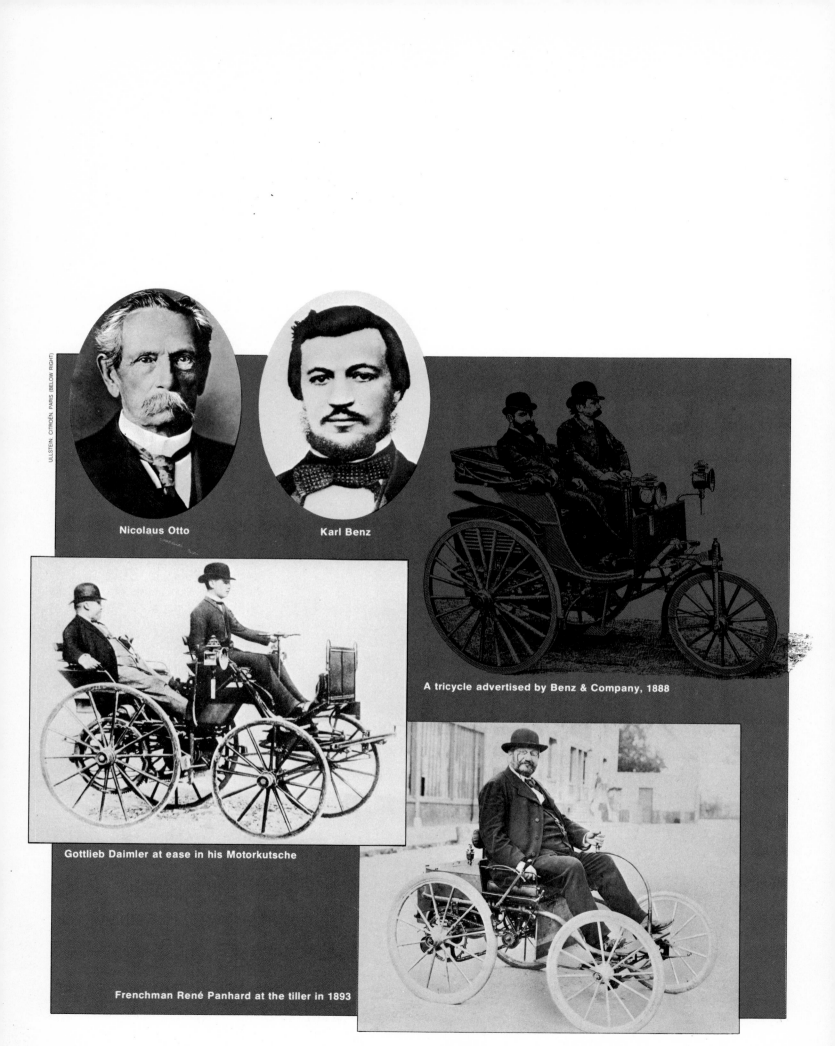

Nicolaus Otto

Karl Benz

A tricycle advertised by Benz & Company, 1888

Gottlieb Daimler at ease in his Motorkutsche

Frenchman René Panhard at the tiller in 1893

Displayed on the facing page are leading European pioneers in the development of the gasoline car. The first such vehicle in the United States may have been the powered tricycle at right, the creation of one John W. Lambert of Ohio City, Ohio. Local photographer Walter Lewis claimed that he took this picture in August, 1891, in the lobby of Ohio City's opera house.

gant use of the adjective) went into production as a stationary engine at the Gasmotorenfabrik Deutz factory near Cologne, the floodgates of innovation opened wide. A former Otto engineer named Gottlieb Daimler and his assistant Wilhelm Maybach produced a gasoline-fueled Otto-cycle engine in 1885 that weighed only 110 pounds and delivered 1.5 horsepower. In that year another German, Karl Benz, built an equally promising light Otto-type engine with water cooling and electric ignition — battery, coil, spark plug — and before the year was out Benz had assembled a three-wheeled powered carriage and Daimler a motor bicycle. By 1891 Benz was manufacturing well-conceived four-wheeled motor carriages, and the French engineering firm of Panhard et Levassor, using the Daimler engine built under license, was developing a configuration that looked less like a carriage and more like a modern automobile: engine in front of the passenger accommodations rather than wedged under a seat, clutch and gearbox, rear-wheel drive. Before 1893 was out, Benz, Panhard et Levassor, and another French firm, Peugeot, would between them sell 220 vehicles.

These European developments were widely reported by the technical and engineering press of the United States, where interest in combustion engines was finally growing intense. Charles and Frank Duryea were only two of scores of back-yard

tinkerers hard at work. An employee of Milwaukee locksmith Frank Toepfer recalled how his boss and a friend, cooper Gottfried Schloemer, "would get a bucket of beer and talk and sketch," groping their way toward plans for a gasoline vehicle. Reportedly, in 1892 they succeeded in building one. A year earlier, claimed German-born machinist Henry Nadig, he and his two sons had operated a motorcar "under its own power" on the streets of Allentown, Pennsylvania. It was in 1891, too, that Indianapolis blacksmith Charles H. Black examined a friend's imported Benz; within two years, so the story goes, he successfully completed a Benz-like machine.

These challengers to the Duryeas for the honor of building the first American gasoline car are not backed by ironclad documentation, but a rather stronger case has been made for John W. Lambert of Ohio City, Ohio. Lambert was a respected businessman and property owner — his holdings included the local opera house and the town hall — who had made a close study of the work of Otto and Benz. In 1891 he assembled a three-wheeled carriage with a fringed top and a one-cylinder gasoline engine, and after a test run in the showroom of his implement store he began driving it on the streets of Ohio City. Lambert was optimistic enough to mail out sales brochures describing his creation, and in August of that year he hired photographer Walter

Lewis to make a set of negatives for him. These pictures, the authenticity of which Lewis affirmed in a 1927 affidavit, are the only surviving record of what the Lambert car looked like. It was destroyed in a fire late in 1891, ending Lambert's plans for manufacture.

Whether automotive historians can ever finally agree on who built the first American gasoline car is an open question. It was a matter of dispute right from the start. On Independence Day, 1894, Elwood P. Haynes of Kokomo, Indiana, an engineer with the Indiana Natural Gas and Oil Company, demonstrated a car he had built in conjunction with the brothers Elmer and Edgar Apperson, Kokomo machinists. Haynes, aware of Lambert's experiments, visited the Ohio City businessman to ask him not to object if the Haynes-Apperson machine was advertised as the first car of its type in America. Charitably, Lambert agreed to keep quiet, and as late as the 1920's Haynes's advertising included the phrase "America's First Car." That this should offend Frank and Charles Duryea is not surprising. Whether or not they knew of Lambert's work, they knew very well that their own motor wagon predated the Haynes-Apperson car. Charles waged a successful battle with the Smithsonian Institution to remove from the 1894 Haynes-Apperson in its collection the designation "America's first gasoline powered vehicle."

Whoever may have been first, there

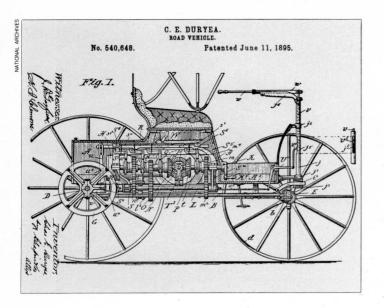

C. E. DURYEA.
ROAD VEHICLE.
No. 540,648.   Patented June 11, 1895.

Fig. I.

In the summer of 1895 Charles E. Duryea had himself photographed, probably in Springfield, Massachusetts, in the motor wagon he and his brother Frank had constructed. This was the vehicle Frank piloted in the fifty-four-mile Chicago *Times-Herald* race that November, the first such contest held in the United States. The patent drawing at left depicts the Duryea brothers' vehicle in cross section, with details of the transmission gearing.

was no shortage of contestants for the garland. In 1895 *The Horseless Age* estimated that to date some three hundred Americans had tried to build —and perhaps even contemplated manufacturing—horseless carriages, and a good proportion worked with gasoline engines. Most of them— machinists or blacksmiths or carriage makers or simply inveterate tinkerers —worked in isolation. In his memoir *Horseless Carriage Days* auto pioneer Hiram Percy Maxim recalled how "blissfully ignorant" he was that anyone else might be "working might and main on gasoline-propelled road vehicles. . . . As I look back, I am amazed that so many of us began work so nearly at the same time, and without the slightest notion that others were working on the problem." For real progress to be made, in steam and electric power as well as gasoline, the lonely experimenters needed an excuse to emerge from their barns and shops to meet and exchange ideas and compare dreams. The excuse was furnished by Chicago newspaper executive Herman H. Kohlsaat.

Kohlsaat, publisher of the Chicago *Times-Herald,* had followed the horseless carriage's halting progress as reported in the newspapers and technical journals crossing his desk. He particularly noted *Le Petit Journal*'s sponsorship of an 1894 race from Paris to Rouen. The *Times-Herald,* he reasoned, could reap benefits by sponsoring a similar contest in the United States. While promotional considerations no doubt influenced him, Kohlsaat seems also to have been genuinely impressed with the motorcar's potential and eager to arrange a test of its merits. On July 9, 1895, in a front-page story headlined "Prize for Motors," the *Times-Herald* announced such a test, with a purse totaling $10,000 for awards and expenses, to demonstrate that "the invention and coming perfection of [motor vehicles] is destined to work a revolution in road transportation." September 13 was set as the closing date for entries, with the trial scheduled "not far from" November 1.

The response was all that Kohlsaat hoped for, but the time limits he imposed caused problems. Of eighty-nine prospective entrants, many pleaded for more time to put the finishing touches on their machines and also for financial support—to be paid back, they assured Kohlsaat, out of their prize money. "If a newspaper publisher thinks it easy to build a motor vehicle in four months," one inventor complained, "then let him provide the means." Kohlsaat finally agreed to a one-month postponement. Competing newspapers stepped up their gibes at the *Times-Herald* for conducting a promotional hoax, but the postponement was supported by no less than Peter Studebaker, of the highly respected Studebaker brothers' wagon and carriage company. In an open letter to Kohl-

saat, Studebaker expressed confidence that few builders had "lost heart or given up" and congratulated him "most heartily on the great success already achieved in attracting attention to the possibilities of the motocycle." (*Motocycle* was more of the *Times-Herald*'s doing. When in July the paper sponsored a competition to replace "that awkward phrase, horseless carriage," G. F. Shaver of the Public Telephone Company of New York proposed "the name motocycle as being as near a perfect definition as is consistent with euphony." He was awarded $500.)

Publisher Kohlsaat was determined to sponsor not a mere race but a wide-ranging international contest designed to prove the motocycle's superiority to the horse. A distinguished slate of judges was impaneled and detailed rules established. All entries had to have at least three wheels and carry at least two people, one of them an officially appointed umpire, and be equipped with three lamps and a suitable warning device, such as a foghorn or a trumpet. Any propellant except muscle power was permitted, with refueling at specified "relay stations" along the course. (The course finally selected ran from Jackson Park, site of the 1893 World's Columbian Exposition, through the city of Chicago to Evanston and back again to the starting point—fifty-four miles in all.)

Most imaginative was a method of actually testing vehicles to rate them

The Chicago *Times-Herald* contest of 1895 was a magnet for automotive inventors eager to display their wares. At the left are Philadelphians Pedro G. Salom (with the beard) and Henry G. Morris in one of the three electrics they took to Chicago. They christened this pared-down model the Skeleton Bat, but in the race they drove their more sophisticated Electrobat II. An important phase of the contest was the scientific testing of the various vehicles to measure them against horse-drawn transport. The photograph at right shows the Duryea motor wagon, with brother Frank up, positioned on the testing apparatus.

against the horse. To simulate road conditions, engineers of the Chicago City Railway Company constructed a platform equipped with a pair of revolving drums rigged to a friction brake to supply output readings. With its driving wheels turning these drums, an entry could be rated for horsepower, load-carrying capacity, and fuel economy. Prize money would be awarded on the basis of speed; "general utility, ease of control and adaptability"; original cost and probable annual repair expenses; economy of operation; and "general appearance and excellence of design."

The "Race of the Century" was rescheduled for Thanksgiving Day, but in deference to the handful of entrants who had hewed to the original schedule Kohlsaat offered a $500 prize to the winner of an exhibition run, from Chicago to Waukegan and back, on November 2. Two entrants agreed to participate—the Duryea brothers with their motor wagon, and Oscar B. Mueller of Decatur, Illinois, who entered a German-built Benz. When the two cars set off, the motor wagon quickly proved the faster, but the Duryeas' elation was short-lived. Attempting to pass a lumbering farm wagon, they ended up in a ditch with a broken differential and a mangled steering linkage. The Mueller Benz completed the ninety-two-mile course and was duly awarded the $500. The Duryeas loaded their damaged machine into a

freight car bound for Springfield, promising to be back by Thanksgiving.

In postponing the contest Kohlsaat's major concern was Chicago's notorious weather. His worst fears were realized. On November 27, the day before Thanksgiving, a foot of snow fell on the city, with high winds piling up great drifts. Nevertheless, six intrepid entrants were at Jackson Park on Thanksgiving morning.

Of three Benz cars on the starting line, only one was a stock model, entered by R. H. Macy & Company, the New York department store. Macy's had hoped to generate publicity by having the car driven all the way to

Chicago, but bad roads and worse weather ended the attempt near Schenectady, New York. It was carried the rest of the way by rail. The Mueller Benz had had its power plant completely re-engineered since its victory in the exhibition race on November 2. The third Benz, entered by the De La Vergne Refrigerating Machine Company of New York, had a special steering gear designed by driver Frederick C. Haas. No steamers showed up, but two electrics did. The well-engineered Electrobat II, with front-wheel drive and rear-wheel steering, was the design of electrician Pedro G. Salom and mechanical engineer Henry G. Morris

Out for a Spin, 1897

After dinner, just as it was turning dusk, I suggested that we all take a bit of a ride around the village. . . . We persuaded [Julia Hamilton], who was willing to venture so that she might be able to say she had had her first ride in a horseless carriage. . . . Everything being ready, I spun the engine over. It burst into speed, as a gasoline-engine will when it is first started with a wide-open throttle, and Miss Hamilton thought the thing had exploded. She made to leave as hastily as possible, but [we] restrained her, shouting—so as to be heard over the roar—that this was merely starting the engine. She reluctantly resumed her seat, casting doubtful

glances behind. . . .

I opened the gas valve wide and the engine caught hold like a little bulldog. It was a gay ride. Miss Hamilton shed hairpins as I had never seen hairpins shed before. We ran around the village, the lady rapidly falling to pieces, after which we climbed the hill back home. When we arrived Miss Hamilton had the appearance of having been passed through a threshing-machine. She had to completely rebuild herself. However, the trip was voted a huge success. I was enormously relieved. The nervous strain had been no light one.

—Hiram Percy Maxim, *Horseless Carriage Days*, 1937

of Philadelphia. The big Sturges electric, weighing in at more than 3,500 pounds complete with batteries, was a slightly modified version of the William Morrison vehicle that had dazzled Chicago three years before. The sixth entry was the Duryea motor wagon, newly repaired and under the command of Frank.

Beginning at 8:55 A.M. the cars were sent off one by one. The storm had passed and the temperature was in the thirties, but driving conditions were miserable. The two electrics suffered the most in the deep snow. Backers of the Electrobat had not been able to deliver replacement batteries to the relay stations because of the storm and announced that they would simply make a demonstration run. The little electric traveled some fifteen miles before its batteries were depleted. The heavy Sturges struggled through the drifts, stopping frequently to lets its overworked motor cool and exuding an odor of ozone; but its driver pushed on bravely.Fred Haas's De La Vergne Benz suffered a fatal breakdown a few miles from the start. Only the two remaining Benz cars and the Duryea seemed capable of finishing.

Frank Duryea and Oscar Mueller had taken the precaution of wrapping sash cord around their tires to gain traction, and the ploy was effective. But it was the Macy Benz, driven with abandon by Jerry O'Connor, that took an early lead. On Michigan Avenue O'Connor skidded into a trolley but suffered only slight damage. A crowd of ten thousand outside the Auditorium Hotel applauded the contestants. Duryea was running second, Mueller third. Crossing the Rush Street bridge the motor wagon's repaired steering arm snapped; Frank was able to forge a repair at a blacksmith's, but the mishap cost him nearly an hour. Mueller meanwhile was having troubles of his own, perhaps from overloading—he carried a passenger, Charles G. Reid, as well as umpire Charles Brady King—and when Duryea resumed the course he was still in second place. Pushing along snow-rutted Lake Shore Drive through Lincoln Park, the three leaders were cheered on by fans watching the University of Michigan—University of Chicago football game; later the crowd sent up a cheer for the laboring Sturges electric, which promptly retired.

Just before 1 P.M., in suburban Evanston, Duryea caught up with the Macy Benz, and O'Connor sportingly pulled over to let him pass. Mueller remained in third place, having to halt once to tinker with his engine and again to repair a balky clutch. Jerry O'Connor was still full of fight, but it was not his day. As he recrossed the Chicago-Evanston line he collided with an overturned cutter. A few blocks later he banged into a hack, damaging a front wheel and his steering linkage. Fortunately the Benz's wheels fitted neatly in the Clark Street trolley tracks, and O'Connor let the tracks guide the unsteerable machine to the next relay station. Repairs cost him eighty minutes. He started out once more, but his battered car's endurance was not equal to his own tenacity, and at 6:15 P.M. he finally called it quits.

In the meantime, Duryea was plodding along toward the finish line, his main problems being ignition troubles, snowdrifts, and a two-mile detour when he made a wrong turn. At 7:18, in the darkness, after nearly eight chilling hours at the tiller, he crossed the finish line the winner. Just before nine o'clock the Mueller Benz limped in. Halfway back from Evanston, passenger Reid had fainted from the cold and been carried off in a sleigh; then Mueller himself collapsed. Umpire King finished the course, supporting Mueller with one hand and steering with the other.

Duryea's actual on-the-road time was seven hours, fifty-three minutes, averaging out to only about 7 mph, but under the terrible conditions to have finished at all was recognized as a remarkable feat. Considering the order of finish and the records of the evaluation tests, the judges awarded the Duryea brothers $2,000; $1,500 went to the Mueller Benz, $500 each to the Macy Benz and the Sturges electric, and the remaining prize money was split among other entrants that had shown merit.

The Thanksgiving Day adventure was fully reported in the nation's press and discussed at length in

The contest it was sponsoring, predicted the *Times-Herald,* would be the "Race of the Century." Here is the scene in snowy Chicago that Thanksgiving Day of 1895 as rendered in gravure by E. E. Goff. Four of the six contestants are on the starting line in Jackson Park. Number 25 is the Sturges electric, Number 5 the Duryea motor wagon, Number 7 the German Benz entered by the De La Vergne Refrigerating Machine Company of New York, and Number 22 the Benz sponsored by Macy's. The inset picture shows the winning Duryea, with Frank Duryea at the tiller, chugging along a street on the outskirts of Chicago. It required some eight hours of driving and two hours of repair work for Duryea to cover the fifty-four-mile course to Evanston and back.

MATTSON JR. HIGH LIBRARY

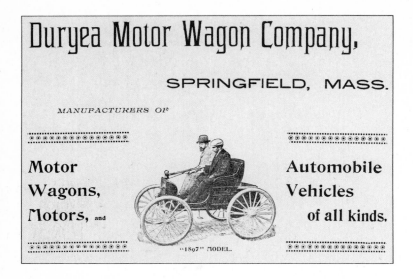

Duryea Motor Wagon Company,

SPRINGFIELD, MASS.

MANUFACTURERS OF

Motor Wagons, Motors, and

Automobile Vehicles of all kinds.

"1897" MODEL.

technical journals. Although the Chicago *Tribune* sarcastically headlined its story "Old Dobbin is Still in the Ring," most papers were more impressed. The remark of an observer in a two-horse rig who had failed to keep pace with the winning car—"No horse on earth could have made those fifty-four miles"—was widely quoted. Publisher Kohlsaat was confident that he had made his point—and delighted that an American car had won—and such automotive experimenters as Alexander Winton, Ransom Olds, and Henry Ford would later say that the contest had reinvigorated their own efforts. The one casualty of the affair was Mr. Shaver's term *motocycle,* which rapidly fell into disuse. L. Scott Bailey, who has closely studied that 1895 happening in snowy Chicago, sums up its importance in *The American Car Since 1775:* "If any single event can be pointed to as the catalyst leading to the ultimate acceptance of the automobile in America and the impetus for the beginning of a new industry, that event would have to be the Chicago *Times-Herald* contest."

The Duryeas were quick to exploit their Chicago triumph. Whether or not they constructed the first American gasoline car, they were unquestionably the first to take the whole business a step further and go into production. In February, 1896, the Duryea Motor Wagon Company made its initial sale (to one George H. Morrill, Jr., of Norwood, Massachusetts),

and before the year was out it built a dozen more vehicles. This was serial production rather than any primitive form of mass production: while based on a single design, each car was separately assembled, each part hand fitted. Advertisements promised perfect control, absolute safety, and handsome carriage styling, "not a 'carriage-without-a-horse look'—and yet not a machine in appearance." (Most early car builders considered the "machine look" uncouth.) On Memorial Day the brothers collected more publicity with a clean sweep of a race from New York City to suburban Irvington and back, winning *Cosmopolitan* magazine's $3,000 first prize. To cap a good year, Frank Duryea led the pack in the London-to-Brighton "Emancipation Day Run" on November 14, which celebrated Parliament's repeal of the notorious Red Flag Act.

For all their pioneering efforts, the Duryea brothers soon faded from the automotive limelight. By the turn of the century they had sold their company stock, quarreled, and gone their separate ways. Frank had modest success with the Stevens-Duryea car before leaving the business in 1915, but Charles had little luck marketing his designs. Charles died in 1938, Frank in 1967, having watched from the sidelines the colossal growth of the industry they founded.

Eighteen ninety-six was a year of automotive milestones beyond the Duryeas' initial production run. In

March, in Detroit, Charles Brady King, the umpire in the *Times-Herald* contest who had driven the Mueller Benz across the finish line, managed to get a gasoline car of his own running and introduced the future Motor City to the motor age. King was also of considerable help to his friend Henry Ford, the thirty-two-year-old chief engineer of Detroit's Edison Illuminating Company, who was building a "quadricycle" in the brick shed behind his house. One night in June Ford impatiently "enlarged" the narrow shed doorway by hammering out a section of the wall with the head of an axe so he could roll his machine outside for a short spin. The quadricycle ran well enough and the engine showed considerable craftsmanship, but it had no brakes and could not be reversed, and there was nothing to distinguish its builder from a hundred other backyard tinkerers of the day. During the summer Ransom E. Olds of Lansing, Michigan, demonstrated a gasoline car that in the opinion of the Lansing *State Republican* successfully resolved "the much mooted question of the horseless carriage." In September a trigger-tempered Scot, Alexander Winton, completed *his* first car in the Winton bicycle factory in Cleveland. And it was in the fall of 1896, wrote F. O. Stanley, that "my brother and I began to make drawings of a steam automobile. We knew but little about steam engines and less about boilers. . . ."

Francis E. and Freelan O. Stanley

This photograph of the Stanley twins, F. E. (foreground) and F. O., was made about 1899. The Stanley steamer was justly famous as a hill-climber par excellence. F. O. and his wife made the first motorized ascent of towering Mt. Washington in New Hampshire's White Mountains in 1899, a challenge soon formalized in an annual contest billed as the Climb to the Clouds. The photograph at right was taken during the 1905 competition. This Stanley finished first in class and second only to a considerably more powerful English Napier in the unlimited category.

were identical twins, upright Yankees from Maine with full flowing beards and bowler hats, so stubbornly (and jointly) individualistic that in automotive history probably only Henry Ford matched them in that characteristic. In the accelerating competition to produce salable horseless carriages in America, they would put the steamer in an early lead.

F. E. and F. O., who made a tidy living manufacturing a photographic dry plate of their own invention, were forty-seven years old when they decided to build a steam car. By 1898 their little machine had been developed sufficiently for them to enter a Boston speed and hill-climbing trial. They easily won the speed test; and on the artificial hill with its successive gradients ranging from five to thirty per cent, recalled F. O., "the Stanley car shot up to the very top of the grade and my brother held it there by the engine. . . . Never, before or since, have I seen such enthusiasm. . . ."

When that enthusiasm brought them two hundred inquiries from would-be buyers, they elected to go into the automobile business. Investing $20,000 in an abandoned bicycle factory in Newton, Massachusetts, and the machinery needed to begin production, they completed their first car in March, 1899. Auto enthusiast John Brisbane Walker, the owner of *Cosmopolitan* magazine, arrived in Newton one day to propose a partnership. "Had he said he had come to buy a half interest in our wives," F. O.

recounted, "I doubt if we would have been more surprised. . . . We had difficulty enough in getting along with each other, and we did not want to increase our trouble by taking in a third party. . . . We were stubborn, and he had to leave greatly disappointed." Walker was soon back, however, pleading with the twins to set a price for selling out. To get rid of him, they asked a quarter of a million dollars in cash; to their amazement, Walker agreed.

That first Stanley design remained in production four years under the names Locomobile and Mobile. The Locomobile (the more widely sold of the two) made Americans conscious of the steam car, but it also left certain bad impressions. A light two-passenger runabout selling for $600 in 1899, it was advertised as noiseless and odorless. "The few moments' attention required when in use," the ad promised, "can be given entirely at your convenience and without so much as removing your cuffs." Indeed, "in use" the Locomobile was sheer pleasure: no gearshift to manhandle, no spark advance to manipulate, no vibration, no noise except a faint hiss of steam, no problems negotiating the steepest of hills. If its water supply was good for only twenty miles, if on a windy day the burner blew out, if on a damp day the car trailed a white fog bank of condensing steam, these were minor inconveniences, certainly no worse than the trials faced by a gasoline-car

owner. The real inconvenience was getting up steam.

The Stanleys loved to drive their cars and drive them fast, and getting one started was to them simply a challenge. To the average owner of one of these early Stanley-designed Locomobiles the challenge was diabolical. The fuel was gasoline, which had to be vaporized before it would fire the burner. The owner's first step was to heat the "firing iron," a U-shaped steel pipe, on his kitchen stove or elsewhere, until it was red-hot. He then carried it to the car, inserted it in the burner, and connected it to a fuel valve. Assuming the firing iron had remained hot enough and the owner had not suffered second-degree burns, the process of vaporizing fuel and firing up the burner could begin. Raising steam seldom took less than half an hour.

In 1901 the Stanleys re-entered the steam-car business (one of the terms of Walker's purchase was that they not compete for at least a year), bought back their Newton factory and their patents for $20,000, and were soon in production. In 1902 Locomobile began the switch to gasoline power, and the five thousand Locomobile steamers became only a memory—a mixed memory.

The Stanleys steadily improved their machines, fitting direct drive to the rear axle, utilizing cheaper kerosene for the burner, developing an acetylene "blowtorch" starter, but always proceeding at their own pace

THE PASSING OF THE HORSE

The relationship of the noble horse to what was sometimes regarded, early in the century, as the ignoble automobile was common grist for cartoonists. Here are examples from popular magazines of the day. The poignant scene below was photographed in 1904 during a test conducted at American Express in New York City to pit delivery trucks against horse-drawn delivery wagons. The horse quite rightly casts a suspicious eye at the newcomer, a Moyea van. It won.

"IT'S RUN DOWN. I'LL GET OUT THE AUXILIARY MOTOR."

"COME ALONG, JENNY!"

"IT MAY BE SLOW, BUT WE'LL GET HOME."

and in their own way, with little regard for the "whims" of the marketplace. When an owner once complained about the small fuel tank, F. O. replied, "But, my dear Sir, three gallons will take you thirty miles, and that is all you will *ever* want to drive in one day." They retained their outmoded little fire-tube boiler because its reserve of steam was always available for bursts of speed, and they refused to fit a condenser until 1916. Scorning advertising, the Stanleys never built more than 650 cars in their best year, regardless of demand. Their machines were designed to suit F. E. and F. O. and their self-admitted "cussed" ways, and that was good enough. But whatever its eccentric shortcomings, the Stanley steamer remained one of the era's most pleasurable cars to drive.

Of the Stanleys' steam competitors, the most successful was Rollin H. White of the White Sewing Machine Company of Cleveland, who in 1901 began marketing a steamer that would in time fully measure up to its advertised slogan, "The Incomparable White." The first Whites were small, in the same class as the Stanley, but they soon moved up in both class and price. By 1904 the Stanley look was gone, replaced by touring-car bodies and even a limousine priced at $2,700. The powerful double-acting engine was compound (steam was admitted to a high-pressure cylinder, then a low-pressure cylinder, compounding its expansive

power), a condenser recycled the steam to extend the car's range, and a "flash boiler" lowered start-up time. In the flash boiler, patented in 1889 by the Frenchman Léon Serpollet, water injected into coils of tubing preheated by the burner "flashed" into steam with considerable speed. The big, luxurious Whites were hardy and powerful and represented the best in steam power in the opening decade of the century. A White was chosen to be among the first official White House automobiles during the Taft administration.

The electric car, like the steamer, bloomed early in America. The electric was simplicity itself. Typically, advertisements pictured the driver as a stylishly turned out matron who could enter her tall electric coupé without disturbance to her ostrich-plume hat, settle herself comfortably at the steering tiller, and proceed down the avenue for "visiting, shopping or a ride in the park" with no more effort than a flick of the controller handle. She suffered no waiting, no cranking, no gear shifting, no tire changing (tires were solid rubber); in motion there was no noise, no jarring vibration, no noxious fumes. "It could not go fast enough to get her into serious trouble," observes historian J. C. Furnas, "and would never bolt in terror of a wind-blown newspaper. . . ." To a man of means, the $3,000 price tag on a 1900 Woods electric brougham, which included accommodation for a

liveried footman, was small price indeed for his wife's motoring ease and pleasure.

Despite the best efforts of its promoters, the electric remained a car of limited utility. It was an urban vehicle, suited for driving only on paved streets at a leisurely pace, and its thirty-eight-per-cent share of the automotive market in 1900 would never be bettered. By 1905 that share had fallen to less than seven per cent. What could not be remedied was the electric's gravest shortcoming—the inadequacy of battery power. The batteries were heavy and expensive and deteriorated rapidly. Motoring range on one battery charge rose from twenty miles in 1900 to about eighty miles a decade later, but charging facilities were rarely available outside cities and expensive anywhere.

Such companies as Baker, Pope-Waverley, Woods, Columbia, Detroit, and Rauch and Lang put the best face on their product by stressing its socially desirable traits of easy operation and clean, quiet power "always ready to go." Woods advertising, for example, was aimed at substituting its "fine carriages in all variety of styles" for the equipages in every gentleman's private stable. Conservative, elegant carriage styling was the rule, with curved glass windows and luxurious interior appointments (including crystal vases for milady's flowers) on enclosed models. A succinct and prophetic

Ransom E. Olds promoted his curved-dash Oldsmobile as a car of many virtues, although it is not stated whether the Olds driver pictured (far left) hub-deep in mud actually made it through. A curved dash was entered in a braking contest (left) held on New York's Riverside Drive in 1902. From 14 mph it required just over 21 feet to come to a full stop; a two-horse victoria carriage needed 36 feet and a large four-horse coach no less than 77 feet. The display at right was a demonstration of the little Oldsmobile's ease of control and responsiveness: the cars were driven to and fro, making the teeter-totter teeter.

verdict on the electric was offered by *Review of Reviews* as early as 1900: "It is the handsomest automobile, the easiest to drive, the pleasantest to ride in; but it is not adapted for general use—say, in rural districts, nor for touring."

It was by no means clear at the turn of the century which power source —steam, electricity, or gasoline— would dominate in the race to produce practical road vehicles. However, the Stanley twins' indifference to the marketplace, the White Company's decision to focus on the luxury trade, and the electric's technical shortcomings meant that the field was wide open to opportunistic proponents of the gasoline car. Ransom E. Olds saw the opening and exploited it.

Of all his fellow experimenters in the gasoline-car field, Ransom Olds seemed among the best qualified to lead the way. He and his father operated the Lansing, Michigan, firm of P. F. Olds & Son, producers of stationary steam and gasoline engines. In 1887 Ransom completed a steam-driven vehicle—he sold a second one for $400 to a London patent-medicine company for export to India —but eventually he turned to the gasoline engine to power the light road carriage he wanted to produce. "A great many persons in this country and Europe are waiting for some one to make a vehicle of this character that is a success," he explained to a reporter after the demonstration of his

1896 machine. "There is no trouble about selling them after you once get the article that class of customers want."

Olds's optimism, as it turned out, was entirely justified. He was one of the first to grasp an essential characteristic of the American motorcar market. Most European models were evolving in the direction of the heavy, powerful, hand-crafted, high-priced touring machine admired by the wealthy "coach-and-four" set for travel on the Continent's good roads. There was undoubtedly some American demand for such vehicles, but a far greater market existed for a literal substitute for the horse and buggy: light, sturdy, economical, adaptable to harsh American road conditions, priced close to the cost of a buggy and Old Dobbin to pull it. Olds's problems were developing just the right vehicle and raising the capital to produce it in quantity.

These were problems not quickly solved. In 1897 the Olds Motor Vehicle Company was incorporated in Lansing, and general manager Olds was "authorized to build one carriage in as nearly perfect a manner as possible." Working capital proved inadequate, however, and in 1899 there was a major reorganization. A new company, the Olds Motor Works, was put together by Samuel L. Smith, an investor who had made a fortune in Michigan lumber and copper. Olds remained as chief executive officer, working capital of $150,000 in cash

was assembled, and on Jefferson Avenue in Detroit ground was broken for a factory. Other cities made bids for the Olds plant, but the primary reason for selecting Detroit seems to have been that Smith, the major stockholder, lived there. For more than a year Olds labored to build that perfect carriage, producing eleven models varying in size, price tag, and power plant. One prototype was a light buggy-type machine with the floorboards swept upward in front to form a snappy-looking curving dashboard. According to historian George S. May, Olds and his restive backers had finally focused their attention on this little runabout when, on March 9, 1901, disaster intervened to seal their decision. A fire ignited by a gasoline explosion all but destroyed the new factory, leaving only the foundry building standing.

The single vehicle saved was the curved-dash prototype, which company timekeeper James J. Brady dragged out of the blazing main building before the walls fell in. There was no assurance that the little car was what America was waiting for, but if the struggling company was to get into volume production in time for the 1901 good-weather selling season it was the only answer. It was simple and easily assembled—important points since much of the work was being subcontracted—and it was "in being" for the making of assembly patterns and jigs. Work was quickly begun. "In exactly thirty days

from the date of our blessed disaster," Smith's son Frederick later wrote with the benefit of hindsight, "the first little Phoenix of a runabout was again trundled out by Jimmy Brady to receive the blessing of the management."

The Olds Motor Works's surviving building, the foundry, was converted into an assembly center. Ransom Olds had scoured the Detroit area for subcontractors, his line-up reading like a future *Who's Who* of the automotive industry. To acquire engines and transmissions he went to the Dodge brothers, John and Horace, a tough, hard-living pair of redheads who had recently set up a machine shop in Detroit. When the Dodges could not keep up with the demand, it was arranged for another local machine shop, Leland & Faulconer, to fill the gap; Henry M. Leland would go on to create both the Cadillac and Lincoln marques. For bodies and upholstery Olds turned to carriage builder Barney F. Everitt, whose list of automobile credits would in time total half a dozen makes. To help fill the Olds order, Everitt hired Fred J. Fisher, the oldest of the six Fisher brothers, future body makers for General Motors. Sheet-metal work—fenders, gas tanks, radiators—was undertaken by Benjamin and Frank Briscoe. Benjamin Briscoe, who late in the decade would assemble a combine to challenge General Motors, contended that these subcontracting arrangements by Olds

"marked the beginning in a real way of the automobile manufacturing business in the city of Detroit."

Olds's promotion of his little car was no less shrewd than his production decisions. He got off to a good start with its name. By the turn of the century the French term *automobile* (literally, self-movable) was in general use, having received the august imprimatur of the Académie française. (This caused some grumbling—a Francophobe complained to *The Horseless Age* that surely "the English language is rich enough to furnish its own terms without any borrowing from foreign or dead languages"—but it found ready acceptance when

compared to such coinages as *automaton, petrocar, motorig, mocle, mobe, viamote,* and the *Times-Herald*'s ill-fated *motocycle*.) By christening his machine Oldsmobile, Ransom Olds was trading on the newest terminology. His advertising directly challenged the major competitor—the horse. Rather than enduring "the danger of the horse's uncertain temper, sudden fright and unruly disposition," an Oldsmobile owner could travel by the slogan "Nothing to watch but the road."

In truth, like all early horseless carriages, an Oldsmobile could exhibit an "unruly disposition" of its own. Eyeing the company's slogan, one

---

Advice to the Pioneer Motorist

Don't take anybody's word for it that your tanks have plenty of gasoline and water and your oil cup plenty of oil. They may be guessing.

Don't do anything to your motor without a good reason or without knowing just what you are doing.

Don't imagine that your motor runs well on equal parts of water and gasoline. It's a mistake.

Don't make "improvements" without writing the factory. We know all about many of those improvements and can advise you.

Don't think your motor is losing power when clutch bands need tightening or something is out of adjustment.

Don't drive your "Oldsmobile" 100 miles the first day. You wouldn't drive a green horse 10 miles till you were acquainted with him. Do you know more about a gasoline motor than you do about a horse?

Don't delude yourself into thinking we are building these motors like a barber's razor—"just to sell." We couldn't have sold one in a thousand years, and much less 5,000 in one year, if it hadn't been demonstrated to be a practical success.

Don't confess you are less intelligent than thousands of people who are driving Oldsmobiles. We make the only motor that "motes."

—Oldsmobile Manual, 1905

SECOND TRIP
NEW YORK to ST. LOUIS

The automobile proved an ideal vehicle for stunts and promotions. Here are a few typical examples (counterclockwise from left): one Oliver Lippincott and friends perched a Locomobile steamer atop Glacier Point in Yosemite in 1900. A Cadillac charged up the front steps of Detroit's County Court House in 1903, and in 1904 an Elmore drew a crowd of Filipinos in the exotic Manila Gardens at the Louisiana Purchase Exposition in St. Louis. Carl Graham Fisher, who would later dream up the Lincoln Highway, reached new heights in 1908 at Indianapolis while promoting Stoddard-Dayton. An overloaded 1903 Cadillac showed its mettle on a steep hill in Detroit, and a 1904 Pope-Toledo showed equal mettle in Washington, carrying a distinguished delegation to the Capitol. Californians saw the elephant in 1909 thanks to the publicity flacks for the Tourist.

35

frustrated owner wrote, "The idea is good, but I get darned tired of watching the same piece of road." For its time, however, it was a simple, reliable vehicle; the advertised boast, "Ladies and children can readily understand its mechanism," was only slightly hyperbolic. The one-cylinder water-cooled engine produced a top speed of about 20 mph and was mounted behind the seat. The planetary transmission was simple to operate, having a two-speed gear lever (plus reverse) and no clutch. Steering was by tiller. The wheelbase was just 66 inches and the weight some 700 pounds. The $650 price tag included mudguards and brass lamps but not the buggy-style top, which was an optional extra, as was a speedometer. In a time before "styling" became a Detroit byword, the little curved-dash Oldsmobile, shiny black with red trim, demonstrated a natural, down-to-earth handsomeness in the best tradition of American carriage building.

Showings at county fairs and special stunts—driving up the steps of the state capitol in Lansing and the United States Capitol in Washington, for example—were part of Olds's publicity campaign, but his boldest coup took place in the fall of 1901. Twice, in 1897 and 1899, Alexander Winton had driven one of his machines the unheard-of distance from Cleveland to New York, and now Olds decided on a similar trial.

On October 29 Roy D. Chapin, a twenty-one-year-old company employee, was sent off eastward from Detroit in a new curved dash equipped with a large box of tools and spare parts. Eight days and 820 miles later he arrived in New York, exhausted and mud-spattered but triumphant. The roads were so atrocious, he reported, that in crossing New York State he had taken to the towpath of the Erie Canal. Olds would later acknowledge that Chapin had endured "all the trouble that could possibly be created by one small car," but at the time that aspect was glossed over. "The owner says his experience has showed that the lightweight automobiles are well adapted to such tours," the New York *Tribune* reported. It was announced that the local Oldsmobile dealership was taking the staggering total of a thousand cars for sale in the New York area.

Orders for the little runabout poured in. Maude Adams, Mark Twain, and the queens of England and Italy were mentioned as satisfied buyers. In Detroit—and later in a second factory in Lansing—production assumed the look of an assembly line. Chassis were placed on wheeled dollies and rolled from one workman to the next, with parts stockpiled at each man's station. Olds predicted an output of 25 cars a day, a startling figure for 1901 but an underestimate of what he would soon achieve. Neither steamers nor electrics could keep pace in sales. The Olds Motor Works turned out 425 curved-dash models that year, 2,500 the next (almost a third of them sold in New York), 4,000 the next, and peaked at more than 5,500 in 1904. This was far and away the largest output in the growing industry. And it was profitable. Samuel Smith and the other original stockholders earned back their investment in dividends alone, and by the end of 1903 the company's capitalization had increased by $2 million and showed a cash surplus of $600,000—all from earnings. Beyond a doubt, this new business had potential.

At the Detroit Automobile Show in 1901, Henry M. Leland and his son Wilfred made a point of visiting the exhibit set up by Oldsmobile, for whom Leland & Faulconer was building transmissions and engines. On the exhibit platform were two engines chugging along side by side, with large dials indicating identical running speeds, testimony to the Oldsmobile's consistent manufacturing standards. A lean stranger standing nearby grinned and beckoned them behind the platform. "Here he pointed out the fact," Wilfred later wrote, "that a brake load had been applied to the fly wheel of one of the motors to hold its speed down to equal that of the slower motor." Amused, the Lelands discovered that the slower engine had been built by the Dodge brothers, the faster (by twenty-three per cent) by Leland & Faulconer; the only difference was superior machining. Several years later the bystander met

In 1932, shortly before his death at the age of eighty-nine, Henry M. Leland was photographed at the crank of one of his early one-cylinder Cadillacs. It was this model that in 1908 won the Dewar Trophy for automotive excellence awarded by Britain's Royal Automobile Club. His young grandson, Wilfred Leland, Jr., nicely filled the large trophy cup (right).

the Lelands again and introduced himself as Henry Ford.

Henry Leland was surely not surprised at the superiority of his engine. Had it been otherwise, he would have descended on his work force with fire in his eye. If the Duryea brothers deserve credit for founding the automobile business and the Stanley twins and Ransom Olds for first demonstrating its potential, it was Leland who taught the industry the necessity of precision craftsmanship.

He was fifty-eight in 1901, with as solid a background in precision machinery engineering as anyone in the United States. Born in Vermont, he was working as an apprentice machinist in a Massachusetts loom works by age fourteen. During the Civil War he built muskets for the Union army and later broadened his experience with interchangeable parts at the Colt arms factory in Hartford, Connecticut. He spent eighteen years in Providence with Brown & Sharpe, the nation's leading maker of precision machine tools. In 1890, with the financial backing of lumber baron Robert C. Faulconer, Leland went into business for himself in Detroit. The Leland & Faulconer machine shop had a growing reputation for producing bicycle gears, steam engines, and marine gasoline engines when Ransom Olds arrived and introduced Leland to the automobile business.

Leland & Faulconer's work on the curved-dash model was a revelation to Olds. Previously, transmission as-

sembly meant hand filing and fitting each gear. Well-machined L. & F. gears needed no hand fitting at all, and their transmissions worked smoothly and quietly. Leland turned next to the standard Oldsmobile engine he had contracted to build. By careful machining and reworking of the intake and exhaust passages, valves, and camshaft, he produced a new engine with nearly three times the power at no increase in displacement. To his dismay, it was rejected. The added power, he was told, would require major revamping of the curved dash's chassis, causing delays in filling the spiraling backlog of orders. Leland decided that someday he would build a car of his own and build it right.

His chance came in 1902. Officers of the moribund Detroit Automobile Company asked him to appraise their corporate assets for liquidation. Leland persuaded them instead to go into production using his new engine. Prototypes were quickly completed and the car, christened Cadillac, was exhibited at the New York Automobile Show in January, 1903. The well-received little Cadillac "one-lunger" runabout was an exceptionally well built and smooth-running car for its day, reflecting Leland's gospel of precision and uncompromising quality. "It doesn't cost as much to have the work done right the first time as it does to have it done poorly and then hire a number of men to make it right af-

terwards," he once wrote; and on another occasion: "There always was and there always will be conflict between Good and Good Enough. . . . One must sweat blood for a chance to produce a superior product."

These were not hollow homilies. Dissatisfied with the work of his casting department, Leland once stormed through the foundry, slamming newly finished castings to the floor and pointing out the defects in those that broke. In his memoirs Alfred P. Sloan, Jr., the brilliant between-wars president of General Motors, recalled an interview with Leland early in the century when he was supplying roller bearings to Cadillac. Patriarchal in his white beard, Leland gestured at a handful of bearings he had checked with a micrometer and intoned with measured emphasis: "Mr. Sloan, Cadillacs are made to run, not just to sell." He had been assured, he went on, that the bearings would be accurate to one-thousandth of an inch; "But look here! . . . There is nothing like that uniformity. . . . You must grind your bearings. Even though you make thousands, the first and the last should be precisely alike." The lesson was learned and never forgotten, Sloan wrote. "A genuine conception of what mass production should mean really grew in me with that conversation."

In 1905 Cadillac produced a four-cylinder engine and began gravitating toward the luxury market where it would become famous, but during its

No other American car on the market in the
first decade of the century was constructed
to higher standards than Cadillac. Pride
of ownership is evident in these faces.
The setting is Leavenworth, Kansas, and the
picture was taken by town photographer
E. E. Henry or his stepson, Harrison Putney;
but the name of the family who owned
this shiny 1903 tonneau model is unknown.

lifetime the little runabout was a major contender in the production race. It was also the first American car to earn international respect.

In 1908 Cadillac was the only entry in a standardization test sponsored by Britain's prestigious Royal Automobile Club to evaluate the theory of interchangeable automotive parts. At the Brooklands motor speedway outside London, three stock one-cylinder models were disassembled down to the last nut and bolt and piston ring; the parts were thoroughly mixed (along with some components drawn at random from spare-part stocks) and then reassembled, using only wrenches, screwdrivers, hammers, and pliers. The three cars that emerged were dubbed the "Harlequins" for their multicolor appearance. To the astonishment of Royal Automobile Club observers, all three Harlequins started promptly and were driven five hundred miles at top speed on the Brooklands track without a breakdown. The feat earned Cadillac the Dewar Trophy, the highest award in motordom, and was an enormous boost in prestige not only for Cadillac but for the American car in general. It was as well a dramatic acknowledgment of Henry Leland's sermon on the proper way to build automobiles.

Leland's congregation was multiplying at a prodigious rate in the first decade of the century. As would-be manufacturers discovered, the rules of the game were far different from what Oliver Evans and his successors had experienced; the industry was now, writes John B. Rae in *The American Automobile*, "as classic an example of free competitive enterprise as could be found."

Ransom Olds established the era's dominant pattern. Early car makers were less manufacturers than assemblers. Components—engines, transmissions, wheels, chassis parts, bodies—were purchased from suppliers who normally granted thirty to ninety days' credit. Relatively modest financing (Henry Ford organized his Ford Motor Company in 1903 with but $28,000 in paid-in capital) enabled the fledgling car maker to set up an assembly center. If his reputation, or his advertising, was good enough to earn him a place in the seller's market, he could demand a cash deposit of as much as twenty per cent from his distributors and dealers, bringing in more operating capital. The rule for shipping finished cars to dealers was payment on delivery. If the combination was right—a well-designed machine promptly assembled and smartly promoted—there would be money in the till in time to pay suppliers' bills as they came due. If the combination turned sour, the receiver was soon at the door. Charles Duryea, in a survey conducted for *Motor* magazine, estimated that by the end of 1908 as many as 515 companies had entered the field and that half of them had failed.

The bicycle business provided a natural springboard from which to plunge into horseless carriage making. In addition to the Duryeas and Alexander Winton, Henry A. Lozier, Thomas B. Jeffery (Rambler), John North Willys (Overland), and Erwin R. Thomas (Thomas Flyer) were other bicycle builders who pioneered famous marques. For a time the Pope Manufacturing Company of Hartford, Connecticut, the nation's largest bicycle builder, was also the leading auto builder. Colonel Albert A. Pope, who displayed a lifelong affection for his rank, a relic of Civil War service on General Grant's staff, was at first dubious about the gasoline car. According to Hiram Percy Maxim, head of Pope's "motor-carriage department," the colonel once announced, "You can't get people to sit over an explosion." Initially the company focused its efforts on electrics, but before long gasoline-car production predominated. Perhaps Colonel Pope relented when the explosion engine was taken out from under the seat and put up front.

Olds, Leland, the Apperson brothers, Jonathan D. Maxwell (and later the Dodge brothers) typified the machinists and engine builders who entered the auto field. A third natural avenue of entry was carriage building, notably the world-famous Studebaker firm and the Durant-Dort company, whose William C. Durant would found General Motors.

The pathway to automotive fame was not always logical, however.

Cloudy Crystal Ball

Our idea was simply that the automobile was and always would be a sport vehicle. Accordingly, the Fleetmobile was built to look as much like a racing sulky as possible, although of course it had four wheels, and patent leather mudguards. We even made an all-weather model with a dashboard ... and a top with fringe around the edges. The fringe was to annoy the flies. ...

Save for the Fleetmobile Company, nobody had the faintest notion of what an automobile should look like. Some of the machines resembled buckboards; others (the electrics) looked like foreshortened hearses; not a few were motorized invalid's tricycles; and the remainder seemed to be iron bedsteads with wheels, seats, tanks and mechanism jutting out in unexpected places. No wonder, then, that we were proud of the Fleetmobile; of its coaster-brakes; of its bicycle-tube frame; of its fire-chief's buggy's bell which went "ting-tang". ... We were proud of its incomplete look — incomplete, because you felt that all it lacked was a pair of shafts with a blooded filly between them. And right there was the Fleetmobile's great sales appeal; it made the transition from horse to motorcar so easy.
— Guy Gilpatric, *Brownstone Front*, 1934

Henry Ford was unusual in that he had no previous business experience at all — but then Ford was as unusual a figure as American industry has produced. David Dunbar Buick's business background was in bathtubs, Rollin H. White's in sewing machines, Howard C. Marmon's in millstones, George N. Pierce's in birdcages and bicycles. James W. Packard was manufacturing electric cables in Warren, Ohio, when he bought a car from Alexander Winton in 1898. Convinced that he had been stuck with what later generations would call a lemon, Packard confronted Winton with his complaints. "All right, if you don't like the car, and you know so much," the testy Winton responded, "why don't you make a car of your own." Packard, of course, did so.

James Packard's role in automotive history was brief. In 1901 his little company was acquired by a syndicate headed by businessman Henry B. Joy and two years later moved to Detroit. Packard stayed behind in Warren, serving as a management figurehead until 1909. Ransom Olds was another pioneer eased out of the company that bore his name. In 1904 the Oldsmobile board of directors voted him out in a dispute over his management policies. Olds moved on to form the Reo Motor Car Company, its name being an acronym of his initials. David Buick, too, was a casualty, lost in the shuffle in one of the periodic reorganizations of the company that had taken his name.

The Buick story is a microcosm of the young industry's growing pains. David Buick's long suit was tinkering, his short suit business affairs. Before he had sold his first car he ran out of money and surrendered control to his major creditors, Benjamin and Frank Briscoe, the sheet-metal suppliers for many early Detroit car makers. The Briscoes, in turn, unloaded the unpromising company on James H. Whiting, manager of a wagon works in Flint, Michigan. Whiting moved the operation sixty-five miles upstate to Flint, where in August, 1904, the first Buick was finally sold. It was a typical buggy-type car of the period, powered by a well-engineered two-cylinder valve-in-head engine. Whiting had no more luck unraveling Buick's tangled affairs than the Briscoes had, and three months after making its first sale the Buick Motor Company was taken over by forty-two-year-old William Crapo Durant.

Billy Durant is unique in automotive history; among his many titles is that of most ambitious promoter. Already a millionaire carriage maker before he entered the automobile business, he was selling 150,000 low-priced Durant-Dort wagons a year through a nationwide network of dealers. In a matter of months he had the Buick operation refinanced and in good health, selling a reported half-million dollars worth of stock to his Flint neighbors in forty-eight hours. Utilizing Durant-Dort dealerships, he sold

(continued on page 45)

SILENT ELECTRICS

Here and on the following three pages is a glimpse of the quiet, always ready-to-go electric car that enjoyed popularity at the turn of the century and then went into a steady decline as the gasoline car surpassed it technologically. The electric's primary devotees were women; these fashion plates appeared in a Rauch and Lang advertisement in 1915.

WOODS MOTOR VEHICLE COMPANY

"VIVIDA VIS ANIMI"

THE GRAY LITH.CO.N.Y. NEW YORK & CHICAGO.

The 1900 Woods sales catalogue, the cover of which featured a hansom cab and a Latin motto testifying to the electric spirit that animated its vehicles, was expensively printed in color and aimed squarely at the conservative carriage trade. The pictures and descriptions of three (of ten) Woods models on the facing page are also taken from the catalogue. Woods started building electrics during 1899 and closed its doors in 1918.

Station Wagon $2,350

"One of the most popular family vehicles in existence, and as an Automobile, has the same features of carriage design and appointment that have always pertained to this character of vehicle. Has 42-inch and 36-inch wheels and 2-inch hard rubber tires. . . . Painted black body, with yellow or Brewster Green gear. . . . Trimmed accordingly. Has electric lights and electric bell."

Theater Bus $4,250

"This vehicle is designed with every reference to luxury of appointment. . . . It has a seating capacity of three on each side of the interior of the vehicle, with room for two on the smokers' seat, and is designed to be used with two men up in full livery. Is painted and trimmed in any desired colors. . . . Tires 2 inch. Cost to operate, about $2\frac{1}{2}$ cents per mile."

Game Trap $1,500

"A light, handsome, park and boulevard vehicle of sidebar design, arranged with game box between the seats for carrying lunches, golf sticks, or other requisites for an outing. . . . Weight complete 1400 pounds. Maximum speed, 12 miles per hour. Mileage capacity on one charge of the batteries, 25 miles. Will climb a 12 per cent grade. Cost to operate per mile, one cent."

Baker Electrics

SHAFT DRIVEN

Because of the limitations of battery power, the electric was typically an urban vehicle that operated on paved streets at low speed. This gave it one important advantage: it could be equipped with a closed body that made it drivable the year round. The more challenging rural road conditions met by gasoline cars early in the century would shake a closed body to pieces. The two ladies in this Baker ad can face a winter storm with aplomb, needing only tire chains to be on their way in comfort. To manage the 1913 Ohio at right, equipped with steering tiller, "magnetic brake," and power controller, was the very simplest of tasks.

Exclusiveness!

Mechanically and Artistically — the Ohio Electric Instantly Suggests It

The Ohio Electric introduced the *double drive* and the *magnetic control*—we hold patents on both ideas. And these two features, in connection with the *magnetic brake*, afford a driving comfort and an ease of operation that no other car has ever approached.

Thousands of satisfied owners endorse that statement—the numerous imitators prove it.

Artistically—in design, finish, upholstery and appointments—the Ohio Electric bears the stamp of aristocracy throughout. It is a car that will worthily enhance the appearance of the best gowned women.

The car itself is, after all, its own best argument. Any Ohio Electric dealer will be pleased to show it to you.

Literature on request.

The Ohio Electric Car Company, 1503 W. Bancroft St., Toledo

Gibson Electrics, Ltd.   Ontario Distributors   Toronto, Canada

OHIO
THE ENVIED ELECTRIC

1,400 Buicks in 1906, 4,600 in 1907, and 8,800 in 1908, second only to Ford. He was a whirlwind of salesmanship and promotion. His famous advertising slogan (as originally written) reflected his confidence: "When better automobiles are made, Buick will build them."

For Billy Durant the future was rosy and his expectations grand. For David Buick, tired at last of tinkering in obscurity in the Buick shops, 1908 was his last year with the company. By 1929, the year he died a poor man, more than two and a quarter million Buicks had been sold. "Just the breaks of the game," he told a reporter a year before his death.

Unlike Packard, Olds, and Buick—and other pioneers less familiar—Henry Ford was not the sort to be levered out of a company bearing his name. From the first, Ford did things his way. Born the son of a farmer in Dearborn township, Michigan, in 1863, he displayed an early genius for anything mechanical, matched only by a distaste for work in the fields. "My toys were all tools—they still are!" he would later write. At age sixteen he apprenticed himself to a Detroit machine shop, repairing clocks and watches as a sideline. Succeeding jobs widened his experience and whetted his fascination with the gasoline engine. Hired by the Edison Illuminating Company in 1891, Ford was soon focusing all his spare-time energies on the quadricycle taking shape in the shed behind

his rented house on Detroit's Bagley Avenue. After its successful trial in 1896, he set his cap for the automobile business. A spare, tidy, friendly man, country-boy unassuming, Ford proceeded with single-minded ambition.

Success came slowly. "It was not at all my idea to make cars in any such petty fashion," he later said of his early experimental prototypes. A dispute over his preoccupation with racing and speed trials to generate publicity led to his angry departure from the Detroit Automobile Company, the firm that under Henry Leland's direction later became Cadillac. Ford vowed never again to put himself "under orders." Finally, in 1902, he found a financial partner in Detroit coal dealer Alexander Y. Malcomson, and on June 16, 1903, the Ford Motor Company was incorporated. Of 1,000 shares of stock, Ford and Malcomson each held 255; among the other 10 stockholders were the Dodge brothers, the new company's chief supplier, and James Couzens, a Malcomson associate with an exceedingly tough, shrewd business mind.

The Ford Model A—the original Model A—was soon in production. A handsome little two-cylinder car of the buggy type, it got the company off to a dashing start. By the fall of 1904, 1,700 had been sold. Early Ford advertising blithely promised "positively the most perfect machine on the market"; more significant was

A 1904 Ford advertisement included a pledge to protect buyers against any legal action brought by the Selden patent holders. The photograph of the N. B. Slack carriage and harness establishment in West Chester, Pennsylvania, was probably taken in 1908. Mr. Slack was a man who saw the handwriting on the wall and added Fords to his sales line. The three cars lined up out front are the successors to Ford's popular Model N— a pair of Model S's flank a Model R—and the immediate predecessors of the famed Model T.

Model A's $850 price tag, placing it, the ads said, "within the reach of many thousands who could not think of paying the comparatively fabulous prices asked for most machines." Like Ransom Olds, Ford had his eye firmly fixed on the mass market, and already he had charted the course to reach it. "The way to make automobiles," he told stockholder John W. Anderson in 1903, "is to make one automobile like another automobile, to make them all alike, to make them come through the factory just alike; just as one pin is like another pin when it comes from a pin factory, or one match is like another match when it comes from a match factory."

The Ford Motor Company, with Ford handling design and production and Couzens administration and sales, quickly made its presence known. In 1906, its fourth production year, it seized the industry sales leadership—and held it for twenty-one consecutive years. Initially Malcomson tried to direct the company toward the higher-priced market, pushing development of the Model B ($2,000) and the Model K ($2,800) over Ford's increasingly strenuous objections. Backed by Couzens, Ford forced a showdown, and on July 12, 1906, Malcomson surrendered, selling him his 255 shares for $175,000. Henry Ford now had complete control of his company and his destiny. Now he could "get the car to the people," he exclaimed. "This is a great day."

The forerunner of things to come

was his Model N of 1906. A neat two-passenger runabout Ford described as "all automobile," it weighed just over a thousand pounds and was powered by an efficient four-cylinder engine of 15 horsepower that pushed it to a top speed of 45 mph. *Cycle and Automobile Trade Journal* proclaimed it "distinctly the most important mechanical traction event of 1906." It was priced at just $600. Output reached a hundred cars a day but could not keep up with demand. In the company's 1906–7 fiscal year, net income shot up to more than a million dollars and a new slogan was coined: "Watch the Fords go by."

By the time the Ford Model N reached the market, the era of the horseless carriage was ending. The ultralight "cyclecars" and solid-tired, buggy-like "high-wheelers" would continue to have their advocates, but the future belonged to standard-sized machines that no longer were mistaken at a distance for farmers' buggies. In 1906 American auto production outstripped that of France, the previous world leader. Figures such as Billy Durant and Henry Ford were on the verge of turning the automobile into very big business indeed. One problem continued to plague the industry, however— George B. Selden's patent.

Year after year Selden had carefully nursed the patent application he

filed in 1879 for a gasoline-powered "road engine." To keep its pending status active he periodically added amendments broadening his claims —but built no prototype—and always took the maximum time allowed for administrative paper-shuffling. Patents then had a life of seventeen years and were nonrenewable, and Selden was too good a patent attorney to want one issued in a nonexistent field. Historian William Greenleaf describes him as "a hawk-like figure lying in wait." Finally, in 1895, the Patent Office tightened its lax regulations and Selden's case was acted upon. On November 5 he was awarded United States Patent No. 549,160, which, the Commissioner of Patents reported, "may be considered [to cover] the pioneer invention in the application of the compression gas engine to road or horseless carriage use."

Selden, of course, had actually "invented" nothing at all. In his patent application he had simply taken known, existing elements, including the Brayton two-cycle engine, and combined them to produce—in theory—an operable road vehicle. When he first learned of it, recalled Hiram Percy Maxim, "I snorted my derision. I pointed out that the engine shown in the patent was utterly impractical and a joke. . . . The claims were so broad they were ridiculous." But whatever the patent's merits, it took on new significance in 1899 when Selden sold his patent rights for

George B. Selden's "road engine" patent brought him wealth if not fame. The handsome little brass model was a part of his application to the Patent Office. The photograph below, taken by Nick Lazarnick in New York City in September, 1907, shows a demonstration run of a prototype of Selden's machine built as a ploy in the long patent battle with Henry Ford. The mechanic jogging alongside had to restart the balky engine so often that he was called Cranky Louis. The controversial prototype did run, more or less, but Selden lost out to Ford anyway.

$10,000 and a share of future royalties to the Electric Vehicle Company.

Perhaps the best explanation for a company so named wanting a gasoline-car patent is that the dominant motives of its organizers were opportunistic and imperial. The Electric Vehicle Company was a combine of Wall Street financial tycoons, including William C. Whitney, P. A. B. Widener, and Thomas Fortune Ryan, allied with Colonel Albert Pope, the bicycle and auto builder. Electric Vehicle's first dream—of filling the streets of America's cities with electric cabs—came a cropper when the cabs' heavy lead-acid batteries proved totally inefficient; all the venture gained the combine was a pejorative press label, "the Lead Cab Trust." The Selden patent thus became an increasingly important asset on the company's books.

In 1900 Electric Vehicle sued Alexander Winton for patent infringement. Lacking the financial resources for a legal battle, Winton sought a settlement out of court. Other auto companies promptly came into line, and in 1903 the Association of Licensed Automobile Manufacturers was organized to coordinate matters. The Selden patent was assigned to the A.L.A.M., with two fifths of all royalties collected going to the Electric Vehicle Company, two fifths retained by the A.L.A.M. to administer patent licensing and to promote the auto industry in general, and one fifth to George Selden.

Motor Age was encouraged by this attempt to stabilize the freest of free-enterprise industries. The A.L.A.M., it editorialized, would restrain the "piratical hordes who . . . flood the market with trashy machines, made only to sell and not intended to go . . . ." Most of the leading car makers were content with this solution to the Selden "threat." But there were exceptions, most notably (but not surprisingly) Henry Ford. When the head of the A.L.A.M. sought to bring the Ford Motor Company to heel, James Couzens brought him up short. "Selden can take his patent and go to hell with it!" he snapped. "You men are foolish," warned the A.L.A.M. man. "The Selden crowd can put you out of business—and will." "Let them try it," was Henry Ford's rejoinder.

They did try it. Their suit brought against Ford in 1903 for patent infringement was prosecuted and defended with great vigor and enormous expense. Ford took his case to the public, with telling effect. He painted a vivid David-and-Goliath picture of a Wall Street "automobile trust" seeking to trample free enterprise by "smart practice and bluff." "I am opposed to the Selden patent first, last, and all the time," he told the press, "and I will fight it to the bitter end." When A.L.A.M. ads warned the public, "Don't buy a lawsuit with your car," Ford countered by guaranteeing purchasers against any legal liability. He was a clear winner on the publicity front, and Ford sales soared. In 1909 the court's decision went against Ford, but in 1911, on appeal, he won the war. The Selden patent was ruled valid—but only for automobiles using the long outmoded Brayton-type two-cycle engine. Neither Ford nor anyone else had infringed the Selden patent.

The A.L.A.M. was clearly an attempt at monopoly by regulation of both production and entry into the automotive field. In the event, however, it suffered the loosest kind of enforcement. The major car makers were too busy competing with each other, and many would-be makers simply ignored the patent. Ford's eight-year battle kept the "Selden crowd" continually off balance and encouraged defiance of their patent claims. As for George Selden, he was well enough rewarded for a decidedly limited contribution to automotive history, earning between $200,000 and $500,000 (estimates vary) in royalties. But the big winner was Henry Ford, who was well launched on his way to becoming that rarity in American history—a millionaire folk hero.

The automobile shed its swaddling clothes during the drawn-out Selden patent war. Americans found themselves facing something entirely new under the sun. Some viewed it as a plaything, others as an instrument of change, still others as a new necessity of modern life. But whatever it was or would become, the automobile was not being ignored in the opening decade of the new century.

2
AMERICA DISCOVERS AUTOMOBILING

The population of the United States in 1900, the Census Bureau reported, was 75,994,575. Whenever 99.99 per cent of these nearly 76 million Americans journeyed any distance domestically, they did so by railroad or interurban or steamboat. Urban transit meant horse-drawn carriage or bicycle or trolley or elevated railroad or (in Boston) subway. Daily life in small towns and rural areas proceeded at the pace of the horse. As the twentieth century began, barely .01 per cent of the population could count the horseless carriage as one further travel option.

The railroad ruled unchallenged as the nation's primary transportation artery, moving people and goods with a speed undreamed of by earlier generations. Urban mass transit, where it existed, tended to be crowded and uncomfortable. For private, individualized travel unfettered by timetables and fixed routes, the average citizen had only the choice of a bicycle or a horse and buggy; and for the two thirds of the citizenry who lived on farms or in small towns, nearly all workaday travel was behind a horse. The typical farm family existed in isolation, its horizons restricted to the distance it could cover by wagon or buggy—a dozen miles or less—and return the same day in time to care for the stock and milk the cows.

Small-towners, too, lived an isolated existence. Except for special occasions—a trip to visit relatives, a holiday excursion, an out-of-town funeral—their contact with the larger world was limited to picking up news at the depot or the steamboat landing or reading the weekly paper. Livery stables, blacksmith shops, and watering troughs were everyday reminders that Old Dobbin was a major fact of small-town life.

The horse was a major fact of urban life, too, and in America's cities he was not a creature universally admired. Sanitation experts at the turn of the century calculated that the average horse produced about twenty-two pounds of manure a day. Over a year this mounted up, in a city the size of Rochester, New York, with a horse population of 15,000, to the equivalent of a one-acre manure pile 175 feet high. In major cities such as New York or Chicago the malodorous mess was almost beyond calculation. Disease-bearing flies bred by the billions in streets and stables. Rain left thoroughfares coated with a foul gumbo of droppings, and in dry weather dust clouds of dried dung filled the air, irritating eyes and nasal passages and carrying "pestilential vapours" in through open windows.

The city horse failed on other counts besides sanitation. William Dean Howells wrote feelingly of the noisome torment of screeching iron-tired wagon wheels and "the sharp

This young lady donned her fur coat, took the driver's seat, and decided that the new American sport of automobiling was worth raising a cheer for. The cheering taking place opposite was in celebration of a very real accomplishment: motoring coast to coast in the record time of just a shade under thirty-three days. The year is 1904, the place is New York City, and the car is an air-cooled Franklin. At the wheel is L. L. Whitman, who made a career of cross-country expeditions, and beside him is C. S. Carris, of the Franklin company.

clatter of the horses' iron shoes." Horse-drawn conveyances took up an inordinate amount of storage and parking space and created sizable traffic jams. "The faithful, friendly horse," sums up urban historian Joel A. Tarr, "was charged with creating the very problems today attributed to the automobile: air contaminants harmful to health, noxious odors, and noise.... The solution to the problem, agreed the critics, was the adoption of the 'horseless carriage.'"

However ironic this solution to urban ills may seem today, it is an accurate reflection of the early welcome the automobile found in America. Thoughtful commentators of the period might tick off the nation's shortcomings — cities bursting their seams, thinning economic lifeblood in too many small towns, the flight of disaffected rural youth to the bright lights of Metropolis — yet their faith in social perfectibility through Progress was secure. Was it not amply demonstrated that technology was the handmaiden of Progress? Witness the advances wrought by the railroad, the trolley, the telegraph, the telephone, the harnessing of electric power, the thousand and one other technological innovations. The automobile, they believed, clearly came from the same mold.

None other than the Wizard of Menlo Park gave it his blessing. "The horseless vehicle is the coming wonder...," Thomas Edison told the New York *World* in 1895. "It is only a question of a short time when the carriages and trucks in every large city will be run with motors." The automobile would enhance the farmer's economic position "and greatly extend the scope and pleasure of all phases of country life," wrote a correspondent for *Harper's Weekly*. Motoring would increase "appreciation of the joys of living, of the beauties of nature, the hallowings of history . . . , that make for that love of country which we term patriotism," *Outing* predicted in 1903. In *The Independent* in 1904 one William F. Dix painted a rhapsodic word-picture of future suburbia: "Imagine a healthier race of workingmen, toiling in cheerful and sanitary factories, . . . who, in the late afternoon, glide away in their own comfortable vehicles to their little farms or homes in the country or by the sea twenty or thirty miles distant! They will be healthier, happier, more intelligent and self-respecting citizens because of the chance to live among the meadows and flowers of the country instead of in crowded city streets."

Such stuff as dreams are made of, certainly. "They had logic on their side," wrote Allan Nevins, "and experience was still unborn." Yet such hopes and predictions *were* logical. Once it was demonstrated that the horseless carriage was more than a noisy, smelly, greasy, vibrating mechanical novelty, that it would actually run, and run with reasonable regularity, its potential for creating real change in American life was plain for all to see. Change, of course, was Progress. This more than anything else explains the clamor of buyers for delivery, the insatiable demand for this most expensive item of consumer "hard goods" that had ever been offered to the public. In 1900 sketchy registration figures suggest a ratio of one car per 9,500 people; by 1910 the figure was one per 200. During the first decade of the twentieth century the majority of Americans did not simply accept the automobile; they smothered it with affection.

In the progression from horse to automobile, the bicycle served as an important way station. In the nineties Americans by the millions had taken with relish to the new "safety" bicycle (the modern geared, chain-driven configuration with wheels of equal size), crowding city streets and country lanes in good weather, reveling in the freedom of truly individualized travel. Such organizations as the League of American Wheelmen campaigned vigorously for better roads. In 1893 their pressure persuaded Congress to appropriate $10,000 for an Office of Road Inquiry — the acorn from which in time that mighty oak, the federal highway program, would grow. As we have seen, a number of pioneer auto makers came directly from the bicycle business. The industrial technology necessary to crank out a bicycle a minute, which Colonel Albert Pope's operation in Hartford was doing at the

American city streets at the turn of the century were not infrequently the scene of major traffic tie-ups featuring trolley cars and horse-drawn transport of every description. The picture below was taken in Philadelphia late in the 1890's. Barely a decade later both horse and traffic jams were on the way out—or so a 1910 poster touting Auto Week in Detroit suggests.

DETROIT

AUTO WEEK
JAN. 24-29
1-5-1-0

"LOOK MAMMA, THERE'S A HORSE!"

America's upper crust was quick to seek out automobiling's pleasures. The couple at upper right swathed their electric in flowers and enjoyed an automobile fete staged for the Four Hundred by the O. H. P. Belmonts at Newport, Rhode Island, in 1899. In the center picture, Mrs. Leslie Carter and pet, attended by footman and chauffeur, take their ease in a custom-built machine. The gentleman in the bowler at the bottom of the page is also well attended. His steamer by Locomobile is a dos-à-dos model, very popular at the turn of the century. Rich sporting types who ignored speed laws were much resented, and this cartoon proposes confining them to a modern Circus Maximus where the minimum speed would be 60 mph.

height of the cycling craze, furnished invaluable lessons. Precision-machined gears, friction-reducing ball bearings, chain drive (widely used on early cars), metallurgically advanced light steels, improved machine tools—and of course the pneumatic tire—were all part of the bicycle's legacy to the motorcar.

A more important part of that legacy was the matter of attitudes. It was the bicycle, Hiram Percy Maxim believed, that first "directed men's minds to the possibilities of independent, long-distance travel over the ordinary highway." Having created this demand, Maxim continued, the bicycle could not fully satisfy it: "A mechanically propelled vehicle was wanted instead of a foot-propelled one, and we now know that the automobile was the answer."

As had been the case with the bicycle in the nineties, the horseless carriage found quick acceptance among the trend-setters of high society eager for a new diversion. The Oliver Hazard Perry Belmonts of New York and Newport initiated the fad by importing a French motorcar in 1897, and by 1899 enough of their friends had acquired machines of their own that Mrs. Belmont could play hostess to "the first automobile event of social importance." Her horseless carriage festival, *Automobile* reported, "finished the summer season of America's 'Four Hundred' in a blaze of glory."

The festival was held on the broad lawns of Belcourt, the great marble "cottage" in Newport that Richard Morris Hunt had designed for the Belmonts to pass their summers in Gothic splendor. Guests in their flower-bedecked vehicles were confronted with a cunning "obstacle park" marked out by golf flags and featuring life-size cutouts of policemen, nursemaids, and other everyday hazards as well as dummy horses harnessed to carriages. Mr. Belmont, with Mrs. Stuyvesant Fish as his passenger, showed the way in a machine "surmounted by an arbor of cat-o'-nine tails bearing a stuffed eagle from whose beak ran blue and yellow streamers festooned to a floral pole, upon which were numerous seagulls." Colonel John Jacob Astor—who was soon to attract notice as the owner of no less than seventeen automobiles—steered his clematis-covered Pope-Waverley electric through the maze "with the same cool-headed dash that distinguished him while serving under fire at Santiago." To the amusement of all, the puckish playboy Harry Lehr concluded the novel gymkhana by deliberately knocking down every obstacle he encountered. After an evening of dining and dancing, *Automobile*'s correspondent reported, the "pageant of fairy chariots" headed home with "every vehicle . . . brilliantly illuminated with countless little glow-lights interspersed among the floral wreaths. . . ."

American Automobile marveled in 1899 at how quickly "the horseless car became the rage" among the elite: "At first when Mrs. Herman Oelrichs appeared in her self-moving car there was a sensation and lots of people talked unmercifully of the utter awfulness of Mrs. Oelrichs' proceedings. Yet some days afterwards Miss Daisy Post got a natty 'auto.' . . . In some inexplicable way Mrs. A. T. Kemp was induced to follow the example of her intrepid contemporaries in society, and she learned very quickly to manage her own Automobile. People rapidly began falling in line then. . . ."

Not everyone, however, mastered the art as easily as Mrs. Kemp. It is recorded that Mrs. Hamilton Fish of New York, on her maiden run in a new electric, knocked down a startled pedestrian and ran over him twice more before she could essay a final and complete stop. More terrified than injured, her victim fled. Mrs. Fish returned home on foot in high dudgeon and ordered the staff to dispose permanently of the offending vehicle.

Such incidents tended to inflame the natural resentment of the lower classes toward the rich and well-born. Arrogant young bloods who drove fast and carelessly were not the motorcar's best image makers, and on meaner streets they could expect a barrage of rocks. In an 1899 article titled "Criticisms Worth Heeding," *Motor Age* observed, "Chicago generally hailed the advent of the horseless carriage with a good deal of

The closing months of 1895 saw something new in the publishing world — the automotive press. *Motocycle* was first on the scene, published in Chicago in October. A month later *The Horseless Age* appeared in New York. That same month the venerable *Carriage Monthly,* based in Philadelphia, put out a special "Horseless Vehicle Number."

rejoicing. The people wanted it. But we doubt if they want it driven over them or over their rights in the public streets, and the warmth of their welcome is going to be a good deal cooled unless automobile owners exercise more care." Such warnings were too often ignored. On September 13 of that year, the New York *Times* reported, the city suffered its first automotive fatality, real-estate man H. H. Bliss being run down on Central Park West by a speeding horseless carriage as he stepped from a trolley.

Not surprisingly, the most vocal booster of the automobile was the newly founded automotive press. The first of these journals was *Motocycle,* which appeared in Chicago in October, 1895, reportedly backed by *Times-Herald* publisher Herman Kohlsaat. The magazine took its name from the winning entry in the *Times-Herald's* contest to christen the horseless carriage, but its editor revealed an uneasiness with the choice by adding "(Automobile)" to the cover. A month later in New York *The Horseless Age* made its debut under the editorship of E. P. Ingersoll. Both journals predated the initial American production run by the Duryea brothers. "The appearance of a journal devoted to a branch of industry yet in an embryonic state, may strike some as premature...," admitted editor Ingersoll in his first issue. "But those who have taken the pains to search below the surface for the great tendencies of the age, know what a giant industry is struggling into being there." If nothing else, E. P. Ingersoll was an unerring prophet.

The number of magazines and trade papers quickly multiplied, eight new ones appearing in 1899 and 1900 alone. "Although the automobile journals were biased partisans of the motor vehicle, they rarely misread public opinion by confusing it with their own...," writes automotive historian James J. Flink, who has made a close study of these publications. "The reporting seems on the whole to have been fairly objective and has the decided merit of having been done by participant observers who had a high degree of technical competence...." The journals reported industry developments (including, in 1897, the first press showing of new models, conducted by the ubiquitous Colonel Pope), explained technical advances, offered driving and servicing tips, covered the organization of new automobile clubs, lobbied for better roads and more realistic traffic laws, and in general served as a sounding board for the new life style they called "automobiling."

Newspapers and general-circulation magazines also reflected the public's intense interest in the horseless carriage, running news stories, special departments, and even whole issues on the subject. As a rule their tone was complimentary, with the inevitable criticisms more constructive than destructive. In 1899 the Cleveland *Plain Dealer* assigned reporter Charles B. Shanks to accompany Alexander Winton on the second of his pioneering Cleveland–New York cross-country drives. Shanks's dispatches, picked up from the *Plain Dealer* by many other papers, were a big publicity boost for the young industry. Winton, of course, was the immediate beneficiary. Before his trip, he reported, "sales were made almost exclusively to engineers..., but after the trip, the sales were made to the public at large." In appreciation he made Shanks his advertising manager.

Newspaper editors of the period followed the general rule of not mentioning the names of advertised products in their news columns, so their automotive coverage tended to publicize the industry as a whole rather than individual car makers. However, there was a more direct publicity windfall if the subject of a legitimate news story — Winton and his trek to New York, for example — happened to market a car bearing his own name. Winton, Ransom Olds, and Henry Ford (especially Henry Ford) understood this trick perfectly and made full use of it. Ford may have fought the Selden patent on principle, but he also recognized that it was worth challenging simply for the enormous publicity benefits.

Another major generator of public interest was the automobile show. What would become the most prestigious of these events, the New York

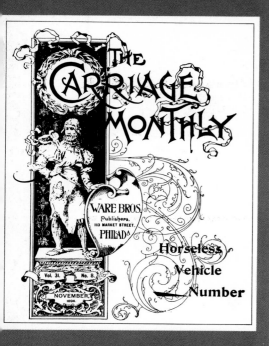

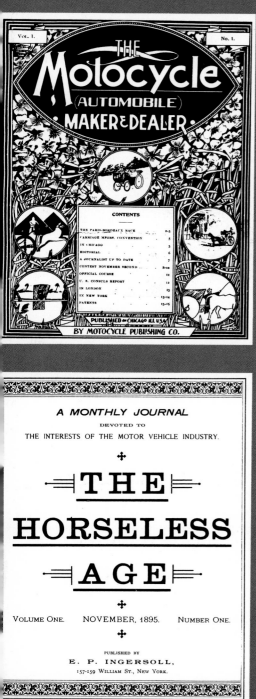

Automobile Show, was inaugurated in Madison Square Garden with a nine-day run in November, 1900. Colonel Pope was on hand to promote his machines, as were Winton, Elwood Haynes, James Packard, the Duryeas, and Harry Knox. In all there were thirty-four models on display, nineteen powered by gasoline, seven by steam, six by electricity, and two by a reassuring gasoline-electricity combination. Suppliers, including B. F. Goodrich, the first tire maker to call Akron, Ohio, home, had displays in the balcony. Stunt driver Joe McDuffee demonstrated the prowess of the Mobile steamer by piloting it up a steep wooden ramp, which included one gradient of forty-six per cent, twenty times a day.

Society turned out in force to view the machines in the Garden, and it may be that many spectators came simply to view the swells. "The handsome gowns of the women and the multitude of snowy masculine shirt fronts reminded one of the Horse Show at its best," reported the *Times*. The William K. Vanderbilts, Kiliaen Van Rensselaer, Whitelaw Reid, D. Ogden Mills, William Rockefeller, and Colonel Astor all appeared one evening. Mrs. Edward Curtis, Jr., and Mrs. John W. Allison competed in a race for electrics on the board track surrounding the exhibits. Sportsman Albert C. Bostwick, one of the Four Hundred, demonstrated steerability on an obstacle course. The more adventuresome spectators availed

themselves of free rides. The *World's* society page headlined its coverage of the show, "The Automobile Vies with Dances in Interest This Week."

One sponsor of the Madison Square Garden show was the New York-based Automobile Club of America, founded eighteen months earlier by what *Motor Age* called "an ultra-fashionable coterie of millionaires." It was not an exaggerated description. A single A.C.A. membership drive, for example, corralled the banker August Belmont, steel master Henry Clay Frick, Wall Street plunger John W. "Bet-a-Million" Gates, and that consummate aristocrat Alfred Gwynne Vanderbilt. Other early big-city clubs were similarly dominated by the socially prominent. Before very long, however, automobile ownership began to reveal an egalitarian, democratic pattern that was peculiarly American. As early as 1901 *Motor World* predicted trouble for clubs that declared themselves "organizations of the elect; self-constituted arbiters of all automobilism and an aristocracy or autocracy to whose sacred membership no man without cerulian sanguinaceousness or millionairish pretentions is to be eligible."

However orotund his phrasing, *Motor World*'s editor could spot a trend. Within three years there were perhaps a hundred clubs scattered across the nation, welcoming (as the Automobile Club of Buffalo put it) "anyone interested in motoring," re-

In November, 1900, the New York Automobile Show made its debut in Madison Square Garden and drew sizable crowds. This first major American show featured a wide array of steam, electric, and gasoline models (right). Below is a show promoter with a show poster. One of the most popular attractions was the Mobile steamer, which was driven up and down a steep ramp at frequent intervals. The photograph above was apparently taken at a trial run inside the Garden; during the show itself the stunt was performed on a ramp atop the Garden's roof. In the inset picture opposite is a trial of a different sort: how to negotiate an obstacle course.

AUTOMOBILE SHOW
MADISON SQUARE GARDEN

Here is Old 16 at work, thundering through Westbury Bend on the way to victory in the Vanderbilt Cup race in 1908. At the wheel of the mighty Locomobile—its 16-liter engine could take it to 110 mph on a straightaway—is George Robertson, and at his side is his riding mechanic, Glenn Ethridge. In taking the Vanderbilt Cup (right), Robertson scored the first win for an American car in this famous series of road races held on Long Island in the first decade of the century. An estimated 200,000 fans cheered Robertson to victory; as the photograph suggests, the crowd control left much to be desired.

gardless of social position, who sought "a rallying point for those causes that motorists favor." In 1902 the American Automobile Association was formed to give national voice to these local clubs. In its early years the A.A.A. suffered ill health brought on by the undue influence of elitist-minded clubs such as the A.C.A. There was much grumbling in the rear ranks about "a small clique of gentlemen" named Vanderbilt, Harriman, Havemeyer, Du Pont, Flagler, Astor, and Rockefeller seeking to dominate automobiling as they dominated so much else in American life. Eventually the levelers won out, the A.C.A. withdrew in a huff, and the A.A.A. gained fresh strength by allying itself with a trade organization, the National Association of Automobile Manufacturers. By 1910 the rejuvenated A.A.A. had more than 25,000 members and affiliation with 225 local clubs in thirty of the forty-six states. Democracy had triumphed.

Without question, Americans at the turn of the century were becoming intrigued by the automobile as a wholly new means of personal transportation. At the same time a good many of them were becoming intrigued by an even more exciting point: how fast could it go?

Early in 1902, while still with the Detroit Automobile Company, Henry Ford spelled out for his brother-in-law his formula for gaining public attention in the infant automotive business. "My Company will kick about me following racing," he wrote, "but they will get the Advertising and I expect to make $ where I can't make ¢s at Manufacturing." Racing was indeed an attention-getter, as Ford and other car makers were discovering.

The attention was not always flattering. During the first American speed contest, held in 1896 at the old Narrangansett Park in Cranston, Rhode Island, a Riker electric won every heat with such monotonous regularity that the crowd began to shout at the also-rans, "Get a horse!"

No such derision was ever aimed at Alexander Winton, whose racing machines set a whole series of early speed marks. On October 10, 1901, in a racer of his own design, Ford challenged Winton's ascendancy in a ten-mile match race at Detroit's Grosse Pointe horse track. Winton was building a solid lead in his more powerful car when suddenly, as a newsman described it, "a thin wreath of blue smoke appeared at the rear of the machine, and it gradually increased to a cloud." Ford swept past the laboring Winton and won going away. "Boy, I'll never do that again!" he exclaimed to spectators. "I was scared to death." He had averaged about 45 mph around the one-mile dirt track.

Before long, car makers were turning out special racers with dashing names to challenge each other's records—Ford's *999* and *Arrow;* Winton's *Bullet* machines; Ransom Olds's *Pirate;* Packard's *Gray Wolf;* Peerless's *Green Dragon;* Baker's electric *Torpedo;* the fast White steamer *Whistling Billy;* the faster Stanley *Rocket.* In 1906 at Ormond Beach, Florida, a Stanley racer captured the world's land-speed record with a run of better than 127 mph for the flying mile. The next year the Stanley people were back at Ormond Beach with the *Rocket* to try to break their record. A quarter of the way through the measured mile the steamer hit a bump, became airborne, and was slammed to pieces. Miraculously driver Fred Marriott survived, but the accident soured the Stanleys' taste for racing. (In his later years Marriott liked to astonish visitors with the tale that his speedometer registered 197 mph at the moment of the crash. The *Rocket,* however, had no speedometer. F. E. Stanley, who was clocking the run, carefully calculated the speed at no more than 150 mph—still no mean feat for 1907.)

The gaudiest American racing competition of the period took place under the banner of millionaire sportsman William K. Vanderbilt. Vanderbilt hoped to see a gentlemanly international competition for the ultimate betterment of the sport of automobiling, but he got more than he bargained for. The Vanderbilt Cup contests run on the back roads of Long Island between 1904 and 1910 were spectacles worthy of ancient Rome, unlike anything the country had ever witnessed. In some years more than 250,000 people jammed themselves alongside the course — and often on it. Only the cry of "Car coming!" and the thunderous exhaust of a racer bearing down like "a shell from a 12-inch gun" cleared the road of bemused spectators. *The Horseless Age* labeled the 1904 contest, in which a riding mechanic was killed, a "barbarous exhibition" in a nation otherwise "marching in the forefront of civilization" — an opinion of auto racing still heard today. Two years later the New York *Herald* headlined the death of a spectator and "Many Marvellous Escapes." But still the thrill seekers came out by the hundreds of thousands to watch. Not until 1908 were they rewarded by an American victory; a powerful Locomobile with "daredevil" George Robertson at the wheel averaged better than 64 mph for four hours around the twisting course. An Alco, the sturdy product of the American Locomotive Company, then won two years in a row. "Call them haphazard, call them bloody, call them tragicomic. . . ," writes a student of these contests, "the Long Island Vanderbilts were singular events."

Road racing — notably the post-Long Island Vanderbilts and the Elgin contest in Illinois — would remain a part of the competition scene, but closed-course racing was taking over in popularity. It was far easier for spectators to see everything that went on. The Indianapolis 500 was inaugurated in 1911, and the moment its first "rolling start" broke for Turn One it was on its way to becoming an American sporting institution. Less pretentious events were run by the hundreds at county fairgrounds and horse tracks all across the country in the automobile's early years. This was rough-and-tumble barnstorming (before that term was appropriated by the pioneer aviators), the direct ancestor of today's stock-car racing.

Lead-footed racing drivers of every stripe became a new species of folk hero, men such as Ralph Mulford, Joe Tracy, Bob Burman, Ralph De Palma, the Chevrolet brothers, the legendary Barney Oldfield. When his number finally came up, the rough-hewn Oldfield once said, "I want the grandstand to be crowded and the band playing the latest rag. I want them all to say, as they file out the gate: 'Well, ole Barney — he was goin' some!'" He always did go some, but he died peacefully in bed in 1946. An echo of those bare-knuckle racing carnivals can still be heard every time a traffic cop snaps, "Who d'ya think ya are, Barney Oldfield?"

The American fascination with speed certainly did not begin with such auto racing events as the Vanderbilt Cup, yet just as certainly it was whetted by these contests. The automobile was a means of personal transportation that obviously could go faster than a horse or a bicycle; and that being the case, it was inevitably going to be driven fast — by some as fast as it would go, by others

Race driver Barney Oldfield (top), cigar in place as usual, oils up his powerful Peerless *Green Dragon.* Nick Lazarnick took the photograph at right at the Elgin, Illinois, road-racing circuit in 1913; Spencer Wishart drove this Mercer to a third-place finish in the race for the Elgin Trophy. The picture below was taken during a twenty-four-hour marathon grind at Brighton Beach, Brooklyn, in July of 1909. The pit crew is at work servicing the victorious Simplex, driven by Vanderbilt Cup winner George Robertson.

THOMAS CARS
EQUIPPED WITH
DIAMOND TIRES

SIMPLEX

MOTOR VEHICLE MANUFACTURERS ASSOCIATION

at least faster than non-car owners (and the law) felt was safe.

But the effectiveness of speed as a sales pitch was from the first a matter of dispute. Billy Durant, who heavily backed Buick's competition efforts, advertised the popular 1908 Model 10 as the car for "men with real red blood who don't like to eat dust." On the other hand, contemporary accounts agree, excessive speed on the open road triggered the public's ill temper faster than any other aspect of automobiling. Commenting on manufacturers entering speed competitions, *Motor Age* questioned whether "even the winners can see any great profit in the outcome, whereas it is certain the losers . . . have lost more by failing to make the showing they expected to make."

As a general rule, early automobile advertising featuring family cars — as opposed to ads for flashy sporting machines — emphasized mechanical reliability over speed and styling; most potential customers were primarily interested in knowing they could successfully get where they wanted to go. Economy and reliability trials, hill-climbing contests, and twenty-four-hour marathons attracted sizable fields, with companies such as Lozier, Marmon, Simplex, Buick, and other major winners making sure the public was aware of the feats of their sturdy "stock models." Marmon, reads a typical ad of the period, was able to defeat "the hottest kind of competition with the highest-priced

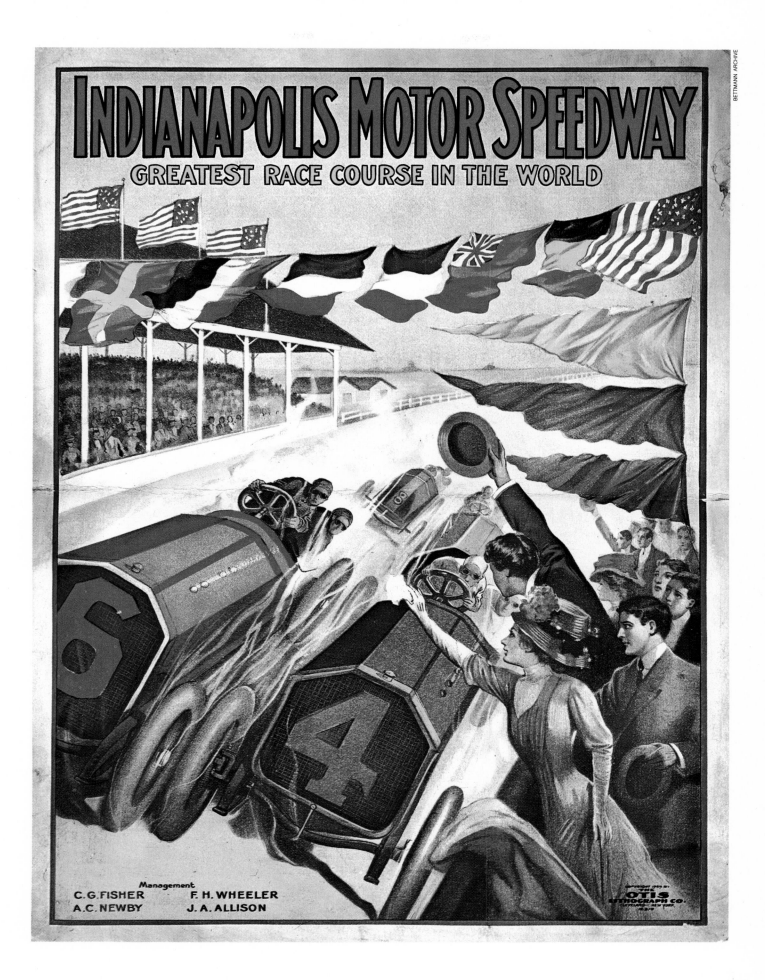

cars . . . simply because it has been better able to stand the pace for long distances."

As Alexander Winton had demonstrated with his Cleveland—New York jaunts—and as Roy Chapin confirmed when he drove his curved-dash Oldsmobile from Detroit to New York in 1901—cross-country expeditions were sure-fire ways to capture the public's imagination and stimulate sales. The supreme test was obvious: coast to coast by automobile. One day in May, 1903, at the San Francisco University Club, Horatio Nelson Jackson, a thirty-one-year-old doctor from Burlington, Vermont, who had wintered in California, was defending the automobile's utility so vigorously that he was challenged to drive one home across the continent. He promptly accepted. That Dr. Jackson's instincts were purely sporting is evident from the paltry wager involved—$50.

In 1903 more than ninety-three per cent of the 2.3 million miles of roads in the United States were nothing better than plain dirt—horse-belly deep in mud in spring, thick with dust in summer, frozen in iron-hard ruts in winter—and of that total, dirt or otherwise, very few miles indeed were west of the Mississippi. No less than thirty-seven automobilists had already failed the challenge Dr. Jackson was accepting. Lord Nelson would have approved his daring. He hired a mechanic, Sewell K. Croker, purchased a used 20-horsepower

Winton "two-chair" touring model, put Mrs. Jackson on an eastbound train with the cheerful promise that he would see her again before the year was out, and on May 23 he and Croker set forth on their adventure. Behind the Winton's tufted leather seats was a mound of tools, spare parts, camping gear, block and tackle, fishing rods, a telescope, and an armory that included a rifle, a shotgun, and two pistols.

Since many transcontinental attempts had come to grief in desert country, Jackson and Croker decided on a more northerly crossing. Appropriately, part of the time they would be following the old Oregon Trail route of the pioneers. But first there was the Sierra Nevada to cross. It was a stiff test of their resolve. Laboring up boulder-strewn tracks and edging along narrow mountainside ledges were bad enough; going downhill was almost worse. The Winton's brakes were as good as those on any car, which is to say they were nothing much at all.

On they went, patching the tires and patching them again until in desperation they wrapped them with burlap. In the empty high-plateau country of eastern Oregon they ran out of gas, and Croker had to walk twenty-nine miles to find fuel. In isolated settlements where people had never heard of an automobile much less seen one, they were greeted like visitors from another planet. The rugged Winton chugged along,

wrote Ralph Nading Hill, that tireless chronicler of Vermont's sons and daughters, "through mountain windstorms and slanting rains, through gullies of red clay, over lava beds of extinct volcanoes and between the boulders of dried-up creeks."

Near Caldwell, Idaho, the travelers were adopted by a stray white bulldog they named Bud. Bud seemed to enjoy the bouncing, wrenching ride and wore a pair of driving goggles with aplomb. Idaho was also the site of a deep bog they christened the "twenty-four horsepower mudhole"— the Winton's twenty horses plus the four-horse team that pulled them out. A sand plain in Wyoming required them to lay out a track of cut sagebrush to give the driving wheels purchase. Sometimes they were able to bump across ravines and deep-cut riverbeds on railroad trestles, but more often they had to winch the car through the worst places with block and tackle. Near the Continental Divide this winching process was repeated seventeen times in a single day.

The Winton stood the rigors remarkably well. Croker was able to make good a front wheel ball-bearing failure with the help of a coal-mine machinist and parts from a mowing machine. There was a five-day layover in Rawlins, Wyoming, while the Winton factory in Cleveland responded to Jackson's telegraphed plea for new connecting rods for the two-cylinder engine. New tires were

(continued on page 73)

Edward Penfield's study for an Oldsmobile ad pictures the Model Z of 1908.

ILLUSTRATING THE AUTO

Devotees of the automobile in the first decade of the century had the good fortune to be living in the golden age of American illustration. Leading artists were commissioned by the press as well as auto manufacturers, and their posters, magazine-cover illustrations, and advertisements—sampled in this portfolio—received wide circulation and spread the gospel of automobiling.

Magazines and newspapers reflected—and stimulated—the public's growing interest in the automobile with articles, illustrations, and an array of special "auto numbers." The 1907 poster for *Scribner's* magazine was painted in vivid art-nouveau style by Robert J. Wildhack. The New York *World* commissioned the painting above for the cover of an automobile section it published in 1908; the setting is Riverside Drive, with Grant's Tomb in the right background. One of the most prolific "automobile artists" was Edward Penfield. In both his 1906 calendar and his *Collier's* cover design, painted in 1907, the motorists are well-garbed and well-born. Automobiling was as yet seldom depicted as a sport of the common man.

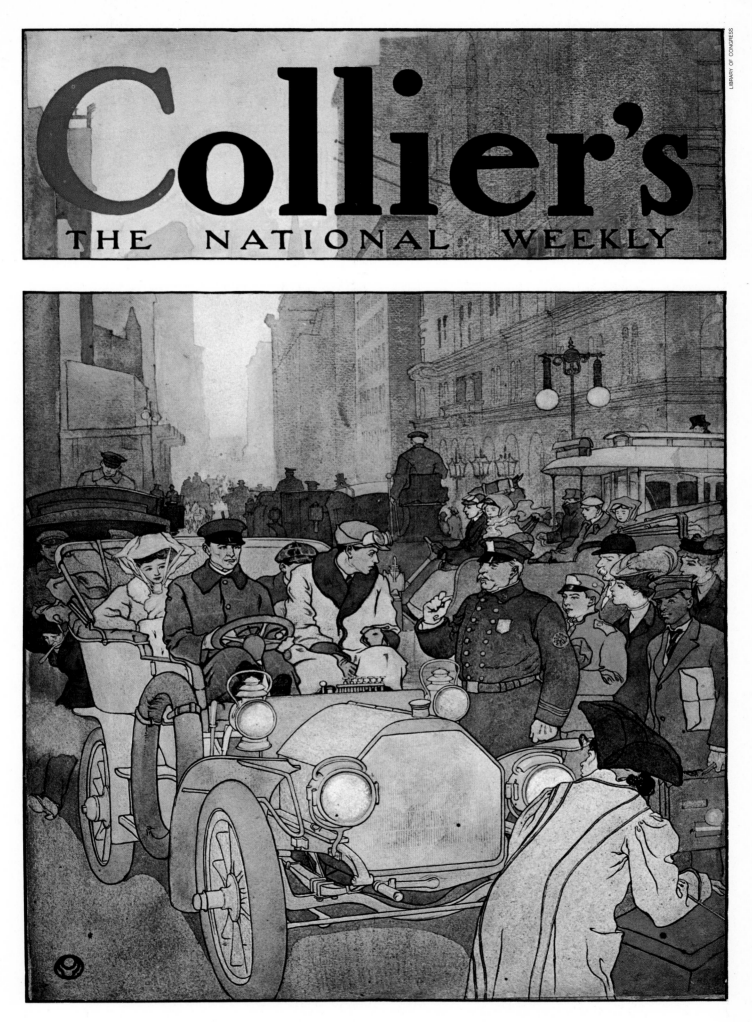

The Pierce-Arrow

Gil Spear

[Shopping with the Pierce-Arrow]

Pierce-Arrow commissioned advertising art with a lavish hand and a light rein. "I don't think anyone anywhere ever had the freedom that the artists for Pierce-Arrow had," a veteran illustrator has recalled. The policy paid off, producing such work as this 1910 ad by Adrian Gil Spear. The Penfield rough sketch below for Oldsmobile dates from about 1906 and challenges the copywriter to do his thing in a small space indeed. Probably the most famous automobile picture—certainly the most widely distributed one—was painted in 1910 for Oldsmobile by William Harnden Foster. At right is the chromolithograph version that hung in garages, saloons, clubs, and of course dealers' showrooms from coast to coast. The car is Oldsmobile's Limited, the train New York Central's crack Twentieth Century Limited. The Packard touring phaeton rendered in an elegantly classical Roman setting is the 1913 model.

SILENCE

COMFORT

Peerless

All That The Name Implies   Catalogue N will be sent on request

THE PEERLESS MOTOR CAR CO.,
2443 EAST 93ᴿᴰ ST., CLEVELAND, O. MEMBER A.L.A.M.

also dispatched from the East. In Nebraska the resourceful Croker jury-rigged a broken front axle with a length of iron pipe so they could limp to a blacksmith's for a permanent repair.

When the adventurers reached the settled areas of the Great Plains, local papers began reporting their progress under such headlines as "From Ocean to Ocean in an Automobile Car." Crowds gathered at each stop to gawk and ask questions endlessly. One boy rode his horse sixty-eight miles to examine their machine. "I have seen lots of pictures of 'em," he exclaimed, "but this is the first real live one I ever saw." A Nebraska farm couple showed no such curiosity. When the Winton came clattering toward them, trailing its customary cloud of dust, they hid under their wagon in terror.

Once across the Mississippi they found the driving easier, except for mud, the usual flat tires, and one nasty accident when the speeding car cracked into an unseen obstacle in a dust-deep road and Jackson, Croker, and Bud were all pitched out of the machine. In Cleveland the smiling Winton people treated them to a testimonial dinner, but their offer to give the car a factory overhaul was turned down by Dr. Jackson for fear his journey would be dismissed as a promotional stunt. On July 26, 1903, after sixty-four days and probably at least 4,500 miles, the weary trio motored down New York's Fifth Avenue.

Jackson, Croker, and Bud were first, but not by much. Less than a month later a factory-sponsored Packard arrived in New York from San Francisco after a crossing of sixty-one days. In September a little curved-dash Olds completed the journey. There were repeated transcontinental crossings in succeeding years as factory teams sought publicity flourishes by lowering the record. (In 1904 Oldsmobile made much of the fact that it was the first to accomplish the westbound trip.) In 1910 a Reo lowered the record to ten days, fifteen hours, a mark that stood for seven years. The year before, in a Maxwell, Alice Huyler Ramsey and three women companions had made the first distaff crossing. "I was born mechanical, an inheritance from my father," Mrs. Ramsey confided in her memoir of the adventure. It was a fortunate inheritance. (A newspaper reporter who interviewed Mrs. Ramsey in California in 1977 found her a spry ninety and still driving. She regularly requalified for her driver's license without trouble.)

The ultimate in long-distance expeditions was the New York-to-Paris contest of 1908—the legendary Great Race. On February 12 a quarter of a million New Yorkers lined the streets to see the six contestants head off westward around the world. One hundred sixty-nine days and 13,341 miles later the lone American entry, a stock Thomas Flyer, was declared the winner in Paris. George Schuster, be-

Instructions for Motoring in Nevada

0	Eureka
0.4	Left fork up canyon . . .
1.5	Left fork (sign)
2.3	Right fork, follow telephone poles . . .
7.3	Water (Pinto)
9.9	Left fork, sign, follow telephone
10.0	Left fork, follow telephone
14.2	Turn right around house across flat, leave telephone
22.9	Summit. Telephone poles come in here
33.8	Coyle ranch
34.0	Take right fork, brush road (best of three roads)
35.0	Left fork (sign) . . .
40.8	Spring, foot of grade
44.3	Ranch
46.8	Fourteen-mile ranch. At end of fence take right fork . . .
68.0	Kimberly. Down the canyon may be seen a small settlement known as Riepetown. Head for this . . . and keep on the road in the bottom of the canyon until you again meet the railroad tracks and follow
73.7	Take left fork leading toward railroad
73.8	Cross tracks and follow main road straight ahead through Lane City to
77.2	Northern Hotel, Ely

—Bellamy Partridge's log of a cross-country journey in 1912, in *Fill 'er Up!* (1952)

The ultimate adventure in automobiling's early days was the long-distance expedition. The well-traveled Winton at left carried Dr. Horatio Nelson Jackson (at the wheel), Sewell K. Croker, and Bud the bulldog on the premier coast-to-coast crossing, in 1903. At the right are some of the trials encountered by long-distance travelers. Tom Fetch and Marius Krarup complete a tire repair in the scorching Nevada desert in 1903; their car is a Packard christened "Old Pacific," and they made it to New York only a month behind Jackson and Croker. The snowscape was taken in Illinois in 1908, during the opening leg of the spectacular New York-to-Paris race. A locally owned Locomobile breaks trail for Italy's entry, a Zust. The Mercer contestants facing muddy prospects were photographed during a transcontinental crossing attempt in 1911.

hind the wheel most of the way, had battled unimaginable terrain and weather on three continents to become an instant national celebrity. "It was something from the pages of Jules Verne, yet it actually happened," remarks *Automobile Quarterly*. The next year Thomas sales jumped twenty-seven per cent.

The typical early car owner might not be ready to tackle the trackless West in imitation of Dr. Jackson and Mrs. Ramsey or the Siberian plains in imitation of George Schuster, yet he was always on the lookout for any chance to test his driving mettle. Local auto clubs and the American Automobile Association found that their memberships responded most enthusiastically to tours and reliability runs. Here was the perfect challenge to that spirit of adventure and independence that seemed to beat in the breast of the early motorist; having thoroughly explored home-town streets and byways, he—and in some cases, she—was eager to explore the outside world. In 1904 the A.A.A. Touring Committee, under the leadership of Augustus Post, a tireless promoter of the motorcar (and later of the airship and the airplane), and Charles J. Glidden, a Bostonian who had retired from the telephone business a millionaire, announced a truly demanding long-distance event: a reliability run of some 1,250 miles from New York to St. Louis, host city of that glamorous centennial fair, the Louisiana Purchase Exposition.

On the morning of July 28, 1904, the main contingent assembled at Fifth Avenue and Fifty-ninth Street in New York. The tour was to head north through the Hudson Valley to Albany, where it would be joined by a group from Boston, then across New York State via the Mohawk Valley, the historic route of the pioneers, to Buffalo, thence westward through Cleveland, Ohio, and South Bend, Indiana, to Chicago, and finally southward through Illinois to East St. Louis. There it would rendezvous with a contingent from the Middle Atlantic states, which was to trace a more southerly route, for a final triumphant parade to the exposition grounds in St. Louis. Seventy-one cars were officially entered, but many additional tourers would cut in and out along the route.

At 9 A.M. Augustus Post was waved off first in his White. There were several other big White steamers in the procession—including one piloted by Laura Lillibridge, the only woman driver on the starting line—but no electrics: the problems of recharging batteries on a cross-country tour were considered prohibitive. Among the other starters, all of them piled high with luggage, spare parts, tow ropes, and extra tires, was a stately Peerless carrying five passengers; a luxurious Pope-Toledo driven by Colonel Pope himself and a Pope-Hartford, its less expensive sister car; a chain-driven air-cooled Franklin; and a hulking French Darracq. There was also an

Oldsmobile light tonneau model, a 24-horsepower Pierce Great Arrow, a Haynes-Apperson, a Buckmobile, a noisy little two-cycle Elmore, and a Yale with solid-rubber tires and detachable top. A bulky Knox Waterless was finally coaxed into life and was a late starter. After the tour officials had left for Poughkeepsie, the first checkpoint—they traveled by train and got there well ahead of the tourers—a little Cadillac "one-lunger" rolled up to the starting line and the driver asked where everyone had gone. Given directions, he waved cheerfully and set off in pursuit.

The first leg to Poughkeepsie was not without event. Beyond the normal complement of tire troubles, Colonel Pope's Pope-Toledo lost its fan belt and the Buckmobile snapped its driving chain. The Yale was crippled when a repairman left a wrench in its planetary transmission. One trolley car was run into and one dog run over. The late-starting Cadillac caught up at dinnertime and afterward kept the pace comfortably. Upon reaching Albany the second day, the tour was joined by the big green English Napier belonging to Charles Glidden, who reported that on the journey from Boston he had hit a horse. The miserable roads across New York State took a heavy toll of tires, springs, and steering linkages. The angry drivers paused in Utica to petition the governor: without doubt, they wrote, "throughout the civilized world there do not exist roads in such

wretched condition." There was a one-day layover in Buffalo to make much-needed repairs and visit Niagara Falls.

Because of the distance and difficult conditions, the tour was declared a "go-as-you-please" event, with no official time limits established between checkpoints. There was considerable indignation at the "ungentlemanly" conduct of Colonel Pope, who persistently drove as fast as possible in order to arrive first in each town and collect the plaudits of each mayor's welcoming committee. Excessive speed—"scorching"—also caused other problems, especially in rural areas. During the Buffalo layover the driver of the Peerless was served a summons for having frightened an allegedly valuable horse. Near Erie, Pennsylvania, Charles Glidden was brought to an abrupt halt by an angry farmer waving a shotgun and was not allowed to proceed until he had paid a dollar compensation for each of the farmer's chickens run over by an earlier driver.

The scatterings of chicken feathers left by such incidents, however, served as valuable route guides on the unmarked roads. Pathfinder cars were supposed to mark out each day's course with confetti, but often they were late or too slow to stay ahead of the scorchers or simply got lost themselves. Suspicious farmers were not overly helpful with directions, and drivers reduced to dead reckoning turned up hours late at every checkpoint. In Illinois a little one-cylinder Rambler simply disappeared. It was marked on the tour log as "dropped out."

Mechanical failures and accidents felled other contestants. Chuckholes broke many a wheel and bent many an axle, and the combination of muddy high-crowned roads and deep ditches caused frequent mishaps. Near South Bend, Indiana, the Peerless, which had been dogged by trouble all the way, was demolished by a freight train at a grade crossing; fortunately no one was hurt. In the village of Pontiac, Illinois, a local mechanic, working on a leaky carburetor by the light of an open-flame lantern, totally gutted the Oldsmobile light tonneau.

In contrast to their often chilly greeting in rural areas, the tourers found a warm welcome in the cities. Local auto clubs in Cleveland and Toledo feted the contestants with splendid banquets, and in Chicago there was a gala parade along Michigan Avenue. Upon reaching East St. Louis the tour directors found that the Middle Atlantic contingent had arrived a day early and proceeded on across the Mississippi's Eads Bridge into St. Louis. Colonel Pope once again jumped the schedule, driving into the grounds of the Louisiana Purchase Exposition and exhibiting his Pope-Toledo under banners proclaiming first place in the two-week New York–St. Louis odyssey. Nevertheless, there was considerable satisfaction evident among the fifty-nine official entrants who completed the journey as they drove their muddy, dented cars in procession into the fairgrounds on August 11 to the cheers of admiring crowds. The mayor proclaimed it Automobile Day.

Charles J. Glidden may have been the most devoted early booster of the automobile in America. The cross-country trip to St. Louis inspired him to establish the celebrated Glidden Tours, which for eight years were premier events on automobilists' calendars. If they were not exactly what Glidden hoped them to be—pleasant "health-giving recreation" for blue-blooded ladies and gentlemen—they did persuade countless Americans that the motorcar was here to stay. They also made certain car makers exceedingly happy.

The initial Glidden Tour was scheduled for July, 1905, the 867-mile course beginning at the Plaza Hotel in New York, proceeding to Bretton Woods, New Hampshire, and returning to the Plaza, covering in twelve days a sizable part of New England. Glidden had wanted to attract owner-drivers interested in a sporting test of their machines, but in fact the tour attracted mostly factory entrants interested in selling cars.

The entry list was distinguished if not exactly blue-blooded. Colonel Pope entered several models, and on hand in person were Ransom Olds in a Reo, Jonathan Maxwell and Ben-

The first Glidden Tour, in 1905, was a social as well as a motoring success. The massive Mt. Washington Hotel at Bretton Woods, New Hampshire, seen here, was the midpoint watering hole for the entrants. The machines are lined up for the return trip to New York. The proper attire for all the socializing required considerable luggage, carried along by the Packard truck at top. This first tour had its mishaps, however, such as the one that befell Jean Newton Cuneo (right). No one was hurt, and her White was saved.

These snapshots were taken during various Glidden Tours. Beginning counterclockwise from left is a scene of alfresco dining near Atlanta, Georgia, in 1911. The driver of the Mitchell paying his due to the lady toll keeper has a horseshoe on his radiator for good luck. The toughest job in touring was marking the route; witness the muddy dilemma of this 1909 pathfinder crew in an E-M-F. Braving unbridged streams was another hazard, and in this rural setting it was apparently regarded as a spectator sport. Even when the going was good there could be problems. The puzzled gentleman below, another one of the pathfinders for the 1909 tourers, is facing a crossroads decision. At right, a small boy perched on a fence post takes in three entries in the 1910 tour. They are (from left) a Cutting, a Cartercar, and a Parry. All three companies were gone by 1916.

jamin Briscoe in a pair of Maxwells, Walter White (Rollin's brother) and Augustus Post in White steamers, and Percy Pierce (son of company founder George N. Pierce) in a Great Arrow. Glidden would make the tour in his Napier. There were a number of women going along as passengers, but only one, Jean Newton Cuneo, was behind a wheel. In the European fashion, heavy, powerful touring cars were in the majority.

The rules laid down by the A.A.A.'s Touring Committee stressed reliability rather than speed. Time limits were imposed for each day's run, with points deducted for early arrival (to discourage the scorchers) as well as late arrival. Contestants were on their honor to report breakdowns, mishaps, and unauthorized aid, such as being dragged out of a mudhole by a team of horses.

This first Glidden Tour had its memorable moments. Near Greenwich, Connecticut, the plucky Mrs. Cuneo, trying to avoid a driver carelessly backing his machine, was forced off a narrow bridge. Although her White steamer ended up on its side in the stream bed, neither she nor her three passengers were more than shaken up. The White was gotten back on its wheels and limped to the next checkpoint. Rather more serious was the fate of a Cadillac entry in New Hampshire on the fourth day. The Cadillac's driver was trying to pass a White — "comparing speed," the official report noted disapprovingly — when a

This is Mangum, Oklahoma, one day in 1910, when every car owner in town, and probably in the nearby countryside, too, lined up for a group portrait taken by an itinerant photographer equipped with a panoramic camera. People in this part of Oklahoma, like people in the nation at large, favored Buicks and Fords.

one-lane bridge loomed up suddenly out of the obscuring dust cloud. The Cadillac was upended and its occupants received "several gashes in the forehead, contusions of the body, and wrenched arm muscles." After a day out for repairs to all concerned, they continued the run. A sudden, violent storm in the White Mountains not only drenched those in open cars — which was almost everyone — but gave Ransom Olds a bad scare. A tree splintered by lightning fell only a few feet from his Reo.

Throughout the run the social amenities were fully observed, with two accompanying baggage trucks transporting the necessary evening wear, and in most places the tourers were received with warmth and friendly curiosity. But not everywhere. In Leicester, Massachusetts, a certain Constable Quinn collected $120 in fines by setting up a speed trap at the foot of a steep hill where the unwary put on a burst of acceleration to make the grade. The constabulary in Dover, New Hampshire, disguised themselves as road workers to catch violators of the local 8 mph limit, a ploy the tourers considered unsporting entrapment. New Hampshirites exhi-

bited the coolest attitude encountered on the tour. The Manchester *Union* — which today as the *Union Leader* continues its bristly traditions — termed the Glidden Tour an "unmitigated nuisance." Inflamed by the Cadillac's speeding accident in the Granite State, the *Union*'s editor demanded vigorous prosecution of all scorchers: "Let a few of them stay in jail two or three days and they and all the rest of us will be the better for it."

Glidden and his fellow tourists — twenty-seven of the thirty-four entrants completed the course — shrugged off such outcries. Percy Pierce was awarded the handsome Glidden Trophy for the best point score, and all finishers received "certificates of performance" suitable for framing. An English Napier was honored for the fastest run up Mt. Washington, with a little Stanley steamer coming in second. The Glidden Tour for 1905, entrant George O. Draper reported to *The Horseless Age,* "has shown the few who took part how delightful their short vacation may be, and it has strengthened our belief in the permanence of the motorcar."

Public interest in the Glidden Tours remained high over the next several years. Each one followed a different course as Charles Glidden sought to spread the gospel of automobiling as widely as possible, and thus uncounted thousands had their first glimpse of an automobile. Author Bellamy Partridge recalled the first time he saw the Glidden tourers

sweep past. "To my youthful eyes," he wrote, "they had an enchanted appearance, as the Crusaders of old in quest of the Holy Sepulcher must have looked to the feudal yokelry." The Pierce people in Buffalo were no doubt content with such an image. A Great Arrow (or Pierce-Arrow, as the marque was called after 1908) won the Glidden Trophy five years running, at no harm whatever to its reputation in the American luxury car market. Yet there were enough additional trophies and awards connected with the tour to keep other manufacturers happy. (In 1908 the Maxwell firm challenged Glidden winner Pierce to a transcontinental endurance contest, putting up $2,500 to back its bid. The offer was ignored, but three years later Maxwell was presumably satisfied after winning the Glidden Trophy outright.)

The 1911 tour ended on a grim note. Sam Butler, one of the directors, was killed near Tipton, Georgia, when the big Cunningham in which he was riding went out of control and crashed. Too few entrants signed up in 1912 to hold a run, and 1913 was the Glidden Tour's last year. It went out with colors flying. With the aid of railroad magnate James J. Hill a course was laid out across the scenic Northwest, with Hill's Great Northern Pullmans serving as luxurious accommodations for the tourers in sparsely settled areas. Metz, Locomobile, and Hupmobile took the honors and everyone had a fine time.

The Glidden Tours were instrumental in introducing Americans to the automobile and helping to persuade them that it was an invention with a future. The very idea of auto touring, of "Seeing America First," was implanted in these years. The need for better roads was spotlighted, and certain technical lessons were learned. For example, Albert L. Clough, an observer on the 1906 tour, pointed out that a major cause of breakdowns was the frail tubular front axles then used by many manufacturers. He listed other areas that needed improvement, notably springs, brakes, and tires. The Glidden Tours—and other tours like them—taught auto makers practical lessons they could not easily learn any other way.

As well-publicized a demonstration of the automobile's durability as racing, cross-country trials, and touring was an entirely unsolicited testimonial in a time of disaster—the 1906 San Francisco earthquake and fire. Officialdom impressed some two hundred privately owned cars for emergency service, evacuating casualties, carrying medical supplies, delivering key personnel where they were needed. The White Company dispatched a cavalcade of steamers from its California dealers to aid the stricken city. The performance record of all these machines was widely applauded. Even when tires were wrecked by the scorching pavement in fire-swept areas, cars continued to

run for days on their wheel rims. That the automobile was "indispensable," reported the San Francisco Chronicle, "is conceded by every man who has had his eyes open during the ten days or so that have elapsed since the earthquake. Old men in the bread lines who had previously occupied much of their time in supper-table denunciation of the whizz-wagons now have nothing but praise for them." Such paeans were widely reprinted in the automotive press.

After about 1906 acceptance of the automobile picked up speed rapidly in every quarter. The most vocal opposition (and some vigilante action) had originally come from farmers who resented having their horses spooked and their chickens run over—or simply resented change itself. No doubt apocryphal is a report that a group of Pennsylvanians calling themselves the Farmers' Anti-Automobile Society demanded legislation to require any automobilist confronted by a nervous horse to disassemble his machine promptly and conceal the parts in the bushes. It was in 1906 that Woodrow Wilson, president of Princeton University, predicted the spread of "socialistic feeling" among country people equating car ownership with the "arrogance of wealth." Wilson quite misjudged both the auto's appeal and its democratizing impact. Farmers' attitudes warmed considerably as they saw more of the automobile and its promise of easing their grinding isolation. Price would remain a barrier until Henry Ford's Model T revolution, but before that day came the demand was there: the American farmer was a ready customer simply waiting for the right machine at the right price.

In these years, too, the automobile was invading popular culture. Tin Pan Alley, never slow to spot a social trend, set automobiling to music in every imaginable tempo. There were marches and waltzes, two-steps and rags, polkas and gavottes, even a light-opera melody by Victor Herbert. Between 1905 and 1907 alone at least 120 pieces of motoring music were published. Some had comic themes: "Get a Horse," "Automobile Breakdown," "Otto, You Ought to Take Me in Your Auto." Some stressed romance: "In Our Little Love Mobile," "The Automobile Honeymoon," and "Come, Take a Spin in My Auto," by a jaunty future mayor of New York, Jimmy Walker. Manufacturers commissioned such long-forgotten numbers as "The Studebaker Grand March" and "The Ford March & Two-Step," but the most celebrated auto song of all, and the best one, was composed in 1905 without factory backing. "In My Merry Oldsmobile," music by Gus Edwards and lyrics by Vincent Bryan, was an instant hit on the vaudeville circuit, and soon the entire country was singing this "Rattling Song of the Road . . . It Glides! It Romps!! It Gallops!!!" (The delighted Oldsmobile people pre-

sented Edwards and Bryan with a car, but they could not agree on which one would use it so they sold it and divided the money.) There were a dozen vocal and instrumental arrangements and a lantern-slide version for nickelodeon theaters. Oldsmobile plugged the song for decades, making it the central theme of its fortieth anniversary celebration in 1937 and devising advertising tie-ins with a 1939 movie biography of Gus Edwards that featured Bing Crosby crooning the famous number.

Rudolph E. Anderson, who delved into the impact of the automobile on American music and drama, noted how quickly it became an accomplished theatrical scene stealer. "The bulb-horn echoed throughout the length and breadth of the American Rialto," he wrote. "The strident 'honk, honk' from the wings giving the cue that an automobile was about to roll onto the stage invariably paralyzed the audience with laughter." The theatergoing public seemed ready to accept the automotive age without hesitation.

The motorcar first reached the stage via vaudeville and musical comedy, but it first achieved stardom in *The Great Automobile Mystery* of 1904. It was the villain of the piece. "Yes, the automobile that has been running down helpless people for so long [this, to repeat, was 1904] is at last branded as a melodramatic vehicle for base cr-r-r-rime!" crowed critic Alan Dale of the New York

American and Journal. The machine exercised an evil hypnotic spell over the heroine, carrying her along the road to depravity and causing her to moan and sigh (as another critic put it) "like a Rambler going up hill." The mechanical villain was booed as roundly when the show went on tour. By the season of 1905–6, however, the automobile was getting better notices as a featured prop in no less than eleven Broadway shows. It played an important part in Shaw's *Man and Superman,* carried the hero to victory in a race with a locomotive in *Bedford's Hope,* and quite stole the show—with the aid of treadmills, moving backdrops, and race driver Barney Oldfield—in *The Vanderbilt Cup;* the celebrated chariot race staged in *Ben Hur,* the critics agreed, had been "beaten to a frazzle."

If the theater's infatuation with these machines continued, critic Dale predicted, Richard III would soon be pleading, "A motor. An automobile. My kingdom for a motor." With tongue in cheek—but foretelling serious criticisms to be leveled at the auto in years to come—Dale went on to observe that the automobile "is the heroine's favorite vehicle for flight; it is the method of locomotion that lures her to her ruin; it is the way in which she compromises herself. It is the hero's hope, and the universal rescuer; it is the villain's delight, and an exquisite means of consummate villainy." All this was already recognized by the writers of boys' adven-

ture fiction and by the makers of flickering nickelodeon films and was about to be discovered in a big way by Hollywood.

With growing acceptance came growing demand, followed promptly by growing sales competition. As we have seen, entering the decidedly free-enterprise automobile business was not particularly difficult. The problem was staying in it. In the first decade of the century "mushroom firms" (as *Scientific American* termed them) sprouted up across America faster than they could be counted. Most of them collapsed nearly as fast. The Colt Runabout Company of Yonkers, New York, was incorporated with high hopes on June 3, 1907; by December it was bankrupt. The Worth high-wheeler disappeared from history when corporate vice president S. R. Hunter absconded with the company's single car and all the machinery used to build it. In 1908 "all visible assets" of the Earl Motor Car Company of Kenosha, Wisconsin, "were seized by sheriff on a claim of $90."

In addition to general business ineptitude, a major cause of failure was a myopic view of automotive technology. For motive power, besides steam, gasoline, and electricity, there were proponents of compressed air (John S. Muir of South Norwalk, Connecticut), water vapor (James A. Charter of Chicago), and liquid air, a propellant suggested at the turn of the century by the Liquid Air Power and Automobile Company, Ltd., of Boston. For those dubious about four wheels there were any number of tricycle configurations, a five-wheeler called the Hicks, and even an electric-powered one-wheel "mechanical horse," the brain child of Charles H. Barrows of Willimantic, Connecticut. Of the more than 4,900 American makes tracked down by the diligent editors of *Automobile Quarterly,* many never got beyond the home-made prototype stage, and the vast majority were gone from the scene by the time of the First World War.

Established companies of every description took a stab at car building. In Massachusetts the Springfield Cornice Works tried its hand; in Newcastle, Indiana, the Safety Shredder Company; in Chicago the Fireproof Covering Company; in New York City the American Chocolate Machinery Company and the Townsend Automobile & Piano Works. The Dormandy was sired by the United Shirt Collar Company of Troy, New York, the Eck by the Boss Knitting Machine Works of Reading, Pennsylvania. Both Montgomery Ward and Sears, Roebuck experimented with selling "motor buggies" by mail order, as did the M. W. Savage people of Minneapolis, who named their car Dan Patch after the celebrated pacer of the day. Buyers of the Car Without a Name (1909) could call their machine whatever they pleased, but anyone who purchased an Eclipse had to supply his own power plant.

There is a certain poignancy to the names bestowed on many of these long-lost marques. The efforts to impart glamour and romance were gallant—Beau Brummel, Luxor, Ben-Hur, Tiffany-Bijou, Peter Pan, La Petite. Community pride sometimes played a role in the naming. The residents of Luverne, Minnesota, insisted on calling their local car the Big Brown Luverne, and their pride was merited: the Luverne, brown or otherwise, stayed in production from 1903 to 1918. The Seven Little Buffalos highwheeler was, of course, a product of Buffalo, New York, and the car built in Dowagiac, Michigan, was named Doe-Wah-Jack. The Kansas City Hummer had a brief existence (1904–5) in Kansas City, Kansas; four years later the Kansas City Wonder turned up just across the state line in Kansas City, Missouri, but its life was even shorter. There is a ring of blunt assurance in Battleship, Steel Ball, Merciless, Self-Contained, Unique, and Devac, an acronym for the Double-Explosion Valveless Air-Cooled automobile, which surfaced briefly in Newark, New Jersey, in 1907 and then sank from sight. The rationale behind such names as Snoburner, Half Breed, and Fifty-Fifty is not self-evident, but there is no doubt what the builders of the Motor Horse, with its horse-shaped body, and the Horsey Horseless, a Haynes-Apperson complete with a dummy horse's head and reins, were about: by arousing "no fears in any skittish animal" they

hoped to ease Old Dobbin gently into the automotive age.

Many early car builders, with pardonable pride, attached their own name to their machines. This practice posed no particular marketing or customer-acceptance problems for the Henry Fords or David Buicks or James Packards, but it does suggest at least one reason why the vehicles named for Messrs. Crock, Krotz, Klink, Foos, Friddle, Izzer, Lunkenheimer, and (at a later date) Neskov-Mumperow made so little impression on the public.

The competition had a Darwinian impact. Only the fittest survived, and as a consequence the motorcar was evolving into a reasonably reliable piece of machinery by the middle years of the decade. This was particularly true of the gasoline-engined car, gaining it ascendancy over the steamer and the electric. Four- and even six-cylinder engines appeared. Fuel, cooling, lubrication, and ignition systems underwent steady improvement. Frames, steering, and brakes were strengthened. The drive shaft began to replace often-troublesome driving chains. The sliding-gear transmission with standardized H-slot gearshift pattern (devised by James Packard, who is also remembered for that famous slogan, "Ask the man who owns one") came into common use—although shifting gears smoothly and quietly remained an art form some drivers never mastered until the synchro-

mesh transmission appeared in 1929. One of the longer-running automobile jokes was the one about the visitor to the motorists' ward of an insane asylum who asks where all the patients are and is told they can be found under their beds fixing the slats; and one of the better-remembered automobile songs, "He'd Have To Get Under, Get Out and Get Under," was written as late as 1913. Nevertheless, just a decade after the Duryeas' initial car sale, automotive technology was showing quite remarkable advances.

This was far less true of tire technology. As John B. Rae has written, "Changing tires was as routine a need as filling the gas tank." Breaking loose the beads of an early high-pressure clincher tire from the rim flanges that hooked over them required brute strength and a high boiling point. In 1904, to motorists' infinite relief, the demountable rim began to come into use, allowing (as a Fisk ad put it) tire removal "without the use of a crowbar or pickaxe."

Tire quality, however, advanced only slowly. Tire company scientists tinkered with the additive "mix" of the rubber and with cord and fabric reinforcement of every description and tread of every design; inventors tried casing "fillers" of vegetable oil, sponge rubber, cork, asbestos, sawdust, animal hair, powdered aluminum, and a hundred other substances; and accessory makers filled their catalogues with allegedly foolproof "outer shoe covers" of steel or

leather or whatever to prolong tire life and with elaborate repair kits and home vulcanizers to fall back on when all else failed. All else failed all too often, and until the twenties the flat tire remained the heaviest cross motorists had to bear.

Some perspective on customer demand may be glimpsed in the fact that buying an automobile in, say, 1905 was not a financial decision lightly undertaken. For the Four Hundred the price tag on a Pierce Great Arrow ($5,000) or a Packard Model N ($3,500) or a victoria-top Peerless limousine ($6,250) might not be any particular barrier. But for the average middle-class American the purchase of one of the popular five-passenger "family cars" such as Maxwell ($1,400), Rambler ($1,350), or even Ford's Model C ($950) was a decidedly major investment. Machines in the intermediate price class cost as much as a small house. This was cash on the line—buying a car on time was then unimagined—in an era when the average schoolteacher saw less than $400 annually, the average factory worker less than $500, the minister $750, the clerk perhaps $1,000.

Beyond the sizable initial cost was upkeep. Early Oldsmobile advertising liked to boast that its little curved-dash model could be run for but $35 a year, whereas "board alone for one horse costs $180.00 a year, so the economy is very evident." This was entirely unrealistic. Gasoline might cost only fifteen cents a gallon in 1905, but maintenance and parts (a set of tires, good for only a few thousand miles, was priced from $100 to more than $300 for the "heavy car type") ran high indeed—"enough," said one owner, "to make a man wild." The motorist who spent less than $500 a year to operate and maintain his machine was doing remarkably well; some contemporary estimates put the figure closer to the original purchase price.

"Capitalists," manufacturers, bankers, and other moneyed types are well represented in any tabulation of early car buyers, yet so are small businessmen, engineers, and country doctors, none of whom could be regarded as affluent. Doctors out-bought every other profession by a wide margin. As one small-town general practitioner with a large rural practice explained, he could make ten calls in the time it formerly took him to make one by horse and buggy and be far less tired afterward. Car makers obliged this demand with a variety of light "physicians' models." In 1905 *The Horseless Age* devoted a special issue to doctors who drove, printing their experiences and passing on their tips. (One doctor advised rigging a piece of canvas under the machine to catch the bolts and fittings that vibrated loose with distressing frequency.) The local doctor was often the first motorist in any town; if not, it was likely to be the local banker. In either case, car own-

What the well-dressed automobilist wore on a typical Sunday outing early in the century. "The many dangers of the open road," one doctor warned, included "poisonous fumes, currents of cold air, or in the summertime, choking dust and swarms of small winged insects." The usual precautionary measure was simply to cover up as much as possible.

ership gained the cachet of respectability.

A wealthy man might buy an automobile to stay abreast of society's protocols, a banker to uphold his status, a doctor to widen the range of his healing, a salesman to cover his territory, a farmer simply to get to town — all to a greater or lesser extent utilitarian reasons and certainly key factors in the motorcar's rapid acceptance. But there was another factor, one not always articulated by prospective buyers. As James J. Flink explains in his important study *America Adopts the Automobile, 1895–1910,* "Motoring had a hedonistic appeal rooted in basic human drives." He goes on to quote a 1901 article in *Motor World:* "To take control of this materialized energy, to draw the reins over this monster with its steel muscles and fiery heart — there is something in the idea which appeals to an almost universal sense, the love of power." To climb behind the wheel of one's own machine was to exercise not only a new form of personal power but also a new form of personal democracy. A car owner was free and independent — free to go (for a reasonable distance, anyway) whenever the mood struck him, with company of his own choosing, independent of the schedules and fixed routes of crowded public transport. Adventure beckoned on even the most prosaic Sunday drive.

This is not to say that one simply climbed behind the wheel and cas-ually drove off to find that adventure. Motoring in the first decade of the century was hardly a cut-and-dried affair. For a typical gasoline-car owner careful preparation was vital.

Step One was a thorough check of the machine. Grease cups, oilers, crankcase, radiator, and gas tank were topped off with essential fluids, the often-contaminated gasoline from the general store being strained through chamois skin. Spark plugs were cleaned, wiring connections secured, nuts, bolts, screws, and fittings tightened, tires examined for cuts and bruises. Renewing a worn leather-faced cone clutch could be time-consuming, perhaps requiring the services of a mechanically inclined blacksmith. Kerosene in the side-lights and the taillight was replenished and the Prest-O-Lite acetylene tank for the headlights recharged if necessary: even the best-laid travel plans for a seventy-five-mile round trip could go awry, requiring navigation homeward after dark. A full tool locker — wrenches, pliers, screwdrivers, files and punches, hammers, a goodly assortment of spares — was as important as a full gas tank. Jack, air pump, mud chains, tire irons, and tire-repair kit (patches, cement, tape, gauge, grater, emery cloth) were positioned within easy reach. The cautious motorist also found room for a few odds and ends that experience had proved useful; several lengths of two-by-four, an axe and shovel, a block and tackle, gum boots, spare containers of gasoline and oil, iron wire, a ball of twine, a folding bucket for filling the radiator at streams or horse troughs and for washing up after roadside repairs.

Step Two was to hazard a weather prediction. Since hardly anyone north of the Mason-Dixon line attempted to drive in wintertime, the primary weather concern was rain. Nothing dampened a Sunday outing more quickly than watching a cloudburst turn a pleasant country lane into a quagmire. Most manufacturers offered folding tops as extra-cost accessories (closed cars were then a rarity), but they were not always the handiest things to operate. As William Faulkner noted, "When rain threatened five or six people could readily put up the top and curtains in ten or fifteen minutes. . . ." Early automotive catalogues offered "storm aprons" ("Small Tonneau, 4 openings for heads. . . . $14.00") for those without tops. At best a sudden summer storm meant considerable discomfort for tourers; at worst it meant paying a smug farmer two or three dollars to extract the machine from a mudhole with a team of horses or mules. (One of the memorable Faulkner characters in *The Reivers* is a Mississippi farmer who keeps "his" stretch of muddy road well plowed and watered and his mules close at hand in full harness.)

Even when the weather was promising, open cars and unpaved roads called for special attire. For men a leather coat or linen "auto shirt," sturdy gauntlets and leggings, cap, and driving goggles were *de rigueur.* For the woman motorist there was a dilemma: how to be fully protected from dust and wind without loss of femininity. As early as 1904 Saks and Company of New York compiled a special catalogue, *Automobile Garments and Requirements,* to resolve milady's problem.

Alice Huyler Ramsey, in *Veil, Duster, and Tire Iron,* described the apparel she and her three companions selected for their historic transcontinental crossing in 1909. "For day-by-day wearing," she wrote, "we had chosen suits of tan covert cloth as being most practical as far as dust and light rain were concerned. With those we wore simple blouses, dusters in warm and dry weather, and for rain, rubber ponchos and hats. Our fair-weather hats were a type of large full cap with stiff visors to shield the eyes in the low western sun, over which crepe de chine veils were draped and came under the chin to be tied in billowing bows." Such motoring garb appears at this distance both comely and practical, but there were those at the time who held contrary opinions. A grumpy contributor to *The Independent,* one Frederick Dwight, complained that "under the new regime, nothing is too ugly. Hatless and coatless or wrapped in linen dusters and huge veils, men and women are reduced to one uninspiring, begoggled level"— a sad

(continued on page 95)

A Matheson is filled up at a portable gas pump as the family watches closely.

OUT FOR A DRIVE

In 1909 *Harper's Weekly* listed some of the pleasures to be found in automobiling: "The feeling of independence. . . , the ability to go where and when one wills, to linger and stop where the country is beautiful and the way pleasant, or to rush through unattractive surroundings, to select the best places to eat and sleep." A few of those pleasures, and a few of the problems that went with pursuing them, are seen on the following pages.

It was a very rare auto outing indeed that did not include at least one tire change. The woman above demonstrates the technique on a Chalmers-Detroit with demountable rims. Crossing a stream usually meant fording it, and the family at left ran into unknown engine trouble in midstream. By cooperative effort, the Ohioans below are attempting to get their White through a rocky defile. Just what is going on opposite is not clear. The setting is rural New Jersey, and the tourers in their Maxwell seem more concerned about the dog by the side of the road than about the sloppy going ahead of them.

90

Whether embarked on an ambitious excursion or only a Sunday drive, car-owning families early in the century seem to have regarded the rewards of touring as worth the trials of getting there. That appears to be true of these two couples camping in New Jersey's wilds. The Rambler that got them there is very much in the picture.

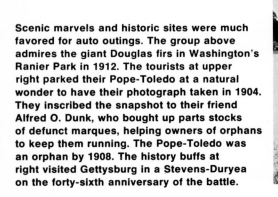

Scenic marvels and historic sites were much favored for auto outings. The group above admires the giant Douglas firs in Washington's Ranier Park in 1912. The tourists at upper right parked their Pope-Toledo at a natural wonder to have their photograph taken in 1904. They inscribed the snapshot to their friend Alfred O. Dunk, who bought up parts stocks of defunct marques, helping owners of orphans to keep them running. The Pope-Toledo was an orphan by 1908. The history buffs at right visited Gettysburg in a Stevens-Duryea on the forty-sixth anniversary of the battle.

94

state of affairs indeed, he added, when compared to "the trim coachman erect on his box" of days past.

Mr. Dwight aside, our typical automobile owner of 1908—call him John Smith—was now properly attired and ready to begin his regular Sunday expedition. Mrs. Smith, in duster and veil, with the A.A.A.'s *Official Automobile Blue Book* in hand to aid navigation, climbed into the front passenger seat. Young John Smith, Jr., perched on the divan-like back seat along with Uncle Harold and Cousin Maude. (Before the summer was out, all the Smiths' relatives in turn, down to the smallest niece, would taste the thrills of automobiling.) Mr. Smith prepared to crank up, first making sure that the spark lever on the steering wheel was in the retard position. This was very important: if the engine was cranked with the spark advanced, warned an early motorist's handbook, "backfiring will occur, resulting in reversal of the operation of the motor and possible injury to the operator." Translated, that meant the crank kicked back, breaking wrist or forearm, which happened with great frequency. But Mr. Smith had his wits about him, and after a turn or two at full choke to prime the cylinders he spat on his gauntlets and gave the crank a hearty wrench—then another—then another. When the engine finally barked into life, he hurried to the driver's seat to adjust spark and throttle; and after a proper warm-up he coaxed the ma-chine into gear and the Smith family rolled off down Elm Street headed for the country.

Sitting up high in the wind stream, bouncing on stiff leaf springs with minimal shock absorbers (or none) on a narrow, high-crowned road, gave an exhilarating impression of high speed—although the prudent Mr. Smith disapprovingly regarded any speed above 25 mph (registered "with unerring accuracy" on his Auto-Meter, "price, complete $75.00") as scorching. He had his hands full with spark, throttle, brakes, gear shifting, and the heavy steering.

While the back-seat passengers marveled at the bucolic scenery flashing past, Mrs. Smith kept a sharp eye out for the landmarks listed in the *Blue Book* and the trip mileage registering on the Auto-Meter. Most of America was yet unblessed with the highway marker or the road sign. The *Blue Book* listed turns to be made at this or that mileage mark at an iron watering trough or a slate-colored barn or a Civil War monument in a town square, and warned of steep hills and interurban grade crossings and treacherous river fords. Half the adventure was finding the way.

At noon the Smith family pulled into a pleasant shady glen and unstrapped the wicker picnic hamper. Everyone brushed at the layer of gray dust that coated him from head to foot. While lunch was laid out Mr. Smith filled the radiator, added oil to the crankcase, checked the grease cups, and replaced a spark plug that had been misfiring. As they picnicked they discussed plans for an autumn vacation excursion, perhaps to the historic Gettysburg battlefield.

For the journey home they decided on a different route, got lost twice, had two flat tires, stampeded several horses, and were mired in a wet stretch of bottom land. With the mud chains in place and with Uncle Harold levering the machine forward with a fence rail under the rear axle, they made it through and arrived home tired and dusty but happy, without having to light the acetylene head lamps. It had been, everyone agreed, an adventure not to be missed.

In the history of the automobile in America, 1908 was a watershed year. By that date the horseless carriage was a thing of the past and the automobile, in the modern sense of that term, was on the scene to stay. Registration figures—not as yet entirely reliable—indicated a nationwide total of at least 194,400 machines. There were 253 companies trying to meet the skyrocketing demand. Automobiling as represented by the experiences of the Smith family was about to enter a new phase. The pioneering days were giving way to the Age of the Automobile, with all that would mean to the basic structures and patterns of American life. This would not happen overnight, but thanks to Henry Ford and William C. Durant it would happen at a speed no one then could even begin to imagine.

3
RISE OF THE GIANTS

The sudden sharp recession known as the Panic of 1907 purged the auto industry of dozens of "mushroom firms." The better-managed companies, however, handled the heavy financial weather without great strain; even a recession hardly dampened the seller's market. The gasoline engine was proving highly adaptable to refinement, pushing steamers and electrics into the background, and the foundations for the new auto age were firmly in place. Raising the structure called for new production techniques and new corporate combinations. The pivotal year 1908 saw both processes begun.

Automotively, 1908 is best remembered as the birth date of Model T. History's most famous, most important motorcar was conceived in a twelve-by-fifteen-foot "experimental room" on the third floor of the Ford Motor Company's Piquette Avenue plant in Detroit. While there is no knowing the exact moment Henry Ford began to dream of a "universal car" (his later reminiscences are unreliable and heavily freighted with hindsight), it is clear that it did not

spring forth full-blown in a sudden inspiration. He had to wait for technology to flesh out his vision. The success of the 1906 Ford Model N (and the subsequent similar but "more pretentious" Models R and S) confirmed the vision. Probably the final piece fell into place in March, 1907, when the first American "heat" of vanadium alloy steel, forty tons of it, arrived at the Ford plant and passed its machining tests. "Charlie," Ford told Charles E. Sorensen, head of his pattern-making department, when they planned the experiment, "this means an entirely new design requirement and we can get a better and lighter and cheaper car. . . ."

Tough, light, shock-resistant vanadium alloy and other advanced heat-treated steels were vital to the equation being worked out in the experimental room. Ford's chief designer, Childe Harold Wills, and his assistant John Wandersee developed gears, axles, springs, and steering parts of great strength and minimum bulk. A Hungarian-born engineer, Joseph Galamb, translated ideas into blueprints. "Mr. Ford first sketched out on the blackboard his ideas of the design he wanted. . . ," Galamb recalled. "There was a rocking chair in the room in which he used to sit for hours and hours at a time, discussing and following out the development of the design." Another Model T insider, George Brown, remarked Ford's non-dictatorial manner: "He'd never say, 'I *want* this done!' He'd say, 'I wonder if

The auto industry was on the brink of big-business status when the photograph opposite was made about 1908. Outside the Ford factory a batch of Model R's and Model S's — direct ancestors of Model T — receive a final test run-in. The Chicago *Tribune*'s cartoonist John T. McCutcheon remarked on the public's rush to invest in cars rather than stocks, much to Wall Street's consternation; at the right is a frustrated J. P. Morgan, at the upper left a pleased oilman John D. Rockefeller.

we can do it. I wonder.' Well, the men would just break their necks to see if they could do it."

As the design took shape in those busy months, Ford repeatedly exhibited what historians Allan Nevins and Frank Ernest Hill, in their monumental study of the man and his company, call "an extraordinary power of divination." By experiment, by self-taught insight, or simply by strokes of pure mechanical genius, he cut through Gordian engineering knots and proposed practical compromises for conflicting requirements. Dozens of men made important and vital contributions to Model T, but let there be no doubt that it was Henry Ford's conception and creation. After his first ride in the completed prototype he was as jubilant as a small boy with a new toy, grinning, slapping backs, giving everyone around him (Brown recalled) "a kick in the pants." "Well," he announced happily, "I guess we've got started." Model T was exactly what he wanted, and he was certain it was exactly what America wanted too.

On March 18, 1908, an "advance catalogue" describing the new car went out to Ford dealers. Their response was ecstatic but nervous: with no deliveries scheduled before October they worried about selling current models when news of the new model got out. Many dealers locked the catalogues away and quietly waited for October. If Model T was all it promised to be, they decided, there

would be no problem selling it. Public response to Ford's full-page ad in the October 3, 1908, *Saturday Evening Post* was strong. According to *Ford Times*, the widely distributed company magazine, "Saturday's mail brought nearly one thousand inquiries. Monday's response swamped our mail clerks and by Tuesday night the office was well nigh inundated." The car's reception at leading automobile shows was equally enthusiastic. By May, 1909, the company was telling dealers to accept no more orders until production caught up.

In its price class ($850 for the touring car) no other automobile on the market in 1909 could touch Model T. Indeed, many cars costing twice as much—and a few costing three times as much—could not touch it. It was nimble as a jack rabbit, tough as a hickory stump, simple as a butter churn, unadorned as a farmer's boot. Plain the T may have been, but not unhandsome: it had the simple Shaker-like look of something designed exactly right for the job.

New foundry techniques enabled the 20-horsepower four-cylinder engine to be cast in one block, a step forward from the common practice of casting cylinders singly or in pairs. Another innovation was a detachable cylinder head, Ford's simple answer to the frequent need in that era to grind valves and remove carbon deposits. Ignition current was supplied by a magneto built into the flywheel. Four body styles were offered that

first model year—touring car, runabout, town car, and delivery car—in a choice of black, green, red, blue, or two shades of gray. (This color option was soon rescinded, all cars being painted Brewster green with black trim and red striping; the famous black-only policy took effect in 1913.) The radiator and head lamps were brass and the seats leather. The steering wheel was on the left—not the first car to have it there, but Ford led the way in making it standard American practice. Model T was just over ten feet long, and with the top up, seven feet tall. Its high ground clearance, short turning radius, and excellent power-to-weight ratio allowed it to go almost anywhere except, said the wits, in society.

A motorist driving off in a factory-fresh Model T proceeded on faith. The cherry-wood dash was barren of instrumentation. There was nothing to tell him the fuel supply, the engine temperature, or the oil pressure (the T had utterly simple "splash system" lubrication). He knew not how fast he was going or, if it rained, where he was going, there being no windshield wiper. Over the years, although Model T underwent a slow evolution, its essential plain practicality remained. One change (to look ahead) was the addition of front doors on the touring car in 1913. Only one functioned, however. The driver's door was a neatly embossed dummy, one of Henry Ford's rare concessions to styling symmetry over function.

"Why should it open, Henry probably thought, when the handbrake obstructed the doorway and the driver could just as easily slide across the seat to get out," writes *Automobile Quarterly*'s Beverly Rae Kimes.

Then there was Model T's planetary transmission, perhaps the best example of Ford's passion for durable simplicity. No sound in motordom in those years was more familiar than the agonizing clash of gears as drivers struggled with their sliding-gear transmissions. Not so a Ford owner. As novelist John Steinbeck would remark, more Americans of the period understood "the planetary system of gears than the solar system of stars." Gears, clutch, and brake were all incorporated within the transmission unit. The principle involved was running the gears constantly in mesh, "the different sets of gears. . . brought into action," the Ford instruction manual explained, by a simple pedal-actuated tightening of the proper transmission friction band. Model T went, stopped, and backed up by means of three pedals sprouting through the floorboards.

No one has better described the fullness of the Model T experience than E. B. White. His memorable essay "Farewell, My Lovely!" appeared in *The New Yorker* in 1936, signed "Lee Strout White," a pseudonym he invented to acknowledge Richard L. Strout's suggestion for the piece. Here is E. B. White on the flivver's planetary transmission:

With its brass radiator, head lamps, and fittings, its cherry-wood dash, and its six color choices, the early Model T was a rather dashing little car. The all-black utilitarian look came later. On the facing page are cross-section diagrams revealing the inner workings of the car in full view (top) and in detail the famed two-speed planetary transmission (lower left) and the tough four-cylinder engine (lower right).

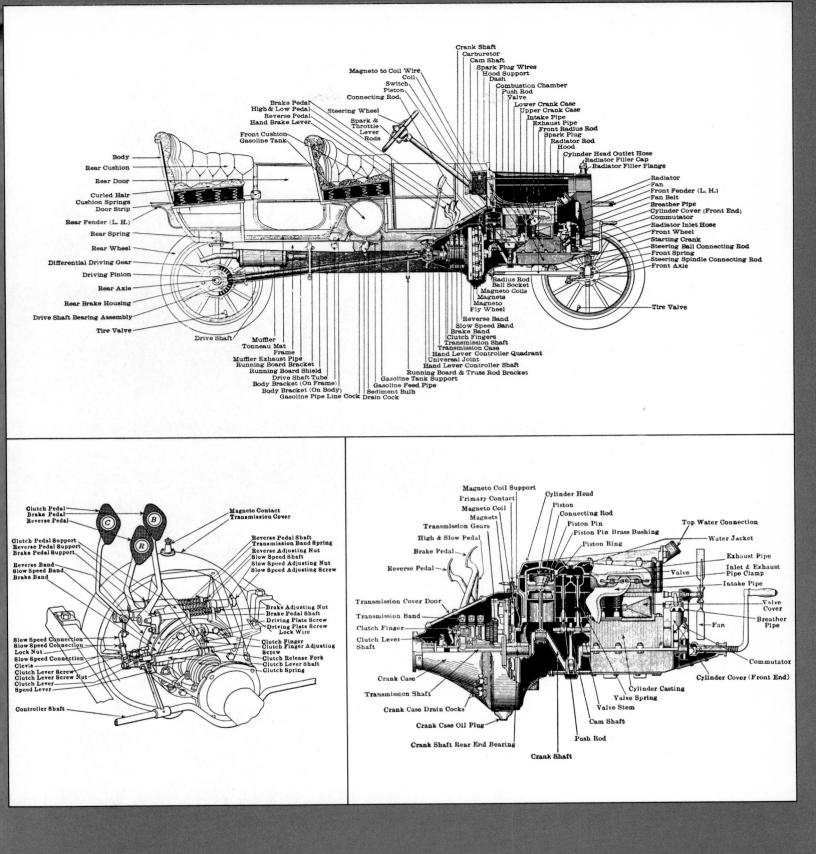

OVERLAND SALES 1911 TWO

In the first decade of Model T's life, the most consistent winner of second place in the sales race was Willys-Overland. It was a very distant second place, however. These photographs are from the album of the proud proprietor of the Clark Vehicles Company, an Overland dealer located in rural Nebraska near the village of Friend. The photographer had to back up to get all the satisfied owners into the 1912 picture.

"Engineers accepted the word 'planetary' in its epicyclic sense, but I was always conscious that it also meant 'wandering,' 'erratic.' Because of the peculiar nature of this planetary element, there was always, in Model T, a certain dull rapport between engine and wheels, and even when the car was in a state known as neutral, it trembled with a deep imperative and tended to inch forward. There was never a moment when the bands were not faintly egging the machine on. In this respect it was like a horse, rolling the bit on its tongue. . . .To get under way, you simply hooked the third finger of the right hand around [the throttle] lever on the steering column, pulled down hard, and shoved your left foot forcibly against the low-speed pedal. These were simple, positive motions; the car responded by lunging forward with a roar. After a few seconds of this turmoil, you took your toe off the pedal, eased up a mite on the throttle, and the car, possessed of only two forward speeds, catapulted directly into high with a series of ugly jerks and was off on its glorious errand. The abruptness of this departure was never equalled in other cars of the period. . . ."

To stop this juggernaut (pushed flat out, a Ford might reach 45 mph), according to the instruction manual, it was necessary only to retard the hand throttle, push the left pedal halfway down to disengage the clutch, and "apply the foot brake slowly but firmly." To *really* stop Model T,

owners soon discovered, the quickest procedure was to stomp hard on both brake and reverse pedals and haul back on the hand-brake lever, which worked a separate set of rear-wheel brakes. The easy alliance between forward and reverse was ideal for rocking the machine out of mudholes. Another of the reverse pedal's attributes was serving as a court of last resort on hills. Reverse's gear ratio gave the maximum pulling power; but more importantly, the regular failure of the T's gravity-flow fuel system on steep inclines—the gas tank was under the front seat—made going up backward the only recourse.

Despite such idiosyncrasies, Ford's Model T was a superior car at a bargain price, very much a quantitative leap forward. Most auto makers would have been content to rest on these laurels. Not Ford: the revolution he was consciously fomenting, to bring the automobile within reach of Everyman, had several essential steps yet to go.

The first step was product standardization. In 1909, in a move that startled his competitors, he announced that henceforth Model T would be the Ford Motor Company's lone model. Several body styles would continue to be offered, but all on a single standardized chassis for maximum economy of production. Step Two was quantity production on a scale previously unimagined, with the avowed purpose of lowering prices. That would take more doing.

Early in 1910 Ford moved his operations from the Piquette Avenue plant to a great complex rising on the sixty-acre site of a racetrack on the northern outskirts of Detroit called Highland Park. It was at Highland Park, over the next five years, that the system of assembly-line mass production—what Nevins and Hill term "a lever to move the world"—was perfected.

What, it may be asked, propelled Henry Ford to the forefront of an economic and social revolution? He was certainly not the first auto maker to try to tap the mass market. Ransom Olds had sought to do that with his little curved-dash runabout as early as 1901. Conceivably the "Merry Oldsmobile" could have undergone the same evolutionary development by which Ford's original Model A became Model T. The Oldsmobile management chose instead to focus on the $2,000-plus market with its higher unit profits, shedding Ransom Olds in the process. Olds himself acknowledged second thoughts about the mass market when he subsequently designed his medium-priced Reo. Thomas B. Jeffery had pioneered one-model standardization with his Rambler. Alanson P. Brush, formerly chief engineer at Cadillac, designed a small runabout selling for $500 in 1907, terming it "Everyman's Car." The Brush, however, was an exercise in false economy: tiny engine, chain drive, solid tires, largely wooden construction. Sales during its five-year

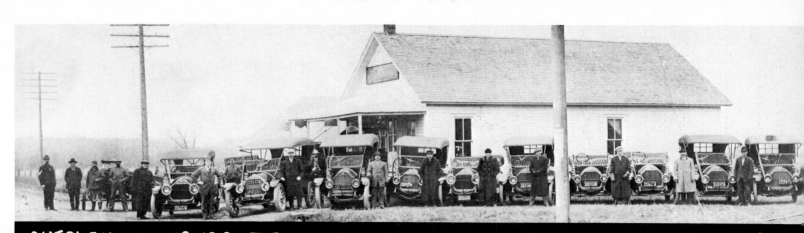

OVERLAND SALES 1912 TEN ARE THE OWNERS SATISFIED? ASK THEM

life were less than fifteen thousand, and it suffered grievously from the alleged but widely circulated owner's lament, "Wooden body, wooden axles, wooden wheels, and wooden run." Detroit engineer Robert Hupp also entered the low-priced field ("I recall looking at Bobby Hupp's roadster. . . ," Ford once remarked, "and wondering whether we could ever build as good a small car for as little money"), but Hupp could not achieve the volume production to maintain the challenge. Many share the credit for introducing Americans to the automobile, but Henry Ford made it possible for almost everyone to step up and try one. In 1909, the first full year of Model T production, he seized such a commanding lead in the low-priced field that eighteen years would pass before anyone caught him.

What set the Ford operation apart was Henry Ford himself. He was uniquely his own man. His indifference to personal wealth resulted in profits being relentlessly plowed back into corporate expansion. Dividends for the company's minority stockholders ranked low in his priorities; outside financial leverage was nil, for no capital was raised by borrowing (countryman Ford despised bankers). No other major automotive entrepreneur of the period—or since, for that matter—could begin to operate with Ford's freedom of action and his disregard for corporate conventions.

He was also held in unparalleled esteem by the car-buying public, thanks to such actions as his challenge to the "interests" in the Selden patent war, and at a later date, his $5 wage. In a day when better than half the nation's population was classified as rural, Ford was seen as the embodiment of the countryman's storied virtues—hard-working, thrifty, respectful of honest value, utterly unpretentious, very much in tune with the Populist reform pressures of the time. And in this period of his life, when Model T was born and grew to vigorous adulthood, the picture was accurate enough. Henry Ford would become a less likable figure and the center of swirling controversy; but just then, in the time of his greatest impact on automotive history, indeed on American history, he merited the trust he and his car received from millions. He was obsessed with building the best possible product for the most people and selling it, thanks to the economies of scale, at the lowest possible price. "I am going to democratize the automobile," he confided to a lawyer during the later stages of the Selden controversy. "When I'm through everybody will be able to afford one, and about everyone will have one. The horse will have disappeared from our highways, the automobile will be taken for granted. . . ." As the lawyer later remarked, "And by God, he was right!"

Like Model T itself, the assembly-line mass production of automobiles

was a case of evolution rather than any sudden "eureka!" inspiration. The essential principles of efficient in-factory movement of materials date back to Oliver Evans's eighteenth-century mechanized flour mill and to nineteenth-century meat-packing plants. The standardized, interchangeable parts equally essential to mass production originated with (among others) arms makers Eli Whitney and Samuel Colt, Connecticut clockmakers Chauncey Jerome and Eli Terry, harvester builder Cyrus McCormick, bicycle builder Albert Pope. Prodded by Henry Leland and his disciples, the American machine-tool industry turned out new precision lathes and grinders, milling machines and drill presses, and then promptly rendered them obsolete with even better designs. Management techniques, raw materials procurement, and factory layout underwent constant refinement as car makers strove to meet the rising demand. When the Ford Motor Company began operations at Highland Park in 1910 it was by no means the only auto company to have developed these manufacturing skills into a high art. Soon, however, it was advancing alone into uncharted waters.

The Highland Park complex, designed by the brilliant industrial architect Albert Kahn and Ford's imaginative construction engineer Edward Gray, was itself a major innovation. Cleanly designed and fully utilitarian, dubbed the "Crystal Palace" for its

103

thousands of panes of glass set in walls and skylights, it was carefully laid out for maximum production efficiencies.

By the end of 1912 these efficiencies were manifest. Cranes, conveyors, and gravity slides moved materials and parts when and where they were needed. Advanced machine tools, including one that simultaneously drilled forty-five holes in an engine block, were everywhere in evidence. An apparatus that painted 2,000 wheels a day—in most auto plants wheels were painted by hand —was only one of scores of specialized devices invented on the spot to resolve particular bottlenecks. That year 170,211 Model T's rolled out of Highland Park and into every corner of the nation and nearly every corner of the world. This was six times the output of the nearest competitor and almost ten times the number of T's built in 1909. The price tag for the touring car was down to $600. The company's net profit was up to $13.5 million. Nothing like it had ever been seen before—and it was only the beginning.

To this point, the subassembly and final assembly of Model T's proceeded sequentially but in a stop-and-go mode, a highly refined version of the process used in Ransom Olds's Jefferson Avenue plant at the beginning of the century. Then a revolutionary change began, quietly enough, in the Ford magneto department. In the spring of 1913 a moving belt was installed: where previously each worker had assembled a complete magneto, each now performed just one operation—inserting magnets, tightening bolts, or whatever— as the belt carried the magnetos past his station. Assembly time promptly fell from twenty minutes to thirteen; further refinement slashed the time to five minutes. With no increase in manpower, the daily output of magnetos was increased fourfold. The same techniques were soon applied to engine and transmission assembly. It was quickly apparent that if the fruit of these experiments was to be harvested, *every* assembly step would have to be put into continuous motion.

Many shared the honors, but primary credit for the moving final-assembly line belongs to Clarence W. Avery, Charles Sorensen's thirty-one-year-old assistant. Avery, who had first come to Henry Ford's attention as his son Edsel's manual training teacher at the Detroit University School, joined the company in 1912. Knowledgeable in the pioneering time-and-motion studies of Frederick W. Taylor, he carefully dissected every job and every phase of final assembly. In October, 1913, he had a rope windlass installed to move the chassis, then, in 1914, an endless chain to haul them along rails at six feet per minute. From frame to finished car, Model T's now emerged in continuous, fluid movement at the completion rate (by April, 1914) of one every twenty-four seconds.

Indeed, all Highland Park was aboil with carefully calculated movement. The body-assembly line alone, noted the contemporary observers Horace L. Arnold and F. L. Faurote, "wends its way over three successive floors..., now running straight for 850 feet at a time, turning right-angled corners—now going down-grade to the floor below, back and across, until finally the terminal is reached. . . ." Output leaped right off the production graphs—more than 300,000 cars in 1914, more than 500,000 in 1915— and the price of the Model T touring car fell to $440. The next good light touring cars on the market cost at least $300 more.

To the modern mind, inured to the commonplace "miracle" of mass production, the evolution of the continuously moving assembly line may seem a simple, even unremarkable exercise in ordinary logic. But the obvious, of course, becomes obvious only after someone thinks of it. What made this new form of mass production such a historic milestone was that in 1913–14 it sprang out of—and helped create—a set of circumstances that had never before existed.

A mass market for automobiles had to be present, and the product (Model T) good enough and cheap enough to sell in volume to that market. Enormous amounts of capital (in this instance, reinvested profits) were required for plant, machinery, and

(continued on page 110)

Ford first applied the moving assembly line to the production of magnetos.

ASSEMBLY LINE

In 1913–14 a giant stride into the modern world was initiated at the Ford Highland Park factory. The newly evolved moving assembly line began spewing forth Model T's in unimagined numbers. "It's wonderful! Wonderful!" exclaimed ex-President William Howard Taft. "I am amazed at the magnitude of the establishment." Here is a glimpse of the "magic method" that so astonished Taft and his contemporaries.

Phases of the Ford system are pictured here. Above are three parallel final-assembly lines about 1914. Tributary assembly lines fed such components as engines, dashboards, transmissions, and axles into these main lines. At left is the assembly point for the mounting of the wheels and radiator. So minute was the subdivision of labor, Ford wrote, that "the man who puts in a bolt does not put on the nut; the man who puts on the nut does not tighten it." At upper right, newly varnished sedan bodies move past drying lamps. An early version of the body drop is seen at right. Bodies were assembled on Highland Park's upper floors, then slid down this chute to be fitted to completed chassis. A runabout body has just been installed; a touring-car body is next.

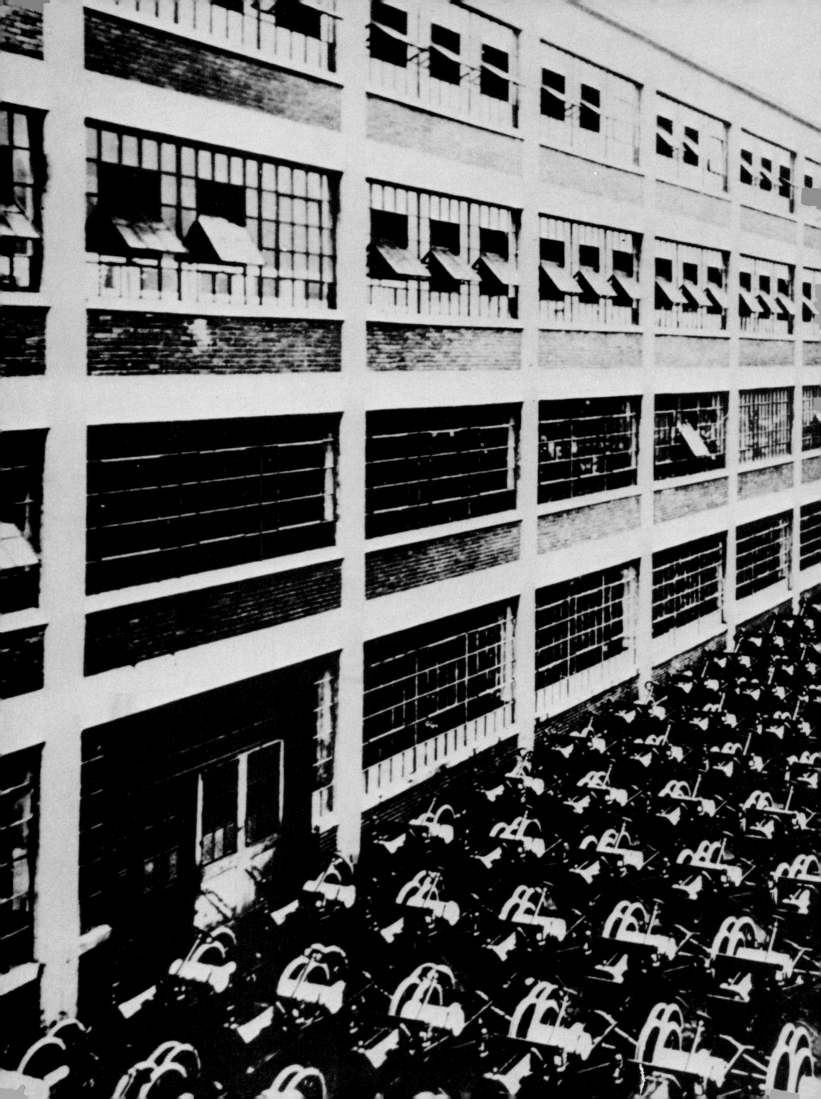

A publicity picture, and a very effective one: a single day's output—a thousand Model T chassis—was photographed in 1915. In July, 1914, Ford had made news by promising a rebate to car buyers if sales over the next twelve months topped 300,000. The goal was reached, and $50 rebate checks, with this picture engraved on them, went out to the Ford owners. The program cost $15.4 million.

Ford described his $5 day as a plan to "add to every man's pay a share of the profits of the house." H. T. Webster's cartoon, from the New York *Globe*, pictures the Ford workers as a new class of plutocrats. The Detroit *Journal* clipping reports the scene at Highland Park on January 12, 1914, the day the new $5, eight-hour day went into effect. Job seekers had begun lining up outside the plant the previous evening.

raw materials. The managerial and engineering skills needed to make it all work were entirely uncodified; there were no textbooks on the subject.

Nevins and Hill devised the apt metaphor of a great river system to describe the Highland Park assembly scheme. "Soon," they wrote, "the scientifically-timed rivers were all being fed by scientifically-timed tributaries. The whole factory became kinetic." It was all interdependent, interconnected, interrelated. And Highland Park was only the center of a wider complex. Huge stocks—a hundred freight-car loads a day by 1914—of raw materials, parts, and machinery were purchased and routed to the scene on precise timetables. Finished Model T's were transported to the marketplace—a network of regional assembly plants was established to save on shipping costs— via seven thousand dealers. Here, in sum, was the ultimate in specialization and interdependence upon which, as Adam Smith had pointed out seven score years before in *The Wealth of Nations*, the Industrial Revolution was rooted.

In a few short years key factors now taken for granted in our industrial society were invented from scratch by an inspired exercise in classical American pragmatism presided over by Henry Ford. Only mass national advertising, today an essential in the equation, was lacking. In those years Model T needed only announcing, not advertising. Assembly-line mass production meant high quantity, low price, and, perhaps most astonishing to contemporary observers, high quality. For all its skills, handcrafting could not match the machine-crafting inherent in the Ford system. All Model T's were alike, and every one performed very well indeed.

Highland Park had one further element beyond machinery and motion that required the full innovative attention of Ford and his managers: its labor force. Although the plant's working and safety conditions were far above average for the period, the Ford company still suffered, like its competitors, severe problems of worker absenteeism and turnover. Late in 1912, for example, Ford's monthly labor turnover was a potentially crippling forty-eight per cent. Ford and James Couzens, head of the business side of the company, sought a prompt solution. Not only for reasons of good business: for all his hard-driving martinet spirit, Couzens seems to have shared with Ford (at least the Ford of this period) a genuine concern for the worker's welfare.

This concern, to be sure, left no room for "coddling," no tolerance of anything less than a full day's honest labor—and no tolerance for unions. Both men paternalistically viewed hard work as the solution to the nation's social ills—so long as the dignity of that work was respected and rewarded. Ford boasted that he could rehabilitate "the most shiftless and worthless fellow in the crowd" in no time at all: "Give him a job with a wage that offers him some hope for the future, some prospect of living a decent, comfortable, and self-respecting life, and I'll guarantee that I'll make a man out of him. All that man needs is an opportunity that has some hope in it. . . ."

With the same intensity Clarence Avery was devoting to the car-assembly process, Ford's personnel manager John R. Lee evaluated work requirements and job classifications and came up with reforms in pay equalization. He also ended the arbitrary firing power of foremen, making it company policy to find jobs in other departments for alleged "misfits." These and similar reforms paid off. Within a year absenteeism was brought under control and monthly turnover was cut to 6.4 per cent. By the end of 1913 workers were better off at Highland Park, in terms of general labor policy and working conditions, than at any other major auto plant, certainly better off than the vast

HIGAN, MONDAY, JANUARY 12, 1914.

PRICE: Detroit and Suburbs—One cent on street and news stands. cents per week delivered. Elsewhere—two cents.

ICY FIRE-HOSE DELUGE STOPS 1,200 IN RIOTOUS RUSH FOR FORD'S JOBS

Five Men Arrested and Three Thousand Soaked With Water In Zero Cold When Crowd Tries to Enter Works.

SMASH WINDOWS; WRECK STANDS

Crowd Irritated at Douch Hurls Stones at Factory Then Angrily Attacks Street Venders' Places— 14,000 Applications By Mail.

of ice cold water, play- tailed his entire force to the Ford firehose in the hands district. Up to Monday, however, Park policemen, stopped inconsequential bottles between men seeking vantage points in the crowd men for jobs at were the only disturbances. nt Monday Monday morning the scene appeared to a ... as any day

majority of American factory workers of the era. Then came the most astonishing move of all.

On January 5, 1914—as the new assembly lines were rolling into operation—Ford and Couzens announced that the company would reduce work shifts from nine hours to eight and raise the daily pay to $5. It was nothing less than a full doubling of wages.

The announcement had the impact of a bombshell. It was front-page news in every city in America and in many cities around the world. The New York *Sun* termed it "a bolt out of the blue sky, flashing its way across the continent and far beyond, something unheard of in the history of business." "An epoch in the world's industrial history," added the New York *Herald*. There were, predictably, howls of complaint from other auto makers. Many business leaders called Ford a traitor to his class. The *Wall Street Journal* labeled the plan an economic crime and predicted that such a disruption of wage patterns would result in "material, financial, and factory disorganization" across the country. But the man in the street and the man on the farm—and certainly the man in the factory— blessed Henry Ford. He who had given Everyman a decent cheap automobile had now given his workers a decent day's wage. In January,1914, Ford himself became for the first time as famous as his cars. So he would remain for the rest of his life.

Thousands rushed to the Highland Park employment office. At one point during the week after the announcement fire hoses had to be employed to halt a near riot among the job seekers. In that week, too, fourteen thousand applications were received by mail. Inside the plant a newspaper reporter sensed a feeling of "universal brotherhood." He quoted laborer Woljeck Manijklisjiski: "My boy don't sell no more papers. My girl don't work in the house of another and see her mother but once in the week no more. Again we are a family." By the end of 1914 nine out of ten Highland Park workers qualified for the $5-a-day rate—or would as soon as new employees among them completed their six-month probation. That meant some $1,500 annually, in a year when the average American manufacturing worker earned $580 and the average federal employee $1,140.

There was a certain amount of cynicism then and since about Ford's motives: he was simply looking for publicity; he was blackmailing his men into quiescence before hiking productivity demands; he was reducing labor turnover and buying labor peace with his great wealth. Self-interest certainly entered into the $5 day. Yet the overall pattern of Ford's labor policies in those years reflects an undeniable sincerity, indeed a generosity, of spirit.

He was the first major American industrialist to regard labor as something more than simply a standard-

ized raw material in the manufacturing process, to be purchased as cheaply as possible. He was a pioneer in authorizing the employment of blacks and other minorities, and of ex-convicts as a means of rehabilitation. He directed special recruitment of the handicapped and crippled—who totaled, by 1917, some seventeen per cent of his work force. He had mandatory classes set up to teach English to the company's many foreign-born workers. John Lee's Sociological Department, established in 1914, initiated detailed personal counseling and assistance to workers and their families in a manner that today would be considered overly paternalistic but by the standards of the second decade of the century was astonishingly enlightened. In short, the record suggests no sham but instead a recognition that both a worker's general welfare—and, equally important, his purchasing power—were as important as his productivity.

The universal car, assembly-line mass production, the $5 day: they are the monuments to Henry Ford's idealism. It has been said that had he then retired, his great work done, and assumed the mantle of elder statesman of industrial capitalism, he would

Detroit was assuming status as Motor City when the photograph opposite was taken about 1908. The square, called the Campus Martius, is dominated by the Pontchartrain Hotel, gathering place of the automotive establishment. Early in that year, at the Pontchartrain, these industry leaders held merger talks. At top is Ransom Olds of Reo, at center Billy Durant of Buick. Flanking them are Ford business manager James Couzens (left) and Henry Ford. Below are Maxwell's Benjamin Briscoe (in the bowler) and his brother Frank, in a Brush runabout. This Big Four merger attempt failed when Ford and Olds balked.

today occupy one of the higher niches in the American pantheon. But of course he did not; and as we shall see, his rank in history became severely and tragically diminished.

In the seven years after 1908, Model T and the method of its production transformed the automotive scene. In that same period there unfolded a parallel tale of almost equal significance. It too has a star actor, Billy Durant, in his own (but quite different) way as remarkable a figure as Henry Ford.

The old Pontchartrain Hotel in Detroit, all marble and gilt and mahogany, was the unofficial watering hole of the automotive fraternity; there gossip was traded, jobs bartered, deals made. On January 17, 1908, in Billy Durant's room at the Pontchartrain, a very big deal was cooking.

Meeting with Durant were Henry Ford, Ransom Olds, and Benjamin Briscoe. Their marques—Ford's Ford, Durant's Buick, Olds's Reo, Briscoe's Maxwell—had taken the top four places in the production race the year before, and Briscoe now proposed that they merge to form "one big concern of . . . dominating influence in the automobile industry, as for instance, the United States Steel Corporation exercises in the steel industry. . . ." There were too many firms, too many marginal producers, in the car-making business; this multiplicity was disillusioning the marketplace and hampering progress. Order must be brought out of the

NATIONAL AUTOMOTIVE HISTORY COLLECTION, DETROIT PUBLIC LIBRARY. MOTOR VEHICLE MANUFACTURERS ASSOCIATION. FORD ARCHIVES, HENRY FORD MUSEUM. MOTOR VEHICLE MANUFACTURERS ASSOCIATION

Billy Durant's spectacular amassing of his General Motors empire inspired this 1909 cartoon. Curiously, the farmer harvesting his vehicular crop — which includes Buick, Cadillac, Oldsmobile, Welch, Ranier, and Alliance truck — is the banker J. P. Morgan, reflecting the mistaken belief that Durant was under the House of Morgan's control.

chaos. The Morgan banking interests agreed, Briscoe added, and were eager to act as brokers for the consolidation. (The House of Morgan was highly adept at promoting industrial order, having already helped assemble General Electric, International Harvester, American Telephone and Telegraph, and U.S. Steel.) After several hours of debate and "gingerly" discussion of the principals' corporate worth, it was decided to initiate formal financial appraisals of the four companies and then meet again.

As the spring of 1908 wore on, there were several more sessions dealing with the proposed combination. Then Ford and Couzens dropped the other shoe. Whatever value the appraisers finally placed on the Ford Motor Company, they announced, they would accept as a down payment nothing less than $3 million — in cash. Upon hearing this, Ransom Olds demanded the same sum. The talks collapsed.

The suspicion remains that Ford was not in dead earnest about consolidation. Model T catalogues had just gone out to Ford dealers, and at this pivotal point in his quest for the universal car it seems out of character that he would consider putting himself "under orders" once more or dealing with bankers of any rank. In the event, the meetings did serve to plant the expansion-through-combination seed in Billy Durant's mind, and there it would flourish.

For a time it appeared that at least

Buick and Maxwell would merge. Then the House of Morgan became suspicious about certain aspects of Durant's role in the scheme and pulled back. Durant did not help his cause by remarking offhandedly that the automotive industry would soon be building half a million cars a year. The 1907 production total had been only forty-three thousand, persuading eastern bankers that the automobile was still in the novelty stage. "If that fellow has any sense," a Morgan partner confided to an aide, "he'll keep those observations to himself when he tries to borrow money."

Durant was not discouraged. Billy Durant was never discouraged by setbacks. He decided to work alone. On September 16, 1908, he filed incorporation papers for a New Jersey holding company he named General Motors. Then he started looking for things to buy. The holding company was the device John D. Rockefeller had used with such success to pyramid his power in the oil industry, and Durant was eager to try it out for himself. Operating under a holding-company umbrella required more salesmanship, promotional skill, and imagination than money, which suited the Durant style perfectly; he was too impatient to wait for growth through reinvested profits in the Ford manner. His basic asset was his popular Buick — G.M.'s first "purchase" — being built in good volume in Flint in what was then the world's largest auto plant. Buick was solidly

in the black and Flint was a boom town: shacks and tents sprouting everywhere to shelter new workers, boarding houses renting their beds in shifts. Around the Buick nucleus Durant intended to assemble an auto empire, using General Motors stock to pay for most of it.

He turned first to Oldsmobile. That pioneering company had fallen on hard times after Ransom Olds was pushed out in 1904, and in November, 1908, Durant was able to take control by paying just over $3 million in G.M. stock and a mere $17,279 in cash. Even at that he wondered what sort of bargain he had made. "That's a hell of a price to pay," he complained, "for a bunch of road signs [billboards]." When he discovered there was no new Oldsmobile model on the drawing boards, he is supposed to have ordered a Buick body quartered, moved the four sections a few inches apart, and instructed Oldsmobile's management to build a car to those dimensions with the regular Olds front-end treatment. Apparently the Oldsmobile name still had magic: some 5,000 of these bastardized Buicks were sold in 1909.

It was a typical bit of Durant audacity. A short, slight, benign-looking man, he was a whirling dervish of activity, up half the night on the telephone, dashing from city to city to talk deals, to close deals, to apply his acquisitive eye to new prospects. Wherever Durant showed up, wrote one of his aides, "it was like the visitation of a cyclone." The exchange-of-stock pattern he had used with Oldsmobile was his favorite ploy. Within just two years he had his General Motors empire, or at least a paper facsimile of an empire: thirteen car and truck builders, ten makers of parts and accessories.

Many of Durant's purchases were new companies struggling to get started or older companies trying to stay afloat. One marque that rolled into the G.M. tent under full power was Cadillac. Henry Leland and his son Wilfred had built Cadillac into one of the soundest companies in the industry, and they (and their fellow stockholders) demanded and got from Durant not only $4.5 million in cash plus stock but a management guarantee as well. "That is exactly what I want," Durant assured the Lelands. "I want you to continue to run the Cadillac exactly as though it were still your own. You will receive no directions from anyone." Since Cadillac's 1909 earnings were $2 million, Durant had struck an exceedingly good bargain. The problem, if there was to be one, would be papering over the considerable cash drain he inflicted on Buick to swing the deal.

His goal was apparently to offer the public a car for every taste and every pocketbook. "Durant sees—actually sees—90,000,000 people just aching to roll along the roads of the country in automobiles, and he wishes to fill that aching void," a Detroit newspaperman remarked in 1909. Buick,

Oldsmobile, Cadillac, and the new Oakland (to be transmuted into Pontiac in the thirties) had sound enough potential—they are today, after all, four of the five automotive jewels in the G.M. crown. But he also acquired what John B. Rae has termed a "strictly ephemeral" string of marques: Ranier, Rapid, Welch, Ewing, Cartercar, Elmore. Some never saw life at all; the longest-lived survived only until 1916. Durant bought Cartercar because he thought its friction drive might be the coming thing, Elmore because its two-cycle engine might somehow displace the four-cycle type then in all but universal use. "I was for getting every kind of car in sight, playing safe all along the line," he said.

Durant also collected some solid parts and accessory companies, such as AC Spark Plug ("AC" was Albert Champion, whose former company kept his name and remains today very much in the business), but in this field, too, he was stung badly. Most painful was paying $7 million in stock and $112,000 in cash for an incandescent lamp patent that turned out to be a fraud. He even tried again, and failed again, to gather in Ford. This time the asking price was $8 million in cash; it is not entirely clear whether Henry Ford was seriously negotiating or simply indulging in one of the little practical jokes he enjoyed.

By the summer of 1910, after this spectacular burst of acquisition en-

Epitaphs

"No Hill Too Steep, No Sand Too Deep" (Jackson)
"No Clutch To Slip, No Gears To Strip" (Metz)
"Ride in a Glide and Then Decide"
"Lexington Leads Because It Lasts"
"Surpasses the Rest by Actual Test" (Cutting)
"All the World Loves a Winner" (Liberty)
"The Only One That Always Won" (Haynes-Apperson)
"The Gem of the Highway" (Columbia)
"The Ace of the Highway" (Kline)
"From a Thinking Automobile Manufacturer to the Thinking Automobile Buyer" (Moon)
"Perfectly Simple, Simply Perfect" (Maxwell)
"Silent as the Stars" (Northern)
"Silent as the Foot of Time" (Mitchell)
"The Car That Obviates the Tow" (Knox)
"The Car That Shuns the Repair Shop" (Thomas)
"The Car of No Regrets" (King)
"The Car You Won't Regret" (Reo)
"The Car with the Punch" (Stephens)
"The Car with a Thousand Speeds" (Owen-Magnetic)
"The Car with a Conscience" (Oakland)
"The Car for Aesthetics" (Peerless)

ergy, Billy Durant found himself in troubled waters. He had built too fast, gambled too recklessly; his corporate ship was full of leaks and was drifting toward the rocks. The bankers watched and waited.

Durant desperately needed time and money to get his creaking, patched-together assemblage all pulling in the same direction. He got neither. He was suffering a severe cash-flow problem. Only Cadillac and Buick among the G.M. marques were making money, and Buick's profits were falling off, due in part to an economic downturn in 1910 and in part to Durant's inattention to its management. When bank loans and suppliers' bills came due there was little cash in the till to pay them. At one point a Buick payroll was met only by subterfuge: a loyal Boston dealer dispatched suitcases full of cash to Flint to avoid the banking channels threatening to bottle up G.M. money to meet outstanding loans. At last, in September, a syndicate of New York and Boston banks took command and dictated the terms of Durant's surrender.

The bankers were at first inclined to bail out only Buick and let the rest of G.M. sink. Henry Leland was then in Europe, but his son Wilfred was equal to the crisis. He won a last-minute stay with an impassioned plea to preserve Cadillac and a pledge that Cadillac's management skills would reinvigorate other G.M. divisions. General Motors would be salvaged, but only on the stiffest of terms. In return for $12.75 million in cash the company was assessed better than $6 million in stock and $15 million in five-year, six-per-cent notes. Thus the rewards of managing risk capital. And Durant himself would have to go. General Motors was put under the command of a "voting trust" headed by Boston banker James J. Storrow.

Under the Storrow regime G.M. underwent a complete turnaround. The weak reeds Durant had acquired were ruthlessly pruned. The Lelands made good on the promise to teach advanced Cadillac production techniques to the other car divisions. Strong management rose to the top in the energetic persons of Charles W. Nash (whom Durant, just before his fall, had installed at Buick) and Walter P. Chrysler, who succeeded to the Buick job when Nash moved up to the G.M. presidency in 1912. Durant's vision of a powerful multi-car consolidation began to come true under other, more disciplined hands. General Motors, however, had not seen the last of Billy Durant.

His expulsion from G.M. did not faze him. What others might consider "an irretrievable misfortune," wrote Arthur Pound in his history of General Motors, was to Durant "but a turn of the wheel on which he expect[ed] to swing round to the top again." Using his personal fortune and his wealth of contacts, he quickly re-entered the auto business. His goal was to find another Buick upon which to rebuild his empire.

In the fall of 1910 Durant put the Swiss-born star of Buick's racing team, Louis Chevrolet, to work with the simple injunction "We're going to need a car." The car the mustachioed racing driver designed—the Chevrolet Classic Six of 1912—was big and powerful and distinctive looking with its vee-front radiator, but its $2,150 price tag put it a long way from the mass market Durant was beginning to eye. By this time, true to form, he had assembled a stable of companies, one of which produced the Little. Its $650 price tag pleased Durant, but not the fact that it ran a poor second to Model T in quality and performance. In any case, its name was hardly a car-salesman's dream. Durant turned to his juggling act, merging here, shifting there, incorporating, reincorporating. "I had found a name for my company—the Chevrolet," he later reminisced. "My next job was to find a car worthy of the name. . . ."

By 1915 he was at the peak of his freebooting form. Chevrolet had absorbed the Little operation and was solidly in the black with its modestly priced Baby Grand and Royal Mail models. It reported a two-year profit of $1.3 million. A new model, the 490, was announced as a direct competitor to Model T. (Louis Chevrolet was not there to share the plaudits. He had parted company with Durant to join the likes of James Packard and David Buick on the sidelines in the rueful pastime of watching others turn his name into a household word.) Durant converted Chevrolet into a holding company with an inflated capitalization of $80 million and launched his most audacious scheme yet—the recapture of General Motors.

Oddly enough, the victim was ripe for the plucking. Many big G.M. stockholders were critical of the Storrow-Nash regime for being too conservative, for failing to market a low-priced competitor to Model T and letting Ford run away with the mass market. Yet the company Durant surrendered to the bankers in 1910 had required nothing so much as conservative, hard-nosed management. The bankers' primary goal was simply to get G.M. back on its feet, if for no other reason than to protect their investment—and to reap the profits thereof. The lion's share of earnings was plowed back into the company, dividends being paid only on the preferred stock. This was good for G.M., good for the bankers, and good for holders of G.M. preferred. It was not good for holders of G.M. common, and that was the breach in the fortress Durant intended to exploit.

Early in 1915 he began adding to his already substantial holdings of G.M. common by buying on the open market in alliance with Lewis G. Kaufman, head of the Chatham & Phoenix National Bank of New York. Another eager buyer was Pierre S. Du Pont, who was anxious to find an investment haven for the enormous profits

Du Pont was beginning to make in the sale of munitions to the warring European powers. During that year the price of G.M. common stock leaped from 82 to 558. Durant was making a lot of friends. He also offered to trade five shares of Chevrolet stock for one of G.M. and was promptly oversubscribed. By September, 1915, his position was strong enough to prevent a renewal of the bankers' voting trust at G.M., and by the spring of 1916 the Durant group and the Chevrolet company held the dominant block of G.M. common. Wall Street watched in astonishment as little fish Chevrolet (fiscal 1915 sales less than $10 million) swallowed the General Motors whale (fiscal 1915 sales more than $94 million). So began the automotive Napoleon's Second Empire at G.M.

What made Billy run? Like Ford, he was a man of imposing complexity. He never ceased to amaze his contemporaries. Walter Chrysler remembered him as having "the most winning personality of anyone I've ever known. He could coax a bird right down out of a tree, I think." A banker acquaintance thought he was plainly a genius, "therefore not to be dealt with on the same basis as ordinary businessmen. In many respects he is a child in emotions, in temperament, and in mental balance, yet possessed of wonderful energy and ability. . . ." Alfred P. Sloan, Jr., who came into General Motors in 1916 and who would eventually succeed to its

presidency, confessed unceasing amazement at "his daring way of making decisions. . . . Durant would proceed on a course of action guided solely, as far as I could tell, by some intuitive flash of brilliance. He never felt obliged to make an engineering hunt for facts." Few people, however, could say they actually *knew* Billy Durant. He had hundreds of acquaintances but hardly any close friends. There is repeated testimony to his charm and his "sweet nature," yet to contemporaries, as to history, he remains an enigma.

James J. Flink, who with Glenn A. Niemeyer has closely examined Durant's career, concludes that at heart the man was an actor. This may be as close to a definition of his character as we are likely to get. Although he lived well, Durant never regarded money as an object in itself; he treated it like the play money in a Monopoly game, buying and selling as if it had no intrinsic value. When Charles Nash, sensing that there was room for only one at the top, resigned as G.M. president in 1916 after Durant regained corporate control, he said that the salary offered him to stay on "was more than any man's worth." Rather than share decision making, Durant tried to buy his executives' loyalty. "We'd fight," Chrysler recalled, "and then he'd want to raise my salary." Finally, in 1919, Chrysler too had had enough and left G.M. "Now, Billy, I'm done," he said, more in sorrow than in anger.

By the same token, power purely for power's sake seems to have motivated Durant no more than money for money's sake. He reveled in making the instant, intuitive decision, in gambling for high business stakes, in testing the mechanisms of capitalism to the hilt (in the twenties he would be the biggest of all the bulls on Wall Street). If his faith in the future of the automobile was boundless, his concept of building a sound corporation to tap that future was decidedly imperfect. He was fascinated by challenge, bored by routine. It was as if he were simply playing a game, or, to return to Flink's characterization, simply playing a larger-than-life role. With unflagging energy he stalked the brightly lit automotive stage, dazzling audiences with his virtuoso skills, seemingly with no concrete thought about the future beyond tomorrow's performance. Whatever the critics might say, he obviously enjoyed the role. And there was never a dull moment when he was on stage.

During these years of Durant's adventuring with General Motors and Ford's production miracle with Model T, the rest of the auto industry was also undergoing a major shakedown. Here too there were attempts at combination and a thinning of the weakest from the ranks.

One of the best examples of this shakedown process, and of the Byzantine nature of the auto industry in its early years, is the tale of Studebaker and E-M-F. The famous Studebaker brothers' firm, founded in 1852 in South Bend, Indiana, was solidly positioned as the world's leading builder of wagons and carriages when it began looking into the horseless carriage at the turn of the century. By 1904 John M. Studebaker had overcome his initial disdain for the gasoline car ("clumsy, dangerous, noisy brutes") and launched the venerable company into the auto age. Studebaker's widespread network of dealerships gave it a running start in the auto business—Durant was then exploiting a similar advantage his Durant-Dort carriage dealers gave him at Buick—and in 1908 it sought a fresh foothold by buying a one-third interest, including exclusive sales rights, in E-M-F for $800,000.

E-M-F was itself struggling for a foothold. *E* was Barney Everitt, the one-time body builder for the Merry Oldsmobile who had staked his fortunes on a car called the Wayne; *M* was William E. Metzger, Cadillac's first sales manager, who had put *his* money on the Northern (then celebrated, with some justification, as the "Silent Northern"); and *F* was Walter E. Flanders, Ford's tough and volatile production straw boss who had moved on to join Everitt at the Wayne company. Their combine, formed early in 1908, discontinued the Wayne and Northern marques (plus a third car, the Deluxe) and in their stead began building the $1,250 E-M-F 30 and the smaller Flanders 20. They were plagued with teething troubles. Certain E-M-F mechanical shortcomings earned it the punsters' epithets "Every Morning Fixit" and "Easy Mark's Favorite," a situation that did not sit well with Studebaker dealers. Intracorporate friction grew until in 1910 Studebaker took over control in a $5-million deal engineered by the Morgan banking interests. (The House of Morgan obviously thought more of the solid old Studebaker firm than of that upstart Billy Durant.) By 1913 the E-M-F and Flanders marques had given way to a single line of cars bearing the Studebaker name. Six marques had become one, and Studebaker was solidly positioned in the scramble for a share of the market left by Ford.

The failure of the E-M-F combination was soon duplicated on a larger scale by the collapse of Benjamin Briscoe's dream company. After seeing Durant leave him to assemble General Motors, Briscoe set up a holding company of his own, which in January, 1910, he christened United States Motor. U.S. Motor was nothing if not ambitious: in one way or another Briscoe managed to assemble a loose alliance of 130 auto and accessory companies. Unhappily for him, the only really strong profit-maker proved to be his own Maxwell, and it could not begin to support the rest of the shaky U.S. Motor line. "Alden Sampson and Stoddard-Dayton were small fry," writes John B. Rae; "Columbia was a lame duck, and Brush was a dead end." By September,

1912, U.S. Motor, with liabilities of $12.25 million and assets of but $9.25 million, was in receivership.

Only the well-engineered Maxwell came out alive. Walter Flanders was brought in and kept Maxwell running smoothly for the rest of the decade, after which it became the foundation stone for yet another combination, this one assembled by Walter P. Chrysler. (The Maxwell would survive vicariously for decades as the cherished radio-land possession of that celebrated tightwad Jack Benny.) Looking back over the shambles of his various companies, Briscoe, the eternal bridesmaid, commented ruefully, "The history of almost every combination will show that the principal motive comes from being hard up."

Neither merger nor monopoly in the form of the Selden patent had succeeded in deflecting auto making from the path of highly competitive free enterprise. In the century's second decade, survival in the business depended, as it always had, on a good product; but increasingly it depended as well on strong personal leadership in promoting cars and in raising the ever-larger sums of capital needed to achieve volume output. Staying price-competitive in the marketplace now required mass production. From 1909 through 1918 Willys-Overland batted .700 in the fight for second place in sales behind Ford.

John North Willys, master salesman and promoter, was cut from the same bolt of cloth as Billy Durant. After making the switch from selling bicycles to selling automobiles, Willys found himself, during the Panic of 1907, deep in a one-man rescue operation of the moribund Overland Automobile Company of Indianapolis. His resuscitation effort included, at one point, persuading a hotel clerk to accept his personal check in exchange for the weekend cash receipts so he could meet a Monday morning Overland payroll. Willys next restored the faith of Overland's creditors, and in a matter of months he had the company on its feet. By 1909 he had transferred operations to Toledo, Ohio, renamed the car Willys-Overland, and was charging into the thick of the production race.

Three other soon-to-be famous automotive marques were born in these years. All were the result of independence movements. A group of Oldsmobile alumni headed by designer Howard E. Coffin and Roy D. Chapin, who had piloted Ransom Olds's little curved dash from Detroit to New York back in 1901, began on their own to build a rakish-looking car in 1909 that ads described as "Strong—Speedy—Roomy—Stylish." It bore the name of Detroit department-store magnate Joseph L. Hudson, who had put up most of the money to get the new company started. (Designer Coffin no doubt had long since resigned himself to the fact that his name would never become a household word, at least in the automobile field.)

(continued on page 128)

Genre art to raise a chuckle, by C. M. Coolidge, admirer of man's best friend

AUTOMOBILIANA

Americans' fascination with the motor vehicle in the early decades of the century was reflected in the wide-spread popularity of automobiliana of every description. This sampling of post cards, valentines, fans, games, books, toys, and miscellaneous oddities and objets d'art—all of it, except for the item above, from the Leo Pascal Collection—indicates that both adults and children were caught up in the fad.

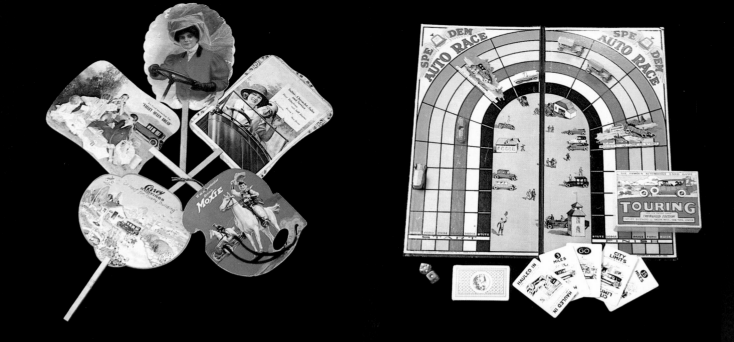

The fans at the upper left were giveaways to promote various products and services. The auto-race game dates from 1922 and the card game "Touring" from 1926. The juveniles feature such heroes and heroines as the Motor Maids, the Auto Boys, and inventive Tom Swift.

The contents of the display at right, listed clockwise from the plate: Easter-egg ornament, chocolate mold, four-wheel meerschaum pipe, jewel box, china car, button, watch fob, harmonica, Santa Claus pin, pincushion, coin bank, matchbox, and silver cigarette case.

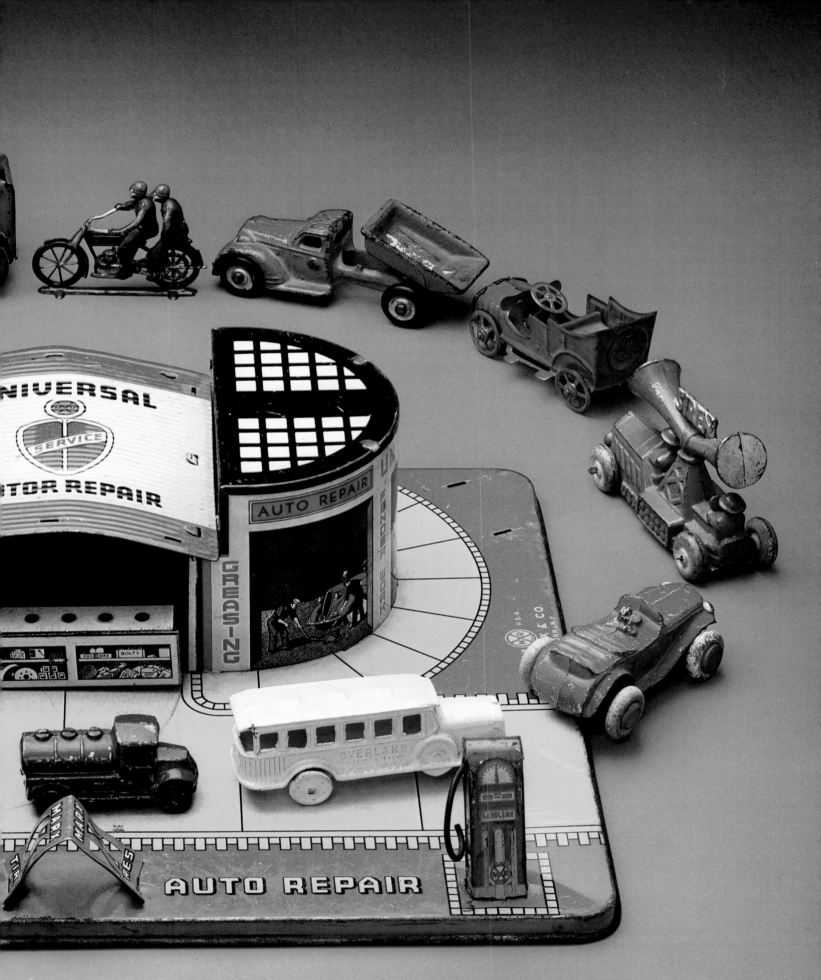

Once upon a time no toy box was complete without
a model service station. This one probably dates from
the thirties, the tin and cast-iron vehicles from
various periods. At the far right is a military siren truck.

The Hudson was a well-engineered car backed by a strong management, and it soon attracted a loyal following in the medium-priced class.

In 1914 John and Horace Dodge declared *their* independence, severing a long-standing supplier tie to Ford to begin producing a car of their own. Their announcement, *Automobile Topics* reported, "swept like wildfire throughout the industry." The brothers had one major advantage that set them apart from other newcomers to auto making: money, in great sums. The Dodges' original 1903 investment in the Ford Motor Company—$7,000 in materials and $3,000 in cash—has to rank as one of the most profitable gambles in the history of American business. Thanks to Ford dividends and to the profits of their parts making, they could pull together $5 million in cash to capitalize a new company with hardly a blink of their collective eye. The brothers' car was as solid and dependable as the brothers' reputation. In the price range just above Model T and matching the T in plain-Jane practicality, the Dodge quickly found a comfortable slot of its own in the marketplace. All the while, of course, the brothers continued to draw dividends from the Ford Motor Company, which —as we shall see—set Henry Ford's teeth on edge.

A $5 million investment was also enough to start a third long-running American marque. Charlie Nash, everyone said, could have been the model for a Horatio Alger novel. At age six the orphaned Nash was "bound out" to a Michigan farmer to "perform whatever labor might be required"; at age forty-eight he was named president of General Motors. After leaving G.M. in 1916 Nash and his fellow G.M. refugee, banker James Storrow, bought the Thomas B. Jeffery Company of Kenosha, Wisconsin. Jeffery had started building the popular little Rambler early in the century, and after his death in 1910 his son took over the management and changed the car's name from Rambler to Jeffery. That change did not take with the public, but the new change did: cars bearing the Nash emblem would remain in production for forty years.

No doubt Charlie Nash and his contemporaries would have been startled, had they been granted a glimpse into the future, to learn that Nash Motors, founded just two decades after the Duryea brothers brought forth the American automobile industry, would be the last of that hardy breed known as independents to make a go of it. Of all the "one-marque" companies started after 1916, none would last more than a few years. Oligopoly was far from being just around the corner, but conditions in this once freest of free enterprise businesses were beginning to take a new course.

In a 1910 newspaper article, the veteran production man Walter Flanders predicted that "henceforth the history of this industry will be the story of a conflict between giants." By 1914 Flanders's giants had emerged (that year automobiles climbed into seventh place in product value among all industries), and by the eve of America's entry into the Great War they were in full cry. In 1916, the last full prewar production year, better than 1.5 million cars rolled out of American factories, a staggering increase of 630,000 over the previous year. Their wholesale value was nearly one billion dollars. Model T was the runaway individual leader with forty-eight per cent of the total, more than five times the output of second-place Willys-Overland. General Motors, which turned out 240,000 Buicks, Chevrolets, Oaklands, Cadillacs, and Oldsmobiles in 1916, was an empire on the move.

To term the automobile's growth rate in the ten years ending in 1916 astonishing is an understatement. Production had increased 4,500 per cent, suggesting that not only had the automobile won an unshakable place in the nation's scheme of things but that it had become far more affordable. This was not due simply to the rise in Americans' disposable personal income in this period. Other factors were at work.

In a pioneering 1928 financial study of the automobile industry, Ralph E. Epstein pointed out that nearly forty-one per cent of the car buyers in 1906 paid between $2,275 and $4,775 for their machines. Ten

It can be supposed that the back-yard builder of the Overland Wind Wagon at left enjoyed some success as an ice racer, but just what the Franklin Wind Machine's owner hoped to gain by fitting a propeller for highway traveling is not at all clear.

years later, however, that price range accounted for but 1.5 per cent of the sales; indeed, nine tenths of the 1916 car buyers paid less than $1,375. Certainly Model T had a great deal to do with lowering the average price (the cost of a T touring car after August 1 of that year was down to $360), yet even when Ford sales were taken out of the equation, Epstein observed, eighty-four per cent of the remaining sales were still in the lowest price brackets. Mass production as executed by Henry Ford and imitated by his fellow producers was rapidly bringing the auto closer to the reach of *every* Everyman.

A second reason for the car-buying surge in these years involved major technological advances. This progress had begun quietly during the Selden patent war. An avowed purpose of the Association of Licensed Automobile Manufacturers, in addition to administering the Selden patent and battling Henry Ford, was to promote the whole notion of automobiling, and it was soon recognized that cars would be far easier to build and repair if there was technical standardization. As it was, if a maker of a unique type of bolt or tubing or washer or whatever went out of business, the car manufacturer was stranded without a key source of supply; conversely, if the car maker went out of business (as so many did), the driver of a suddenly orphaned marque was in a quandary trying to locate one-of-a-kind replacement parts.

Working with leading suppliers, the A.L.A.M. made some progress in standardization before it turned the campaign over to the Society of Automotive Engineers in 1910. The S.A.E.'s first president, Howard E. Coffin of Hudson, stated flatly that the lack of standardization was "responsible for nine-tenths of the production troubles and most of the needless expense entailed in the manufacture of motorcars." Between them, the A.L.A.M. and Coffin's S.A.E. made great strides in persuading auto makers to specify such things as standard-thread bolts and screws and spark plugs and (for example) to build their wheels to take a stock range of tire sizes offered by all tire makers.

This achievement, and a patent

cross-licensing agreement ratified in 1915, were of particular help to the smaller firms—giants such as Ford and G.M. had already begun standardizing as a necessity of mass production. But the big winner was the car owner. He found prices lower and repairs easier and cheaper, and if he was stuck with, say, a Big Brown Luverne (d. 1918), he knew that he had some hope of keeping his orphan alive. And of course today's loving restorer of an antique car has frequent cause to bless Howard Coffin and the S.A.E.

The technological revolution quickened in 1908 when Charles F. Kettering, a thirty-two-year-old engineer with National Cash Register in Dayton, Ohio, decided to focus his spare-

A Peerless Peerless

The "Salon-Sedan," a car with an interior resembling a cozy and luxuriously furnished drawing room, is the feature of the Peerless exhibit. The carefully harmonized and tasteful fittings are imported. . . .

The interior colors of the car are dark mahogany, ivory, and green, blending from the darker to the lighter shades. Dark green linoleum covers the floor boards and is bound with German silver moulding. The carpet is high-piled English Axminster. At the floor and the side walls is a baseboard of mahogany about four inches wide. Above this is wool frieze cloth and a chair rail of the same design as the

baseboard, only smaller. Around the windows is a veneering of ivory enamel and the sash-less panes are set in a veneer of three quarters of an inch wide mahogany. The shades are silk taffeta. The festooned draperies are silk broché lined with silk taffeta. The dome ceiling is lined with plain wool tapestry laid in a panel with flush lights in each of the four corners. Pillows are of Italian brocade with silk tinseled velvet border. A toilet case is of mahogany with fittings of silver and mahogany-colored goat skins. All the interior metal parts are quadruple silver plated. . . . Compartments are furnished for gloves, books, papers and slip covers.
—*Automobile Trade Journal*, 1914

time energies on the automobile. An acquaintance who worked for Cadillac told Kettering of the troublesome electrical ignition system then in wide use, and before long "CFK," an assistant noted in his diary, "was full of auto ignition project." Working evenings and weekends in a Dayton barn with a team of like-minded colleagues from National Cash Register, Kettering developed a system that supplied a single, intense, precisely timed spark for ignition rather than the usual erratic "shower of sparks." When Henry Leland of Cadillac ordered eight thousand ignition sets from this "absolutely unknown young electrical genius," Kettering formalized his barn research center as the Dayton Engineering Laboratories Company (Delco) and moved into the auto business to stay.

The next challenge to engage his attention was the one major problem still plaguing the gasoline engine— getting it started. The hand crank was universally condemned as an invention of the devil, reducing strong men to tears of impotent rage if it did not break their bones first and often leaving the fair sex literally helpless. The story goes that Cadillac's Leland was galvanized into a crash starter program when, in 1910, his friend Byron T. Carter of Cartercar was fatally injured cranking a lady's stalled Cadillac in Belle Isle Park in Detroit. The tale loses authority, as Beverly Rae Kimes points out, due to the fact that Mr. Carter had died two and a half

years earlier of pneumonia. Nevertheless, Leland's interest in the problem *was* triggered in some such fashion about this time, and he immediately put his engineering staff—and Kettering—to work to resolve it with the admonition, "The Cadillac car will kill no more men if we can help it."

From the day the gasoline car became a practical reality, inventors had been at work to persuade it to start "automatically." There were experiments with compressed air, with tanked acetylene, with exhaust gases stored under pressure, with spring-wound contrivances of Rube Goldberg complexity. None of them worked very well, if they worked at all. An obvious starting device was an electric battery-driven motor, but the consensus of the experts was that such a motor would have to deliver up to 5 horsepower to do the job, and the typical 5-horsepower electric motor of the time was very big and very heavy.

Kettering was a man of great enthusiasms and entirely unconventional turns of mind, and when he tackled a new problem there came over him an engaging touch of the mad scientist. "All human development, no matter what form it takes," he once observed, "must be outside the rules; otherwise, we would never have anything new"; less formally he liked to say, "Never mind about the experts." This attitude was never better displayed than in his work with the electric starter.

His solution to the problem was classically pragmatic. As he had discovered in developing a small electric motor for cash registers, what was needed in this situation was a high-torque, high-voltage motor that could be made small and light because it worked in bursts short enough to preclude overloading and burning out. But that was only part of the need. Kettering and the Cadillac engineers rightly foresaw no great problem in obtaining a small heavy-duty lead-acid storage battery to power the starter; what had to be developed was a generator driven by the car engine to charge the battery, plus some sort of voltage regulation of the charging system. With these requirements in mind, "Boss Ket" and his "barn gang" set to work with a will.

By February, 1911, the Delco prototype system was ready to demonstrate to the Cadillac management. Kettering had combined the starting and generating functions in one unit (modern usage separates the two, but the principle is the same). To start the car, the driver switched on and pressed a starter pedal; pulling 24 volts from the battery, the starter motor engaged teeth on the flywheel rim to turn the engine over. Once the engine burst into life, the starter motor disengaged and the generator, driven off the engine's timing gear, produced a regulated 6 volts to operate the ignition system and charge the battery. Kettering himself drove the Cadillac equipped with the

The automobile evolved far more rapidly in the first two decades of the century than the roads it was driven on. In the backdrop photograph of this display a Packard leads a trial drive on the first mile of concrete rural highway in the nation. It was built outside Detroit in 1909 at a cost of $13,534. Such modern construction techniques were rare in an era dominated by the concept of locally built roads for local use. The crude roadbed at right, photographed about the same date, was more typical; the car is a Packard Glidden tourer. At the left, convict laborers work on a Georgia road about 1912, and a horse-drawn grader is put to use in rural Kentucky. Only gradually did machine power replace manpower. Below is a grader, photographed in central Iowa in 1916, pulled by a steam traction engine.

new starting system to the Dayton railroad depot for shipment to Detroit, stopping the engine every block and restarting it to assure himself that all was well. On February 17, 1911, the starter passed all its tests at the Cadillac plant. Leland's commitment and Kettering's genius had put the hand crank on the road to extinction.

Boss Ket was not done yet. His goal was an *all*-electric system, and he promptly carried his revolution to its logical conclusion by making the car's lighting system electrical as well. Soon the Prest-O-Lite acetylene tank on the running board would join the hand crank in limbo. The 1912 Cadillac Model Thirty had the first "all-electric" system: starting, ignition, lighting, generating. At $1,800 for the five-passenger touring car it was the best automotive buy of the season. Advertisements pictured the car head-on above the simple caption "The Car That Has No Crank." Britain's Royal Automobile Club recognized the Leland-Kettering achievement and for the second time awarded Cadillac the Dewar Trophy for automotive excellence.

By 1914 fully ninety per cent of America's auto makers were offering electric self-starters as standard equipment. The primary holdout was Ford. Although electric lights were installed on Model T late in 1914, a starter was not offered as an option ($75) until 1919 and was not made standard until 1926. For the rest of its production life Model T would appeal

This impressive line-up, photographed with a panoramic camera in 1913, is the newly equipped motor division of the Cincinnati police department, featuring motorcyclists, patrol cars, and a paddy-wagon brigade.

primarily on its unbeatably low price and durability while the rest of the industry moved ahead technically (and stylistically). The self-starter meant that anyone—young or old, male or female, strong or weak—could operate a car. The automobile's appeal was now universal. It was the beginning of a new era.

The self-starter was also the final symbolic nail in the coffins of the steamer and the electric. True progress in steam-car technology was already languishing, a fact acknowledged by the White people when they completed the switch from steam to gasoline in 1912. By the time progress was renewed in the person of Abner Doble, whose brilliantly engineered Doble steamer blossomed in 1917 and reached full flower in the twenties, it was too late. By then steam could no longer hope to compete with the solidly entrenched gasoline engine. Abner Doble was the Henry Leland of steam, but as the auto enthusiast and historian Lord Montagu observes, what the "steam crowd" really needed was a Henry Ford.

As for the electric, it had enjoyed a turnaround of sorts after about 1908 when its particular handiness as an urban vehicle began to be appreciated, but the self-starter nipped the

brief renaissance. No longer could the electric claim to be the only vehicle "always ready to go" when a woman was at the controls. For better or worse, the internal-combustion engine was the unchallenged king of the American road.

From the beginning, the gasoline car had found its widest acceptance in the Middle West, where soon enough Detroit was ensconced as Motor City. ("Detroit," in this context, encompassed the whole southeastern quadrant of Michigan and included such production centers as Flint, Lansing, and Pontiac.) To be sure, other cities were sharing in the new automobile-bred prosperity— notably Cleveland, Toledo, Indianapolis, South Bend, Buffalo, Kenosha, Wisconsin—but Detroit quickly went to the top and stayed there. This phenomenon had come about, as we have seen, mostly by chance: the happenstance that Ransom Olds and his financial backer Samuel Smith, followed by Henry Leland, Henry Ford, and Billy Durant, all launched their enterprises in that quarter of Michigan gave Detroit a commanding lead. Then, like Topsy, it "just growed." As George S. May observes, the old boosters' slogan, "Detroit the Beautiful," soon gave way to "Detroit the Dynamic."

A wide range of ancillary industries struggled to match Detroit's furious growth. These will be examined in more detail in Chapter 5; suffice it to say here that auto production was en-

tirely dependent on their keeping pace. Those one hundred freight cars arriving daily at Highland Park by 1914, for example, contained everything from pig iron and sheet steel to leather, brass, wood, glass, and paint (black). The tire industry multiplied manyfold to meet the demand. American machine tools reached a volume and variety unmatched anywhere in the world. For the petroleum industry, confronting at the turn of the century a saturation of the market for kerosene and lubricating oils, the automobile was a godsend. The spectacular strike at Spindletop, near Beaumont, Texas, in 1901, was symbolic assurance of the (seemingly) unlimited supply of American crude oil. The automobile triggered comparable booms in such fields as road building, service facilities, accessories, insurance. . . the list is endless. Putting America on wheels, in this second decade of the century, was a huge, complex undertaking.

The auto boom slowed only momentarily when it encountered global war. While the industry made notable contributions to the American war effort in 1917-18, there was no total mobilization as there would be in World War II. To be sure, production of civilian cars in 1918 fell some 800,000 below 1917's record total of 1.75 million, but this was due more to material shortages than government edict. Far and away the car makers' most important wartime role was doing what they did best — building

motor vehicles. In other roles their record was uneven.

Trucks and ambulances composed the lion's share of the approximately 160,000 American-built vehicles mobilized for the Great War. Additional military hardware — helmets, shells, artillery carriages and mechanisms, for example — was also produced with good success. Considerable innovative skill got the newly designed Liberty aircraft engine into production and into combat use before the Armistice.

Other auto-industry production programs were less successful. The plan to manufacture tanks and submarine chasers in quantity shifted into high gear too late for any of them to see action, and a major effort to mass produce warplanes bogged down badly. Military manpower rather than military materiel was the prime American contribution to the defeat of the Central Powers, but considering that the nation was at war only nineteen months, the overall production record of the automobile industry was a strong one.

The industry's three best-known figures, Billy Durant, Henry Leland, and Henry Ford, were all strongly affected by the Great War. Durant's 1909 pledge to Leland not to interfere with the running of Cadillac had always been scrupulously honored, a policy that helped produce not only the "all-electric" 1912 Cadillac but also a superior V-8 engine, introduced in 1915 models, that was

the first American power plant of that type suited to quantity production. The nation's entry into war in 1917, however, brought the two men to a clash of wills. Leland vehemently demanded that G.M. plunge full-bore into war work. Durant, just as vehemently pacifist, dismissed arguments that it was everyone's battle as "platitudes." "This is not our war," he fumed, "and I will not permit any General Motors unit to do work for the government." Durant would soften his attitude and allow the company to fulfill military contracts, but not before Leland resigned. "The Cadillac has been dearer to me than any other one thing in the world except my home," he explained at a farewell banquet in his honor, "but there has arisen now a claim on my loyalty that is nearer and dearer still." The seventy-four-year-old Leland promptly formed the Lincoln Motor Company and began an ambitious program to bring the Liberty aircraft engine into production. As usual, the dean of the auto industry was acting for principle rather than only for profit.

Henry Ford was equally principled, and as usual, his actions gained worldwide attention. From the moment the conflict began, he wore his pacifism on his sleeve, pleading with Europe's warring powers to end this "murder, desolation, and destruction" and submit to a negotiated peace. In the winter of 1915–16 the industrialist became a magnet for a variegated collection of what Nevins

WE ARE ALL FOR PEACE.

1ST DAY OUT.

WHAT KIND OF PEACE?

2ND DAY OUT.

BRYAN PEACE! WILSON PEACE!
PREPAREDNESS! TAFT PEACE!
ROOSEVELT PEACE

3RD DAY OUT.

PEACE AT ANY PRICE!

4TH DAY OUT.

Henry Ford's pacifistic idealism led him to launch his Peace Ship crusade in 1915–16 in an effort to end the fighting in Europe. The derision heaped on the crusade by the press is typified by this cartoon sequence printed in the Minneapolis *Daily News.* Once America entered the war, all the auto makers (including Ford) turned to the production of military equipment, primarily trucks, ambulances, and other vehicles. On the opposite page, at the top, are Ford ambulances collecting British wounded on the Western Front in 1917. At center are trucks and ambulances mobilized to support the American Meuse-Argonne offensive in 1918. The Model T truck at the bottom is assisted across a stream by British and Indian troops campaigning in Mesopotamia.

and Hill term "social evangelists" whose one (and only, as it turned out) common denominator was seeking peace of any sort. The result was the infamous voyage of the "Peace Ship," the liner *Oscar II* Ford impulsively chartered to carry this strange delegation to Scandinavia for the purpose of establishing an international mediation commission to try to end the bloody conflict.

The Peace Ship crusade was an instance of Ford's idealism running aground on the shoals of wider reality when applied to events outside his auto plants. His fellow pacifists aboard *Oscar II* were tinged with more than a bit of eccentricity, and reporters traveling with them were more than a bit unsparing of this band of "nuts, fools, and maniacs." The tone was set early. "Great War Ends Christmas Day," headlined the New York *Tribune;* "Ford to Stop It." Cartoonists and editorial writers ridiculed the "impossible effort to establish an inopportune peace." The Hartford *Courant* charged that "Henry Ford's latest performance is getting abundant criticism and seems entitled to all it gets." "Mr. Ford's visit abroad will not be mischievous only because it is ridiculous," ex-President Theodore Roosevelt predicted. Not surprisingly after such an inauspicious beginning, the odyssey of *Oscar II* withered into nothing.

Henry Ford was undaunted but quietly bitter. He sensed correctly enough that millions of "little people"

in Europe and America agreed with him on the insanity of the war. How then, he asked, could anyone criticize his efforts? "I wanted to see peace," he later remarked. "I at least tried to bring it about. Most men did not even try." The logic was sound enough, but it seems not to have occurred to him that his inept management had much to do with the ignominious reception his scheme received. (Like Durant, Ford changed his stand after the United States entered the war and filled military orders.) The naturalist John Burroughs, Ford's close friend, viewed the incident with sad resignation: "His unfortunate Peace Ship expedition did more credit to his big heart than to his judgment." Burroughs might well have noted another end product of the dismal failure of the peace crusade: an embittered darkening of Henry Ford's character.

The Peace Ship episode was not the only outgrowth of Ford's pacifist stance to have repercussions. In the "war scare" in 1916 precipitated by Pancho Villa's freebooting adventures along the Mexican border, the superpatriotic Chicago *Tribune* charged (incorrectly) that Ford refused to pay any of his workers honoring a National Guard call-up. The *Tribune* mounted its soapbox in an editorial headlined "Ford Is an Anarchist": "If Ford allows this rule of his shop to stand, he will reveal himself not merely as an ignorant idealist, but as an anarchistic enemy of the nation which protects him in his wealth."

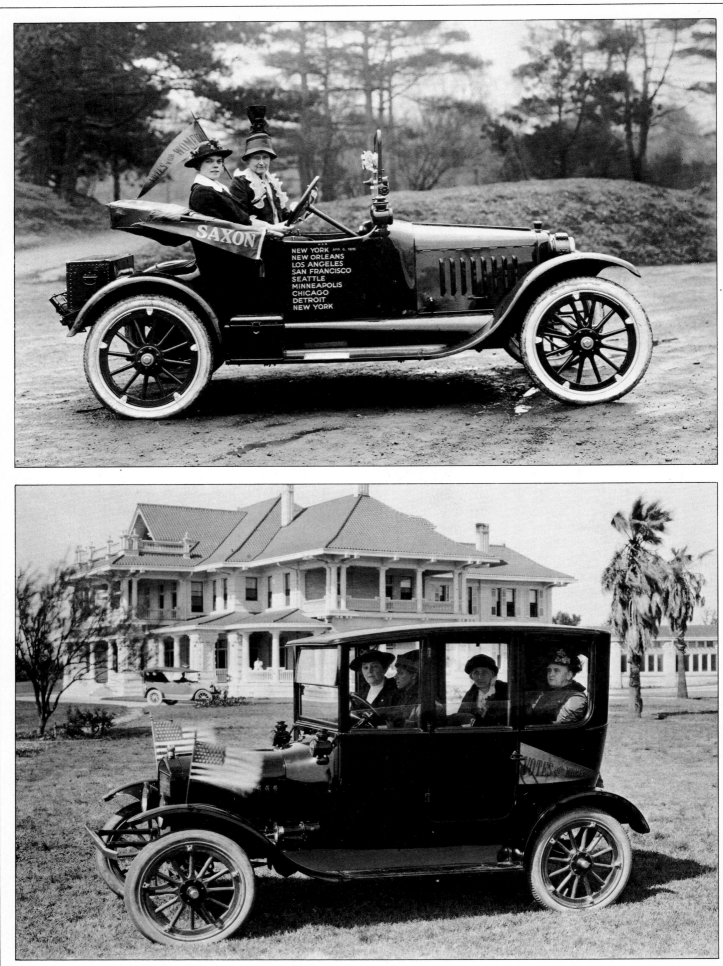

The World War I era also saw the automobile mobilized for a campaign of another sort, the fight for women's suffrage. The pair at top carried the banner from one end of the country to the other and back again in their Saxon runabout in 1916. The four suffragettes in the well-cared-for Tin Lizzie were photographed in Texas. The campaign ended triumphantly in 1920 with the passage of the Nineteenth Amendment.

Ford filed a million-dollar libel suit against the newspaper.

When the case finally came to trial in 1919, Ford's lawyers served him badly by failing to narrow their suit to the "anarchist" charge, a term clearly regarded in common-law precedent as libelous. Instead, they left the door wide open for a freewheeling inquisition by *Tribune* lawyer Elliott G. Stevenson, who pinned Ford on the witness stand for eight days to "prove" him indeed "an ignorant idealist" unfit to render opinions on anything beyond car making. It was a mortifying public humiliation for Ford. He had last seen the inside of a not-very-good country school at sixteen, and he could not begin to cope with Stevenson's questions on such things as social policy, politics, and American history—especially American history. The New York *Times* was more charitable in its phrasing than most newspapers when it reported that the industrialist "has not received a pass degree." The jury found the *Tribune* guilty of libel, but awarded Ford six cents in damages.

Ford's "history is bunk" dictum, which gained notoriety during the *Tribune* trial, was pounced on gleefully by the auto maker's contemporaries and is still a bone worried by modern commentators. The barbed phrase may be one reason, theorizes historian John A. Garraty, that "while praising his talents as a manufacturer, historians have not dealt kindly with Ford the man. . . ."

Indeed, Ford seems to have suffered a bum rap. During the trial, Stevenson asked him to comment on a newspaper interview in which he was quoted as saying, "History is more or less bunk. It's tradition." "I did not say it was bunk," Ford replied. "It was bunk to me [referring to his school days] but I did not need it very bad." The number of students, in Ford's generation and since, similarly numbed by dullard teaching and catalogues of dusty facts is beyond counting; in recent years, instead of "history is bunk," their refrain has been "history isn't relevant." Ford told an aide, after the trial, that he was going to "give the people an idea of real history. I'm going to start a museum. We are going to show just what actually happened in years gone by." Today a good deal of relevancy may be found in Dearborn's Henry Ford Museum and Greenfield Village.

Thus was more scar tissue added to Ford's changing character. The trial, wrote Nevins and Hill, "which did not break the closed system of his thought or persuade him to seek a broader cultivation, tinged his mind with wariness, bitterness, and cynicism and strengthened the arbitrary and arrogant elements in his nature. . . ." The world's most powerful industrialist now facing a host of new challenges was far different from the man in 1908 who had looked in happy innocence at his fledgling Model T and proclaimed, "Well, I guess we've got started."

Mr. Ford's Mercurial Turn of Mind

There is about him the fascination of an unlimited uncertainty. No living being knows what he is likely to do or say next. . . . As in every other man, there is in Henry Ford the mingling of opposing elements. In him, however, the contrast between these elements is more pronounced than in the average man. Phenomenal strength of mind in one direction is offset by lamentable weakness in another. Astounding knowledge of and insight into business affairs along certain lines stand out against a boasted ignorance in other matters. Sensational achievements are mingled with equally sensational failures. Faith in his employees and, at times, unlimited generosity toward them are clouded on occasion by what seems to be an utter indifference to the fate and feelings of men in his employ. There seems to be no middle ground. . . . There is no line discernible that I have ever been able to detect, that marks the resultant of the opposing forces within him, and to which one may point and say, "this is the general trend of his life." . . . His moral qualities . . . have never been compounded and blended into a stable, unified character.

—Samuel S. Marquis, *Henry Ford: An Interpretation,* 1923

139

4
THE WORLD OF TIN LIZZIE

The ancestry of two of the automotive world's most famous coinages, *Tin Lizzie* and *flivver,* has never been satisfactorily explained. Etymologically, these so-briquets for Model T carry "origin obscure" labels. The best guess on *Tin Lizzie* is that it was someone's pet name—Model T was called many things, some affectionate, some not—that caught on. As for *flivver,* Rudolph E. Anderson, a devoted collector of automotive oddities, ran across this 1914 limerick:

> There was a fat man of Fall River
> Who said as he drove his Ford flivver,
>   This bumping and jolting
>   To me is revolting!
> It's hell, but it's good for the liver.

It could be deduced from this verse, Anderson continued, that the term's origin was biological. Model T's bumpy ride was excused as being at least healthy for one's liver: *for the liver* had eventually become *f'th liver* and finally *flivver.* (Anderson did not vouch for this explanation, and in fact it does seem strained.) Be that as it may, both terms promptly entered the vernacular, testimony to Model T's impact on American society.

In 1929 the journalist Charles Merz described Ford's flivver as "the first log cabin of the Motor Age." It is an appropriate metaphor. Like the log cabin, Model T was simple, sturdy, and utilitarian, and like so many of the people who owned it, it was hard-working, frugal, and practical. And it was likely to be found anywhere. For the eighteen full calendar years of Model T production (1909 through 1926), its share of the auto industry's total output averaged 42.9 per cent. In six of those years its share topped 50 per cent, and in 1921 it led the production race with an astonishing 61.6 per cent. All told, nearly 15.5 million flivvers were built.

These statistics have a significance beyond their sheer weight. If today a single Chevrolet model (for example) were to capture fifty per cent of the auto market, the achievement would affirm that marque as the big winner in Detroit's annual popularity contest. Only a small segment of its buyers would be coming of age and purchasing their first automobile; the rest would be replacing their old cars with Chevy's latest rather than someone else's latest. But whenever Model T won half the market (the first time was in 1914), it signaled something more: a huge expansion of the market itself.

Tin Lizzie was the first car a substantial majority of its buyers had ever owned. Henry Ford created an

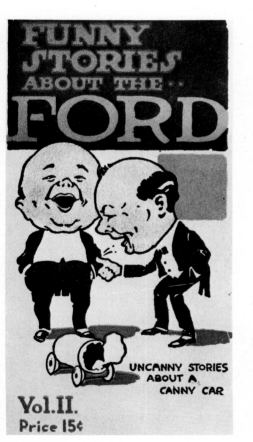

FORD ARCHIVES, HENRY FORD MUSEUM

The Ford phenomenon was beginning to hit full stride when the cheerful Californians opposite clowned it up for a family portrait in their Tin Lizzie in 1914. In that year one of every two new-car buyers selected a flivver. Ford jokes proliferated almost as fast as the cars themselves. This collection of outrageous puns, limericks, and knee-slappers was published in 1915.

The new look of small-town America—this
happens to be Henderson, Texas—on a
Saturday in the twenties: it is farmers'
day in town, and most arrived in flivvers.
Will Rogers observed in 1924 that "Politics
ain't worrying this Country one tenth as
much as Parking Space." The parking
pictured here was common in towns where
Main Street had originally been laid out
wide enough for teams and wagons to turn.

entirely new market for the automobile, and each time he cut prices he uncovered yet another layer of that market. This process was accelerated by the fact that as his prices fell the buying power of the American family was rising. During Model T's lifetime, average annual earnings across the nation multiplied about two and a half times, while the cost-of-living index was approximately doubling. By 1925, when a new Lizzie touring car could be had for $290 (its all-time low price tag—approximately $995 in 1977) and a used one for considerably less, the automobile was coming ever closer to the reach of every family that wanted one. True to his promise, Ford led the way in democratizing car ownership. When his flivver first appeared, there were some three hundred thousand cars of all makes on America's roads; when the last one was built there were some twenty million.

That Model T introduced so many millions of Americans to the auto age goes far toward explaining the folklore and nostalgia that surrounded it. A proud owner's first day with his new machine was an occasion to be remembered and treasured: collecting it from the Ford dealer and intently absorbing the instructions for its care and feeding, settling behind the wheel for the nervous but exhilarating solo drive, finding a hero's welcome awaiting him at the home place. Countless family albums contained snapshots of kith and kin posing in a shiny new flivver, as often as not dressed in their Sunday best for the occasion. Over the years the snapshots multiplied. There were views of Tin Lizzie parked at a family reunion, loaded down with gear at a fishing camp, filled to the overflow mark with collegians on Homecoming Day, perched on the rim of the Grand Canyon. Lizzie's world was a large and varied one.

Everyone, it seemed, had a favorite story about the little car. "I have never in all the world . . . seen so much to cause me to laugh and weep, to wonder and rejoice, as I have at the Ford," said the journalist Ida Tarbell. Many an owner could tell of the time he forgot to set the hand brake before cranking his T and was gently pinned to the barn wall when the machine started and edged forward in high gear. Others might recall losing their way on a rainy night and plodding wearily along in low gear with the engine racing to keep the flickering headlights bright enough to search for road signs and familiar landmarks. The size of the mudholes Model T wrenched itself out of grew with each telling, as did the steepness of the hills it climbed and the depth of the streams it negotiated.

Model T folklore, like folk medicine, was rich in home remedies. Many of these remedies were applied to the problem of starting Lizzie in cold weather The days were ending when owners put their cars up on blocks the moment the snow flew. The T was tough and agile enough to handle winter driving conditions—once it was started. Some owners favored heating the engine's intake manifold (to hasten vaporization of the fuel) by dousing it with boiling water, emptying what was left in the teakettle into the radiator for good measure. Others achieved the same result with a flaming corncob or a blowtorch. The more fastidious might invest in a Hot Spot Generator ($1), a small tray mounted under the manifold in which gasoline or alcohol was burned, or in a Simon Primer ($5), an electrically heated manifold that allegedly would "start any Ford in 10 seconds in the coldest weather!"

Among other remedies for winter starting troubles were a splash of highly volatile ether in the carburetor or the cylinders, heating the spark plugs red hot, or jacking up a rear wheel to produce the effect of an extra flywheel and ease the labor of cranking the engine. (The code name assigned the starting crank on Ford's parts list was singularly appropriate: HERNIA.) Eventually one of these ploys or some combination of them would succeed and Model T would bark into life, one cylinder at a time, with a sound "like a thresher trimming the nap off an acre of barbed wire," as Floyd Clymer, an avid collector of flivver lore, put it. However inconvenient all this must have been—and winter starting problems, it should be noted, were by no means limited to Model T owners—it was accepted as

Model T came from the factory in full running trim but without a flair or flourish to its name. A large "add-on" business quickly sprang up to remedy this failing. These are entries from the Ford section of a 1916 Sears, Roebuck automotive catalogue. The couple pictured in their Ford in 1918—the admonition on the radiator refers to World War I Liberty bonds—are Mr. and Mrs. Arthur Telfer, of Cooperstown, New York, who believed in keeping a car in good repair. Telfer, the town photographer, drove this flivver for thirty-seven years and did not relinquish the wheel until age ninety-four.

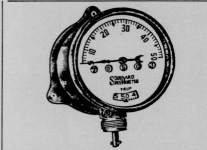

Standard Speedometer

The Standard is accurate. The hand is steady. Miles per hour, trip and total mileage easily read. Fifty-mile dial, 100-mile trip and 10,000-mile automatic repeating season register. Attached in ten minutes. Used on over 150,000 Fords. Bearings all steel with hardened and ground ball cups pressed in. Finished in black.

61R7921—Weight, 12 pounds..**$7.25**

Quick-Cool Radiators
Including Streamline Hood

Has 25 to 30 per cent greater cooling capacity than most Ford radiators. Will not break when frozen. It is a cellular radiator with copper tubes, three-inch core top and bottom tanks, brass casing and auxiliary water tank which gives total capacity of 2 gallons, 1 quart, 1 pint. Triple japanned, 20-gauge steel hood with six louvres on a side. Extended starting crank and bonnet clamp brackets, and hood edges with models prior to 1915. Mention model and year of car when ordering. Shipping weight, 80 pounds.

261R5752—Nickel finish **$32.50**
261R5773—Brass finish 31.50
Shipped from factory in Southern Michigan.

Wind Shields

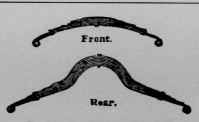

For Fords prior to 1915. Strictly high class construction. Frame is best quality steel, black enameled. Adjustable ball bearing hinges. Shield adjusts automatically. Will not rattle or loosen. Heavy imported glass, perfectly clear and set in rubber channels. All attachments included. Top strap loops to fasten top to shield included. Straight type shield for 1911 or 1912 models. Zigzag type for 1913, 1914 and early 1915 models. Shipping weight, 50 pounds.

161R5659—1911-12 Models **$8.25**
161R5660—1913-14-15 Models.. **8.25**

Springs for Fords

Ford front or rear springs, for models N. S. R. and T. Special alloy steel of high quality. The tension and flexibility are perfect. Buying cheap springs to save money is like stopping a watch to save time. Our springs not only combine quality and workmanship, but fit perfectly as well.

161R5757—Front Spring. Shipping weight, 24 pounds............**$1.95**
161R5758—Rear Spring. Shipping weight, 36 pounds............**$7.**

Pre... elt fr... ng off... f car. Eve... Ford owner should have one, and be always assured that his fan is working. Easily attached. Fastened to fan belt bracket. Length, 2½ inches; width, 2 inches.
61R7532—Weight, 4 ounces....**12c**

Shock Absorbers

Thousands of high-priced, heavy touring cars have been equipped with shock absorbers, with beneficial results. It is an acknowledged fact that the lighter the car the greater the necessity for a shock-resisting device. Eliminates practically all the shock before it can be transmitted to the body spring. Works directly over the axle, and no matter how light the shock, its action is instantaneous. They make a car surprisingly smooth-riding, even with the lightest load. They prevent the car from going down too hard, when on a rough road or crossing, and greatly reduce the rebound.

The springs are packed in grease, and will lubricate automatically, requiring attention not more than once or twice a year. Steel spring encased in a neat steel housing.

The entire absorber is finished in baked black japan. Can be applied without machining. Full instructions for attaching included with each set. Come in sets of four. Weight, per set, about 20 pounds.

61R5807—Touring Model Set..**$4.45**
61R5808—Roadster Model **4.45**

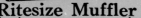

Ritesize Muffler

No back pressure—no noise. A duplicate of the Ford muffler, arranged so that it may be attached to any Ford automobile (except 1915 models), by simply removing the old muffler and attaching the Ritesize in its place.

If the muffler on your Ford is worn out, rattles, or has blown to pieces, use this and get the best results at a low price. Furnished complete with tail pipe as shown.

61R5202—Weight, 10 pounds..**$1.70**

Henry Ford, an advocate of mechanizing agriculture, heavily promoted Tin Lizzie as the "farmer's car." "Having been born and raised a farmer," he wrote in 1922, "I know what it means to work long hours for pretty small returns." The two flivvers plowing and harrowing are equipped with special traction wheels available in the add-on market. Water tanks atop the engines provided additional cooling for the slow going. The pair in the inset on the opposite page are using their Model T to gather the harvest. The Michigan farmer below delivers a spectacular load of hay in 1921.

Ford "fire cars" were commonly used as auxiliary vehicles by fire departments across the country, and in small communities as replacements for horse-drawn apparatus. This is the fire-fighting corps at an army post in the wide-open expanses of Texas, ladder truck (left), pumper, and hose carts all well polished and ready for action.

family from the slavery of tedium and isolation.

For his study *Henry Ford and Grass-Roots America*, Reynold M. Wik examined thousands of farmers' letters preserved in the Ford Archives. Typical is one from a Georgia farm wife written in 1918: "You know, Henry, your car lifted us out of the mud. It brought joy into our lives. We loved every rattle in its bones. . . ." And in 1938 a reminiscent Ohio farmer wrote Edsel Ford, "Until your father provided low-cost transportation, the vast majority of [farm] families had scarcely been five miles from home. I can truthfully say that every time such a family group met my eyes, I would reverently say, 'God bless Henry Ford. . . .' "

Tin Lizzie brought the farmer to town—not only more often than ever before, but to far more towns than he had been able to reach in horse-and-buggy days. On any Saturday in the teens and twenties, thousands of Main Streets would be crowded with mud-spattered flivvers groaning under their burden of wide-eyed children or their cargoes of garden produce to be sold for much-needed cash. Farm families came to shop, to transact business, to visit, to watch a Fourth of July parade, to take in one of the newly popular moving pictures, or simply to see the sights. The flivver multiplied the chances to attend a circus or a traveling Chautauqua, a revival meeting or an amateur theatrical, a harness race or a ball game.

The rural dweller's horizons, which in 1910 had been limited to five or a dozen miles, were suddenly expanded manyfold, with all the attendant wonders that implied.

Nowhere did Model T demonstrate its toughness and its versatility more often than down on the farm. The flivver played an important role in American agriculture's conversion from horse power to mechanical power. Its ability to navigate the muddiest lane and the rockiest pasture became legendary. It hauled produce and livestock and milk cans to market and returned laden with barbed wire, feed, fertilizer, and other essentials. Farmers unable to afford Ford's Fordson or another make of tractor drove their flivvers into the fields to pull harrows and hay rakes. The Forma-Tractor ($178) was one of several kits that turned the car into a full-fledged weekday tractor with heavy cleated steel "traction wheels"; a simple thirty-minute reconversion, claimed Forma-Tractor's ads, restored the car to its weekend role "as a pleasure vehicle or for carrying produce to the market." Many a farmer put his T to work as a stationary engine. When a belt pulley was attached to a jacked-up rear wheel, almost no job—grinding grain, filling a silo, sawing lumber, pumping water, even washing clothes—was beyond Lizzie's capability. As Wik notes, "One farmer said his Model T would do everything except rock the baby to sleep or make love to the hired girl."

The years between 1914 and the mid-twenties saw Henry Ford at high noon. His cars sold themselves, without dependence on advertising, and they sold as fast as he could turn them out. His personal fame grew apace, thanks in no small measure to his Barnum-like penchant for publicity. "Ford is news," admitted a newspaper editor, and Ford was the master at making news.

Newspapers and magazines were filled with articles about the man, about his company, about his interests. The camping trips he made with his cronies Thomas Edison, naturalist John Burroughs, tire maker Harvey Firestone, and President Warren Harding were widely reported. His pronouncements and maxims on everything from the single tax to soybeans and square dancing received an equally good press. He inspired Edward Stratemeyer to create young America's favorite inventor, Tom Swift. In 1918, without campaigning, he nearly won a seat in Congress as senator from Michigan, and there was widespread support for his candidacy in the 1924 presidential contest. "Why Not Ford for President?" the *Wall Street Journal* asked. The opinions he expressed in his newspaper, the Dearborn *Independent,* however eccentric and simplistic and ignorant they often were, added to his popular following. Even his reprehensible anti-Semitic tirades against a conspiracy of "international Jewish banking power" failed to loosen

Ford's grip on the imagination of the common man. He was the millionaire folk hero and he could do or say no wrong.

Less widely noticed in these years—and far more important to the history of the automobile in America—was the degree of personal control Ford achieved over his industrial empire. It was a control unmatched in the annals of American business. Henry Ford became, quite literally, master of all he surveyed, answerable to no one.

This drive toward absolute power can be traced back to 1906, when he steamrollered his estranged partner Alexander Malcomson into selling

out, but the final rush to the peak began in 1915. In that year James Couzens, whose business and financial acumen had been vital to the Ford Motor Company's growth, resigned in protest over Ford's pacifist stance on the war in Europe. The split between the two men ran far deeper, however. It was essentially a matter of Ford's growing absolutism. "I was, and am today, willing to work with any man," Couzens told reporters. "I will be willing to work with Henry Ford, but I refuse to work for him." A year later, in November, 1916, Ford's relations with his remaining two most powerful stockholders and company directors, John and Horace Dodge,

reached the breaking point. The Dodge brothers filed a lawsuit challenging Henry Ford's "reckless" one-man management.

When the Dodges started their own auto company in 1914, they had financed it primarily with their profits as Ford's largest parts supplier and with dividends from their two thousand shares of Ford stock. The auto-buying public greeted the Dodges' car enthusiastically, boosting it into third place in the production race in 1915, and the brothers promptly drew up plans for plant expansion—to be paid for by their anticipated millions in Ford dividends. This scheme went squarely against Henry Ford's grain.

Ford regarded any stockholders' profits beyond a reasonable return on their investment as "parasitic," and he said so repeatedly. In any event, he had earmarked the company's earnings for a massive expansion program of his own. Future dividends would be mere tokens, he said. He intended to corral raw-material sources (timber lands, iron mines, rubber plantations) and transportation links (railroads, lake freighters) to make the company integrated and self-sufficient, and to construct an industrial colossus on the River Rouge in Dearborn township, southeast of Detroit, that would astonish the world. The Ford Motor Company, he believed, must reinvest the bulk of its profits in continuous growth or it would wither. The Dodge brothers demanded that a substantial share of those profits go

Investment Opportunity

The General Motors Company today occupies a unique position in the automobile industry and in the opinion of the writer, with proper management will show results in the future second to none in any American industry. Mr. Durant perhaps realizes this more fully than anyone else and is very desirous of having an organization as perfect as possible to handle this wonderful business. . . .

Mr. Durant's association with [the Du Pont interests] has been such as to result in the expression of the desire on his part to have us more substantially interested with him, thus enabling us to assist him, par-

ticularly in an executive and financial way, in the direction of this huge business. The evolution of the discussion of this problem is that an attractive investment is afforded [us] in what I consider the most promising industry in the United States. . . .

Rather than have a coterie of our directors taking advantage of this in a personal way . . ., it would be far preferable for the Company to accept the opportunity afforded. . . .
—John J. Raskob, memorandum to the Finance Committee of the Du Pont Company, December 19, 1917. (Two days later Du Pont's board authorized the purchase of $25 million in G.M. stock, giving it nearly one quarter of the shares outstanding.)

to stockholders. The stakes in the conflict were enormous. The company's latest fiscal-year statement, issued in mid-1916, reported net profits of $57 million plus a cash-on-hand surplus of $52 million.

The Dodge suit was finally decided in February, 1919. A ruling of the Michigan superior court affirmed Ford's right to pursue corporate expansion and found no grounds to term his management reckless. The court declared, however, that any corporation is "organized and carried on primarily for the profit of the stockholders," and that the Ford Motor Company was sufficiently solvent to pursue expansion *and* pay dividends — specifically, a special dividend totaling (with interest) $20.8 million. Some $2 million of this sum was to go to the Dodge brothers. Ironically, Henry Ford, the largest stockholder, would have to pay himself some $12 million.

Ford was increasingly determined to be rid of "outside interference," by which he meant meddling stockholders. Already he had initiated a startling gambit. On December 31, 1918, he resigned as president of the Ford Motor Company, his twenty-five-year-old son Edsel taking his place. Then, a month after the superior court's decision, the Los Angeles *Examiner* printed an exclusive interview headlined, "Henry Ford Organizing Huge New Company to Build a Better, Cheaper Car." What would happen to the old company?

the reporter had asked. "Why," Ford replied, "I don't know exactly what will become of that. . . ."

In 1906 Ford had used this same gambit of starting a new company — and leaving the old one in the lurch — to increase pressure on his partner Malcomson. Thirteen years later it worked again. Fearing that the value of their holdings would plummet if Ford did indeed build a "better, cheaper car" to compete with Model T — and suspecting that he was enough of a maverick to try it — the minority stockholders began negotiations to sell out. In July, 1919, it was announced that all had agreed to terms. The total cost to Ford would be $105.8 million. The Dodge brothers would receive $25 million, James Couzens $29.3 million. Ford had to go to the eastern banking community he despised to finance the stock purchases, but he was content. He, his wife, and his son Edsel were now the sole owners of the Ford Motor Company.

Never before or since has one man so totally controlled a major American corporation. The year 1919, in which he turned fifty-six, marked the beginning of a new era in Ford's life. As we have seen, the public humiliation of the Chicago *Tribune* libel trial that year helped solidify "the closed system of his thought." His seizure of absolute corporate control and the departure of three more of his once-most-trusted lieutenants increased his self-imposed isolation. Designer C. Harold Wills, personnel man John

R. Lee, and sales manager Norval A. Hawkins resigned in rapid succession. Ford professed no regrets. He preferred facing the future entirely dependent on no resources but his own — resources that were increasingly corrupted by power into an arrogant inflexibility.

It was as if his mental outlook on the world — which by 1915 had produced a universal car, a revolutionary way of building it, and an enlightened view of those who built it — became immutably fixed in amber. As the automotive scene shifted rapidly during the twenties, Ford would demonstrate an inability to change his thinking to shift with it or to influence it in any significant way.

While personal absolutism became the order of the day at Ford, its great rival, General Motors, was moving in exactly the opposite direction. Like so much else in G.M.'s early history, this action was in reaction to Billy Durant.

After his dramatic recapture of G.M. in 1916, Durant charged back into the fray as if he had never been away. In his Second Empire he set new records for wheeling and dealing. Initially, at least, he had a firm ally in the Du Pont interests. By 1918 their holdings of G.M. stock had risen to almost twenty-four per cent of the total, giving them not only a major voice in management but a receptive market for Du Pont paints, varnishes, and artificial leathers. Pierre S. Du Pont, president of the Du Pont company,

The export market was a profitable one for American car makers. Both Ford and General Motors built overseas assembly plants, and in the twenties G.M. purchased the Vauxhall firm in England and Opel in Germany. The cover painting of an overseas edition of Ford's house organ reproduced opposite offers a wry view of Model T's impact on the English countryside. Racing triumphs by the American Duesenberg — particularly Indianapolis 500 victories in 1924, 1925, and 1927 — inspired its German distributor to publish the ad shown at left.

headed the General Motors board of directors, and Du Pont treasurer John J. Raskob chaired its finance committee. Raskob was assigned the post to act as a counterweight to the free-wheeling Durant. In the event, however, Raskob proved to be as much of a freewheeler in finances as Durant was in operations.

Durant's Second Empire revealed the same combination of dazzling intuition and sloppy administration that marked the First. In 1916 he assembled a subsidiary of parts and accessory manufacturers called United Motors that would bring into G.M., among others, the brilliant and innovative Charles F. Kettering of Delco and, most important to G.M.'s future, Alfred P. Sloan, Jr., of Hyatt Roller Bearing. Another key Durant acquisition was Fisher Body, which the six Fisher brothers had made into the world's largest builder of auto bodies. Durant diversified into refrigerators (Frigidaire) and farm tractors, and added two new auto marques, Scripps-Booth and Sheridan, to the G.M. line. Corporate net profits jumped from $14.8 million in 1915 to more than $60 million in 1919.

Anticipating a massive growth of the auto market in the postwar era, Durant and Raskob girded for it by rapidly expanding production facilities. Ever the incurable optimist, Durant expected to finance this expansion through stock offerings and rising sales to a car-hungry public and did not bother to build up a liquid

reserve for emergencies; the word *emergency* was not in his business lexicon. Nor, apparently, was it in Raskob's.

In 1920–21 a sharp economic recession sent tremors through the auto industry. Henry Ford met the crisis by slashing car prices, ruthlessly cutting production and overhead costs, and raising the cash he needed to pay off his debt to the bankers by forcing thousands of unwanted Model T's on his dealers, who had to scramble frantically to borrow the money to pay for them. At General Motors the tremors produced an earthquake so severe that had it not been for the Du Pont connection the company might have foundered.

Durant recognized the warning signs too late; G.M., "out of balance" due to the headlong expansion policy, was rocked when car sales fell alarmingly. Unchecked by the loose-rein Durant administration, the various divisions failed to adjust production and inventories to the sagging demand and "before the dust settled" had to write off losses of $85 million. (The corporation as a whole would lose $38.7 million in 1921.) Working capital became critically short. A new stock issue did poorly in a declining market.

Most serious from Durant's standpoint was the collapse of G.M.'s com-

mon stock during the crisis. He sought desperately to shore up the market, in part to protect his own huge holdings — 2.5 million shares — and those of his investing cronies. Foreseeing calamity for both General Motors and the financial community, a thoroughly alarmed Pierre Du Pont called on the House of Morgan to try to arrest the stock's slide. Before long the two efforts were in conflict. Durant was precariously close to personal bankruptcy when he finally admitted defeat. In a complex series of maneuvers, the Du Pont interests acquired his stock and paid off his welter of brokerage and bank debts. Their price was his resignation. On November 20, 1920, for the second time, Billy Durant left his post as head of the company he had founded. Pierre Du Pont assumed the G.M. presidency (he had resigned as Du Pont's president in 1919, retaining the chairmanship of its board) and appointed Alfred P. Sloan his lieutenant in charge of bringing order out of the chaos. So effectively did Sloan perform that three years later he was named president.

Durant's fall from grace failed to sour him in the least. Within six weeks of leaving General Motors he was right back in the auto business, raising in just forty-eight hours $5 million to start Durant Motors from a select group of investors eager to board his latest bandwagon. He also solicited the small investor by selling stock on the installment plan; by the time

Durant Motors was two years old only American Telephone and Telegraph among publicly held companies had more stockholders.

The four-cylinder Durant, priced below $1,000, went into production in the fall of 1921, followed early in 1922 by the Star, which Durant grandly proclaimed a direct competitor to Model T. He bought bankrupt Locomobile in hopes that the famous marque, which had begun life in 1899 as a steamer designed by the Stanley twins, still retained enough magic in its name to give him entry to the luxury-car field. Later the medium-priced Flint was added to the line. A half-dozen factories were built or bought across the country. In 1923 Durant Motors turned out 172,000 cars, making it the nation's fourth largest auto maker (behind Ford, G.M., and Willys-Overland).

That was the peak, however. True to form, this newest Durant empire contained as much paper as substance. The financial writer B. C. Forbes scanned the company's 1923 balance sheet and began asking hard questions. A major asset item of $23.4 million, for example, turned out to be a set of "participating contracts" that two Durant divisions had signed with each other. "When you know how," Forbes observed, "it is thus delightfully easy to make money—on paper." Even so, Durant Motors might well have held or improved its position under vigorous management. That is precisely what it did not get.

By the mid-twenties Durant's attention had wandered away from automobiles and was fixed instead on his long-time love, the stock market. As his biographer Lawrence R. Gustin puts it, "He abandoned himself to its charms." While Billy Durant and his "bull consortium" of cronies spent their time playing the market, Durant Motors grew progressively weaker. It would be an early victim of the Great Depression.

On balance, considering the record of his two roller-coaster regimes at General Motors, Billy Durant must be ranked second only to Henry Ford as a pioneer of the American "car culture." His conception of offering cars "for every purse and purpose" proved to be a more accurate prediction of the realities of the marketplace than Ford's conception of a single unchanging universal car. With boldness and imagination he staked out the dimensions of one of the world's great corporations; all five of the present G.M. marques and many of the company's parts and accessory divisions were his creations or acquisitions.

Perhaps because he never sought personal publicity as Ford did, or perhaps because he was ultimately a loser in the corporate wars, his achievements were soon forgotten. His death on March 18, 1947, went virtually unremarked, in striking contrast to the tributes paid Ford upon his death three weeks later. Economic historian Dana L. Thomas ob-

No one else in auto making in the 1920's operated with more business acumen than Alfred P. Sloan (left) and Charles W. Nash. Sloan's relentless drive for efficiency and organization pushed General Motors to record-breaking profitability; Nash, a former G.M. president, directed the most fiscally sound of all the independents.

serves that Billy Durant "was drunk with the gamble of America, obsessed with its highest article of faith —that the man who played for the steepest stakes deserved the biggest winnings." Twice Durant played for those stakes at General Motors and lost, and then lost again in his final fling at the automobile business. But for twenty-five years—the formative years of the auto age—he made things happen.

Alfred P. Sloan, Jr., was assuredly not cut from the same bolt of cloth as Billy Durant. If anyone ever addressed the aloof Sloan as Al it has escaped history's notice. He was the first "gray man" (as James Flink calls him) in a business long dominated by colorful promoters and mechanics, the first of a cool breed of managers who recognized the need for new businesslike approaches in an auto industry entering the age of oligopoly. In 1920, wrote Sloan in his memoir *My Years with General Motors,* G.M. "was in need not only of a concept of management but equally of a concept of the automobile business." The management part of that equation was already on paper, drafted by Sloan himself the year before and ignored—at his peril, as it turned out—by Durant. Sloan's "Organization Study" has served as the constitution of General Motors to this day.

Sloan had been a close observer of the auto industry from its earliest beginnings. After graduating from the Massachusetts Institute of Technol-

ogy with a degree in electrical engineering in 1895, he raised Hyatt Roller Bearing to solid profitability by supplying many car makers. When Hyatt entered the G.M. orbit in 1916 as part of United Motors, Sloan was tapped for the high executive echelon. He was, he recalled, of two minds about Billy Durant: while admiring his flashes of intuition, he was appalled by his one-man rule and administrative chaos. In Sloan's unblinkingly analytical view, General Motors was far too big and complicated to depend upon any individual's genius—or hunches. It must be run instead as a congress of intellects, the best available, to capitalize on the rich resources of group judgment.

With the solid backing of Pierre Du Pont—himself a pioneer of modern management techniques—Sloan's goal in the early twenties was to graft the system of group management onto the essentially decentralized structure left behind by Durant. The idea was to maintain the autonomy and operational independence of the various car divisions, yet at the same time run a tight corporate ship from the top. Never again, if Sloan could help it, would General Motors be caught rudderless as it had been in the 1920–21 economic crisis.

Clear lines of authority, tight fiscal and inventory control, market forecasting, and basic technical research on a company-wide basis (presided over by Charles F. Kettering) became the order of the day at G.M. Essentially, this structure was comparable to the military's line and staff organization, except that authoritarianism at the top was replaced by group decision. Sloanism, as it came to be called, was truly a management revolution. Just as Ford's production revolution became standard in the auto industry—and indeed standard in many other industries as well—Sloan's management system was widely copied throughout the business community.

A revolution as comprehensive as this one took time to carry out, and not until about 1925 did General Motors begin to operate as Sloan intended. One of the first tasks the Du Pont-Sloan regime set itself was pruning "excess baggage." The weak Scripps-Booth and Sheridan marques were lopped off, as was Durant's expensive adventure in tractor making. Pricing brackets were established to focus each of the car lines on a specific segment of the market.

The biggest challenge was the Chevrolet division. Its sales in 1921 were less than 62,000, a mere four per cent of the market, and its losses reached $5 million. A consultant group's report advised lopping that marque from G.M.'s line as well. Sloan, however, was convinced that General Motors's future depended on having a strong entry in the mass market, and he persuaded Du Pont to reject the report and give Chevrolet a second chance. Never in automotive

history has a second chance been more brilliantly exploited.

William S. Knudsen, another of the growing army of embittered Ford alumni, was given the task of restoring Chevrolet to good health. The tall, rugged, efficient Dane, who had set up Ford's network of regional assembly plants, overhauled Chevrolet production methods root and branch. The results were startling. Output topped 200,000 for the first time in 1922, and by 1926 it was nearly 590,000. In the production race Chevrolet easily captured second place behind Ford in each of these five years. The strategy was not to try to challenge Model T head-on in price—Ford's production economies at Highland Park and the growing River Rouge colossus remained unbeatable—but in the marketplace. Knudsen and his colleagues calculated that an increasing number of car buyers were willing to pay $100 or $200 more for a better-looking, better-riding, more technically advanced car than Model T, and Chevrolet's rising share of the market was proving them right. The day was coming, Knudsen promised his dealers in his Danish accent, when Chevrolet production would match Ford's "vun for vun."

The 1920-21 crash not only triggered the fall of Durant and the rise of Sloan, but was responsible for the founding of the third of today's Big Three of auto making. The founding father was Walter P. Chrys-

ler, and it all came about, he tells us in his memoir *Life of an American Workman,* because in 1920 his wife became fed up with seeing her house full of tobacco smoke and cluttered with her husband's cronies. "I wish you would go to work," Della Chrysler told her husband. "This isn't a home any more. It's just a place crowded with men. A sort of railroad station."

Walter Chrysler had grown up on the Kansas plains and was apprenticed as a Union Pacific machinist at age eighteen. He rose rapidly through the railroad ranks to the post of works manager at American Locomotive in Pittsburgh, where in 1912 General Motors found him and persuaded him to come to Buick. When he left G.M. in 1919 frustrated with Durant's mismanagement, he was earning $500,000 a year. A big, rough-hewn man whose English, a *Fortune* writer later declared, "was not so much the King's as the shop foreman's," the forty-five-year-old Chrysler tasted retirement and found it unpalatable. His wife obviously agreed.

Chrysler's idea of getting out of the house was to hire on as a corporate "doctor" at troubled Willys-Overland at a salary of $1 million. In 1921, having restored Willys-Overland to health, he moved on to Maxwell, which was also suffering from the economic downturn. The old Maxwell firm had survived the collapse of Benjamin Briscoe's ill-fated U.S. Motor in 1912, and for the next eight

(continued on page 169)

164

Insouciant youth, flask, fast roadster: the 1920's personified by John Held, Jr.

MOBILE SHEIKS AND SHEBAS

The Jazz Age, it is said, was created by two men—F. Scott Fitzgerald wrote it, John Held, Jr., drew it. So persuasive were Held's satires that they became models for social behavior, and this selection of his work makes it clear that the automobile was a Jazz Age essential.

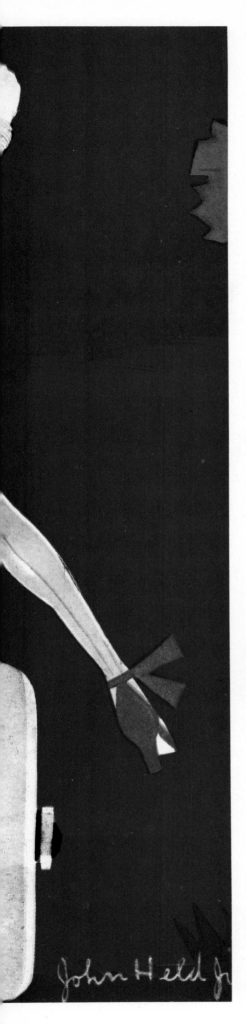

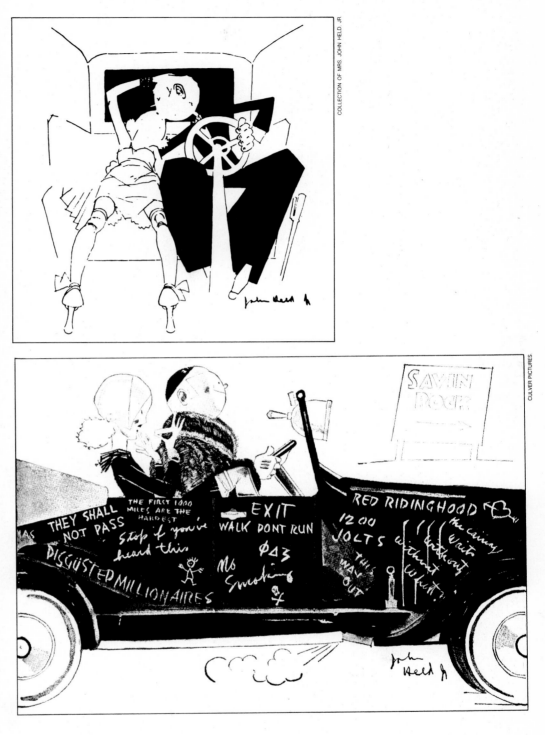

The most widely circulated of Held's works, such as these examples of his "insatiable neckers and social bootleggers," ran in the humor magazines of the twenties, particularly *Life* and *Judge.* Sometimes his sheiks and shebas appeared in snappy roadsters; on other occasions (as seen here) they favored well-decorated old jalopies. Whatever the vehicle, they necked and made whoopee.

Among the Held caricatures that have gained currency as classic twenties clichés — girls in slickers and galoshes, saxophone players with slicked-down hair, collegians in bell-bottom pants and coonskin coats — one has assumed a life of its own: the scatterbrained woman driver. "Shifting for Herself" is one way clichés get started.

years it slogged along in the middle of the pack under Walter Flanders's care, turning out an average of forty thousand cars or so annually. However, in 1921 production was only sixteen thousand units, and its solid reputation was suffering from shoddy engineering. Chrysler obtained fresh capital, reorganized production, beefed up the frail rear axle that was the cause of most owner complaints, and vigorously advertised the car as "The Good Maxwell." Equally important, he brought with him from Willys-Overland three talented engineers whom he was soon calling his Three Musketeers: Owen R. Skelton, Carl Breer, and Fred M. Zeder.

While Chrysler continued his revitalization of Maxwell, the Three Musketeers developed one of the notable engines of the twenties, a light, powerful, high-compression six that was a performance match for the power plants in some of America's most expensive cars. The high-compression six was combined with such advanced mechanical features as four-wheel hydraulic brakes, encased in a handsome body quite rakish for its day, and a new marque — Chrysler — was born.

When the proud parent attempted to introduce this latest entry in the medium-priced field at the prestigious New York Auto Show in January, 1924, he was turned away because space was alloted only to marques already on the market. Undaunted, Chrysler rented the lobby of the Commodore Hotel in mid-town Manhattan for the debut and attracted more attention than he could have gotten at the crowded auto show. The car was an immediate hit with the public, and in 1925 the Maxwell Motor Company was rechristened the Chrysler Corporation.

At this point Chrysler was regarded as one of the stronger independents, ranked in the same breath with Nash, Packard, Hudson, or Studebaker. But Walter Chrysler sensed the winds of change beginning to reshape the auto industry: the future, he believed, belonged to powerful, multi-car giants such as General Motors that were strong enough to weather economic fluctuations and the whims of public taste. Competition was sharpening as the auto market ceased the limitless expansion that had marked the palmy days of Model T. Chrysler began to consider how to widen his range of offerings.

His chance came in 1928 when the New York banking house of Dillon, Read & Company came to him and offered to sell Dodge. John and Horace Dodge had both died in 1920 in the influenza epidemic that swept the country, and in 1925 their widows sold out to Dillon, Read. The bankers' enthusiasm for the auto business soon soured as Dodge sales started to slip. After five days of intensive, round-the-clock bargaining with Chrysler in a suite at the Ritz-Carlton Hotel in New York a deal was struck: for Chrysler stock with a market value

A Marque is Born

Those three young automotive engineers were wizards. They seemed to be the parts of a single, extraordinary engineering intelligence; their names were Fred M. Zeder, Owen Skelton and Carl Breer . . . [and] they were the ones who were going to design the new car. . . .

Although we experienced a good deal of frustration . . . , nevertheless a couple of these cars were made, a part here, a part there, until they were complete — and costly. We tested them on the roads, too. Those were exciting times.

Under an old car's shabby hood we had hidden the unsuspected power of our new high-compression engine. Zeder and his boys had outdone themselves. You could tell that any time a traffic cop's uplifted palm stopped you in a group of cars. It was the most fun if this shabby old testing car was halted between a couple of big ones, with snooty chauffeurs at their wheels. At the whistle's sound we would be past the cop and on our way, while behind us, open-mouthed, our chance rivals would just be getting ready to go into second gear. . . . Nobody had heard about a Chrysler car [in 1923]. But we had dreamed about it until, as if we had been its lovers, it was work to think of anything else.
— Walter P. Chrysler, *Life of an American Workman*, 1937

At left, Walter Chrysler (in the plus fours) and film star Thomas Meighan pose with a sporty new Chrysler roadster in 1925, the year the Chrysler Corporation was formed. The photograph opposite, taken in the office of Henry M. Leland, commemorated the sale of the Lincoln company to Ford in 1922. Ford stands behind his son Edsel, signing the sale document with a quill pen; Leland stands behind his son Wilfred. Leland was clearly an admirer of Abraham Lincoln.

of $70 million and the assumption of Dodge debentures valued at $56 million, the "Dependability Car" and the excellent network of Dodge production facilities and dealers became part of the Chrysler Corporation.

Within hours of the closing of the deal late on the afternoon of July 31, 1928, big signs reading "Chrysler Corporation, Dodge Division" adorned the newly acquired facilities. The transaction was proclaimed the biggest in the thirty-two-year history of the auto industry. By 1929 two fresh Chrysler marques were on the assembly lines, De Soto in the medium-priced field, and Plymouth, a new challenger in the mass market. As *Fortune* would phrase it a few years later, "Rarely in any industry at any time does a late starter, entering competition at a time when the windward berths are all occupied and stretches of open water are scarce, drive so quickly into a commanding position." One-time railroad roundhouse mechanic Chrysler might not have appreciated the fancy yachting metaphor, but by any measure his rapid climb to third place behind General Motors and Ford was remarkable.

Errett Lobban Cord was an entrepreneur who marched to a different drum. Before the thirty-year-old Cord arrived at the Auburn Automobile Company in Auburn, Indiana, in 1924, he had tried among other things auto racing, car servicing, alkali trucking in Death Valley, and selling Moon cars in Chicago.

His dazzling sales and promotional skill restored life to struggling Auburn; by 1926 he had bought control of the company and introduced a new line of handsome, well-engineered models with enough sales appeal to boost profits to almost a million dollars. The "boy wonder" of auto making also acquired Duesenberg, destined to become the most celebrated of all American marques.

Fred and Augie Duesenberg were German-born, Iowa-raised brothers who had made a high art of automotive engineering. Three times during the twenties their racing machines won the Indianapolis 500. Their passenger cars were the first in America to have a straight-eight, overhead-cam engine and hydraulic brakes; with pardonable pride, the brothers touted them as "built to outclass, outrun and outlast any car on the road." Whether or not the boast was true of these Model A Duesenbergs, it became undeniably true late in 1928 with the introduction of the fabled Model J. "The vital fact about a Duesenberg," wrote the auto aficionado Ken W. Purdy, "is that it has an absolute and unique aura of its own." E. L. Cord put no financial restraints on the Duesenberg brothers' efforts to achieve that aura, and in fact the marque never made a penny for its proprietor. He was content to see it serve as a prestige builder for his less expensive — but equally well designed — Auburn and for the innovative front-wheel-drive Cord marque

he introduced in 1929. By that year Cord had amassed from scratch a budding empire with assets valued at $28.5 million. Uncompromising quality, exciting design, and limited production were his trademarks; that he achieved this enviable plateau on the eve of a crippling depression was his misfortune.

The achievements of Walter Chrysler and E. L. Cord are all the more remarkable when viewed against industry trends in the twenties. Even though car output rebounded to new highs between the end of the 1920–21 crash and the onset of the far greater crash in 1929, the number of producers fell by some sixty per cent. The twenties was a bad decade for small independents, whether new or old.

Major figures in the industry were among the fallen. Henry Leland's attempt to revive his past glories at Cadillac with a new luxury marque, Lincoln, collapsed in receivership in 1922. Henry Ford snapped up the company for $8 million, telling the press, "We have built more cars than anyone else, and now we are going to build a better car than anyone else." It was a prediction not far off the mark. Leland himself was forced out after only six months in a dispute over Ford production methods, but he might have taken solace on his deathbed a decade later, age eighty-nine, from the fact that Lincoln had won an enviable reputation as one of America's finest motorcars.

170

Hudson led the shift from open to closed cars in the twenties by pioneering the mass production of practical closed bodies for its Essex line. Below is Hudson's assembly line for the wood-framed bodies in 1921. The antithesis of mass production is seen at right: the Doble factory in Oakland, California, about 1924. Here the magnificent Doble Series E, the aristocrat of steam cars, was painstakingly assembled by hand. Doble was driven under by the Depression.

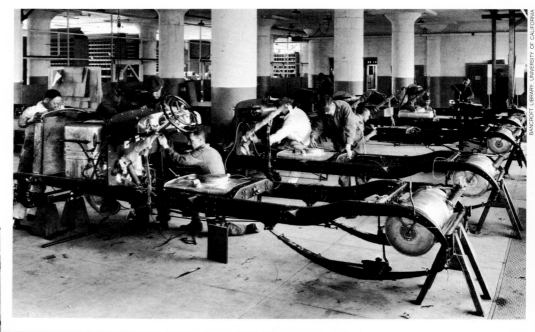

An equally distinguished design, the Wills Sainte Claire, was not so fortunate in finding a rescuer. C. Harold Wills, highly regarded as a designer and metallurgist when he was at Ford (where one of his lasting contributions was the stylized script of the Ford logo), promoted his new creation as ten years ahead of its time. It was unquestionably a superb piece of machinery, but far too few could be built under Wills's nit-picking direction, and those that were proved to be beyond the capacity of any but the most skilled mechanic to repair. The Wills Sainte Claire soon expired, a victim of excess perfectionism.

From 1922 to 1927 Barney Everitt, whose industry credentials went back to the Merry Oldsmobile, fought gallantly to raise the Rickenbacker into the select top fifteen marques. The "cracker jacker Rickenbacker," as a Tin Pan Alley lyricist termed it, was named for the celebrated World War I air ace Captain Eddie Rickenbacker, but even such technical advances as four-wheel brakes and the tireless promotional efforts of Captain Eddie could not sell enough cars to keep the company afloat in the rising tide of competition.

Other noteworthy pioneers who dropped out of auto making in the twenties included that intransigent Scot Alexander Winton, who refused to acknowledge the trend toward less-expensive cars. Nineteen twenty-four saw the end of Winton production in Cleveland. At about the same time, the citizens of Kokomo, Indiana, were witnessing the demise of their two famous home-grown marques. Elwood Haynes retired in 1921, and soon afterward the Haynes "Character Car" also retired, stubbornly clinging to its advertised boast as "America's First Car" to the end. Elmer and Edgar Apperson, the constructers of that alleged first car back in 1894, had been turning out cars of their own in Kokomo since 1902. The company fell on hard times following Elmer's death in 1920, and soon the distinctive Apperson name plate with its bounding jack rabbit was seen no more.

As in past years, business ineptitude alone was enough to drive some smaller independents from the field. As the twenties wore on, however, financial inability to maintain the ever-stiffer competitive pace became the dominant cause of bankruptcies. Automotive technology—indeed the entire automotive scene—was changing very rapidly, requiring greater and greater sums of capital to keep up. Increasingly, the smaller producers found their resources stretched beyond the breaking point.

For the average auto buyer, the most revolutionary change was the arrival of the closed car. In 1919 only one of ten purchases was a closed car, most of them in the luxury field; by 1929 closed cars accounted for nine of every ten sales. An all-weather car meant an all-season car, to the great relief of motorists. Those who lived in the northern half of the nation had grown tired of the spartan constitution required to drive a touring car in wintertime, and drivers everywhere were equally tired of leaky tops and flapping side curtains on rainy days.

The problems with the enclosed body before 1920 had been its excessive weight, its high manufacturing costs, and its tendency to shake literally to pieces on the abominable roads of the period. Gradually both roads and manufacturing techniques improved. The pioneers of this revolution were Roy Chapin and Howard Coffin of Hudson, who used their new Essex line to test the concept of the closed car in the popular-priced market. Competitors dubbed the boxy 1921 Essex coach the "packing crate," but they stopped laughing when they saw its price tag: $1,495, just $300 more than an Essex touring car. Before long Chapin and Coffin had pared the price differential to $100, then in 1925 to parity with touring models. By that time every manufacturer was on the closed-car bandwagon. Larger, more sophisticated stamping presses and the availability of sheet steel in greater widths made the steel sedan body a reality by the end of the decade.

The Zeder-Breer-Skelton high-compression six, which powered the maiden Chrysler of 1924, was another twenties landmark. Except in the lowest-priced market, where the four continued its sway, six- and eight-

BRIAN O'BRIEN
IF IT'S BROKE I CAN FIX IT

The servicing and repairing of cars grew to such proportions in the twenties that even Hollywood noticed, and gave O'Brien's Garage (above) and its boastful owner star billing in a 1923 film. Crosby's Garage in Minneapolis could boast a lady grease monkey, shown (left) at work on an Essex. Mechanics at the Ford Garage in Edgar, Wisconsin (upper right), had their picture taken in 1922. Clark Hay (lower right) handled tires and general repairs in Trenton, Nebraska.

cylinder engines were the rule by the late twenties. Sixes even broke through the $1,000 barrier. Shatterproof safety glass (pioneered by Stutz) and four-wheel mechanical, then hydraulic, brakes also became commonplace. (So did adjustable seats, a belated recognition of the obvious fact that drivers came in different sizes and lengths.) Independents began to offer so-called light models to broaden sales appeal (Willys's Whippet, Studebaker's Erskine, Hudson's Essex), and in 1926–27 General Motors went a step further by adding two all-new marques to its line, Pontiac and La Salle, companion cars to Oakland and Cadillac respectively. Such rapid changes in technology and in chassis and body layout meant frequent and expensive retooling—and ever-larger advertising budgets—which only the bigger, wealthier companies could afford.

Charles Kettering, renowned for the electric starter and the "all-electric" Cadillac, was much in the news during the twenties. Backed by the coordinated research facilities of General Motors and Du Pont, he created an Edison-like, inventions-to-order atmosphere rich in cheerful pragmatism. "We can make the future almost anything we want to make it," he said. Out of these efforts, for example, came the tough, fast-drying lacquer Duco, marketed by Du Pont, which not only gave car makers a rainbow of colors to choose from but slashed body-finishing time from as

much as two weeks to a matter of hours. Even Henry Ford was persuaded: the 1926 Model T came in a choice of colors, the first such option in twelve years. Boss Ket and his colleagues were responsible for many engineering refinements in the twenties, but they were probably best known for their adventures with no-knock gasoline and the copper-cooled engine.

The cause of the ominous metallic thumping known as engine knock was imperfectly understood, but not its dangers: attempts to increase the power output and efficiency of an engine by raising its compression ratio much above 4:1 (approximately the figure for Model T) produced severe knocking that could ruin the engine. Kettering and his right-hand man, chemist Thomas H. Midgley, Jr., finally pinpointed the problem as an unwelcome surge of combustion after the spark plug fired, a failing of the low-octane gasolines of the day. They initiated a laborious trial-and-error search for a fuel additive to suppress this abnormal combustion.

Immediate success evaded them. Certain compounds did the job well enough, but they produced such foul odors that the G.M. laboratory became all but uninhabitable, and one of the test cars was christened "the Goat." At last, late in 1921, an eminently satisfactory anti-knock agent was found in tetraethyl lead. The Ethyl Corporation was set up by General Motors in partnership with Standard

Oil of New Jersey to produce the new no-knock gasoline, with Du Pont (not surprisingly) getting the tetraethyl lead contract.

This sunny outcome of the Kettering-Midgley experiments soon turned cloudy, however. In October, 1924, newspapers reported that five workers in Jersey Standard's ethyl plant had suddenly gone wildly insane and died in states of violent delirium. Fellow workers became ill with similar symptoms. Ethyl fuel was condemned as "loony gas" and had to be taken off the market. (Not made public were a rash of the same symptoms, and several deaths, among workers at the Du Pont facility producing the tetraethyl lead.) It was soon evident that the problem lay not with the fuel itself but with inadequate safety precautions in its manufacture, but a year would pass before the "loony gas" uproar quieted enough for ethyl gasoline to go on sale again.

Kettering's "copper-cooling caper" is of less interest for what it achieved —which was nothing lasting—than for what it tells about the impact of Sloanism on General Motors. As early as 1918 Kettering became a convert to the air-cooled engine. That only the expensive Franklin among American cars had made a success of air cooling did not dampen his enthusiasm. He was eager to mate the air-cooled's simplicity and light weight with its economies and conveniences—no radiator, no water pump, no "plumb-

Car makers in the Roaring Twenties devoted
much hoopla to the introduction of their
new models at auto shows across the country.
At a show in Louisville, Kentucky, the
sales people for Lexington hired a quartet
(violin, mandolin, guitar, jug) and an
ingénue to promote their "Minute Man Six."

ing," and of course no water or antifreeze—to produce a Chevrolet capable of challenging Model T head-on in price.

Boss Ket's notion was to weld fins of copper—chosen for its high heat conductivity—to the cast-iron cylinders electrically and carry off the heat with an engine-driven fan. "It is the greatest thing ever produced in the automobile world," he assured General Motors president Pierre Du Pont, and he went on to propose copper cooling for other G.M. marques as well. Over the vehement objections of the division heads, management decreed full-scale development and production plans for the copper-cooled engine. Public announcement of the radical new Chevrolet was made in January, 1923.

Six months later the copper-cooled Chevrolet was quietly taken off the market and all cars (a total of 759 were built) recalled to the factory. Both production and performance "bugs" had shown up, serious enough to return the copper-cooling concept to the drawing board. Alfred Sloan, newly installed as G.M. president, regarded the matter as the acid test of his management concepts. He promptly killed the copper-cooled engine. Millions of dollars and two and a half years had been invested in the project, he noted, and any possible pay-out was still well in the future. Chevrolet with its conventional water-cooled engine was on the way to a 400,000-plus sales year and was

A 1929 banquet of the National Automobile Chamber of Commerce attracted a banner crop of auto industry leaders. On the dais are (counting from left) Albert R. Erskine (1), Walter P. Chrysler (5), Charles Nash (7), Alfred P. Sloan (9), William C. Durant (12), Ransom Olds (13), and Walter C. White (15).

clearly in no need of rescue. In the future, Sloan stated, management would act only on tested facts, not on intuitive "engineering dreams." Anything new and innovative would be judged on the basis of cost effectiveness and would have to be "sold" to the various G.M. divisions rather than forced on them by edict. That Sloanism meant rule by committee and organizational chart was thus affirmed.

It is interesting to speculate on what Billy Durant would have done had he still been in charge. Most probably the copper-cooled engine would somehow have seen the light of day, for it was just his sort of challenge. How it might have fared in the marketplace can only be surmised. It remained for Volkswagen's celebrated Beetle to vindicate the Kettering gospel of an air-cooled engine for the mass market. Boss Ket died in 1958, too soon to see Chevrolet finally put an air-cooled car, the Corvair, into full production.

Among the automotive innovations of the twenties most welcomed by American motorists, the balloon tire was ranked right alongside the closed car and no-knock gasoline. The straight-sided, high-pressure tire

with demountable rims had vastly simplified tire changing, but its riding properties were no great improvement over the old clincher tire. Firestone began test-marketing a new balloon design in 1923, stressing its cushiony, doughnut profile, low pressure (twenty-five or thirty pounds, half the inflation of the high-pressure type), and long mileage (a predicted fifteen thousand miles or more). A trial balloon, the wags said. Cole promptly installed balloons on its Aero-Eight, followed by many other car makers on 1924 models. By 1927 better than half of all the tires manufactured in the United States were the balloon type. The improvement in riding comfort astonished car owners and made long-distance touring far less fatiguing. Of equal importance, the low-pressure tire was less susceptible to blowouts, an unparalleled blessing for a motoring population long resigned to tire changing as one of the grim facts of life.

Those commentators of the twenties who spoke unblushingly of the "romance of big business"—"The man who builds a factory," intoned Calvin Coolidge, "builds a temple"—pointed with especial pride to the auto industry. Indeed, its growth was unprecedented. The 1923 output of 3.6 million passenger cars was valued at more than $2.4 billion, moving autos past steel into first place in the business community. In 1926, reported economist Ralph Epstein, more than 3.3 million workers were employed in

building, distributing, and maintaining automobiles. General Motors topped $1 billion in sales that year, and its net profit of nearly $300 million (a tidy twenty per cent return on sales) two years later was the largest ever recorded by an American company. Auto exports passed the 200,000 mark at mid-decade, exclusive of the output of the overseas plants of multi-national giants General Motors and Ford. (By contrast, yearly imports of foreign models averaged only in the hundreds.) Well behind G.M. and Ford but substantial profit makers nonetheless were Chrysler, Dodge, Hudson, Studebaker, Nash, Packard, and Willys-Overland, whose combined net profits in 1925 reached $124 million.

The rapid pace of technological change, as we have seen, was one factor in a growing trend toward that form of "imperfect" economic competition called oligopoly (from the Greed *oligos,* meaning "few": thus "few sellers"). A more fundamental factor, however, was a shift in the marketplace. After about 1926 auto makers discovered that they were dealing with a buyer's market rather than the seller's market they had grown fat on. Henry Ford, who did so much to create the seller's market in the first place, was hardest hit by the shift.

Put simply, the first-car market—traditionally Model T's basic market—was approaching saturation. Replacement sales took its place. The 3.6 million sales plateau reached in 1923 would remain unchanged, on the average, until the onset of the Great Depression. Real market growth ceased—and in fact did not resume until 1949. Sales gains of individual marques were made at the expense of the competition. The losers were on the one hand the smaller independents, and on the other the Ford Motor Company. By 1926 Tin Lizzie sales were running 450,000 below their 1923 peak of 1.8 million, a situation that was anathema to Henry Ford's philosophy of continuous expansion.

At first Ford tried to meet the market saturation problem with his well-tested technique of price cutting. It was not enough; the flivver's low price and celebrated practical utility had become less and less important in the minds of potential buyers. That *every* car on the market was mechanically sound and reasonably reliable was now taken for granted. Speed, comfort, appointments, and styling became prime selling points. This was particularly true among women, whose opinions carried increasing weight with car makers and their advertising managers. As Bill Knudsen was demonstrating so dramatically at Chevrolet, many Americans were willing to pay a few hundred dollars extra for the features that Model T so conspicuously lacked. Flivver owners, remarked Frederick Lewis Allen, were increasingly exasperated at having to labor up hills "with a weary left foot jammed against the low-speed pedal while robin's-egg blue Chevrolets swept past."

Despite the pleadings of his dealers, his managers, and his son Edsel (still figurehead president of the company), Ford refused to recognize that the days of his beloved flivver were numbered. "It was as essential for Ford to have faith in the Model T," remarked economic historian E. D. Kennedy, "as for the Fundamentalist to have faith in the Flood." This stubborn faith blinded Ford to the changing desires of his automotive constituency.

Other car makers were quick to pursue new strategies to deal with the saturation problem. Walter Chrysler spoke confidently of the "American doctrine of the multi-car family," a sentiment Hoover Republicans made part of the political rhetoric in 1928 by espousing two cars in every garage as well as two chickens in every pot. The rising popularity of installment buying (detailed in the following chapter) eased the financial pain of buying a new car.

The auto industry's most revolutionary response to market saturation was the annual model change. Alfred Sloan explained the technique to the car-buying public: General Motors was constantly searching for "the most advanced knowledge and practice" in auto manufacturing in order "to make you dissatisfied with your current car so you will buy a new one.

. . ." J. H. Hunt of the Society of Automotive Engineers was more blunt: he suggested simply improving "the appearance of automobiles frequently [so] as to obsolete those in hands of owners."

This philosophy of planned obsolescence was embraced most fervently at General Motors, becoming an inherent feature of Sloanism. Mechanical refinement and regular restyling, even if only cosmetic, were institutionalized at G.M. by the late twenties. There was certainly no attempt to build in physical obsolescence. Rather, the sales technique was a psychological one: to cajole buyers into regularly trading in their cars on newer models, or trading up to something better—and G.M. had a whole range of "something better" to choose from. The fact that a well-cared-for car in the twenties might have an expected life of six or eight or more years was quietly ignored.

No other corporate policy has had a more lasting impact on the history of the automobile in America. For almost two decades Ford's concept of the unchanging universal car had been dominant, carrying the car culture into maturity. The new concept of the "temporary car" that took its place has yet to be dislodged.

The public's lackluster response to the 1926 Model T—despite the nickel-plated radiator shell, the choice of colors, and the inclusion of a starter and balloon tires as standard equipment—at last persuaded even Henry Ford of the need for a replacement. "Yes, you can paint up a barn, but it will still be a barn and not a parlor," one of his disgruntled dealers complained. (Seven out of ten Ford dealers lost money that year.) Serious planning for the new car, however, seems to have started only in the late summer of 1926; neither the recalcitrant Ford nor the company managers he had cowed by his iron-fisted, one-man rule had any real notion of what to replace Model T with.

Tentative specifications and rough blueprints were not completed until January, 1927, but at least by that time the sixty-three-year-old Ford was devoting all of his still-considerable energies and talents to the project. It was not unlike the scene in the "experimental room" at the old Piquette Avenue plant two decades before when Model T was born. Even a few of the old-timers were on hand to help: Joe Galamb at the design blackboard, Charlie Sorensen in the plant planning production. Edsel Ford played a major role in styling the new car.

Beyond this inner circle there was a news blackout except for repeated denials of the frequent rumors of Model T's impending demise. Finally, on May 25, 1927, the company announced that an entirely new car was in the works. Model T production ceased two days later. Every newspaper in the country put the news on its front page. Editorials and cartoons

"Had the talents of the late P. T. Barnum, the brothers Ringling, and Tex Rickard been united in one grand effort it is doubtful whether they could have brought to pass any such spectacle." The object of that 1927 observation was Henry Ford, and the spectacle was his introduction of a new car to replace Model T. These are two of scores of similar cartoons that appeared in American newspapers that year. When the new Model A finally went on public display, the New York *World* conceded that it "was worth all the commotion it was causing."

generated an instant nostalgia cult for Tin Lizzie. The Roanoke, Virginia, *News* was moved to predict that it would be a long time "before America loses its affectionate, if somewhat apologetic, remembrance of the car that first put us on wheels. We probably wouldn't admit it to anyone, but deep in our hearts we love every rattle...." The *News* was exactly right in saying that Model T would not be quickly forgotten: in that year of 1927 eleven of every twenty cars on the American road were flivvers.

Following the May 25 declaration, a "golden silence," as David L. Lewis describes it in *The Public Image of Henry Ford,* descended over the great Ford industrial complex on the River Rouge, where production of the new car would be concentrated. Frantic and widespread speculation about the car's specifications, its appearance, and the date of its arrival roused only vague company promises of an official announcement "within a few weeks." The faithful would have been shocked to learn that Henry Ford had had no new model waiting up his sleeve and simply did not know how soon the tremendous task of retooling and revamping production facilities could be completed.

Nevertheless, his silence generated a mountain of free publicity and whetted the public's anticipation as no other event in automotive history has ever done. Newspaper editors gave full play to every rumor and

181

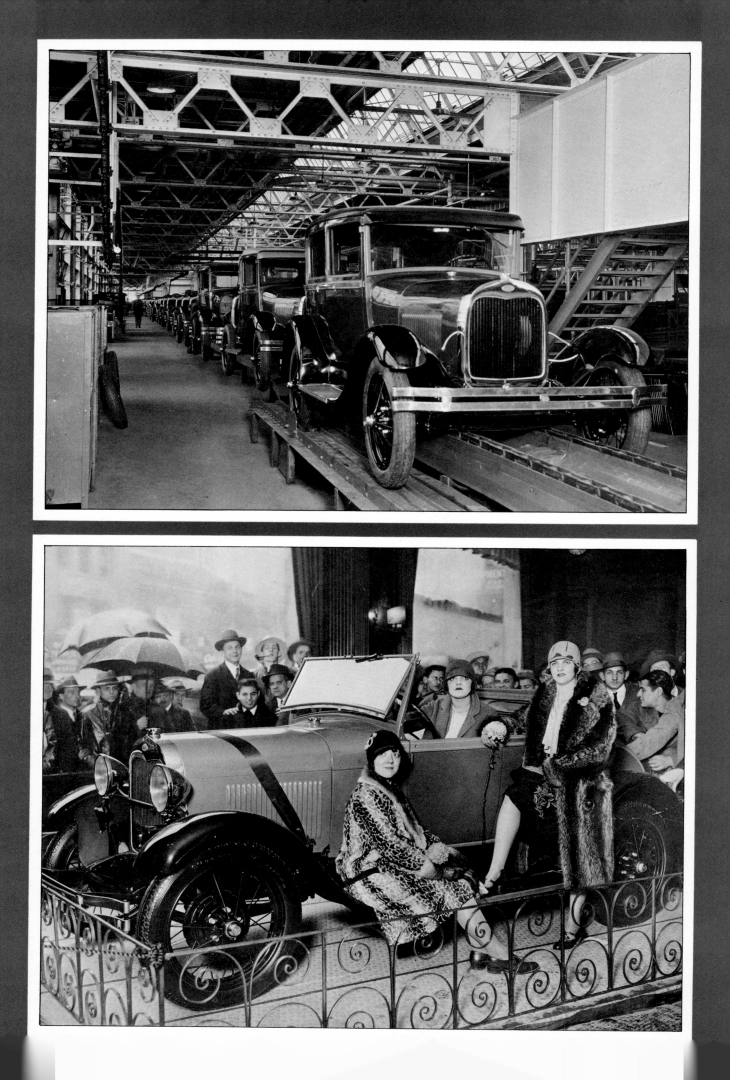

"authoritative" prediction. Ford dealers accepted 125,000 down payments on the new car, sight unseen. Although Chevrolet sales jumped 200 per cent when the Ford assembly lines shut down, taking over the individual sales leadership, overall car output in 1927 slumped by more than 750,000. Prospective buyers were waiting to see what Henry Ford would bring forth. St. Peter, so the popular story went, was questioning every Detroiter who reached the pearly gates, promising quick admittance to anyone who could tell him what the new car looked like. Will Rogers thought he knew: "Here is what you have been waiting for for years: get ready, everybody. HE HAS CHANGED THE RADIATOR!"

The new car, christened Model A, became a reality in October, 1927, as the Rouge assembly lines creaked into motion. Late in November the first of a series of five "teaser" advertisements broke the news the country was anxiously awaiting. Like the rumors, they too made the front pages of many newspapers, complete with the selling copy. The Pittsburgh *Press* said of Mr. Ford's shiny new Model A, "There hasn't been as universal a desire to see anything since Lindbergh came home."

The point was well taken. If Americans of the seventies find it hard to appreciate the tremendous impact Lindbergh's flight had on Americans of the twenties, it is equally hard for

us to grasp the incredible enthusiasm these same people displayed in trying to get a look at the new car created by the Messiah of Dearborn. In city after city police had to be called out to restrain frenzied crowds at Ford showrooms. In smaller communities brief exhibitions were arranged to display one of the scarce sample models, which was then hurried off for showing in the next town. Where no car was available, people lined up simply to peer at photographs of it. It has been estimated that 25 million Americans—about one of every five men, women, and children in the country—examined one of these Model A's at a dealer's or a special showing within a week of its introduction. Within two weeks orders totaled 400,000.

A dispassionate observer, looking back fifty years at the Model A phenomenon, might well be excused for asking what all the shouting was about. To be sure, Model A was an excellent, durable little car. Its four-cylinder engine was the best in the low-priced field, furnishing good power and peppy acceleration. It was right up to date with a sliding-gear transmission and four-wheel mechanical brakes, and it stole a march on its competitors with such innovations as a safety-glass windshield and hydraulic shock absorbers. It gave nothing away in up-to-date styling, either, and the price range of its various models ($385 to $570) comfortably undersold the competition. The new

Model A had the same integrity as the old Model T, and that was no mean accomplishment. This fact alone reaffirmed the common man's faith in the genius of Henry Ford, which goes far toward explaining the enthusiasm that greeted the car.

In the longer view, however, Model A was not the quantitative leap forward that Model T had been when it was introduced in 1908. "There is nothing radical about the new car," Edsel Ford acknowledged. In 1929 Chevrolet came out with a tough six-cylinder engine—to be affectionately known as the Cast Iron Wonder—that put the two marques on a parity basis. Unbiased contemporary observers saw clearly that when it came to building automobiles, Henry Ford was no longer in a class by himself.

The Roaring Twenties saw the American automobile industry assume many of the basic characteristics—in production and management techniques, in marketing strategies, in impact on the nation's economy—that mark it today. If because of sheer numbers alone the decade must be termed the era of Tin Lizzie—the flivver, the flask, and the flapper are the enduring symbols of the 1920's engraved on the popular mind—it was as well a time of basic industry restructuring that endures to this day. And in this same decade the automobile was reshaping a great deal of the basic fabric of American society. The changes it created were both dramatic and lasting.

5

A NEW NECESSITY, A NEW CULTURE

In 1931, when Charles F. Kettering and Allen Orth, his associate at the General Motors research laboratory, completed a book about the automobile's place in the American scheme of things, they decided to title it *The New Necessity*. It was a fair statement of the case. Even as early as the mid-twenties a full-fledged "car culture," as James J. Flink describes it in his book on the subject, was flourishing in the United States, "the backbone of a new consumer-goods-oriented society and economy that has persisted into the present." The automobile as a necessity, as a social and cultural phenomenon, is today taken for granted; that it was already widely regarded as such half a century ago is testimony to the swift progression of the auto age. With few exceptions, every aspect of our present-day car culture—the ill as well as the good—became visible in the 1920's.

One essential of this new age, as we have seen, was the perfection of mass production, enabling the auto industry to supply reliable vehicles within the financial reach of a majority of the population. But even as tough a customer as Model T had limited utility if it could not be driven from here to there with some speed and regularity in any weather. Before the auto age could take another step toward maturity it was necessary to upgrade the nation's miserable road

network completely. That task would prove to be one of twentieth-century America's major undertakings.

The federal Office of Road Inquiry's first "highway census," in 1904, had reported that of the 2.35 million miles of roads throughout the nation, fewer than 154,000 miles could be labeled "improved"—that is, considered more or less passable in most weather thanks typically to a gravel dressing. How well they would stand up to motor traffic, however, was another question. With the exception of 141 miles surfaced with brick or "high type" macadam, paved roads were nonexistent outside the cities.

Each new buyer of an automobile added a voice to the chorus demanding highway improvement, and if he happened to be a farmer literally stuck in the mud, that voice was loud indeed. During the second decade of the century, when car registrations zoomed from less than half a million to more than eight million, the chorus grew deafening. Early in the nineteenth century the noted Scottish highway engineer John Loudon McAdam, for whom the paving surface is named, had written, "Roads must be built to accommodate the traffic, not the traffic regulated to preserve the roads." A century later his dictum was being obeyed from one end of the United States to the other.

Progress was halting at first. The six years after 1904 saw an increase

The Sunday drive had achieved status as an American institution by the time of the First World War, and on the opposite page it may be examined in its full flowering. The setting is St. Louis's Forest Park. In an era when the nation's highway network was unequal to the demands placed on it, auto travel required navigational skill of a high order. Motorists out for a spin in Wisconsin in 1925 confronted the display at left when they approached Manitowoc.

of only fifty thousand miles of "improved" roads. The age-old notion of locally built highways for local use died hard. It was not at all unusual for a rural road to end abruptly at the county line, with nothing more than a faint pair of ruts leading off into the distance for the traveler to follow. The pace accelerated somewhat after 1910. That year California voters approved the state's first highway bond issue ($18 million), symptomatic of a growing awareness that highways were more than a local concern. In 1912 Congress brought the federal government into the picture by offering states matching funds for the improvement of rural postal routes, but the sum appropriated was only $500,000. What the drive for better roads needed was some dramatic focal point, even if only a symbolic one, to capture public imagination and stimulate government action. Carl Graham Fisher set himself that task.

Carl Fisher was a man of many parts. After a fling at dirt-track racing, he founded the Indianapolis Motor Speedway in 1909 and two years later inaugurated the Indianapolis 500. His Prest-O-Lite company, before the advent of the "all-electric" car, had a corner on the car-lighting market as the leading supplier of acetylene for headlights. A promoter of vivid imagination, Fisher developed Miami Beach into a winter playground and was midwife at the birth of the Florida land boom in the twen-

ties; it was he, Will Rogers claimed, who "rehearsed the mosquitoes till they wouldn't bite you until after you'd bought." Carl Fisher, in other words, thought big, and he never thought bigger than when he conceived the idea of a paved, all-weather, no-toll route from coast to coast to be called the Lincoln Highway.

Fisher kicked off his crusade in September, 1912, with a dinner for leading automotive figures at the Deutsches Haus in his home town of Indianapolis. He spoke glowingly of a massive campaign to raise funds from auto makers and their suppliers — present company in the Deutsches Haus included — and from the motoring public at large. According to his timetable, twenty-five thousand Americans would be driving cross-country in comfort to visit the San Francisco Exposition when it opened in 1915. "A road across the United States!" he exclaimed in his peroration; "Let's build it before we're too old to enjoy it!" Before his guests were a night older he had extracted from them pledges totaling $300,000, and before many months passed the campaign had raised $4 million. That sum included $5 donated by President Wilson but not a penny from Henry Ford, whom even the resourceful Fisher could not move.

Fisher did, however, manage to interest other important industry figures in the project, including Hudson's Roy Chapin, Goodyear Tire's Frank A. Seiberling, and Packard's Henry B.

Joy, who became head of the newly christened Lincoln Highway Association. The name was an inspiration. "A man who wouldn't support something named after Lincoln," observes M. M. Musselman in *Get a Horse!*, "would beat his own mother." In 1913 Fisher led a car caravan westward from Indianapolis to investigate the best route for the proposed highway. The publicity windfall was worth every mile of wretched driving they encountered. At each stop Fisher was received with open arms and fulsome pledges of support.

Ironically, this support proved to be a severe problem. In a situation reminiscent of the planning of the transcontinental railroads, half the cities and towns in the United States expected the Lincoln Highway to pass by their doorsteps and enrich their local economies. Mayors, governors, senators, and congressmen bombarded Fisher and Joy with pleas, petitions, and outright demands. As a result, progress on the great highway was slow and erratic. The Lincoln Highway Association put out slogans — "Follow the path of progress," "See America first" — and seeded the route with "demonstration miles" of concrete paving, but many more miles remained rutted dirt tracks bogged down in local politics. "The tourist must be prepared to put up with a few inconveniences . . .," one of the association's pamphlets admitted, although "no real hardships nor dangers which would make the trip

disagreeable to women will be encountered."

In the end — and in a foretaste of the future — it was the federal government that completed the transcontinental highway. Beginning in 1923, funded from Washington, the route was refurbished and the gaps closed. In the process bureaucracy attached various route numbers to many of the segments rather than christening the whole as Fisher had intended. Unhappily, too, neither Lincoln, Nebraska, nor the centerpiece of Lincoln country, Springfield, Illinois, was on the route. Nevertheless, as a symbol the Lincoln Highway was entirely successful. It helped persuade Americans that interstate highways were as essential to the nation's economic well-being as interstate railroads. And the Lincoln Highway, like the Glidden Tours of years past, demonstrated to a growing army of motorists that they might actually be able to see America first.

While the automobile provided the immediate stimulus for highway improvement, the need for good roads ran much deeper than just making life easier for tourists and Sunday drivers. As John B. Rae points out in *The Road and the Car in American Life*, any society "provides roads and streets because they are required for social needs, which existed long before the automobile appeared and would continue to exist even if the automobile had never been invented." This was as true for

the United States as it had been for the Roman Empire. Adequate roads were needed by the farmer to get his crops to market, by the businessman to produce his goods and serve his customers, by the government to provide the logistic framework for defense, by the citizenry at large to communicate for essential social and civic needs. By the twentieth century the nation's waterways and railroads were patently inadequate for these multiple tasks, a fact vividly demonstrated during the First World War when the railroad system broke down under the strains of defense demands and an accelerated wartime economy. However, simply to improve or pave existing roads was not enough; a coordinated system of interstate arterial highways was needed. As the crusade for the Lincoln Highway revealed, this need could not be left to the tender mercies of local parochialism but instead had to be a responsibility of the federal government.

Two landmark federal highway acts, passed in 1916 and 1921, recognized this reality. A total of $150 million in matching grants was appropriated, to be administered through state highway departments — which forced laggard states to establish such departments in order to be eligible. The 1921 act directed the Bureau of Public Roads (successor to the old Office of Road Inquiry) to pursue only "such projects as will expedite the completion of an adequate and connected system of highways,

interstate in character." Billy Durant was inspired to offer up one of his characteristic visions of the future. "Most of us," he told *Automotive Industries* in 1922, "will live to see this whole country covered with a network of motor highways built from point to point as the bird flies, the hills cut down, the dales bridged over, the obstacles removed."

If they were not quite that dramatic, the changes made during the twenties were nonetheless considerable. Total road mileage increased only about three per cent during the decade, but the mileage of improved roads nearly doubled. There were major engineering advances in road surfacing and bridge building. A coherent scheme of highway numbering — even numbers for east-west routes, odd for north-south — replaced the old lick-and-a-promise marking system of painting stripes on telephone poles. (Some of the original names demonstrated staying power, however. The Lincoln Highway, in places, was still called the Lincoln Highway. Vacationers headed south on the Dixie Highway, another Carl Fisher project. Such local coinages as the Hockaday Highway and the Cannonball Road died hard. El Camino Real, with its mission-bell signposts, reminded Californians of their state's Spanish heritage.) Certainly in 1930 much remained to be done — and learned — about an adequate highway network. There were still "roads" to be found in the Great Plains that

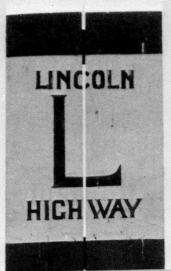

Highway signs and markings in the twenties had a certain eclectic charm all their own. The Lincoln Highway marker below was posted west of Salt Lake City, where the transcontinental route traced the old trail of the Pony Express. Among the miscellany of signs at the right, it may be noted that potential speeders were very politely warned in Azusa, California, and thoroughly warned in nearby Covina, including a reminder to close their muffler cutouts. Waubonsie's Trail ran through Illinois and Iowa. The Jefferson Highway was a more ambitious route, running north-south "from pine [Winnipeg] to palm [New Orleans]." The billboard at the bottom of the page was erected in Nebraska by the Automobile Club of Southern California as a promotion to attract tourists to the Golden State.

were little more than furrows in the prairie grass. The three-lane highway (center lane for passing) was proving a deadly design error. But it can be fairly said that at least Americans were emerging from the mud.

These developments took money, in very substantial amounts. In 1921 highway expenditures nationally (for maintenance as well as construction) came to $1.38 billion, in 1930 to $2.85 billion. These sums ranked second only to spending on public education. Americans accepted the additional tax burden with remarkable equanimity. A growing proportion of the extra cost was raised through what economists call "benefit taxation." Historically, the average citizen in a democracy objects least to taxes that are equitable and that promise direct, tangible benefits. The vehicle fees and the gasoline tax devised in the twenties seemed to most people to meet both criteria. They were equitable because every car owner paid registration and license fees, and every one "paid as he went" via the gasoline tax—and in fact paid in fairly direct ratio to how much he drove on the roads he was financing. Oregon was the first state to levy a gasoline tax (one cent per gallon), in 1919, and by 1929 every state had followed suit. And to motorists long resigned to eating dust and struggling out of mudholes, the benefits derived from paved or improved roads were direct indeed.

What today is sometimes condemned as the "highway lobby" enjoyed a lusty birth in the twenties. Construction contractors, suppliers of concrete and other paving materials, manufacturers of heavy road equipment, highway engineers, bridge builders, road-sign painters—all of them, large and small, found full employment and good profits. And highway construction was but one of a myriad of ancillary industries becoming irretrievably linked to the fortunes of the automobile culture. When auto making captured first place among American industries in 1923, it was a case of only the tip of an economic iceberg being visible. The health of the automobile industry had become vital to the health of the nation's economy as a whole.

During the Roaring Twenties auto manufacturing regularly absorbed one fifth of the yearly production of steel, one quarter of the machine tools, three quarters of the sheet-glass production, and four fifths of the rubber industry's output, plus varying proportions of such products as leather, cloth, paint, and even soybeans (which Henry Ford used for making enamel, horn buttons, and shock-absorber fluid). And of course the total output of scores of entirely new auto-created industries —batteries, spark plugs, carburetors, frames, axles, to list only a handful— poured into the car plants.

No other major industry was more strongly affected by the boom than petroleum. Until the early twenties the rising demand for gasoline was tied in a fairly constant ratio to the rising number of cars on the road. That number rose so rapidly that it produced fears of a serious gasoline shortage. Prices reacted accordingly. Before 1916 gas prices did not fluctuate greatly, averaging about fifteen cents a gallon. Then they jumped sharply upward, reaching almost thirty cents a gallon in 1920. Such prices could be a real burden for some car owners in a year when the average American production worker was making $26 a week. Cartoonists suggested that motorists rig sails to stretch their gas mileage and wondered if the coal-fired steamer was due for a comeback.

Wartime military needs and inflation played roles in the price hike, but the major factor was a lag in fueling the growing tide of auto travelers. Eventually the petroleum industry caught its second production wind, the specter of lining up to buy gas disappeared, and prices began to fall. By the end of the decade they averaged about twenty-two cents a gallon nationwide (including the new gasoline taxes). Once the crisis was over, the oil companies discovered a new growth pattern: fuel demand was accelerating at a faster rate than car sales. With closed cars and all-weather roads, Americans could at last drive the year round. By 1929 the average motorist was covering seventy-five hundred miles a year, a sixty-six-per-cent increase over the

1919 figure, and using half again as much gasoline in the process.

Due to new discoveries in Texas and California, the oil industry suffered no shortage of crude oil in the twenties. The challenge lay in the efficient distillation of the crude into gasoline and automotive lubricating oils — and into considerable amounts of petroleum asphalt for road paving. The solution was the complex process known as thermal cracking, pioneered by research chemist William M. Burton of Indiana Standard, by which increasingly large yields of gasoline were derived from each barrel of crude. As fresh cracking technology was grafted onto the refining process, there was much intercompany battling over patent rights — undertaken in what one study of the industry calls a "cloak and dagger atmosphere" — but eventually these difficulties were ironed out and production rose to ever greater heights. By the end of the decade about three quarters of the petroleum industry's output (measured in product value) was flowing in one form or another into the auto culture, the largest share of course going into the gas tanks of 23 million passenger cars. In 1929 motor vehicles were driven the staggering total of 198 billion miles. Big Oil — bigger even than anything imagined by John D. Rockefeller when he was assembling Standard Oil — was on the scene to stay.

The American mania for drive-in services grew, logically, out of this insatiable demand for gasoline. In the early years of automobiling a car owner bought his gasoline at the same places he had always bought his kerosene: general store, hardware dealer, drug store. When garages began to appear in some numbers, they included fuel in the list of automotive services they offered. The driver pulled up at the curb and a portable tank was rolled alongside, from which the attendant filled 'er up using a simple hand pump. Improved pumps featured a metering device to produce one gallon at each stroke of the handle, but motorists remained suspicious about being shortchanged from these "blind pumps," especially when touring deep in the sticks. They welcomed the arrival of the "visible supply" gasoline pump in the twenties. A graduated glass cylinder holding at least five gallons was affixed to the pump and filled by the attendant; the driver could then actually see how much gas was going into his tank. Sales were made by the gallon rather than by the dollar. A request for, say, two dollars' worth of ethyl would produce much head scratching and labored calculation.

Increasingly, these new pumps appeared at drive-in locations coming to be known as filling stations. *The Gasoline Retailer*, a trade paper, cre-

Styling Breakthrough

The new [1920] Mitchells set a new stride. . . . The revelation came at the National Automobile Shows. And now the nation over, added respect, greater admiration is accorded Mitchell designers and engineers. . . .

Mitchell introduces to car design a logical advancement.

All tendencies of recent years, as you know, have been towards motive lines. Yet many awkward lines remained.

Someone had to conceive the final step; bringing the radiator into harmony with other body lines. It alone remained straight up and down.

It has been Mitchell's opportunity to introduce this inevitable feature — and the result must be seen to be fully appreciated — for it appeals not only to the eye but to one's sense of logical proportions of a swift moving object. . . .

Some will say [a slanted radiator] is a minor thing — that it is not radically different.

Mitchell has not aimed for the freakish nor to attract those of passing fancy. What is offered is a basic development, just like the slanting of the windshield, just like the other many items which make today's cars so different from those five years ago.

— Mitchell Motors Company advertisement

dited Standard Oil of Ohio with erecting the first true filling station (Cincinnati, 1912), but other claimants for the honor have surfaced in Seattle, St. Louis, and Dallas. In any event, the typical early station was described as "an ordinary sized lot" large enough "for a half dozen or more machines to maneuver in," surfaced in gravel or cinders and containing underground storage tanks, a drive-up "island" with one or two gas pumps, and some sort of shelter for the attendant. As often as not they presented a decidedly seedy appearance and were condemned as eyesores by their neighbors. Competitive pressures brought improvements, especially among stations operated or leased by the large oil companies. *National Petroleum News* offered an annual $100 prize to promote station design, stressing architecture, cleanliness, and flora.

The number of drive-in stations grew steadily but slowly until after World War I; then came an explosive expansion. In 1919 as much gasoline was still being sold through the general-store type of outlet as through garages and filling stations; by 1929 the latter accounted for ninety-two per cent of all sales. The number of stations multiplied tenfold, to over 121,000, during the twenties. Motorists grew accustomed to free air, water, and rest rooms and expected to have their windshields cleaned and their oil checked. They brought their cars in regularly for lubrication

and repairs. The filling station was now the service station. Its architecture was sometimes broadly eclectic, dazzling (or numbing) the eye, and its advertising was everywhere to be seen. The corner service station quickly became a basic institution of the car culture, as much a part of the American scene as the corner drug store. A young writer coming to Sinclair Lewis for advice on gathering impressions for the great American novel was told to spend his time at a service station.

If the service station was the most common of the new "highway businesses" springing up across the nation under the stimulus of the auto age, it was by no means the only one. As we have seen, supplying parts and accessories for Model T alone, through retail outlets and mail order, was generating high volume by the mid-twenties, and there were as well millions of owners of other marques who wanted the same sort of add-ons and accessories to make *their* cars look distinctive or run better.

Repairing the growing horde of vehicles was another field rich in opportunity for the small businessman. As a class, farmers were automotive do-it-yourselfers, putting their familiarity with farm machinery to good use to repair the very repairable Tin Lizzie. But there were uncounted other car owners who possessed no mechanical aptitude at all and who had to find help the moment something went wrong. While most new-car dealers

supplied repair services, there was plenty of work for mechanics who chose to go into business for themselves. Skills varied widely, from those with factory training — Packard had pioneered the training of mechanics in 1903 — down to the untutored, trial-and-error blacksmith-mechanic trying to shift from the age of the horse to the age of the auto.

One characteristic common to all these small-business service facilities — which included not only garages but tire dealers, body-repair shops, and specialists in such areas as painting, auto glass, and radiators — was their wide geographical spread. The 1930 census reported some ninety-three thousand repair establishments nationwide. The striking improvement in the road system during the twenties not only made car ownership practical in virtually every corner of America but also greatly multiplied the range of the auto tourist. As a result, any crossroads village that in 1900 had boasted a smithy and a livery stable was likely by 1930 to have in their place a service station and a garage.

See America first" the Lincoln Highway boosters had urged, and car owners everywhere did just that. A traditionally mobile people now had in their hands an instrument of incomparable mobility. The twenties was the common man's age of exploration, the automobile his ship of discovery. Retracing old transcontinental Route 40 for *Sports*

Specialization run rampant: in 1929 a Memphis "lubritorium" offered motor oil blended for thirty-nine cars and trucks.

Illustrated in 1976, Bil Gilbert ran across an old-timer in Kansas with vivid memories of his first touring expedition, undertaken in a 1923 Ford. "Touring was so new that anybody driving became a member of the same club . . .," he told Gilbert. "In the evening it would take an hour or so to unload and arrange our tent, stove and blankets. At night people would get together to talk about their machines, tell about adventures they had had and exchange information about road conditions. It was a gypsy atmosphere. Maybe it was like the emigrants when they drew up their wagons at night. The thing I remember very clearly about that first trip is the great sense of freedom I experienced. . . . We were footloose and fancy-free."

Traveling simply for pleasure was something very new on the American scene, at least for the larger share of the population. To be sure, renting a horse and buggy for a Sunday afternoon jaunt and wheeling a bicycle down country lanes were well-established traditions, but never before had so many possessed a vehicle that truly made them "footloose and fancy-free." "Having a car," writes Bellamy Partridge, "they simply could not resist the call of the open road."

For "auto outings" the more ambitious might hammer together a trailer or even a wood and canvas camp body for their touring cars—the ancestors of today's specialized recrea-tional vehicles—but the majority simply strapped camping gear, tent, sleeping bags or cots, and cartons of supplies on the running boards and fenders of their faithful Ford or Willys-Overland and drove off to see the sights. They spent convivial evenings with fellow tourists in the campgrounds beginning to dot the landscape or enjoyed the seclusion of unspoiled lake shores. (There was always plenty of room; America's population in the twenties was less than half what it is today and there were less than one quarter as many cars.) They rigged their tents and slept on the ground and cooked over open fires and discovered nature as they had seldom seen it before. "The joy of it," a car camper wrote to *Outing:* "We spend hours on the lake, watching the changing lights on sky and hills; we fish, explore, take pictures, and study plants, birds, and squirrels. Nowhere does food taste so good, are fish and chickens so fresh, or bacon and potatoes just the right brown." And when they returned home they developed their snapshots and sometimes mailed them along with lyric accounts of their travels to Henry Ford so he might share the sense of freedom his universal car had given them. Looking back now, leafing through the tattered picture albums, old-timers may with justice recall it all as a lost idyll.

Not only was the choice of destination almost unlimited for the tourist in the twenties, but the cost of touring, if one was willing to rough it and live close to nature, was exceedingly low. Reynold M. Wik reports that in 1920 a family of five could finance a month-long "automobile vacation" for as little as $100, with most of that sum going for gasoline and groceries. Bearing a full load of vacationers and supplies, a Ford might still get eighteen or twenty miles to a gallon of gas, and repairs were not likely to cost much thanks to the little car's durability and the easy availability of parts. One flivver owner boasted that he drove from California to Ohio in 1918—a time, be it noted, when little progress had been made in upgrading the highway system—with a total repair bill of $3.50. Most travelers were not that fortunate, of course, but all things considered, the automobile was proving to be a remarkable recreational bargain.

Since not every traveler enjoyed sleeping under canvas or cooking in the rain, the twenties gave birth to still another auto-related new industry—the care and feeding of tourists. The hotels and inns of small-town America that had easily accommodated the occasional out-of-town visitor and the drummer trade proved wholly inadequate to house the flood of new customers. First into the gap was the tourist home, a private residence whose owner hung up a sign and rented out one or two upstairs bedrooms to tired motorists. Then came something new under the sun— the tourist cabins that sprouted like

(continued on page 202)

Opened in 1922, Denver's Overland Park offered tourists 160 acres of campsites.

AUTO CAMPING

In the 1920's, for the first time, the nation's natural wonders came literally within the reach of millions of Americans, thanks to the automobile and the burgeoning highway network. Auto camping was all the rage. As seen in these pictures, some vacationers loaded their gear into and onto their cars; the more ambitious chose specialized recreational vehicles. All of them appear to be enjoying themselves.

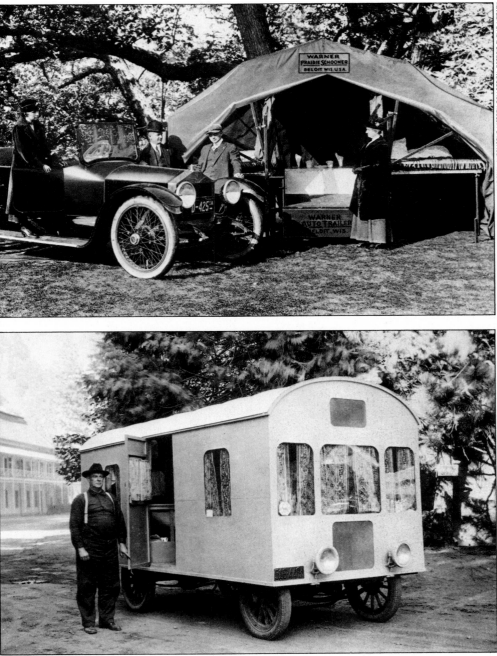

The well-established campsite at left was photographed in the mid-twenties. While the menfolk enjoy pitching ringers, the lady of the camp tackles the work that is never done. At the top of this page is a publicity shot for Warner's Prairie Schooner, an intricately contrived trailer-borne tent. Parked alongside it is a luxurious Roamer. Above is Mr. R. E. Jeffery at Yosemite in 1921, displaying his home-built mobile home, which had started life as a Pierce-Arrow.

The auto campers above pose amidst the
spectacular beauty of Montana's Glacier
National Park, an area described by the
Blackfeet as "the backbone of the world."
They have pitched their tents in the Many
Glacier campground. The setting at right
is rather more prosaic. Not all nature
lovers shed their ties, even while napping.

The Peach Lake Tea Garden in Brewster, New York, typified roadside America in the twenties. The highway culture beginning to put its imprint on the national scene was mapped in 1928 by John Held, Jr., as a public service for *New Yorker* readers.

weeds on the outskirts of towns across the nation. Like the early filling stations, they started crudely: jerrybuilt shacks offering little more than a halfhearted promise to keep the rain off. Gradually, under the pressure of competition, they evolved into more pretentious tourist courts renting at reasonable rates decent accommodations with full facilities. (The term *motel* seems to have been coined in the mid-twenties, but it came into widespread use only after World War II.) Floridians, alert to the promise of the tourist dollar, took an early lead in building such accommodations, claiming 178 tourist camps and courts in operation as early as 1925. Other states with scenic wonders also saw the tourism bandwagon and jumped aboard.

Hand in hand with the tourist court came the roadside eating place, offering to the hungry traveler meals that ranged from a quick hot dog to a full-course Sunday dinner and ranged just as widely in quality. Most of these restaurants were the "Mom and Pop" variety, and if they did nothing else they introduced visitors to the rich variety of American regional cooking. The automobile has been credited with helping to break down regional isolation and prejudices in the United States, but—at least at first —it also revealed many unique regional menus to the uninitiated. The advent of nationwide highway restaurant chains in the years since, however, has reversed this trend and pro-

duced instead a national palate of universal blandness.

In and of themselves, the highway businesses spawned by the auto culture served necessary and socially useful ends. They provided accommodations and services to the millions exercising the new freedom that went with automobile ownership. (In 1929 the number of Americans vacationing by auto reached forty-five million.) They created hundreds of thousands of new jobs and millions of dollars in tax revenues. They made it convenient for Americans to experience the natural bounty of their land and to appreciate the richness of their shared culture. Yet in the process they began, during the twenties, to spread a blight on the land.

There was no inherent reason why a service station, for example, could not be neatly arranged and architecturally pleasing; why a roadside restaurant could not stress an aesthetically inviting atmosphere; why a tourist court could not be handsomely landscaped to complement its setting. Indeed, many roadside businesses were all these things. But others were prime examples of gimcrack ugliness. The blight was still small, but it was growing.

There were two primary reasons for this development. The first was a widespread lack of community zoning regulations, which permitted those interested only in quick profits to throw up gaudy tourist traps in the midst of residential areas or to con-

struct gauntlets of shoddiness along the highway approaches to cities and towns. The second reason was the roadside business's need for instant recognition. The bigger the sign and the brighter the lights, owners believed, the better the chance of capturing the eye of the speeding traveler. Outdoor advertisers, never noted for the tastefulness of their displays even in the pre-auto age, now added to the blight spreading into the countryside by plastering their messages for everything from accordions to zippers on billboards and barn walls and boulders from coast to coast. To be sure, not all roadside advertising had to be unsightly; but much of it was. One exception, to the delight of generations of motorists, was the Burma-Shave verse.

As Frank Rowsome, Jr., points out in his admiring chronicle *The Verse by the Side of the Road,* Burma-Shave— a brushless shaving cream— achieved what very few advertisers ever come close to accomplishing: the buying public looked for its messages eagerly, read them avidly, and tried hard to remember them. The familiar red and white five-sign verses —a sixth sign was always reserved for the name of the product—utilized the witty, amiable soft sell in an age of the often deadly serious hard sell, and America loved them.

The first Burma-Shave signs went up in 1925 around Minneapolis, the company's headquarters; within five years they could be found na-

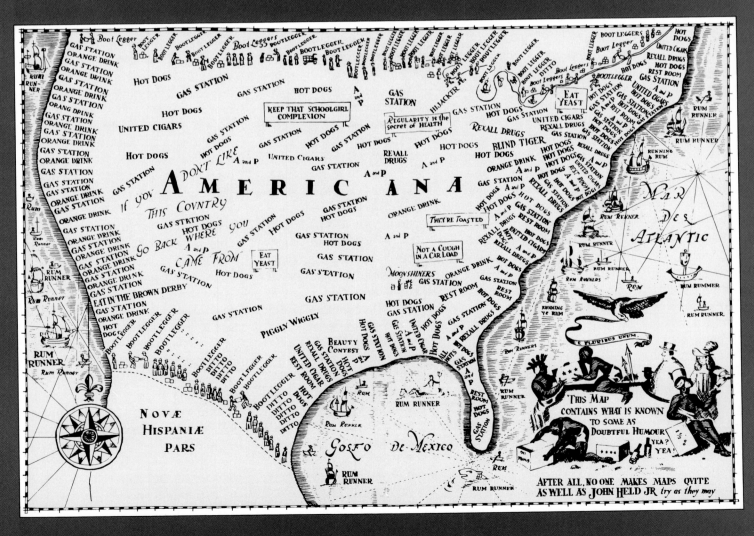

tionwide. Spaced about a hundred feet apart, the signs were easily legible at 35 mph, the best average speed most drivers could manage on the narrow highways of the period. Motoring families delighted in reading the serial verses in unison, shouting out the punch lines, and youngsters in the back seat prided themselves on the tricky art of unscrambling the messages when they faced the other way on the far side of the road. The critic Alexander Woollcott remarked that it was about as easy to read only one Burma-Shave sign as it was to eat only one salted peanut.

In the early years the owners of the family business, Clinton Odell and his sons Allan and Leonard, composed all the Burma-Shave jingles themselves, but as their inspiration ran dry they began to sponsor annual contests, offering $100 for each winning verse. They were swamped. A sampling of the six hundred verses that adorned America's roadsides for nearly four decades appears at the right, but some of the more entertaining ones, such as LISTEN, BIRDS / THESE SIGNS COST / MONEY / SO ROOST A WHILE / BUT DON'T GET FUNNY, were reluctantly rejected by the Odells; unhappily, so was THE OTHER WOMAN / IN HIS LIFE / SAID "GO BACK HOME / AND SCRATCH / YOUR WIFE," as well as THE WIFE OF BRISTLY / BRUSHMUG ZAYMER / BOUGHT TWIN BEDS / WHO CAN / BLAME HER?, both adjudged a shade risqué for family viewing in that more innocent era.

Maintaining the jingles intact against the ravages of fraternity-house collectors and grazing horses who snapped off signs when scratching their backs on them (elevating the messages a foot resolved that particular problem) kept the company's sign crews busy, and there were other contretemps as well. Frank Rowsome interviewed a crew foreman who recalled an occasion in rural New England when, after installing a set of signs reading OLD MC DONALD / ON THE FARM / SHAVED SO HARD / HE BROKE HIS ARM / THEN HE BOUGHT / BURMA-SHAVE, he happened to notice the mailbox of the farmer whose land had been leased by the company's advance man; the name on the box was, of course, McDonald. "I didn't know what to do," he said. "I figured that we probably ought to take down the whole set, even though it was getting on toward dark. Finally we nervously hunted him up. He was a big man, kind of solemn. When I explained, he just looked at me for a long moment. Then he burst out laughing. Turned out that he got a big kick out of it, and of course the whole neighborhood did too."

In the rapidly changing automotive scene after World War II the chatty little Burma-Shave signs were overwhelmed by progress. Highways had become superhighways, and auto speeds soared far above Burma-Shave's sedate reading pace. And perhaps the idea had finally worn thin. In 1963 the company was bought

out and the signs disappeared. Before they went, however, the Smithsonian Institution had the foresight to ask for a set for its American cultural-history exhibit. The Odells obliged with this gem: WITHIN THIS VALE / OF TOIL / AND SIN / YOUR HEAD GROWS BALD / BUT NOT YOUR CHIN / BURMA-SHAVE.

Burma-Shave is the best remembered of the advertisers who began to pitch their messages at automobilists during the twenties; at the same time, the automobile itself was generating boom times for the advertising fraternity. Advertising, in fact, must be added to the list of growth industries beholden to the auto culture. As early as 1915 the automobile moved past foodstuffs into the lead in advertising outlays. By 1929 auto makers were spending $86 million on magazine and newspaper ads, which was some seventeen per cent of all the advertising dollars spent on promoting products nationally in these media.

As David M. Potter points out in *People of Plenty,* advertising assumes real importance in the economy only "when potential supply outstrips demand—that is, when abundance prevails." Between 1917 and 1923 Henry Ford's enviable problem was raising output, not selling, and he stopped advertising entirely. When the first-car market approached saturation, however, Ford and his fellow auto makers faced a quite different situation: consumption rather than production became their primary concern. Indeed, this condition faced the nation's entire economic system in the twenties as mass production spread rapidly through the consumer-goods sector.

In an effort to generate higher consumption, automobile advertising took two fresh lines of approach. The traditional nuts-and-bolts technical slant, whose most skilled practitioner was Claude Hopkins, copywriter for Hudson, Willys-Overland, and Reo among others, gave way to the "new-and-revolutionary" school of ad writing. This concept was at the heart of the annual model change / planned obsolescence philosophy. More power, greater speed, new features, and fresh styling promised to do more than simply enable Mr. Smith to keep up with Mr. Jones; they would put him one up on Jones. By 1927 General Motors was offering no less than seventy-two models, with extensive choices of colors and accessories, and its establishment that year of an Art and Color Section under Harley Earl promised an even stronger emphasis on styling in the future—and on the new-and-revolutionary advertising pitch.

The second fresh advertising approach may be described as the nonspecific. To be sure, such luxury marques as Pierce-Arrow had long featured ads redolent with understated elegance. Theodore F. McManus's famous 1915 Cadillac ad, "The Penalty of Leadership," was so nonspecific that it never once mentioned the car, focusing instead on the company's trials as a front runner (life lived "in the white light of publicity, . . . a target for the shafts of the envious few, . . . fierce denial and detraction" from the also-rans). In the twenties, however, auto maker Edward S. Jordan gave the nonspecific ad an entirely new twist.

Ned Jordan's target was the woman motorist, his creed, "To hell with the mechanical chatter." As Tim Howley writes in *Automobile Quarterly,* Jordan's advertising copy, most of which he wrote himself, "was pure poetry—emotional, rhetorical, illogical, wildly inexplicit, but irresistibly flattering." A car for her as well as him meant an entirely new market, which Jordan pursued with bold imagination. The Jordan Playboy was touted as the car for "the girl who loves to take the open road with top down in the summer time"; for the broncho-busting, steer-roping girl from "somewhere west of Laramie"; for "the golden girl from somewhere, . . . going to the place where fairy tales come true." (*Field and Stream* awarded Jordan a $1,000 prize for the effectiveness of his "out-of-doors appeal.") There was actually nothing exceptional about Jordan's cars, yet he managed to invest them with the aura of the Roaring Twenties: readers of his ads could easily envision Scott Fitzgerald, Zelda at his side, careening off to their next party in a Venetian green Playboy. Ned Jordan himself went into eclipse late in the decade

and his company suffered receivership in 1931, but his impact on the marketing of cars, and on advertising in general, was a lasting one.

Advertising that stressed the romance of auto travel and the hedonistic pleasures of auto ownership no doubt brought customers into dealers' showrooms. So did the general lowering of car prices (most notably by Ford) and the general rise in the disposable income of Americans (some nine per cent, on a per capita basis) during the twenties. The most important new selling factor, however, was the very rapid spread of the installment plan. The notion of paying on time did not originate in the auto field—Isaac Singer began the practice on a national scale in the 1850's to move his sewing machines—but never before had it been used so widely or for such an expensive consumer item.

For years individual car dealers, and a few banks, had made credit available to favored customers, and in 1911 Studebaker made the practice company policy; then, in 1916, John North Willys's Guaranty Securities Corporation made it big business. Auto buying on the installment plan received its final imprimatur in 1919 when the Durant-Raskob regime at G.M. established the General Motors Acceptance Corporation to furnish customers with credit. A disapproving Henry Ford railed against the practice, but most of his dealers employed it anyway.

The idea of average middle-class Americans purchasing something as expensive as an automobile without, at the moment, having the cash to pay for it shocked the conservative souls of many bankers. They foresaw the end of traditional habits of thrift, of saving nest eggs for rainy days. In 1925 a small-town banker informed readers of the *Atlantic Monthly* that he himself had seen a "small tailor" of uncertain means trade up from a Ford to a $1,500 touring machine, and a policeman go into debt for half his monthly salary to purchase a car. A struggling restaurant owner fell under the spell of a slick salesman and "plunged into debt for $1,200" to own a big sedan; "the result," the banker wrote, "is that all he earns must be applied to his debts. . . . Before, he was sure of his ground and free from anxiety. Now, he must not only work, but he must also worry."

Despite such dire warnings, millions of Americans seemed intent on hazarding debt to participate in the car culture. In 1925 seventy-five per cent of new car purchases were made on the basis of $2.5 billion in installment paper. Customarily, the down payment was one third of the purchase price, with balance and interest spread over a year. There is no doubt that this practice entailed sacrifices on the part of many buyers, yet the evidence suggests that the sacrifices were accepted willingly; the repossession rate on those 1925 time purchases was only 2.09 per cent.

Buying on time—which spread rapidly from autos to other consumer items such as refrigerators and vacuum cleaners—was now a permanent fixture of Americans' consumption-oriented way of life. Increasingly the automobile was seen as a necessity rather than a luxury, and thus an overactive Puritan conscience need not balk at the idea of going into debt to have one.

The used-car business is another phenomenon dating from the twenties. Every car, of course, had always become a used car the moment it left the dealer's showroom, and from the earliest days virtually every one radically depreciated in value. Two factors, however, caused the auto industry to view the used car as a growing "problem" during the decade: the thesis of planned obsolescence, and the rise of installment buying. It was a classic case of the solutions to one problem—inducing people to buy new cars in a saturated market—creating a fresh problem.

Car makers invested considerable advertising money in persuading average motorist Smith, instead of clinging to his car for its full useful life, to trade it in on a new and improved model or trade up to a costlier model with more style and more luxurious appointments; and if he did his trading every two years or so, his old car could serve as the down payment on the installment purchase of the new one. Should motorist Smith aspire to a new 1927 Oldsmobile

While Rube Goldberg appears to have been given a free hand with this Ford, it actually represents a major step forward in crime prevention. It was the first radio-equipped police vehicle in Detroit.

($925), for example, he might drive one away with no outlay of cash at all, leaving his old car with the dealer as a down payment and committing himself to installments of about $12 a week for a year. Alternatively, Smith might sell his old car to an independent used-car dealer and use the proceeds for the down payment on his new Olds. In either case, there was that used car to be disposed of—and by 1929, for every five new cars sold, four old ones were taken in on trade.

From the Oldsmobile dealer's standpoint, the trick was to grant Smith a high enough trade-in allowance to clinch the sale without jeopardizing his own profit margin and then sell Smith's trade-in at a profit. He also had to be prepared to take a trade-in on that trade-in. Peddling one or two used cars for each new one sold called for considerable staff, time, and effort on the dealer's part and brought him small returns—a unit profit of $25 was considered good in 1927—or perhaps even a loss in a highly competitive situation. Manufacturers fretted about such diversion from dealer efforts to sell their new cars, and they fretted even more about the used car's tendency to drain customers from the new-car market.

Ford and General Motors made some effort to assist their dealers with the used-car problem, but other manufacturers left them to resolve it as best they could. Dealers often re-

sorted to high-pressure tactics to move the goods. The used-car lot, ablaze with gaudy signs and fluttering pennants, became a part of the everyday scene in the twenties—and a blot on the landscape that is with us still—and selling used cars was on the way to becoming one of America's more maligned professions.

However much discomfort the used car caused auto makers and their dealers, by the late twenties it was as much of a democratizing force in car ownership as Model T had been earlier in the decade. A survey taken in 1927 indicated that while one tenth of the nation's families owned two or more cars, families in the lower-income brackets, despite reduced prices and the spread of the installment plan, still found buying a new car an expensive proposition. Early statistics on used-car sales are imprecise, but there is little doubt that of the more than seventeen million cars on the road in 1927 not bought new that year, a large proportion had been purchased off used-car lots. Except for the more expensive marques, the average four-year-old car sold for about $100. The buying of used-car "basic transportation" quickly became a permanent subculture of the auto culture. It is testimony to the great disparity in family income in the Roaring Twenties that despite these generally low used-car prices, thirty-six per cent of all American families could not afford (or did not want) an automobile as late as 1927.

The automobile's influence on popular culture underwent a sea change during the decade. As its novelty value wore off, its impact on popular music and the Broadway stage lessened. Although Tin Pan Alley continued to crank out scores of "auto songs," many were promotional and none compared with the success of those earlier hits "In My Merry Oldsmobile" and "He'd Have to 'Get Under, Get Out and Get Under." Livewire car dealers stocked the sheet music for such numbers as "Ray and His Little Chevrolet," "The Studebaker Craze," and "In a Hupmobile for Two." Sixty-odd songs mentioned Henry Ford or his flivver in their titles, including "The Little Ford Rambled Right Along," probably the most popular; "The Love Song of the Packard and the Ford," a coy account of a mechanical romance that produced a litter of Buicks; and "Henry's Made a Lady Out of Lizzie," a musical tribute to Model A.

The last of the auto-related stage successes were a pair of comedies, *Six Cylinder Love* (1921) and *Nervous Wreck* (1923). *Six Cylinder Love,* the longer running of the two, told the cautionary tale of a newlywed couple who went in over their financial heads to own an automobile and endured all manner of trials before it all came right in the last act. At least the theme had staying power: *Six Cylinder Love* became a silent movie in 1923, a "talkie" in 1931 (starring Spencer Tracy, Edward Everett Horton, and

Una Merkel), and was remade for the screen in 1939 as *The Honeymoon Is Over.*

As the automobile's role as a Broadway stage prop declined, its stock was rising rapidly in Hollywood. It quickly became an essential motion-picture action prop. The zany car chase was as much a Mack Sennett trademark as the pie in the face. In one Sennett comedy after another, the Keystone Kops piled into their Ford patrol wagon and bumbled their way through hair-raising scrapes with trolley cars, locomotives, and carloads of scoundrels. Laurel and Hardy were only two of the many film comedians who enriched their routines with automotive sight gags; their specially built "breakaway" Model T squeezed between passing trolleys and telescoped into tight places and disintegrated spectacularly on cue. The perils Pearl White endured in motorcars were beyond counting. No gangster movie was complete without a high-speed shoot-out, and rare indeed was the director of twenties film melodrama who could resist the car chase as a device for bringing audiences to the edge of their seats. (That is no less true half a century later, as witness the spectacular car chases in such modern films as *Bullitt, The Seven-Ups,* and *The French Connection* — and during almost any evening's television fare.) Hollywood, of course, found other uses for cars besides vehicles for the chase. They became

stereotypes of social rank—a chauffeured limousine, for example, instantly signified the arrogant rich—as well as handy devices for locale changes and for intimate tête-à-têtes.

One may debate the accuracy of the mirror Hollywood holds up to life, but in its widespread inclusion of automobiles in screen depictions of the American scene during the twenties it was accurate enough. *Recent Social Trends in the United States,* a federal study undertaken by the Hoover administration, reached this sweeping conclusion about the auto: "It is probable that no invention of such far reaching importance was ever diffused with such rapidity or so quickly exerted influences that ramified through the national culture, transforming even habits of thought and language. . . . Imperceptibly, car ownership has created an 'automobile psychology'; the automobile has become a dominant influence in the life of the individual and he, in a real sense, has become dependent upon it." A similar but more succinct verdict was rendered by a resident of Muncie, Indiana. "Why on earth do you need to study what's changing this country?" he asked the sociologists Robert and Helen Lynd when they were conducting their exhaustive study of Muncie (*Middletown*) in the 1920's. "I can tell you what's happening in just four letters: A-U-T-O!"

What the Hoover report found on a national scale the Lynds confirmed in detail in Muncie. By 1929, they wrote,

car ownership in what they considered to be a typical American community had "reached the point of being an accepted essential of normal living." For some, it appeared to be *the* essential. "We'd rather do without clothes than give up the car," a working-class mother of nine told the investigators. "I'll go without food before I'll see us give up the car," said another woman. "The car is the only pleasure we have," said a third. Opinion was all but unanimous among Muncie's citizens that the automobile was a necessity for getting to work, for shopping, for seeking recreation and entertainment outside the home place.

The acceleration of life's daily pace attributable to widespread automobile ownership created a kind of culture shock in such places as Muncie. For example, the Lynds observed that the institution of the front-porch social gathering was going the way of the buggy whip and the feather duster. In the good old days neighbors had dropped by at day's end to have a chat, spread the newest gossip, or perhaps harmonize some old favorites. "The younger couples perhaps would wander off for half an hour to get a soda but come back to join in the informal singing or listen while somebody strummed a mandolin or guitar," a housewife remembered. Now all that was changing. An evening's spin or a Sunday drive in the family car, speeding off to the Wednesday movie in the next town or

to a weekend at the lake, were more popular than front-porch sitting. The change was most noticeable among Muncie's youth once content with a soda and a song or two, the Lynds noted: "Joining a crowd motoring over to dance in a town twenty miles away may be a matter of a moment's decision, with no one's permission asked."

This instant mobility raised serious concerns among parents and other keepers of traditional family values. In the eyes of a great many Americans, the general tenor of morality in the twenties was already bad enough (short skirts, bobbed hair, ragtime jazz, bootlegging, speakeasies) without the additional worry of knowing that their sons and daughters might be, in historian John A. Garraty's phrase, "careening about the countryside in automobiles in search of pleasure and forgetfulness"—and of not knowing what went on in the back seats of those automobiles after dark.

How much sexual license actually occurred in those back seats could only be surmised. It was no doubt far less than parents imagined and certainly nothing like the picture painted by a Muncie juvenile judge, who asserted that "the automobile has become a house of prostitution on wheels." The question might be asked, James J. Flink points out, whether anyone "has ever proved that the back seat of a Model T was more convenient or comfortable than a haystack." Nevertheless, once courtship

Mack Sennett set the style for Hollywood's use of the automobile as a comic prop by putting his Keystone Kops (right) on wheels at every opportunity. Below, cast members of *Pleasure Bound* encounter an unusual kind of Model T tire trouble; and an outsize Lizzie passenger faces a dilemma of a different sort. Across the bottom of the spread, from left, Laurel and Hardy try to laugh off their troubles before an unmoved audience; Charlie Murray pays a visit to a dress shop, accompanied by Louise Fazenda on a motorcycle; Harold Lloyd discovers that his new "Butterfly Six" is a lemon; and Laurel and Hardy overmatch their Tin Lizzie.

355 463

The new, allegedly lapsed morality of the Roaring Twenties car culture caught the eye of *The New Yorker*'s irreverent Peter Arno.

"We want to report a stolen car"

was undertaken elsewhere than in the front parlor or on the front porch, much worry was generated about the whole matter.

Another concern, expressed primarily by men of the cloth, was the replacement of the churchgoing habit with the Sunday-drive habit. This may well have been the case in individual congregations, but the evidence on church attendance nationally is sketchy; at least church membership, as averaged among Catholics and the leading Protestant denominations, rose somewhat faster than the rate of population growth during the twenties. Whatever the truth of the matter, the point has often been made that an automobile is an inanimate object—on Sundays it could just as easily deliver a family to church as to a picnic ground in the country. Possibly the reasons for lagging attendance lay in the pulpit rather than in the garage. (Will Rogers suggested holding services "on rainy days, and days when they are fixing the roads, and they will pack 'em in.")

The automobile's impact on family life had its defenders as well as its critics during the twenties. To some observers, the family that motored together was the family that stayed together. Vacations, camping trips, and visits to scenic wonders and historic sites were all regarded as useful cement for family ties. That most revered tradition, the family reunion, was a certain beneficiary of car ownership. Writing in the *North American*

Review in 1929, Albert R. Erskine, president of Studebaker, stoutly defended the automobile, claiming that it greatly enhanced the quality of life and the material well-being of the average family; those who said otherwise were "second-raters, who are always in danger of developing an inferiority complex which leads to a hostile attitude."

Any assessment of the automobile's influence on family life and habits during the twenties was necessarily subjective. Few aspects could be measured statistically. The Lynds' *Middletown* study is doubly valuable because it stands almost alone in its field. Their evidence suggests that, for the most part, Americans in this pivotal decade of the auto culture accepted—indeed welcomed—the automobile's role in modern life. It generated concerns, to be sure; yet as John B. Rae comments, such concerns "exemplified man's propensity to blame his technology rather than himself for whatever evil consequence it might produce." It seems clear that many of the reservations stemmed from an uneasiness with the *pace* of change the automobile was helping to generate.

A further aspect of car ownership was beginning to be noticed in the twenties. "The make of one's car is rivaling the looks of one's place as an evidence of one's 'belonging,' " the Lynds wrote. Sinclair Lewis turned his perceptive eye on the same phenomenon. "In the city

of Zenith. . . ," he wrote in *Babbitt,* "a family's motor indicated its social rank as precisely as the grades of the peerage determined the rank of an English family. . . . There was no court to decide whether the second son of a Pierce-Arrow limousine should go in to dinner before the first son of a Buick roadster, but of their respective social importance there was no doubt."

However caustic social critics might be, such status seeking was hardly new to the American scene. The impulse to express vanity in material possessions is very much a part of the human condition. Carriage makers for the carriage trade (for example) had long flourished by recognizing this impulse. Auto makers were no less perceptive. The "Three P's" (Packard, Peerless, Pierce-Arrow) consistently pitched their advertising toward the social exclusivity of their luxury marques. But as we have seen, from its earliest days the automobile was a democratizing force in the United States. The wide range of marques and models available in the twenties permitted finer distinctions—what might be regarded as more democracy—in the expression of social rank than ever before. Those reaching up for a handhold on the social ladder in the Roaring Twenties grew self-conscious about driving a Model T, the same make that farmers with manure on their boots drove into town every Saturday afternoon. If they could not yet afford a Packard, they could at least aspire to a Pontiac, and after that perhaps step up to the middle-class respectability of a Buick or a Hudson or a Studebaker. Once, in the years before the First World War, ownership of any kind of an automobile was regarded as the American dream come true. Now the dream was amended to mean ownership of the "right" kind of car, symbolic of the "right" social status.

For those who sought the best in motorcars, for whatever reason, the twenties offered a rich selection. The age of the "Olympian cars," as Richard Burns Carson calls them, began about 1925. At the peak, just before the Crash, these marques constituted perhaps five per cent of the market, but the impression they made — and the impression they still make — exceeded their numbers. They were the grandest, most glorious automobiles that have ever traveled the American road.

The elect whose wealth was old, whose outlook was conservative, and whose carriages had always been ordered from Brewster & Company gravitated toward such marques as Cunningham, Pierce-Arrow, Lincoln — which exhibited a dignity and reserve that belied its recent (1921) origins — or the American Rolls-Royce (some twenty-nine hundred were built in Springfield, Massachusetts, from 1921 to 1931) with coachwork by Brewster. Newer, less established wealth showed a preference for Cadillac, Stutz, the air-cooled Franklin, or

Walter Chrysler's Imperial. For the bold few who insisted on the very finest American road machine available, there was only one choice: the mighty Duesenberg Model J.

Among the Olympian cars of those pre-Depression years, however, Packard dominated the field by a large margin. It was the most widely owned, and the most widely desired among those striving for an automotive symbol of status and success. Over the years, under Henry Joy and then Alvan Macauley, Packard built up a strong tradition of excellence and a loyal following, and its 1920's designs were superbly executed. "The Packard of that day was a 'classic' — aesthetically and otherwise," admitted Cadillac's long-time chief engineer, Ernest W. Seaholm. "It was our bogey for many years." The car's long hood enclosing the powerful straight-eight engine gave it proportions that were sleek and rakish yet not too radical for the carriage trade. Packard was "a gentleman's car, built by gentlemen," and it was a gentlemanly success: in 1928 it achieved sales of fifty thousand, far and away the best of the Olympian era.

These premier marques were engineered and built to the highest standards, and many of them were further enhanced by custom coachwork. Specially ordered bodies from Derham, Dietrich, LeBaron, Murphy, Brunn, Rollston, Fleetwood, Brewster, Weymann, or Judkins, beautifully pro-

portioned and richly appointed, exemplified craftsmanship of the highest order. The best of these machines exhibited aesthetic standards of automobile design that have never been surpassed.

Among these designs, and indeed among some less prestigious marques, were models with a decidedly dashing, personal flavor. Spiritual offspring of those legendary sporting machines of the teens, the Mercer Raceabout and the Stutz Bearcat, they were as much symbols of the flaming youth of the twenties as hip flasks, raccoon coats, and rolled stockings. They tended to be open two-seaters, low slung and brightly painted; they might have rumble seats, massive spotlights, golf-bag compartments, boattail rear decks, and exhaust cutouts. These were the cars that carried Fitzgerald heroes and heroines to yacht clubs and dinner dances and secluded roadhouses, and their owners were the sort that scandalized Babbitt's neighbors in Zenith. The actual number of such jaunty machines was small, just as the flaming-youth fraction of the total population was small, but in their time (and in ours) they lent color to the legend of the Jazz Age.

Behind the building and buying of these highly distinctive motorcars, whether Duesenberg or Kissel Speedster, lay a web of motives. Their designers shared a strong sense of individuality, a fascination with the adventure of high-performance driv-

ing, a rejection of the colorless neutrality of mass production, and an emphasis on quality before profit. The long hoods, the sweeping fenders, the gleaming massive grilles, the side-mounted spare tires, the big headlights, the proud badges and hood ornaments — taken together they bespoke an arrogant disregard for practicality and the "hopelessly utilitarian" virtues symbolized by Tin Lizzie. These were motorcars unblushingly designed as prize possessions.

And what of those who possessed them? Ownership of, say, a Packard dual-cowl phaeton was a clear statement of wealth and social status; the flamboyant custom models favored by Hollywood movie stars represented a sheer flaunting of success. The motives for owning an Olympian car, in short, might range from the heartfelt desire to have only the best to the most blatant materialism, yet the cars themselves transcended even the most crass rationale for their existence. Historically, they marked the climax of the bold pioneering days of automobiling. All of these truly Olympian cars would die out during the Great Depression, their like never to be seen again. In their own and very special way they were as honest as the humble Model T, and that may be why they were treasured in their day and are still treasured by aficionados in ours.

"Think of it," boasts twenties' auto magnate Alexander Kynance in Sinclair Lewis's *Dodsworth;* "by making

During the late twenties and early thirties Hollywood's movie kings and queens were often posed with their selections from the line-up of America's grand marques. At upper left is Clark Gable's Packard Twin Six roadster, at upper right Gary Cooper's Duesenberg with coachwork by Derham. Below is Jean Harlow's Packard phaeton.

autos we're enabling half the civilized world to run into town from their pig-sties and see the movies, and the other half to get out of town and give Nature the once-over. Twenty million cars in America! . . . Why, we're pulling off the greatest miracle since the Lord created the world!'' Beneath the hyperbole was a kernel of truth. The automobile's rising impact on the economy, on recreational habits, on consumer spending, on popular culture, on family life, on social status during the twenties, was matched by its reshaping of the most basic patterns of living.

Almost single-handedly, as we have seen, Ford's flivver lifted the farmer out of the mud and broke through the shell of isolation that had encased rural and small-town life for generations. Rural Free Delivery, undergoing an enormous expansion sparked by the automobile and improved roads, was servicing more than 1.3 million miles of mail routes by 1930, revolutionizing rural communications. Rural education underwent a similar revolution. The one-room schoolhouse of nostalgic memory was patently inadequate for the educational needs of the twentieth century. The school bus made possible the consolidated school and a consequent upgrading of educational standards. Automotive transportation also enhanced the quality of medical care for the farming population by multiplying the range of doctors and increasing access to hospitals. Old habits were transformed. The new mobility gave farm families far wider purchasing choices than just the mail-order catalogue and the general store, which in turn sharpened competition among small-town merchants and led to increasing specialization in retail selling. The old country store appeared doomed to oblivion.

Changes in the urban scene during the twenties were nearly as dramatic. Possession of an auto enabled both white-collar and working-class families to break out of the tight housing restraints imposed by limited transportation. Where once the store clerk or the factory hand could live no farther than a trolley ride from his job, he could now live on the other side of town or even in the countryside. This produced not only a decentralization of housing but a decentralization of industry as well. No longer need a factory be located at the center of an urban area so that workers could reach it; in fact, such central locations often became handicaps as the volume of urban traffic increased.

During the twenties, reported the Hoover administration's *Recent Social Trends,* "the motor car, bringing the country nearer in time, has caused an unprecedented development of outlying and suburban residential subdivisions." The investigators included a study of population trends in four sample cities (New York, Chicago, Cleveland, and Pittsburgh) that documented this substantial out-ward shift. "Center city" Pittsburgh showed the smallest population loss (6 per cent), but the central areas of the other three lost an average of 24 per cent. Conversely, the "adjacent territory" of the four cities registered a population increase ranging from 25 per cent in Pittsburgh to 115 per cent in Cleveland.

The suburban phenomenon was not the creation of the auto age but rather of the railroad age; yet its enormous growth and expansion across the nation was clearly a product of the automobile. Before the auto became commonplace, suburbs—customarily wealthy suburbs—were spaced along commuter rail and interurban lines like "beads on a string," and indeed this pattern can still be discerned in such cities as New York, Philadelphia, and Chicago, where rail service survives. As the auto age took hold, however, this radius-line pattern began to fill in even around "railroad cities." On the fringes of other cities from coast to coast once-isolated villages became suburbs, and entirely new communities sprang up in the once-empty countryside. There were even three pioneering shopping centers erected in the twenties, one near Kansas City and two on the outskirts of Philadelphia, to serve the new suburban lifestyle.

No other major city in the nation exhibited greater physical changes in this period than Los Angeles, and the shape of those changes was dictated by large-scale automobile ownership. The pattern of decentralization was both dramatic and deliberate. During the 1920's, writes Mark S. Foster in the *Pacific Historical Review,* "City leaders consciously and confidently committed themselves to a decentralized pattern of development as a positive goal." The planners, supported by the thousands of newcomers flooding into the city—its population doubled during the decade—expressed fears that downtown Los Angeles would become as cramped and crowded and traffic-ridden as the older cities of the East. (In fact, traffic congestion in Los Angeles was already in a class by itself.) The centralized city was widely regarded as "old-fashioned." In 1924 Los Angeles voters passed over proposals to expand the city's rapid-transit system in favor of a plan to construct highways in outlying areas. "The great city of the future," prophesied a leading civic group, "will be a harmoniously developed community of local centers and garden cities, a district in which need for transportation over long distances at a rapid rate will be reduced to a minimum."

The rush away from central Los Angeles was on, and for real-estate brokers and land developers it was a gold rush. Before 1920, as Foster points out, area maps showed few residential streets located farther than walking distance from trolley or interurban lines. By the mid-twenties, however, subdivisions were sprout-

(continued on page 226)

Even in the grim year 1931 Pierce-Arrow pictured its cars in a serene setting.

GRAND MARQUES

Grand marques, Olympian cars—by whatever term they are known, American luxury cars attained a peak of engineering and design during the late 1920's and early 1930's that sets them apart from their brethren of other eras. The advertisements reproduced here and on the following pages reflect the same elegance and concern for quality as the cars themselves.

PIERCE - ARROW

Open Cars $5250, Closed Cars $7000, at Buffalo
Government Tax Additional

Dual-Valve Six

The simple, understated soft sell was as
much a long-standing trademark of Pierce-Arrow
advertising as the car's distinctive fender
headlights, which appeared on every model
from 1913 onward. These are 1925 ads.

PIERCE-ARROW
Dual-Valve Six

Open Cars $5250, Closed Cars $7000, at Buffalo
Government Tax Additional

A frequent element in Packard advertising
was "analogy" paintings. In the 1930 example
below, the conquering Norsemen are analogous
to Packard's conquest of the fine-car field.
The series opposite, displaying the 1927
cars, has a thematic focus, with Joan of Arc
(lower left) representing Packard's leadership.

Luxurious Transportation

The valiant Norsemen sailed to new continents in the staunchest, swiftest and most luxurious craft known to their civilization

FROM its first pioneering efforts Packard has built its motor cars for conquest—conquest of the fine car field! And as the fine car market grows with the natural increase of taste and discrimination among motorists, Packard leadership becomes more marked.

The slender grace of Packard lines has always attracted the favor of the discerning—contributed to the winning of a distinguished clientele. And in the Packard Eight Phaeton—so popular in the open-air, open-road seasons—Packard beauty reaches its most graceful

expression. It is only natural that the characteristic Packard design should appeal so strongly. For behind Packard beauty itself lies the satisfying assurance that Packard does not depreciate cars in the hands of owners by frequent and radical changes in appearance. Every Packard—whether new or old—is always unmistakably a Packard!

Supreme safety, the luxury of superb performance and *beauty that is always modern* will be yours in a Packard for many long years of truly distinctive transportation.

ASK THE
MAN WHO
OWNS ONE

PACKARD

"The supreme com-
bination of all that
is fine in motor cars"

Simplicity ~ More than ten years ago Packard started not only the modern trend in body lines but the intensive simplification of design so universally sought after today. The mechanical simplicity of Packard cars has since been as much copied as has their famous beauty.

True engineering genius, years of research and experiment, are required to reduce any machine to its simplest and most efficient form. But once achieved, as in Packard cars, such simplicity is of the greatest value. It means lower first cost, exceptionally low maintenance expense and long life.

Packard simplicity and high precision workmanship, together with such features as "Instant" chassis lubrication, are responsible for the years of luxurious mileage every Packard owner enjoys.

PACKARD
ASK THE MAN WHO OWNS ONE

"The supreme com-
bination of all that
is fine in motor cars"

DEPENDABILITY ~ ~ Thousands of families have not been without the faithful service of a Packard for a generation.

To these and many other families of more recent ownership Packard cars have come to mean far more than fine, efficient machines of transportation. They have gained some part of that affection men feel for faithful dogs and high-bred horses.

For the Packard is, above all, *dependable.*

Owners learn to trust the unfailing performance of this fine car—day after day—year after year—with its surprisingly small maintenance cost and simplest sort of routine care.

The famed beauty and distinction of the Packard, its roomy comfort, great power and long life—all have had a part in establishing its priceless reputation. But underlying all these is the Packard dependability which for twenty-seven years has made the name Packard synonymous with quality motor cars.

ASK THE MAN WHO OWNS ONE
PACKARD

"The supreme com-
bination of all that
is fine in motor cars"

LEADERSHIP ~ Packard's position in the vanguard of automotive progress has been consistently maintained for twenty-seven years.

Packard leadership is the result of a deliberate intent backed from the first by means more than adequate to permit engineering research and the highest degree of precision manufacture.

For a generation Packard has been the great automotive laboratory from which have come most important develop-

ments in the evolution of the modern car.

Today, Packard-powered planes, surviving gruelling military and naval tests; Packard-engined racing boats, champions of their class; Packard cars, outstanding as the most imitated cars in the world; proclaim Packard leadership on land, in the air, and on the water.

And Packard owners, themselves leaders in every field of human endeavor, know that their cars cannot but reflect a compliment upon their taste and judgment.

PACKARD

"The supreme combination of
all that is fine in motor cars."

Prestige ~ ~ The Packard owner, however high his station, mentions his car with a certain satisfaction—knowing that his choice proclaims discriminating taste as well as a sound judgment of fine things.

For the Packard is one of the world's few fine cars universally approved by the enthusiastic owners of other famous makes.

Recognized everywhere, as supremely typifying America's genius for perfection

in things mechanical, Packard cars go further in possessing to a marked degree that subtle attribute—prestige.

Packard prestige, sensed if not defined by every Packard owner, is reflected in the car's aristocratic beauty, its distinction, its luxury and comfort, its superb performance—unexcelled in traffic or on the open road.

PACKARD
ASK THE MAN WHO OWNS ONE

THE ALL-WEATHER BROUGHAM

Outstanding among all fine cars on famous avenues and boulevards, Lincoln appearance unmistakably suggests Lincoln quality and fineness. Lincoln character and reputation do not need the emphasis of showy embellishment—that which is genuinely fine wins universal recognition without display—those who design Lincoln bodies—famous custom body designers—seek with beautiful body lines to express the innate fineness of Lincoln quality and performance.

A glance at this beautiful Brougham (by Brunn) reveals Lincoln distinction—it is as perfect in line and form as a sculptured masterpiece—its simplicity and genuine elegance appeal most invitingly to the educated tastes of people who invariably buy the finest things.

The interior of the Brougham is like a corner in the perfect home—comfortable, restful, unobtrusively rich in fabrics and costly fittings. There are two folding armchairs for the extra guests. The driver's compartment —entirely separate—may be open or closed—an arrangement quite vogue in this season's fine closed cars

L I N C O L N   M O T O R   C O M P A N Y
Division of Ford Motor Company

Although they represent two distinctive campaigns, these advertisements emphasize Lincoln's custom coachwork—at left a brougham by Brunn (from *Country Life,* 1928), at right a sport roadster by Locke and a cabriolet by Holbrook (both from *Vanity Fair,* 1925). Brunn's brougham featured "two folding armchairs for the extra guests."

For the growing number of people who prefer an open car for personal use, there is none so satisfying nor of more unmistakable style than the powerful Lincoln Sport Roadster with body by Locke.
LINCOLN MOTOR COMPANY
Division of
Ford Motor Company.

The fully collapsible Cabriolet by Holbrook.
LINCOLN MOTOR COMPANY
Division of
Ford Motor Company

Of all the reasons why the Cadillac V-16 has met with such favor, none is more important than the fact that it permits complete expression of the purchaser's preference as to body style and appointments. Fleetwood has executed more than thirty V-16 body types, each one highly distinctive in its basic design, and available in a variety of finishes and interior fabrics. In addition, special custom creations may be had in any mode the purchaser specifies. Any Cadillac-La Salle dealer will gladly provide complete information.

CADILLAC V 8 12 16

The classic Cadillacs were at their most opulent when this stylish advertisement ran in *Fortune* in 1931. The town brougham with V-16 engine and canework appliqué was priced at $9,700. Duesenberg, the elite of American motorcars, did not advertise in color or, in this classic example of snob appeal, even bother to show the automobile.

She drives a *Duesenberg*

· 47 ·

ing up in parts of the San Fernando Valley (for example) that were miles from the nearest Pacific Electric interurban line. The car was king. "So prevalent is the use of the motor vehicle," wrote the City Planning Commission's Gordon Whitnall in 1927, "that it might almost be said that Southern Californians have added wheels to their anatomy." During the twenties auto registrations in Los Angeles County multiplied five and a half times (registrations nationally multiplied three and a half times), more cars per capita, by a wide margin, than in any other city in the United States. Los Angeles has yet to surrender that title. Elsewhere in the nation the one-car garage was becoming a new feature of suburban architecture; around Los Angeles, increasing attention was being paid to building two-car garages.

As was true in the early railroad suburbs, the well-to-do were the first to combine country and city living, or to abandon the city altogether, during this auto-age suburban boom. Exclusive residential communities underwent dramatic growth between 1920 and 1930: the population of Beverly Hills, outside Los Angeles, increased almost 2,500 per cent; Shaker Heights, outside Cleveland, 1,000 per cent; Grosse Pointe Park, outside Detroit, 725 per cent; Elmwood Park, outside Chicago, 717 per cent; Richmond Heights, outside St. Louis, 328 per cent. Middle-class families who had bought a car joined

the exodus as fast as their financial health permitted. The poor, the minorities, and the elderly stayed behind; inability to afford a car was a major barrier to suburban living for those who might have aspired to it in the twenties. Thus the typical pattern of the suburb as a white, middle- or upper-class enclave took root, and automobile ownership was a formative factor.

Another key component in the decentralization of living, working, and buying patterns was the motor truck. The number of trucks jumped from just over 1.1 million in 1920 to better than 3.6 million in 1930. Just as the automobile and the bus offered more flexible personal transport than the railroad, the truck was a more flexible means of short-haul freight transport; and like the automobile and the bus, the truck came into its own only with improvements in the road network. Most suburbs, especially the newer ones, were heavily serviced by trucks. They were also instrumental in the dispersal of industry from city centers. (Long-haul trucking, however, remained in its infancy during the twenties, in part because of the relatively late development of practical pneumatic truck tires.) The farmer's new economic flexibility stemming from the improvement in farm-to-market roads was apparent in his rapid adoption of the motor truck: a quarter of the trucks on the road in 1930 were farmer-owned.

During the Roaring Twenties the

The auto-fueled rush to the suburbs during the twenties was nowhere more apparent than in Los Angeles. The developers of the Westwood subdivision, below, were quick to advertise the accessibility of their tract to car owners. In 1922, the year this picture was taken, more than a thousand such subdivisions were laid out in the Los Angeles area. The country club was one of the features of the suburban lifestyle; Willys-Knight used a country-club setting for the public relations photograph at left.

The rush-hour traffic in New York in the
mid-twenties was regulated by traffic
light towers such as this one, overlooking
the intersection of Fifth Avenue and
42nd Street. The view is north along Fifth.

benefits, or seeming benefits, of the car culture were easily visible. The automobile had a high social profile: it was, writes social historian Blaine A. Brownell, "a more impressive piece of machinery than a radio, more personal in its impact than a sky-scraper or dynamo, and certainly more tangible than electricity. Thus it was generally more legible as a symbol and more apparent in its consequences." By the same token, the flaws beginning to emerge in the car culture stood out in bold relief.

We have already examined the "visual pollution" that accompanied the growth of highway businesses. (The pollution of air quality was neither recognized nor apparent in the twenties.) Expectations early in the century that the automobile would relieve the urban congestion created by horse-drawn transport proved ephemeral. Traffic regulation and the traffic light—first installed as early as 1914 in Cleveland—were inadequate to cope with what was becoming an American institution: the traffic jam. In most cities parking was so limited that a second institution was born: circling the block to search for a parking space. Massachusetts governor Alvan T. Fuller suggested banning "pleasure cars" from downtown Boston during working hours. The Chicago Plan Commission suggested a master scheme "to widen streets and extend boulevards, open more through streets, eliminate jogs, straighten the Chicago River, and connect up the whole street system so that automobile traffic may be conducted with convenience." Whatever course might be chosen, the problems defied easy solution. Cities that had demonstrated an inability to cope with the horse culture did not seem good bets to tame the auto culture.

The cost to the taxpayer of crime prevention rose substantially as the criminal element took to the automobile and, in self-defense, the police followed suit. Small-town constables might make do with a flivver, but big-city gangsters would have made short shrift of such Keystone Kop vehicles. Prohibition-era gunmen drove high-powered Packards, Lincolns, Cadillacs, or Imperials, with Chicago crime czar Al Capone favoring a specially built 1928 Cadillac with, among other features, quarter-inch boiler plate armor; it cost a reported $30,000. The police countered with fast pursuit cars of their own, the Lincoln being a particular favorite. Car thefts, for criminal purposes or just for joy-riding, were assuming major proportions by the end of the decade.

No other serious problem generated by widespread auto ownership, however, was more visible than safety. While the ratio of traffic deaths and injuries to the number of cars on the road and the miles driven remained fairly constant during the twenties, in absolute terms the toll rose alarmingly—from 12,500 deaths in 1920 to 32,900 a decade later. Mechanical failure was seldom the cause of accidents, and in fact substantial mechanical improvements, in brakes, suspension, tires, steering, and safety glass, were made during the twenties. Poor roads, poor road design, and poor weather could be identified as causes of some crashes. But the large majority of auto accidents—then as now—were caused by a dreary catalogue of driver or pedestrian failures: speeding, alcohol (despite Prohibition), carelessness, simple stupidity. Governmental regulation of licensing and registration left much to be desired. The automotive press, the popular press, and uncounted special commissions expressed their grave concern about the number of deaths and injuries and the amount of property damage resulting from auto accidents. To little avail: here again, sadly, a pattern established in the 1920's would hold true in the decades to follow.

By October, 1929, when the world of the Roaring Twenties began to tumble down, the car culture was in full cry. For future good or ill, it was remaking the face of America and reshaping the way Americans lived. On balance it was a revolution well received; whether the automobile was still a progressive force for change might be a matter for debate, but without doubt the celebrated love affair between Americans and their cars was well launched. As the nation faced its greatest trial since the Civil War, the car culture would also be put to the test.

6 YEARS OF TRIAL

In the closing months of 1929, had anyone cared to tackle the logistics, it would have been possible, with a bit of crowding, for every man, woman, and child in the United States to go riding in an automobile at the same moment. (The exact figure was 5.27 persons per car; perhaps it occurred to those trapped in the ever-more-frequent traffic jams of the period that the stunt *was* being tried.) Detroit was on its way to a new one-year production record of 4,455,000 passenger cars. That came out to one new car for every 27 people in the country—a mark, it might be noted, not all that far behind 1976's production rate of one new car for every 21 people.

Despite those seemingly rosy figures, there was a feeling of unease in many auto company board rooms well before Wall Street's plunge late in October. After eclipsing all records early in the year, car sales began to slip badly early in the summer. The car-buying public had suddenly grown cautious. It had also grown parsimonious, investing primarily in low-priced models. Analysts detected a lopsided quality about the apparent auto boom: Henry Ford, now that he finally had Model A production in full swing, was doing extremely well; but most other car makers were barely matching their 1928 figures, and many were falling

well below them. When the year's totals finally came in, this trend would be confirmed. Auto production in 1929 was indeed greater (18 per cent) than in 1928, but the increase was due primarily to Ford's massive output gain—138 per cent, almost 874,000 cars. The Chrysler Corporation registered a respectable increase of almost 20 per cent, thanks to Walter Chrysler's rejuvenation of his new acquisition, Dodge, and his two new car lines, Plymouth and De Soto. However, sales at General Motors, except for Chevrolet and Oldsmobile, were down substantially, and beyond the Big Three the picture was not in the least rosy. Of the leading independents only Hudson showed a significant sales gain (7 per cent). The independents as a whole sold nearly 200,000 fewer cars in 1929 than in 1928.

The automotive trade paper *Motor* pointed to credit as the villain. "With the Federal Reserve Board constantly stressing the dangers of the credit situation," it commented in July, 1929, "and with the entire nation jumpy because of its frequent warnings, the automotive industry—more completely dependent than any other upon the use of credit for the merchandising of its products—is feeling a real pinch." Early in October L. A. Miller, president of Willys-Overland, announced that he was "gearing pro-

Photographer Dorothea Lange found the public service message opposite in California's San Joaquin Valley in 1937. Even during the Depression automobile ownership represented in visual shorthand the American Way. About the same time, in Sacramento, the Bank of America was promoting auto buying by rolling a shiny new model up to the loan counter—where spelling was secondary.

231

duction schedules to the legitimate absorptive capacity of the market." Since Willys-Overland was suffering the worst sales slump of any car maker, Miller's cutback order was not unexpected and lacked the impact of a fire bell in the night. At almost the same moment, however, the alarm *was* being sounded—and in the halls of the giant. In a directive issued on October 4, General Motors president Alfred P. Sloan warned that efforts "so lavishly expended on expansion and development should now be directed toward economy in operation. . . . It is impossible to assume that the percentage increase from year to year will equal what we have enjoyed during the recent past."

"As it turned out, I was not, of course, pessimistic enough," Sloan would later write. Indeed he was not, but astonishing prescience would have been required to predict the dimensions of the automobile industry's coming collapse. That collapse would produce profound changes—in the line-up of auto producers, in the pace of innovation in car design, in the relationship between worker and employer. The car culture, however, would prove to be too deeply rooted for even the ravaging Depression to dislodge.

No other major American business, in the twenties, had grown as dependent on consumer confidence as auto making, for no other business, as *Motor* pointed out, leaned so heavily on credit. Car owners suddenly nervous about the future were thinking twice about new-car purchases and the installment payments that went with them. As a consequence, auto sales in December, 1929, were the worst for that month since the recession year of 1921. By mid-1930, as the Great Depression began to take grim shape, it was clear that the American car-buyer's confidence in the future was sounding bottom. At the beginning of the year, remarks economist E. D. Kennedy, the auto industry was not sure whether it was suffering from a sprained ankle or a broken neck. By the end of the second quarter it suspected the worst. During the Coolidge years people had generally ignored the fact that an automobile was a durable-goods item that did not *have* to be replaced every couple of years—a fact papered over by the theory of planned obsolescence. In the Hoover years growing numbers of car owners found unthinkable the prospect of going into installment debt to replace a car that still ran well enough; and since two of three new-car purchases were made on the installment plan, the effect on Detroit was stunning. Output for the year was down more than thirty-seven per cent. This was a disastrous plunge for the nation's leading industry; then the disaster was multiplied by the ripple effect on the huge network of ancillary industries dependent on Detroit's good health.

For the thirty-odd auto makers active when 1930 began, reports from the field varied from bad to terrible. Sales of Ford's Model A declined substantially, although they still totaled well over a million, a forty-one per cent share of the market. Every other manufacturer also built fewer cars than in 1929, and many of them built far fewer. Willys-Overland produced less than a third as many, Hudson and G.M.'s Pontiac-Oakland division just over a third. The medium-priced marques took a particularly severe beating.

By now hope was all but gone, in Detroit and elsewhere, that the Depression (ironically, a term favored by President Hoover as sounding less alarming than *crisis* or *panic*) would be as short-lived as the sharp economic break of 1920–21. During 1931 the automobile industry continued to lead the downward spiral. Production was off another thirty per cent. Ford alone fell more than six hundred thousand cars short of his 1930 mark. The industry as a whole plummeted from first to fourth place in value of product sold. Employment in auto factories was down to two thirds of the figure for 1929. Payrolls were half what they had been as companies cut wages, shortened the work week, and instituted periodic shutdowns. "Any further decline in [auto] production," *Fortune* announced in its December, 1931, issue, "will represent an appreciable decline in the American standard of living." A Packard ad in the same issue sounded a pleading note:

"Dollars spent for automobiles, which draw on every state in the Union for materials and parts, will do more to revive prosperity than dollars hoarded against better times."

Nineteen thirty-two was rock bottom, for the nation and the auto industry. Bank closings were everyday occurrences in that cruel year. Nearly a quarter of the country's work force was jobless. Thousands literally did not know where their next meal would come from. Auto production was less than 25 per cent of its pre-Depression high. Giant General Motors sold a mere 5,810 cars during the month of October; in 1929 G.M. dealers had sold that many cars on an average weekday.

With so few people in the market for a new car, the Big Three stopped producing entirely for long periods. Journalist Harrison Salisbury visited Detroit during one of these shutdowns. "Chrysler was dead," he later recalled. "So was G.M. So was the Ford Dearborn works, the greatest of them all. All locked and shut behind high wire barricades and along the Detroit River miles and miles of lean-tos and shacks, tin-can towns, caves hollowed out of the clay sides of the riverbanks. Shantytown, U.S.A. . . . . The glow of the campfires was amber in the dusk and it silhouetted the hulks of the great factories. Dead. Devastated. . . . I was getting in on the apocalypse of the American dream."

The tidy mind of General Motors president Alfred Sloan had no room for contemplation of the apocalypse. G.M. might be down, but it was not close to being out. As Sloan later put it, "The contraction was orderly." In 1932 G.M. stock was selling at only eight per cent of its 1929 high, but no dividends were missed even when payment meant dipping into capital reserves. The company's 1932 profit was a mere $165,000 (compared to $248.3 million in 1929), yet $63 million was paid out in dividends as Sloan bent every effort to maintain shareholder confidence in even the darkest days. The poor-selling Viking and Marquette, companion cars to Oldsmobile and Buick introduced in 1929, were dropped. The venerable Oakland, which Billy Durant had brought into General Motors in 1909, was dropped, its slot in the G.M. pricing line-up taken over by Pontiac. To aid dealers in the hard-hit medium-priced range, the sales organizations of Buick, Oldsmobile, and Pontiac were combined into one unit (B.O.P.) during the worst years of the Depression so that dealers could offer more than one make. Sloan's management revolution, activated during the economic slump of 1920–21, fully earned its keep during the far greater slump of the thirties.

The Chrysler Corporation, by all odds, should have been severely crippled by the Depression. Walter Chrysler, however, was a man who went against the grain of probability. The economic collapse seemed to be striking Chrysler at the worst possible

When You
BUY an AUTOMOBILE
You GIVE
3 Months' Work
to Someone

Which
Allows
Him to
BUY
OTHER PRODUCTS

BUY A CAR NOW—HELP BRING BACK PROSPERITY

moment. He was in the midst of trying to restore buyer loyalty to Dodge, which had suffered a decline in the years between the death of the Dodge brothers and Chrysler's takeover in 1928. His two new marques, Plymouth and De Soto, had had little time to develop customer loyalty before the bottom fell out of the car market. Yet seen in retrospect, Chrysler's decisions in the late twenties were his company's salvation during the Depression. "Had we lacked Dodge," he wrote in 1937, "there is no telling what our situation would be today. For one thing, there would be no Plymouth car."

Plymouth was the key. Acquisition of the excellent Dodge production facilities enabled Chrysler to manufacture enough of the Plymouth's parts under his own roof— rather than buying from, and paying a profit to, outside suppliers of such essentials as forgings and castings—to allow him to challenge Ford and Chevrolet in price. The first Plymouths had been simply derivatives of the old Maxwell-Chrysler line, but in 1931 an entirely new model was introduced that was a true mass-market competitor. Featuring such innovations as "floating power" (rubber engine mountings that drastically reduced vibration), Plymouth output topped the one hundred thousand mark and captured third place in the sales race. By 1933 production reached a quarter million, and a Plymouth could be custom-ordered as to

such things as color, upholstery, and accessories. This novel new procedure required thirty-five copies of the sales order so that the factory could get all the right parts to the assembly line in the right sequence at the right time, but it was worth the mound of paper. Buyers were delighted to be able to get exactly the car they wanted, and in one week's time.

To be sure, Plymouth's sales climb did not erase red ink from the corporate balance sheet. In 1932 losses topped $11 million. The rewards would materialize in the future. Chrysler had solidly positioned himself in the mass market alongside Ford and General Motors with a car competitive in both quality and price. At the same time, he was reducing the debt incurred in the Dodge purchase. In 1935 he retired, and a year later the Dodge debt was also retired. It had taken Walter Chrysler just a decade—half of which was spent in a debilitating economic crisis—to win and hold ranking as one of the Big Three.

The impact of the Depression on Ford was more severe and complex than on either General Motors or Chrysler. The economic collapse pressed the company into a steady decline that would not be arrested until after World War II—a slide that was paralleled, and intensified, by the failing powers of Henry Ford.

Ford, sixty-six at the time of the Wall Street crash, promptly made the front pages with characteristically

dramatic moves. In November, 1929, he announced Model A price cuts ranging from $5 to $35, and in December he increased the daily minimum wage of his workers by a dollar, to $7. To cure the slump, he told the press, wages must be raised to augment buying power. "It is all as plain and familiar as a copybook maxim . . .," he said; "if every one will attend to his own work, the future is secure." Had the nation been suffering only a slump, the gesture might have been influential. But like the $5 day of 1914, the $7 day of 1929 had no emulators. Other auto makers, suffering severe losses in sales and profits, regarded a wage hike as a form of altruism they could ill afford. Ford could be altruistic primarily because he was being spared the worst pressures of the Depression by the continuing popularity of his Model A. By 1931, however, the day of reckoning was upon him. Model A demand collapsed, layoffs were heavy, and those lucky enough to remain on the payroll typically worked only three-day weeks. In October he cut wages back to $6 a day. Ford's 1930 profit had been $40 million. Over the next three years his losses totaled $120 million.

During the Roaring Twenties Henry Ford had been an almost mythical figure to millions of Americans. He was *the* symbol of the age of mass production; single-handedly he had liberated the farmer, raised the quality of everyday life, made the benefits of the auto culture available to all. As

the Depression deepened, however, the common man's faith was shaken. Once Ford had seemed to have all the answers. Now he seemed to have no answers at all.

To expect Ford to turn the nation's stricken economy around by himself was of course entirely illogical, yet so ingrained was his image as the Messiah of Dearborn that the disillusionment was widespread. To many people, Henry Ford in the thirties was less the symbol of the failures of capitalism — Wall Street presented numerous candidates for that role — than the symbol of the failures of modern industrialism. He was the spokesman for the fruits of Progress, which in the depths of the Great Depression seemed sour indeed. Aldous Huxley plumbed this disillusionment in his bitterly satiric fable of the future, *Brave New World*, published in 1932. In Huxley's sterile new age worshipers pray to Our Ford; their Bible is Ford's autobiography, *My Life and Work;* their labor is performed by assembly-line workers decanted as a semi-moronic working caste.

Certainly Ford did not enhance his image with such thoughtless statements as "These are really good times, but only a few know it" (1931), and "If you lost your money, don't let it bother you. Charge it up to experience" (1934). Gone was the adulatory tone that had once marked the letters arriving in Dearborn. Could not Mr. Ford see what was happening? his

correspondents asked. Could he not see the bread lines and the soup kitchens and the foreclosed mortgages and the desperation on the face of America? How could he make "light of ills he never felt," a Michigan farmer wondered. "Stick with your pistons and gear grease," a Californian advised him bitterly. "As a prophet of the Lord you never would have got out of old Egypt land." In a sense, of course, Ford had been out of touch with the realities of the world around him — or at least out of sympathy with many of those realities — since the early days of Model T. Company spokesman William J. Cameron was asked how Ford was taking the Depression. "I don't know," Cameron replied. "He doesn't talk about it much. It's so terrible that I believe he doesn't dare let himself think about it." Fewer and fewer homilies and copybook maxims issued from Dearborn.

However muddled Ford's thoughts on the calamity that had overtaken the nation, he remained as clear-headed about automotive engineering as ever. In February, 1932, he set Detroit buzzing with the announcement that his next line of cars would be powered by a V-8 engine. This was a radical innovation, in the view of his production boss Charles Sorensen, Ford's "last mechanical triumph."

The first American V-8 to go into quantity production had appeared in Cadillac's 1915 models, and this

powerful, smooth-running engine type won increasing favor for higher-priced marques in the 1920's. Until Ford's announcement, however, the V-8 was regarded as too complex and costly to manufacture for the mass market. Ford was not deterred by such pronouncements. The key to a cost breakthrough was casting the entire vee-shaped engine block as a single unit. (Ford's single casting of a four-cylinder engine block, back in 1908, had been a major element of Model T's success.) It could never be done, said the experts; it could be done, said Ford. It was done, and done well. "I've just got my old determination back, that's all," Ford confided to a reporter.

The first models of the new V-8 Ford appeared in March, 1932. Like both Model T and Model A, it had a very favorable power-to-weight ratio, and its 65 horsepower made it a formidable performer. Just how formidable was soon evident in winning sweeps at racing events across the country. Testimonials arrived from unexpected sources. "You have a wonderful car. It's a treat to drive one. . . . I can make any other car take a Ford's dust," wrote John Dillinger, at the time considered Public Enemy

"Even if my business hasn't been strictly legal it don't hurt anything to tell you what a fine car you got in the V-8," read one of the letters sent to Henry Ford after his new model came out. The writer was the murderous Clyde Barrow. He and gun moll Bonnie Parker took pictures of each other posing with their pride and joy, a 1932 V-8 they had stolen in Texas.

No. 1. "I have drove Fords exclusively when I could get away with one," wrote the notorious bank robber Clyde Barrow. "For sustained speed and freedom from trouble the Ford has got ever other car skinned. . . ."

Once certain teething troubles were eliminated, such as overheating and a tendency to burn oil, the V-8 proved to be a fine, well-engineered car. By this time Ford had quietly bowed to the inevitability of the annual model change, but he petulantly refused to adopt any innovations his competitors thought of first. Only once before World War II, in 1935, would he wrest the individual sales leadership from Chevrolet. To meet the V-8 challenge, Chevrolet cut prices until the two marques were virtually identical in cost. Plymouth, too, sold in the same price bracket. For the first time in a quarter century, Ford faced the mass market without his traditional pricing advantage. The old dominance was gone, and the aging Ford, clinging stubbornly to the reins of his absolutism, grew increasingly incapable of reasserting it. The company slipped to third place in overall sales behind General Motors and Chrysler.

As far as the Big Three were con-

cerned, 1933 was the year the nation's economy turned the corner. Car sales rose almost half a million over the 1932 low and continued to rise steadily through the mid-thirties. In 1936 General Motors came within $10 million of matching its 1929 profit of $248.3 million. This recovery rate was not matched by other segments of the nation's economy. Autos had paced the collapse from mid-1929 on primarily because of sharpened public concern about buying on credit. Four or five years later that concern no doubt persisted. Yet old cars were wearing out, threatening to impair an automotive lifestyle that millions considered essential. In 1935, for example, when one fifth of the nation's work force was still unemployed, Detroit turned out more than 3,273,000 cars, just 9 per cent below the average annual figure for the best years of the Roaring Twenties. This buying surge was mainly in the middle-income brackets, where those still employed or otherwise able to scrape up a down payment were renewing their membership in the auto culture.

However much this surge of recovery encouraged the Big Three, it came too late for many of the independents. By the mid-thirties some of the most celebrated American marques had succumbed, others were gravely or fatally ill, and none was in good health.

Such marques as Jordan, Kissel, Ruxton, Moon, Doble, Gardner,

Stearns, and the American Rolls-Royce were gone before the 1933 upturn. Peerless, once a member in good standing of the "Three P's" (with Packard and Pierce-Arrow), was defunct; with the repeal of Prohibition its Cleveland plant would be converted to producing ale. Marmon, DuPont, and American Austin were in their death throes. Franklin, that finely engineered exemplar of air cooling, succumbed in 1934, the dashing Stutz in 1935. The distinguished Locomobile name plate was gone too, along with the rest of Durant Motors, flailing to the end in the corporate confusion characteristic of Billy Durant. Durant declared personal bankruptcy in 1936, listing assets of $250 (his clothes) against liabilities of $914,000. Nineteen thirty-six was also the last year for Cunningham and Ransom Olds's Reo, which thereafter devoted itself to truck building.

Some of those firms were in trouble even before the Crash, and were as much victims of oligopoly as depression. An attempt in 1934–35 to merge Reo, Hupp, Graham, Pierce-Arrow, and Auburn came to nothing. Hupmobile, once ranked in the top ten for its 1925 output of 129,000 cars, struggled painfully through the Depression, "running down like a clock that someone had forgotten to wind" (in E. D. Kennedy's phrase) before expiring in 1940. Graham limped alongside, also building its last car in 1940. Once-mighty Pierce-Arrow expired in 1938. To lovers of fine cars, perhaps the saddest loss was the collapse of E. L. Cord's distinguished little automotive empire. The last Auburn was built in 1936, the last Cord and Duesenberg in 1937.

Ironically, in their last years a number of these companies produced some of the finest engineering and most distinguished designs of the era. Reo's striking Flying Cloud and Royale models were design pacesetters. Advertisements for the 1933 Graham Blue Streak claimed, with some justice, that it was "the most imitated car on the road," and a year later Graham introduced supercharging for the first time in a medium-priced car. Pierce-Arrow displayed prototypes of a beautifully streamlined Silver Arrow, promising to "give you in 1933 the car of 1940," but could not afford to put the design into production. Pierce-Arrow's V-12 engine and the V-16's of Marmon and Peerless were marvels of engineering. Auburn's Speedster models, the bold and innovative front-wheel-drive Cord 810, and the glorious last Duesenberg Model J's and supercharged Model SJ's were truly classic automobiles. But for company after company there was not enough demand, not enough dealerships, not enough capital to ride out the storm, and the classics became collector's items.

While the "Little Five," the leading independents, rode out the Great Depression, they did not emerge unscarred. Tightfisted Charles W. Nash,

who never forgot the fearful poverty of his childhood, somehow managed to keep his company solvent despite dismal sales. In 1932, producing fewer than eighteen thousand cars, he turned a profit of $1 million, six times that of General Motors. He built no cars without firm advance orders, slashed prices, and watched every penny like a hawk. When he merged Nash with refrigerator-maker Kelvinator in 1936, he still had corporate liquid assets of $30 million. Having achieved that financial miracle, Charlie Nash retired from active management of the merged companies. Hudson, too, was salvaged by strong personal leadership. In 1932 its losses reached $5.5 million and there was talk of receivership. Company founder Roy Chapin was then serving as secretary of commerce, but upon Hoover's defeat he returned to Hudson and set about raising money. A low-priced model called the Terraplane was successful in the marketplace, Chapin was successful in the financial community, and the company was saved. The effort cost Chapin his life. Weakened by strain and overwork, he fell victim to pneumonia in 1936.

Careful management and price cuts also kept Packard afloat, despite several losing years. To offer a Packard for less than $1,000 was to risk affronting the marque's traditional "lap-robe" clientele, but company president Alvan Macauley saw no alternative. "We have an Epis-

copalian reputation and we want to do business with the Methodists," he admitted. Proudly conservative Packard even stooped to sponsoring a radio variety show—and promptly replaced headliner Jack Benny with a "less controversial" comedian. In 1937 Packard sold more than one hundred thousand cars, twice its 1928 high.

Willys-Overland, meanwhile, had run hard aground, which came as no surprise to industry insiders. Under flamboyant John North Willys the company had never been renowned for stability. Like Durant, Willys was an incurable optimist, incurring heavy indebtedness to maintain high output and viewing future profit prospects through rose-colored glasses. By 1933, after four years of severe deficits, Willys-Overland was at the end of its tether, facing the same predicament Willys had found at the original Overland company in 1907: it could not meet its payroll. This time he had no answers, and receivership was declared. Willys died two years later, on his annual pilgrimage to the Kentucky Derby. The company was reorganized in 1936, but for the rest of the decade it remained a poor fifth among the major independents.

Far more unexpected was the collapse of Studebaker. Although complete opposites in temperment, John North Willys and Studebaker president Albert R. Erskine shared one fatal trait—a hyperactive optimism. Erskine's acquisition of Pierce-Arrow

The architecturally distinguished facade of
the Detroit Institute of Arts was a
fitting backdrop for the distinguished
Pierce-Arrow special project of 1933—the
Silver Arrow. Five handmade prototypes
of the streamlined fast-back design won rave
reviews at auto shows and exhibits, but
neither Pierce-Arrow nor Studebaker,
its parent company, had the resources for a
production run, and the project died. The
five cars were sold off for $10,000 each.

in 1928 proved to be more beneficial to Pierce-Arrow than to Studebaker. His attempts to enter the mass market with the Erskine and then the Rockne (named for the famed Notre Dame football coach) were costly failures. Equally costly was his Depression policy of bolstering stockholder confidence by paying dividends out of capital. Giant General Motors had the resources for such a policy; Studebaker did not. Still stubbornly confident that the Great Depression was a mere recession, Erskine pursued expansion by attempting an expensive merger with White Motors, the Cleveland truck builder, in 1932. By March, 1933, a month after Willys-Overland's collapse, Studebaker was also in receivership. Four months later, facing personal bankruptcy and broken in spirit, Erskine shot himself. "I cannot go on any longer," his suicide note read.

Studebaker might have died along with Albert Erskine but for the brilliant efforts of sales manager Paul G. Hoffman and production head Harold S. Vance. They persuaded the receivership court that the best chance for paying off creditors lay not in liquidation but in a reinvigorated sales and production program. Pierce-Arrow was sold, bringing in $1 million in much-needed working capital. Some $800,000 was authorized for advertising and retooling, and by the end of 1933 there was even a modest profit ($55,000). Two years after entering bankruptcy, Studebaker, with Hoff-

man and Vance firmly at the wheel, was released from the court's jurisdiction. Planning promptly began for another assault on the mass market. The result was Studebaker's Champion, introduced in 1939, a fine little car fully competitive with Chevrolet, Ford, and Plymouth. In the three years before America entered World War II, Studebaker sales were comfortably back over the one hundred thousand mark.

The winning struggle of the Little Five to stay in business was a remarkable achievement — and to their loyal customers a heart-warming one as well. Yet the number of those loyalists was shrinking. As the Depression thinned the ranks of car makers, the grip of the Big Three on the marketplace became almost a stranglehold. In the final years of the Roaring Twenties the independents had held twenty-five per cent of the market; in 1941 they held just ten per cent.

Industry observers wondered how long the Little Five could continue in business if they had to do battle for a mere ten per cent of the auto market. Oligopoly's "imperfect competition," first visible in the 1920's, was shaped into a seemingly permanent condition by the pressure of the Great Depression. Economist E. D. Kennedy was not optimistic about the independents' future. "It does not at the moment seem likely that they will ever again become major factors . . . ," he wrote in 1941. "The crystallization of the automobile industry into its

present form appears to have become extremely solid."

The patterns of change in the auto industry went beyond a shrunken line-up of producers. To try to capture the elusive Depression-era customer, car makers initially stressed styling less and practical virtues more. Low price, economy of operation, and durability dominated the selling copy in car advertisements in the early thirties. In 1930, for example, Studebaker started the widely copied vogue of "free wheeling," a device that by shifting the transmission into neutral when the driver took his foot off the accelerator allowed the engine to coast and thus use less fuel. (In fact, the elimination of the engine's braking effect could be dangerous on hills and also greatly increased wear on brake linings. Free wheeling was abandoned after a year or two by most car makers.) More genuine gasoline economy was achieved by the use of overdrive, a fourth or cruising gear. General Motors made much of "knee action"—independent front suspension—and the "turret top," a one-piece, all-steel body top. Nash claimed improved engine efficiency with "twin ignition"—two spark plugs per cylinder. Less publicized advances were made in metallurgy and machining, resulting in tougher and more efficient power plants. "When I started making parts for Ford," G.M.'s William Knudsen observed in 1938, "a sixty-fourth of an inch was the smallest tolerance we used; now we

(continued on page 246)

Charles Sheeler titled his 1930 view of River Rouge *American Landscape*.

INDUSTRIAL COLOSSUS

Visiting Ford's complex of factories sprawled across 1,115 acres adjacent to the River Rouge in Dearborn, the English historian J. A. Spender wrote, "If absolute completeness and perfect adaption of means to end justify the word, they are in their own way works of art." Artists Charles Sheeler and Diego Rivera concurred, depicting Detroit as a centerpiece of America's technological landscape.

Sheeler's belief that "a picture could have incorporated in it the structural design implied in abstraction and be presented in a wholly realistic manner" is strikingly evident in these two works, *City Interior* (above), painted in 1936, and *River Rouge Plant,* dating from 1932. Both derived from a documentary photographic study of River Rouge that he made in 1927. "Forms existed on their own terms," Sheeler insisted; seldom do human figures intrude upon his majestic visions of the industrial process.

242

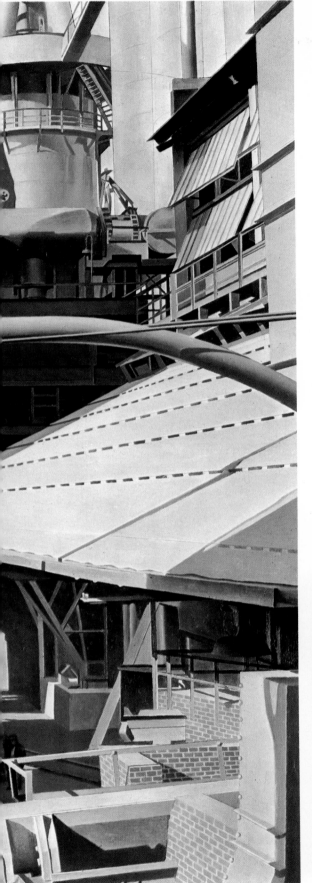

In contrast to Sheeler, Mexican muralist Diego Rivera regarded the human element in the industrial process as paramount. This is a panel from a set of frescoes Rivera did for the Detroit Institute of Arts in 1932–33 under the patronage of Edsel Ford. Combining meticulous observation, allegory, and compression of design, Rivera captured the drama and demonic movement of the assembly line. The scene is the staging of chassis, engine, and body for the final assembly; at right is a huge stamping press.

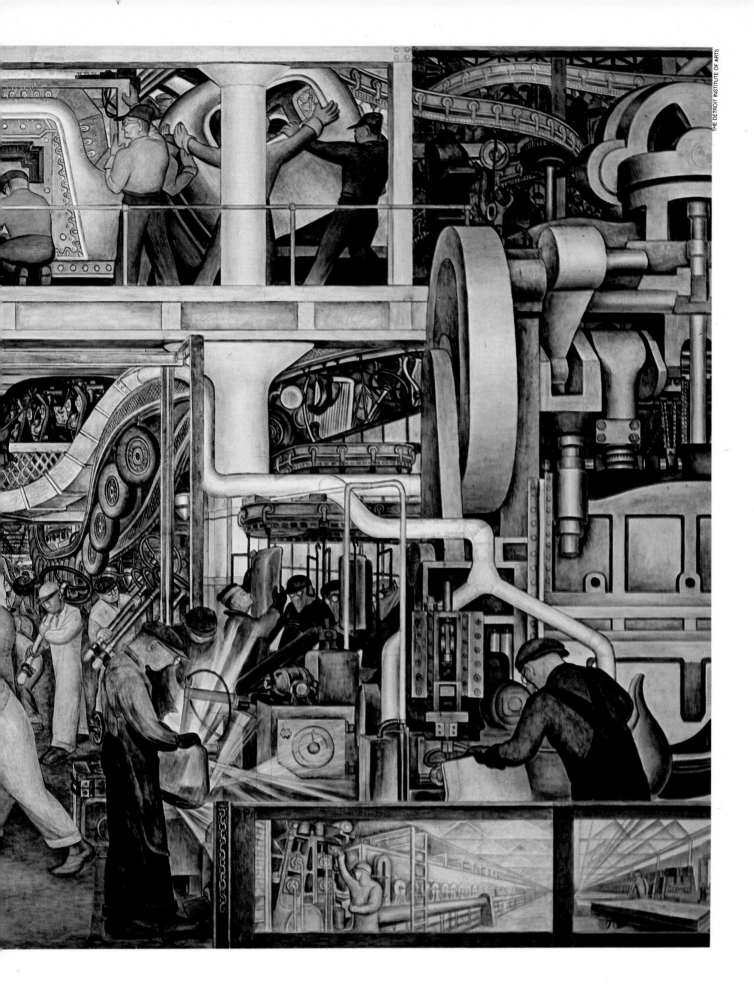

work in ten-thousandths." By the end of the decade hydraulic brakes were universal (the stubborn Henry Ford finally converted from mechanicals in 1939), and the gear-shifting lever was off the floor and on the steering column or, in some cars, replaced by an automatic transmission.

At the same time, automotive styling was changing, especially after the industry's upturn in 1933, at a more rapid pace than ever before. In part this was a natural outgrowth of the annual model change, in part it stemmed from the desperate attempt by smaller independents to attract customers with "tomorrow's car today." Some changes were primarily functional, such as widening the passenger compartment so that three could sit in the front seat, or replacing the outside luggage rack with the built-in trunk. Others were matters of aesthetics. One of the labels applied to the thirties is the "Streamlined Decade," and automobile designers were determined not to be left behind by their peers in other fields.

At first streamlining consisted of rounding off the square corners and softening the rigid upright profile of the typical twenties' machine in the name of aerodynamics for better road stability and fuel economy. Reo, Graham, and Pierce-Arrow's Silver Arrow set the pace with their sleek designs. Then, surprisingly, one of the normally conservative Big Three, Chrysler, took the lead. The result was the startlingly different Airflow designs of

the 1934–37 Chryslers and De Sotos.

The Airflow, the creation of Walter Chrysler's Three Musketeers—Fred Zeder, Carl Breer, and Owen Skelton —was radical in more than just its streamlined styling. The company called it the "first real motorcar since the invention of the automobile." The engine and passenger compartment were moved well forward, producing better handling by distributing the car's weight more evenly between the front and rear wheels and vastly improving riding comfort. At last rear-seat passengers were spared the jouncing that came from riding atop the rear axle. The Airflow was one of the roomiest and most comfortable cars on the road. Its exterior styling, however, was its downfall. The charitable called it too far ahead of its time. Others dismissed it with more pointed comments. As Paul C. Wilson notes in his study of automobile design, *Chrome Dreams*, they derided the Airflow as an example of "rhinocerine ungainliness." That was apparently the majority opinion. Less than thirty thousand were sold in four years.

Despite its reception, the Airflow proved to be the most influential auto design of the thirties. By the end of the decade streamlining prevailed. Bodies became lower and wider,

swallowing up the running boards. The spare tire disappeared inside the trunk. Headlights were faired into fenders, and fenders faired into body sides. Windshields sloped, front-end elements were "unified," rear ends were lengthened, sloped, rounded. The car of 1940 looked nothing at all like the car of 1930.

These changes were not universally admired. Visibility in many streamlined cars was exceedingly poor—"about the same as from a tank with its periscope shot away," in Wilson's phrase. Traditionalists deplored the loss of the handy running board and complained of the contortions required to negotiate the low door openings. Industrial designer Walter Dorwin Teague criticized the chrome moldings "now hung on our cars like beads on a Zulu chief." E. B. White, who confessed a fondness for the Model T's simplicities, concluded that the cars of 1940 "look like a badly laid egg, or a torpedo that didn't quite jell. They are a mass of unrelated chromium bands and miscellaneous ellipses." But for good or ill, streamlining had carried the day, permanently changing automotive design.

The realities of the Depression left the sensible family car the dominant vehicle on the American road. By the

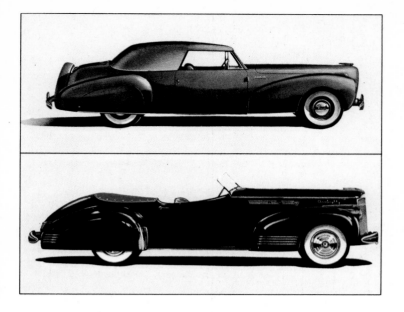

On the opposite page is a teaser photograph released to the automotive press in 1933 by the Chrysler Corporation to hint at the look of its forthcoming wind-tunnel–tested, streamlined design, the Airflow. These are De Soto engineers; none of the test models gave away the exact design of the Airflow, of course, but the one being held came the closest. On this page are ads from 1941 issues of *Fortune* depicting two of the last American classics, the Lincoln Continental (top) and the Packard Victoria.

late thirties, writes Paul Wilson, "the rakish, utterly impractical expressions of wealth and power . . . which had made men's pulses race" were seldom to be seen. The high noon of the Olympian cars was long past. Only three luxury marques remained. Packard had managed to stay solvent only by tapping the $1,000 market. The greatest of the Olympian Lincolns, the KB model, was discontinued in 1934. Cadillac kept its mighty V-16 in production until the 1940 model year, primarily as a prestige "loss leader," but well before then its Olympian look was gone. Many custom coachmakers went out of business for lack of demand. Before going under in 1938, Brewster turned out a number of custom town cars— on lowly Ford chassis. Two examples of last-of-breed may be noted, the custom Packard Victorias designed by Howard Darrin, and the Lincoln Continental, a collaboration between Edsel Ford and designer E. T. Gregorie. The Continental, introduced in 1939, was one of the most graceful automotive designs ever executed, a fitting aesthetic sign-off for the age of the American classic car.

The turbulent thirties witnessed one more change in Detroit's automotive world, the most fundamental one of all. Big government and big labor stepped onto the stage. Their entrance was heralded by New Deal fanfare.

One of the legislative centerpieces of Franklin Roosevelt's "Hundred Days" was the National Industrial Recovery Act (NIRA), passed in June, 1933. Its purpose was to stimulate the manufacturing sector by regulating competition, prices, production, and business practices by means of industry-wide codes, and one of its primary targets was the all-important automobile industry. It received a decidedly lukewarm response in Detroit. The auto manufacturers dutifully drew up the necessary code and with one exception dutifully displayed the Blue Eagle insignia that signified compliance; but they pointed out that the abuses the act was supposed to correct—overproduction, price instability, low wages—were not what had driven them into the economic doldrums. Auto making, they claimed, was a well-organized, well-regulated industry suffering only one problem— a shortage of customers; and in fact during 1933 car buyers were beginning to trickle back into show rooms across the country.

Maverick Henry Ford flatly refused to sign the auto code, terming the Blue Eagle "that Roosevelt buzzard." "Hell," he said, "I wouldn't put it on the car." His stance prompted a public shouting match with a blustering former cavalry general named Hugh "Ironpants" Johnson, head of the National Recovery Administration set up to carry out the NIRA provisions. Ironpants Johnson threatened "a sock in the nose" to nonsigners and traded his Lincoln in on a Cadillac, but Ford did not budge. In truth, the only real difference between Ford and his fellow auto makers on this issue was his outspoken candor. At the root of their universal mistrust of the NIRA was its Section 7(a), a provision that gave labor the right to organize and bargain collectively. That, in the view of every automobile manufacturer, was anathema.

Detroit was one of the most determinedly open-shop areas in the nation and had been so since the day Ransom Olds's first auto factory went up there at the turn of the century. (To repeat, "Detroit" in this usage refers to the entire automobile industry and its primary suppliers; in 1933, geographically, its head and heart encompassed Toledo, Ohio, South Bend, Indiana, and Kenosha, Wisconsin, as well as most of southeastern Michigan, and included by extension assembly plants all across the country.) Management opposition was not the only reason trade unionism had failed to win any sort of meaningful toehold in the industry. The American Federation of Labor was a craft-oriented union, and little organizational effort was expended on auto workers, who fitted into no recognizable craft. Finally, the workers who manned the machines and assembly lines were singularly innocent of trade-union experience. During the teens and twenties they had poured into Detroit—white dirt farmers, black sharecroppers, urban poor, penniless emigrants from Europe's cities and farms—as into a land of milk and honey that paid wages they had only dreamed about. There were grievances, to be sure, but the fat paychecks of the Roaring Twenties had a way of smoothing the rough spots; and in any case they knew there were very few other industries where they could do as well. Sociologists and reformers might express concern at their apathy, but, as John B. Rae remarks, "it may be doubted whether they were as much bothered by monotony and routine as the people who studied them."

Management's attitude toward the worker was essentially paternalistic, a viewpoint harking back to Ford's $5 day and his enlightened employment policy. During the twenties giant General Motors set the trend, which other auto companies generally followed, of developing a system of "welfare capitalism" for its employees: savings and investment programs, bonus plans, subsidized housing, group insurance, educational offerings, recreational activities. G.M.'s motto was "One happy family." There was no place in the family, however, for "union agitators" intent on interfering with management's prerogatives. Henry Ford, characteristically, was the most outspoken foe of unionism, but in his quiet, aloof way Alfred Sloan was just as intransigent. In his memoirs he wrote, in a singular example of understatement, "As a businessman, I was unaccustomed to the whole idea."

The Depression brought the auto worker face to face with harsh reality. Pay cuts, short work weeks, and layoffs were endemic. Job security was nonexistent. Seniority counted for nothing. Men with twenty or thirty years' experience were fired along with the newest recruit, and in rehirings older men were passed over in favor of supposedly more vigorous younger ones. There was incessant pressure to cut labor costs by speeding up the lines. "All they were interested in was production," a Chevrolet worker related. "They treated us like a bunch of coolies. 'Get it out. Get it out. If you cannot get it out, there are people outside who will get it.' That was their whole theme." A fellow worker articulated this universal complaint simply: "I just don't like to be drove."

Labor unrest swelled into protest marches, union organizational drives, wildcat strikes—and violence. Much unrest was centered in the plants of independent parts and accessory makers, where working conditions were particularly bad and where the principle of welfare capitalism had not penetrated. At the Briggs auto body factory in Detroit, for example, wages in 1932 fell to a low of ten cents an hour; after a day's exhausting labor in a "speed-up" atmosphere a worker might take home as little as eighty or ninety cents. Unrest engulfed the major auto companies too. In 1932 a march on Ford's River Rouge complex organized by the tiny Communist-dominated Auto Workers Union resulted in a bloody battle with police in which four were killed and scores injured. A few strikes produced limited worker gains; others were crushed by strikebreakers and police action. Management successfully held the trade-union movement at bay.

Several of the auto makers deflected the NIRA's Section 7(a) by establishing company unions—G.M. called them "employee associations"—which, although they provided useful grievance machinery, were predictably docile on the more volatile issue of exclusive bargaining rights. In May, 1935, the NIRA was declared unconstitutional by the Supreme Court. If Detroit breathed a collective sigh of relief at this news, it viewed with genuine alarm the passage by Congress of the Wagner-Connery Act a little more than a month later. The so-called Wagner Act established the National Labor Relations Board (NLRB) and gave it strong teeth to enforce collective bargaining and insure union elections without management interference. Alfred Sloan condemned the Wagner Act as "most unfair and one-sided"; it would, he predicted, "promote the exploitation of the American worker for the benefit of a comparatively few professional labor leaders. . . ."

The passage of the Wagner Act and Roosevelt's sweeping re-election victory in 1936 set the stage for a showdown between labor and the auto industry. John L. Lewis, a leader of the Committee for Industrial Organization, newly formed to seek unionization in the mass-production industries, was confident that the President "would hold the light" while the unions "went out and organized." There was no doubt that the government, through the NLRB, had established the vehicle by which trade unionism might come to Detroit. There was also no doubt that the great auto manufacturers were going to fight unionism tooth and nail with all the considerable power at their command. This would be an all-out war, one in which the worker was the soldier in the trenches who would have to win it for himself.

A major weapon employed by the companies in their war on unionism was the labor spy. The most notorious spy system was operated by the innocuously named Ford Service Department, whose thuggish director, Harry Bennett, instituted a literal reign of terror at River Rouge. Bennett's "standing army" was made up of men as thuggish as he. "They're a lot of tough bastards," he said, "but every goddam one of them's a gentleman." Any Ford worker exhibiting the faintest tinge of union sentiment was summarily fired and stood a good chance of being roughed up in the bargain by Bennett's gentlemen. Less blatant in method but no less effective was the General Motors spy network. A congressional committee headed by Senator Robert M. La Follette, Jr., charged G.M. with operating

"the most colossal super-system of spies yet devised in any American corporation." Documents obtained by the La Follette Committee indicated that over a two-and-a-half-year period in the mid-thirties the company had employed at least fourteen detective agencies at a cost of $1 million; the well-known Pinkerton agency, for example, counted General Motors its number-one industrial client. So many spies infested G.M. plants on the look-out for union activities that they trod on each other's toes. The worker, the committee concluded, lived in constant fear: "Fear harries his every footstep, caution muffles his words. He is in no sense any longer a free American."

In this shadowed atmosphere the union that would carry labor's banner against the auto industry, the CIO-affiliated United Automobile Workers, took root. The UAW chose as its target General Motors. Go after the giant first, it reasoned, and the rest of the industry would have to conform. The main point of attack would be Flint, Michigan. Flint, once Billy Durant's home base, was a G.M. town, the key production center for both Chevrolet and Buick. Of the 47,200 G.M. workers in Flint, some 10 per cent were enrolled—most of them secretly—in UAW Local 156. It was a small army to do battle with a giant, but the UAW was about to employ a powerful weapon—the sit-down strike.

The sit-down tactic, an importation from Europe, had been tried pre-

Storm Troops at Ford

There are about eight hundred underworld characters in the Ford Service organization. They are the Storm Troops. They make no pretense of working, but are merely "keeping order" in the plant community through terror. Around this nucleus of eight hundred yeggs there are, however, between 8,000 and 9,000 authentic workers in the organization . . . who have been browbeaten into joining this industrial mafia. There are almost 90,000 workers in River Rouge, and because of this highly organized terror and spy system the fear in the plant is something indescribable. During the lunch hour men shout at the top of their voices about the baseball scores lest they be suspected of talking unionism. Workers seen talking together are taken off the assembly line and fired. Every man suspected of union sympathies is immediately discharged, usually under the framed-up charge of "starting a fight," in which he often gets terribly beaten up.

Harry Bennett's power extends beyond Dearborn. . . . Judges and other State officials cannot run for office without a petition. . . . Bennett simply puts such petitions on the conveyer belt, and in one afternoon the prospective candidate has all the signatures he needs.
—Benjamin Stolberg, *The Story of the CIO,* 1938

Scenes from the sit-down strike phenomenon that revolutionized labor relations in the auto industry. At left, strikers take their ease in G.M.'s Fisher Body plant in Flint, Michigan, early in 1937. Below is the struck Dodge plant. The UAW's women's auxiliary (bottom) turned out to support the strike and call for equal pay.

viously by American labor, but against General Motors it received its trial by fire. Although it was of dubious legality — and would later be branded an unconstitutional violation of property rights by the Supreme Court — the UAW regarded it as the only possible counterweight to the company's union-breaking stance. In a sit-down, rather than walking off the job the strikers barricaded themselves inside the factory, holding valuable company machinery hostage against any attempt to remove them by force. On December 30, 1936, UAW sit-downers seized two Fisher Body factories in Flint. With these key plants, plus a third Fisher Body plant in Cleveland shut down two days earlier, the union was in a position to cripple General Motors, notably its Chevrolet and Buick divisions. Chevrolet was G.M.'s bread, Buick its butter.

The company promptly secured an injunction against the strikers, only to squelch it in embarrassment when the Flint judge who issued it was discovered to be the owner of $220,000 worth of G.M. stock. A second injunction was also ineffectual; its threatened penalty of $15 million was so ludicrously high as to be unenforceable. "If the judge can get fifteen million bucks from us," a striker remarked, "he's welcome to it." On January 11, 1937, Flint police attempted to recapture one of the struck plants. The strikers met guns and tear gas with such "popular ammunition" as

fire hoses, rocks, bottles, and heavy auto-door hinges. When the furious conflict finally ended, more than a score of persons had been injured, fourteen of them by police bullets, and the attackers were routed. The strikers derisively termed it the Battle of the Running Bulls. Michigan governor Frank Murphy dispatched the state national guard to Flint. Vowing never to be known as "Bloody Murphy," he ended any further threat of force against the workers. The strike, he insisted, must be settled at the bargaining table.

The company instead took its case to the public. Charging "widespread intimidation," Alfred Sloan defined what he saw at stake: "Will a labor organization run the plants of General Motors . . . or will the Management continue to do so?" It was repeatedly asserted that a small minority of strikers was depriving an overwhelming majority of contented workers of paychecks. It was also frequently charged that the sit-down was a "Red plot." Communists were indeed prominent in the strike, but, as Sidney Fine points out in his definitive volume Sit-Down, "it would be a mistake to interpret the strike as a Communist plot or to assume that the Communists and their friends pursued policies that conflicted importantly with the organizational interest of the UAW." G.M. circulated petitions and convened mass meetings to promote its position. Any hopes the company had for its public-pressure cam-

paign, or for resuming limited production, were dashed on February 1 when the sit-downers suddenly seized a third plant in Flint, one that produced all of Chevrolet's engines. As reluctantly as a "skittish virgin" (in Fortune's phrase), General Motors went to meet the UAW at the collective bargaining table.

The negotiations lasted more than a week, with Governor Murphy the chief mediator. Finally, on February 11, 1937, the strike's forty-fourth day, a settlement was announced. Few grievances were actually resolved, but on the key issue, the right of the UAW to be the workers' exclusive representative, the union won the day. "Even if we got not one damn thing out of it other than that," a worker exulted, "we at least had a right to open our mouths without fear."

In Sidney Fine's view, "The GM sitdown strike of 1936–37 was, all in all, the most significant American labor conflict in the twentieth century." The fortress had been breached, the unionization of the great mass-production industries begun. In April, after a sit-down, the Chrysler Corporation made its peace with the UAW. One by one the other auto makers fell into line — all except Ford.

"We'll never recognize the United Automobile Workers Union, or any other union," said Henry Ford. "We will bargain until Hell freezes over, but they won't get anything," added Harry Bennett. They were whistling in the dark. The Ford Motor Company

The Battle of the Overpass, May 26, 1937: on the facing page, a Ford strong-arm squad approaches union organizers and leaders (from left) Robert Kanter, Walter Reuther, Richard Frankensteen, and J. J. Kennedy outside River Rouge. Suddenly the UAW men were set upon and severely beaten; Frankensteen is the victim in the picture at the left. The attackers also pursued the press cameramen present, but enough of their photographs survived to receive prominent display in newspapers and national magazines.

was fighting a rear-guard action against the law of the land as spelled out by the National Labor Relations Board, and the outcome was foreordained. It was not a graceful retreat. In May, 1937, on an overpass leading to the Rouge plant, a group of UAW organizers that included union leaders Walter Reuther and Richard Frankensteen were passing out leaflets when they were systematically and brutally beaten by a gang of company thugs. The public outcry over the Battle of the Overpass went unheeded. The union-breaking tactics of Bennett's Service Department "storm troopers" became more repressive than ever. Internal power struggles on both sides prevented compromise. At Ford a war of succession raged between Bennett, production chief Sorensen, and Edsel Ford. The UAW was similarly rent by leadership battles.

Finally, in May, 1941, the NLRB forced a union election on the company. Rouge workers voted in the UAW by a two-to-one margin. The nonunion vote was a mere 2.6 per cent, a figure that profoundly shocked Henry Ford. He had believed to the end that his men's sentiments were nonunion. He abruptly threatened to shut his plants rather than sign a union contract, then just as abruptly reversed himself and not only signed but gave more generous terms than those granted by either General Motors or Chrysler. Probably the change of heart was forced on him by

his wife's threat to leave him if he did not end the labor war. After fifty-three years of marriage the auto magnate's beloved Clara was the one person he would listen to.

Henry Ford was the last of the first generation of auto captains still at the helm. The decade saw the deaths of, among others, James Couzens, John North Willys, Hudson founders Roy Chapin and Howard Coffin, Packard's Henry B. Joy, Studebaker's Albert Erskine, Henry Leland, Alexander Winton, and, in 1940, Walter Chrysler. Ransom Olds, Charlie Nash, and Billy Durant retired from auto making. In 1937 Alfred Sloan became G.M.'s board chairman, turning the presidency over to William Knudsen. Ford, however, clung stubbornly to his command, despite suffering two strokes. Those declining years were marked with tragedy, especially in his relationship with his son Edsel.

Edsel Ford possessed many of the qualities so conspicuously lacking in the elder Ford. He was compassionate, public-spirited, talented in administration and in automotive design, sensitive to the times in which he lived. His father, however, persisted in the totally mistaken belief that he lacked the toughness to run the company and turned more and more to the brutal Bennett, who was toughness personified. Edsel, the crown prince, was played off against Bennett, and both were played off against the hard-driving Sorensen.

The company drifted erratically, sometimes on the right course (in 1938 it finally challenged its competitors in the medium-priced field with the Mercury), sometimes off course (the embittering and pointlessly drawn-out battle with labor).

Edsel's health broke under the strain, and in 1943 he died. The cause of death, write Nevins and Hill, was "a complication of ailments: stomach cancer, undulant fever, and a broken heart." He was forty-nine. The son's death seemed to hasten the father's decline. Henry Ford sensed, Nevins and Hill continue, "that his own days were numbered. Like a great oak half-undermined by subterranean waters, he shook, careened to one side, and stood at the point of toppling." One era was ending, a new one about to begin.

All the while the auto industry was suffering these trials and dislocations, the auto culture was proving to be astonishingly "depression-proof." It was evident that the American people, whether out of necessity or a stubborn adherence to an accustomed way of life, ranked the family car high on their personal priority lists. During the thirties cars continued to outnumber both telephones and bathtubs in the United States, and if *Fortune* magazine is to be believed, more people used an automobile daily than a toothbrush. Will Rogers remarked that "we are the first nation in the history of the world to go to the poorhouse in an automobile."

Whatever the case, it was done by choice. The common man might be critical of Henry Ford for failing to reverse the Depression, but he embraced without complaint the car culture Ford had brought into being.

Particularly revealing are the statistics for automobile registrations. In 1932, Detroit's worst year, new-car production dipped to only 24.7 per cent of the 1929 high. That same year, registrations were 90.4 per cent of the 1929 figure. Following a further fractional decline in 1933, registrations began a slow upward climb, surpassing the previous high in 1936. Those who could not afford a new car kept their old ones running, and when they wore out, bought in the used-car market. Car use barely slackened. There was a slight fall (7 per cent) in gasoline consumption in 1932 compared to 1931, but then demand began rising once more. The level never fell below the 1929 figure. Gasoline, like food, shoes, or soap, was regarded as one of the necessities of life.

To be sure, numerous fluctuations were averaged out in these national figures. For the 18 per cent of the population living in suburbia, car use was well above the national average and growing. At the other end of the scale were rural dwellers, who were among the hardest hit by the Depression. Farmers' purchases of new cars plummeted from 650,000 in 1929 to 55,000 in 1932. Uncounted farm families put their cars up on blocks in barns and outbuildings because they had no money for gasoline or repairs. It was reported that in North Carolina old flivvers were truncated, hitched to mules, and derisively named "Hoovercarts." And not all Depression-era motoring included in the statistics was undertaken by choice. Some of the most searing visual images of the thirties are the photographs of the Dust Bowl dispossessed struggling westward in processions of old jalopies and dilapidated trucks toward the supposed milk and honey of California. For them, their vehicles were literal necessities of life; for the nation, their hegira was a frightening symbol of the breakdown of the system.

In 1935 sociologists Robert and Helen Lynd returned to Muncie, Indiana, and in *Middletown in Transition* renewed their examination of life in the average American community. They found few changes in the impact of the auto culture since their first study in the twenties. New-car sales in Muncie in 1932 were down seventy-seven per cent from 1929, but gasoline sales were down only four per cent. "The depression hasn't changed materially the value [Muncie] people set on home ownership," a local banker told them, "but *that's* not their primary desire, as the automobile always comes first." The Lynds concluded that the city's blue-collar families wanted "what Middletown wants, so long as it gives them their great symbol of advancement—an automobile. Car ownership stands to them for a large share of the 'American dream'; they cling to it as they cling to self-respect, and it was not unusual to see a family drive up to the relief commissary in 1935 to stand in line for its four-or-five-dollar weekly food dole." Among factory workers—half of Muncie's labor force was involved in the making of automotive parts and equipment—car ownership "symbolizes living, having a good time, the thing that keeps you working." "So long as they have a car and can borrow or steal a gallon of gas," a UAW organizer complained to the Lynds, "they'll ride around and pay no attention to labor organization; and if they can't get gas, they're busy trying to figure out some way to get it."

The car culture's transformation of the American scene continued unabated. In 1932 one Carl C. Magee of Oklahoma City applied for a patent on a parking meter (it was granted him four years later), and in 1935, in Massachusetts, one Howard Johnson had a string of roadside restaurants with distinctive orange roofs. The first drive-in movie theater went up in 1933. The number of gas stations rose steadily, nearly doubling (to 227,000) between 1929 and 1941. The "super service station" appeared. One of them in Cleveland covered two acres and cost half a million dollars to build; another, in Washington, had fifty-two pumps. Competition was fierce.

The number of tourist accommo-

(continued on page 263)

Arthur Rothstein photographed a determined farmer moving on in 1936.

THIRTIES CAR CULTURE

Beginning in 1935, under the aegis of the Farm Security Administration, a team of photographers directed by Roy E. Stryker compiled a powerful visual image of Depression-era America. This portfolio of FSA pictures focusing on the car culture suggests, even in that grim time, the nation's continued dependence on the automobile and the permanence of the elements that made up the highway landscape.

Russell Lee made the study above of a family of agricultural day laborers near Vian, Oklahoma, in 1939. A year later he visited an all-day community sing at Pie Town, New Mexico, where he recorded the lunch-time break (upper right). The vacationing couple enjoying a sea breeze close by their Oldsmobile were photographed at Sarasota, Florida, by Marion Post Wolcott in 1941.

The text on the car reads:

HANDLE THE GUNS
SEE CLAUD THORNTON'S CRIME MUSEUM
LIFE SIZE FIGURES OF THESE CRIMINALS & GUNMEN
FIRST TIME SHOWN IN THIS COUNT[RY]
ADMISSION 10¢
PRETTY BOY FLOYD (GEORGIA MAN) KILLED 100 MEN ROBBED 3000 BANKS
LEO FRANK - JOHN DILLINGER
BABY FACE NELSON - MA BARKER
BONNIE PARKER (TEXAS BAD WOMAN)
RICHARD BRUNO HAUPTMANN
WILLIAM EDWARD HICKMAN
HEAR THEIR HISTORIES EXPLAINED
SHOWING DOWN TOWN ALL WEEK
SEE THE G. MEN AND POLICE WHO CAPTURED AND KILLED THE[M]

Even in hard times car ownership continued to reflect individuality. The labeled Tin Lizzie opposite was spotted in Louisville, Kentucky, by Marion Post Wolcott in 1940, the derisive radiator cap in Laurel, Mississippi, by Russell Lee in 1939. The mobile billboard promoting Thornton's traveling side show was photographed near Fort Bragg, North Carolina, by Jack Delano.

One of the assignments Roy Stryker gave his FSA staff was the depiction of roadside America. Wolcott took the photograph of the novel tourist court at upper left in Bardstown, Kentucky, in 1940. Ben Shahn found the highway gas station and sandwich shop at lower left in Ohio in 1938; the figure had once been a roadside sign that invited tourists to visit a local Indian burial mound. Walker Evans's study of the Cherokee Garage in Atlanta dates from 1936.

In the thirties the gas station was at
center stage in small towns. Dorothea Lange
memorialized the Fourth of July, 1939, in a
village near Chapel Hill, North Carolina.

dations, too, grew without pause during the Depression until they became a commonplace fixture of roadside America. In 1934, in *It Happened One Night*, Clark Gable and Claudette Colbert titillated movie audiences by posing as a married couple and sharing a tourist cabin; nothing untoward happened, of course. Nevertheless, the fact that such liaisons could, and did, take place in real life did not go unremarked. A study of tourist courts around Dallas, conducted in 1936 by a team of sociologists at Southern Methodist University, concluded that "the growth of these institutions and their toleration by the community are evidences of a changed public attitude toward non-marital intimacies." No such calm assessment would do for J. Edgar Hoover, head of the Federal Bureau of Investigation. The tourist court, he wrote in outrage, is "a new home of disease, bribery, corruption, crookedness, rape, white slavery, thievery, and murder." In 1940, when Hoover issued this indictment, there were some fourteen thousand tourist courts nationwide. There were also fifty thousand tourist homes, presumably under better management.

The scope of highway businesses rapidly broadened beyond simply accommodating and feeding tourists and servicing their cars. Most common were stands displaying farm produce, but there seemed to be no limit to the variety of other roadside offerings. The result was a "transcontinental bazaar," writes Lloyd Morris in *Not So Long Ago*. The motorist was importuned to buy "lawn furniture, 'artistic' weathervanes, sundials and garden sculpture, assorted antiques, boxes of nuts assembled from the ends of the earth, golf hats and clubs, fish-worms and tackle, picture postcards of places he had passed without seeing, domestic pets." The highway blight was spreading fast.

Observing such vistas, some commentators concluded that half the population was made up of tourists and the other half of purveyors of tourist services. In fact, nearly all those who could afford a vacation during the depressed thirties went by car, and their number rose from 45 million in 1929 to 52 million in 1937 — if not half the population, at 40 per cent not that far from it. The Automobile Club of Southern California remarked on the continued brisk sale of its touring guides even in 1932, and it was estimated in the mid-thirties that Americans spent nearly 5 per cent of their income on auto vacations. The national parks were the single most popular vacation attraction, and by 1941 total park attendance had topped the 21 million mark. The overwhelming majority of visitors arrived by automobile.

The car culture, as we have seen, flourished in proportion to the quality of the nation's road network. This was very much the case in the thirties. Despite the economic collapse, the American road received an overhaul. This seeming paradox is explained by two factors — the American motorist's determination to "drive as usual" straight through the Depression, thereby keeping the gasoline-tax coffers full; and the New Deal's equal determination to put the jobless to work.

Between 1929 and Pearl Harbor, yearly receipts from the gasoline tax more than tripled, reaching almost $1.4 billion. By driving more, motorists accounted for something over half of this increase. They paid the balance in higher state gas-tax rates and in a new federal gasoline tax, imposed in 1933. (The gasoline tax was, in fact, one of the nation's very few depression-proof revenue sources. Faced with shrinking receipts, many states could not resist the temptation to dip into the gas tax to bolster their general funds.) The other major share of the highway-construction funds flowed, and flowed freely, from Washington. The total came to $4 billion in the first ten New Deal years.

There was a checkered pattern to this massive effort. As John B. Rae observes in his important study *The Road and the Car in American Life*, "The most regrettable omission . . . was that nothing was done at the national level to begin work on a system comparable to the present interstate highways." What was lacking was a coherent national highway policy, yet what was required to activate such a policy was probably impossible within the grim realities of the Great Depression.

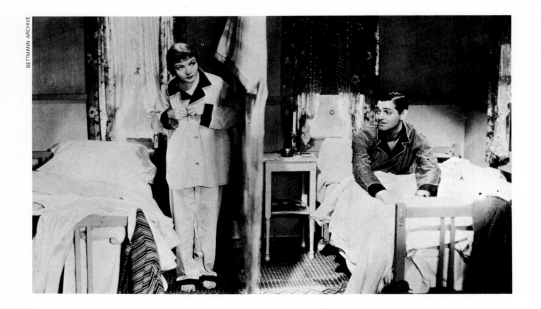

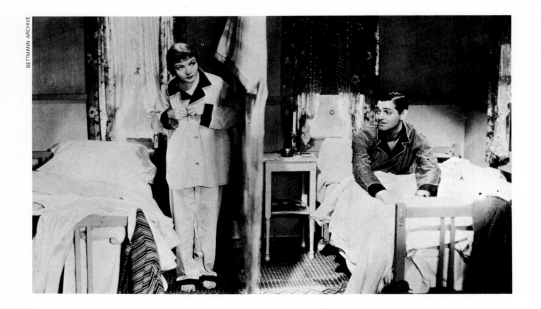

Roadside America comprised a good part of the setting for *It Happened One Night,* the award-winning 1934 film by Frank Capra. In its most famous scene, Claudette Colbert and Clark Gable, both single, shared a tourist cabin; a blanket on a clothesline (the "Wall of Jericho") served to make it all uncensorious. The movie might have played at the first drive-in (opposite), erected in 1933 at Camden, New Jersey.

No more pressing human need confronted the Roosevelt administration when it took office in 1933 than the plight of the jobless. One answer to the crisis was "make-work" projects at the local level that employed the maximum number of people, especially projects with more lasting social benefit than raking leaves or washing courthouse windows. As a consequence, a great many county roads were blacktopped and a great many wooden secondary-road bridges were replaced by concrete structures. For the first time, urban routes became eligible for renewal through federal financing. A variety of agencies supervised these efforts—the Public Works Administration, the Works Progress Administration, the Civilian Conservation Corps, the Tennessee Valley Authority—and without question they produced many benefits. The mileage of paved roads more than doubled between 1933 and 1941. The task, begun in the twenties, of extracting the American farmer from the mud was finally all but finished. Innumerable urban highways were rebuilt to handle modern traffic loads. Access roads were constructed in national parks and other public recreational areas. And perhaps most important in the context of the times, family breadwinners received paychecks when their need was most desperate.

There was, to be sure, a certain amount of political expediency in such locally oriented programs. Their primary purpose was public relief. In 1939, for example, four fifths of all federal highway funding fell into the "relief and recovery" classification, a category that accounted for forty per cent of *all* highway spending, federal, state, and local. "There would undoubtedly have been an outcry against spending money on superhighways," Rae writes, while local unemployment was high and the need for local improvements obvious. In the affluent twenties Americans had been persuaded of the need for such interstate routes as the Lincoln Highway; in the crisis-ridden thirties, they reverted to the old dogma of local roads for local needs. Thus no modern multilane arterial highway network—comparable, say, to the *autobahnen* system built by Nazi Germany—emerged during the New Deal years. Such a project would have to wait for a more affluent society, for a second return to "normalcy."

The thirties, however, were not barren of precedents for the shape of road travel in the future. The impetus came not from Washington but from the state and local level. What was then the world's longest suspension span, the George Washington Bridge, was completed across New York's Hudson River in 1931. Another Hudson crossing, the Lincoln Tunnel, was opened in 1937. (The neighboring Holland Tunnel, the first underwater vehicular tunnel anywhere, had been opened a decade earlier.) Among other thirties' engi-neering spectaculars were San Francisco's Bay and Golden Gate bridges, completed in 1936 and 1937 respectively. Like the Lincoln Tunnel, they leaned heavily on federal financing.

The concept of limited-access "motorways," as they were first called, also advanced several important steps in the Depression years. The initial step had been taken in New York during the twenties when a seventy-five-mile-long metropolitan parkway system was laid out through Westchester County suburban areas adjacent to New York City. So impressed was Lewis Mumford by such "townless highways" that in 1931 he and Benton Mackaye wrote in *Harper's* of a day to come when a motorist could drive "with less anxiety and more safety at 60 miles an hour than he used to have in the old road-town confusion at 25." When that fine day arrived, the automobile would be "an honor to our mechanical civilization and not a reproach to it." (For Mumford the day never came, and he would become one of the car culture's severest critics.)

Inspired by New York's system, and linked to it, was Connecticut's Merritt Parkway, built in 1934–37. A later extension, the Wilbur Cross Parkway, nearly doubled the Connecticut motorway's length, to sixty-seven miles. The Public Works Administration aided in financing construction. The purpose of the Merritt-Wilbur Cross was to relieve the fearsome conges-

tion on the Boston Post Road (U.S. Route 1), which made its tortuous way through the hearts of Connecticut's coastal cities. Both intercity and local auto travelers—commercial traffic was banned—enthusiastically welcomed America's first limited-access, high-speed toll road. Among other precedents, the Merritt-Wilbur Cross route established high standards—unhappily, not always honored by later highway designers—for roadside and median landscaping and for architecturally pleasing related structures, such as the cross-over bridges that carried local traffic. In 1940 Los Angeles took *its* first step into the motoring future by constructing the Arroyo Seco Parkway, later rechristened the Pasadena Freeway. It was the first urban freeway in California. Three years before, a traffic survey in metropolitan Los Angeles had revealed that the citizenry preferred auto travel to public transport by a four-to-one margin.

The prototype cross-country expressway was another Depression baby. In 1935 the Pennsylvania legislature authorized the construction of an east-west toll road the length of the state. The primary purpose was to create jobs, and ironically the project was considered feasible only because of a curious leftover from the buccaneering days of railroading. In the 1880's the Pennsylvania and New York Central railroads had engaged in a bitter power struggle, as one result of which

the Central laid out, graded, and bored nine tunnels for a rail line through its rival's prime territory in southern Pennsylvania. Before the line could be completed, a truce was enforced by financial baron J. P. Morgan—Morgan disapproved of such cutthroat competition—and the project was halted as part of the peace settlement. Fifty-two years later the abandoned right of way became the foundation of the Pennsylvania Turnpike.

The project nearly foundered at the starting gate. Turnpike bonds sold slowly because investors feared that a toll road would not attract enough traffic from nearby toll-free routes to be profitable. To complete the initial 160-mile section required $70 million in federal loans. The new limited-access, divided expressway quickly achieved a traffic flow that astonished even its strongest boosters. When the turnpike opened in 1940 traffic was predicted at an average of 715 vehicles a day; within two weeks it was carrying 26,000 a day. Truckers in particular found it attractive. They saved some 50 per cent in both fuel and time compared to previous routes, making their toll payments a highly profitable investment.

For those who had visited the popular General Motors "Futurama" exhibit at the New York World's Fair the previous year, the Pennsylvania Turnpike was an obvious step toward the world of tomorrow. Designer Norman Bel Geddes's Futurama revealed the

America of 1960: a landscape crisscrossed by nonstop, 100-mph turnpikes; great sparkling metropolises pierced by 14-lane expressways; teardrop-shaped cars fully air conditioned and costing a mere $200. There were no accidents, no traffic jams, no roadside clutter—and no parking spaces either.

Such a magical future suddenly seemed light years away as the threat of war shadowed the nation. The conflict in Europe and Asia daily grew more virulent. In the early months of 1940 the Roosevelt administration sought $4 billion in rearmament funds, and the nation began shifting from neutrality to nonbelligerency. "We must be the great arsenal of democracy," the President announced in a Fireside Chat on December 29. The task would be enormous; the Dutch collapse that spring had raised the United States Army one notch in world ranking—to nineteenth place. Yet modern war was reshaping the old adage that God was on the side of the big battalions. Now He seemed to favor the side with the big factories, and in that category the United States ranked first. At the theoretical center of the arsenal of democracy was the automobile industry.

Detroit, however, was exhibiting a reluctance to shift from civilian production to armaments production. Henry Ford took the high road of pacifism and neutrality—although he did grandly announce, in May, 1940, that "if it becomes necessary" his company could, within six months, "swing into the production of a thousand airplanes of standard design a day." Other auto makers quietly went ahead piling up car sales and profits while the demand held. They realized it was highly unlikely that auto production would be allowed to continue, as it had in 1917–18, if the nation went to war. The industry was still climbing out of the deep hole into which it had plunged during the sharp "Roosevelt recession" of 1938 —output fell to about half what it had been the previous year—and there was a determination to renew depleted profits. Car production in 1940–41 averaged 3.75 million, just 180,000 below the Depression high in 1937, and would have gone even higher except for a growing shortage of strategic materials. In 1941 General Motors earned the highest net income before taxes in its history.

It was not a case of the auto makers refusing to attempt to produce guns and butter simultaneously. They were reluctant to choose between the two, and butter was then far more profitable than guns. So long as the nation remained at peace, they shared the general big-business view that, in the words of historian Geoffrey Perrett, "the new arsenals should be built from scratch, alongside the consumer-goods economy rather than on top of it, and that government should pay for everything." The War Department, which was letting the contracts, seemed content with this solution.

Detroit was represented in Washington's highest councils during this period, most notably by G.M. president William Knudsen, who with labor leader Sidney Hillman headed the peacetime mobilization effort centered in the Office of Production Management. For all his production skills—almost single-handedly he had raised Chevrolet from the doldrums to sales leadership in the twenties—the bluff and unsubtle Knudsen was miscast in a role that required delicate priority juggling and highly political skills of persuasion. (Knudsen would perform far more usefully as a wartime production trouble-shooter for the War Department.) Yet perhaps the task was beyond solution by anyone. The OPM was an agency without authority, without a clear-cut policy. It was asking for voluntary compliance on the part of the auto industry (for example), which would result in a loss of profits and markets during peacetime. That might have been too much to expect of *any* industrialist beginning at last to see daylight at the end of the long Depression tunnel. In any event, when it was vaulted unexpectedly into war by Japan's attack on Pearl Harbor, the nation was far from ready to fight. To be sure, vitally important groundwork had been laid during the OPM period in such areas as retooling and new plant capacity, but the weapons themselves were not at hand.

The confidence with which most

Americans looked to Detroit to furnish the tools of war was nicely summed up fifteen days after Pearl Harbor in *Time*'s remark that "the U.S. need only step on the gas." It would not be that easy. The prewar failure to develop a comprehensive blueprint for the mobilization of the industry resulted in painful delays. "Aside from truck production," a congressional committee reported, "it is questionable whether as much as five percent of the existing automotive facilities of the industry have been used on [defense] contracts. Instead, many new plant facilities are still under construction. . . ." Yet in the end what has been justly termed a "production miracle," in Detroit and elsewhere, produced military hardware in a volume and a variety that astonished the nation, its allies, and its foes.

The miracle was essentially a big-business achievement. "We are going to have to rely on our great mass production industries for the bulk of our increase under the war program," Donald M. Nelson, the new "czar" of war production, announced in January, 1942. America's total manufacturing output in 1940 had been divided in a 30–70 ratio between the 100 largest firms and some 170,000 smaller ones; by March, 1943, the output had doubled and the ratio was exactly reversed. At the top of the list stood the auto industry. General Motors was by far the largest wartime defense producer, fulfilling contracts almost double the value of

The most popular exhibit at the New York World's Fair of 1939 was G.M.'s Futurama, by industrial designer Norman Bel Geddes. Below is a scale model of the turnpike of the future (1960), with controlled-access interchanges, complete lane separation, and radio-regulated, 100-mph traffic. When it opened the next year, the Pennsylvania Turnpike (left) demonstrated that the future was now, if in a less ambitious form.

those of second-place Curtiss-Wright aircraft. Ford held third place, Chrysler eighth. The Little Five independents also made massive contributions to the war effort. It was the combination of plant capacity, production and management know-how, strong credit lines—and effective lobbying—that made the great corporations the favored choices for defense orders. And the device of the "cost-plus" contract insured that the jobs would get done, for the sure-fire incentive was money. As historian John Morton Blum notes, cost-plus "guaranteed large profits without risk."

For two months after Pearl Harbor automobile production continued at its usual pace while mobilization plans were hastily formulated. On January 30, 1942, the last Chevrolet rolled off the line, on February 10 the last Ford, and the great plants momentarily fell silent. Most of this two-month output was impounded by the government and parceled out during the war years on a priority basis—to defense officials, country doctors, and the like. Anyone who acquired a 1942-model car before or after Pearl Harbor was regarded with envy by his neighbors.

Retooling was completed most quickly for the production of trucks and other military vehicles. More challenging was the adaptation of automotive technology to the building of complex aircraft engines, either by utilizing existing facilities or by throwing up entire new plants, such as the huge government-built Dodge factory near Chicago for the production of B-29 Superfortress engines. Detroit also undertook to manufacture a highly varied list of war materiel that had little relation to auto making, such as aircraft, munitions of every sort, cooking pots, life rafts, sandbags, and binoculars, to name only a handful. Such variety was by no means limited to the resource-rich Big Three. Hudson, for example, turned out landing-craft engines, machine guns, anchors for naval mines, and aircraft subassemblies for the Curtiss Helldiver, B-29, and Bell Airacobra. When the totals were added up in 1945, it was found that the auto makers and their prime subcontractors had turned out $29 billion worth of the tools of war, one fifth of American industry's entire output.

Everything imaginable was adapted to assembly-line production. In a one-time cornfield outside Detroit, Chrysler operated a massive factory with an assembly line a third of a mile long for the production of Sherman tanks. The Swedish-designed Bofors and the Swiss-designed Oerliken were the finest rapid-fire antiaircraft weapons in the world, but before Detroit got hold of them they were expensive and, more important, their production was limited by extensive hand-crafting. Chrysler engineers completely revamped Bofors manufacture into a step-by-step mass-production mode

so that a gun that had taken the Swedes 450 man-hours to build could be turned out by a relatively unskilled work force in 10 hours. The Pontiac division of General Motors performed the same sort of radical surgery on Oerliken production techniques, greatly increasing output while cutting the cost per gun by almost a quarter.

The Jeep is something of a case study of the role of big business in the arsenal of democracy. In 1940 the army had asked auto makers for bids on a light four-wheel-drive scout car, and in just over eight weeks the immortal Jeep was born. (The name seems to have been a GI invention, most likely stemming from the car's General Purpose, or G.P., designation.) The design was submitted by the American Bantam Car Company of Butler, Pennsylvania, a nearly moribund builder of the tiny Bantam subcompact, and the army's evaluator called it "absolutely outstanding. I believe this unit will make history." So it did, but not under Bantam's banner. By the time contracts were let, Willys had developed a very similar design, although equipped with its own rugged four-cylinder engine, and it underbid Bantam. From 1941 to 1945 Willys, with a major assist from Ford, turned out some 650,000 Jeeps. Tough, durable, ubiquitous, the Jeep became the battlefield symbol of American know-how. American Bantam's lone reward was the honor of creation; it built fewer than 3,000.

A prime symbol of American know-how on the home front was Ford's Willow Run bomber plant. It is not surprising that Willow Run should have captured the public's imagination. For one thing, it was immense, "the damndest colossus the industrial world has ever known," said columnist Westbrook Pegler; for another, it promised to turn out big four-engine bombers, B-24 Liberators, on a moving assembly line at a pace that boggled the mind; and for a third, it was presided over by Henry Ford. "The nation had come to expect production miracles from Ford as routine," *Business Week* commented in February, 1942. "When Henry went to war—well, Berlin was the next stop." Willow Run *did* produce a production miracle, but only after more than its share of agonizing delays and bitter conflicts.

Under the driving direction of Charles Sorensen, ground was broken for the bomber plant along little Willow Run creek, thirty miles from Detroit, in April, 1941. The cost, eventually to reach $65 million, was borne by the government. On the eve of America's entry into the war the partially finished factory was producing some bomber parts. During the grim days of frequent military reverses in 1942, public hopes were brightened by reports that "soon" B-24's would be pouring out of Willow Run in "unbelievable" and "unprecedented" numbers. In fact, the first "flyaway" Liberator did not appear until Sep-

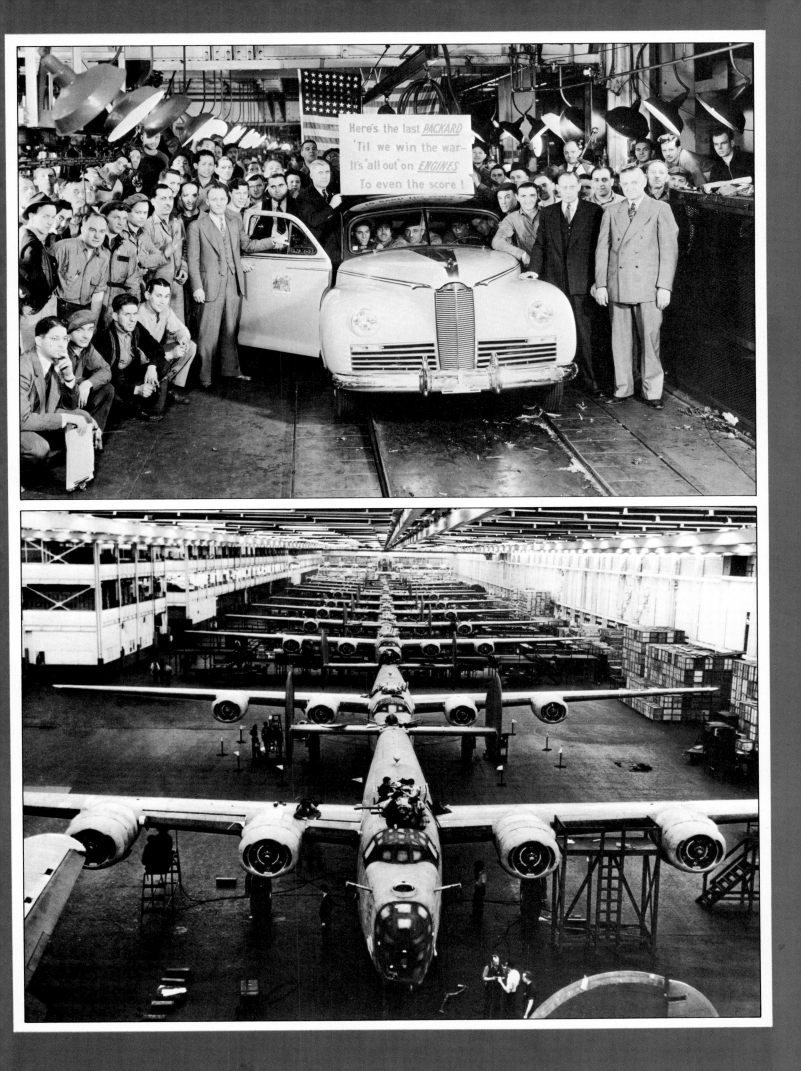

tember, and total production in 1942 was only fifty-six. Criticism mounted. J. H. Kindelberger, the outspoken president of North American Aviation, took aim at the " 'great and god-fearing' automobile makers" for their lack of know-how in aircraft building. "You cannot expect blacksmiths," he said of the Ford operation, "to learn how to make watches overnight." Across the country Willow Run began to be called "Willit Run?"

There was some merit in Kindelberger's charges. Sorensen and other Ford experts badly underestimated the difficulties of producing something as complex as a heavy bomber on a moving assembly line. Too, they were plagued by high labor turnover (the plant was a two-hour round-trip commute from Detroit, and its on-site wartime housing was as bad as any in the country), poor public relations, and plain mismanagement. For a time in 1943 the government considered deposing the failing Henry Ford and taking over the running of the plant.

During the latter half of 1943, however, the situation was sorted out and output grew rapidly. In 1944 the rosy promises came true at last, two years after they were made. Liberators began rolling out of the factory at the rate of one per hour. Their cost was slashed 40 per cent, to $137,000 per plane. At last Willow Run was "Superplant," "one of the world's great monuments of production genius." The wartime output tally was 8,685 B-24's. The blacksmiths had finally learned to make watches.

World War II had meanwhile put a severe crimp in what the 1941 owners of 29.6 million cars regarded as (to quote journalist Richard R. Lingeman) "every American's sacred right to drive an automobile as fast and as far as he liked." For the most part they took the shock with good grace. After all, went the saying, there was a war on. Never in its history had the nation been so unified in a single objective: to get the war over with whatever the cost. If their auto-oriented way of life had to suffer in the process, the large majority saw the sacrifice as necessary and proper.

It would take some getting used to, however. The one comparable experience had been in the depths of the Depression, when economic deprivation put new cars out of reach, but even then the right to drive one's old car was never in jeopardy. Now, by government edict, there were no new cars at all; and worse, heavy restrictions were about to be placed on car use.

The problem was tires. Japanese victories in the Far East had deprived the United States of ninety-seven per cent of its prewar rubber supply. Stockpiled rubber at the time of Pearl Harbor totaled about one year's peacetime supply, which was promptly earmarked for military use.

The Last Chevrolet

It was snowing that afternoon in Flint, Michigan. . . . At 3:18 P.M. a few men stood around a new black Chevrolet coupe in Assembly Plant Number Two. Someone with a sense both of drama and of history had scrawled on its rear window in white chalk: *last Chevrolet off Jan. 30, 1942.*

A reporter and a veteran Chevrolet workman climbed into the car. The reporter stepped on the starter, drove off the assembly line, turned the lights on and off, honked the horn. The strident little beep, echoing through the acres of suddenly silent machinery, signaled the end of an epoch in U.S. industrial history. . . .

A passing workman gave the last Chevrolet an affectionate kick in the rear—as might a farmer slapping an old horse. They knew that a chapter in their life was over. Some current of emotion—half-abashed, self-conscious, a sentiment that seemed a little ridiculous when dedicated to inanimate machinery—moved through the crowd, finding its outlet in the horseplay, the offhand talk, the what-the-hells with which American workmen cover up what they feel.

It was the same at Dodge, at Plymouth, at Pontiac. Throughout the vast automobile industry . . . civilian manufacture had ended.
—*Time,* February 9, 1942

Although gasoline for essential trucking was not rationed, the rubber shortage was a primary cause of the forty-three per cent wartime decline in the volume of intercity freight carried by truck. John Vachon posed a truck driver under an exhortative poster in Lynchburg, Virginia, in 1943.

Production of synthetic rubber was pushed at top speed, but here again the military would be the primary customer. Early in 1942 strict rationing of new and recapped tires for civilian use was decreed by the Office of Price Administration. Only the most iron-clad priority could pry a new tire out of the OPA during the war years. An unknown wit captured the dilemma facing the average motorist:

1940 — No running boards
1941 — No gear shift
1942 — No tires
1943 — No car

In a burst of patriotism, many car owners donated their old tires, even their spare tires, to scrap-rubber drives, a decision they came to regret. (There was also a fad for donating car bumpers to scrap-metal drives, and a San Francisco judge made the papers by accepting bumpers as payment for traffic fines. The usual bumper replacements were pieces of two-by-six lumber.) Left to their own devices, however, motorists made little change in driving habits to save their tires. During 1942 car registrations fell by some 1.6 million, due in part to men going into the service and putting their cars up on blocks for the duration. Gasoline use per car fell only 13 per cent. Part of this drop was attributed to the gas rationing started in the Northeast in May, the result of the devastation by German U-boats of the tanker fleet supplying the region.

There could be no question of let-ting Americans run their tires down to the rims. A series of surveys indicated that for millions engaged in vital war production an automobile was as much of an essential as food and shelter. In southern California, center of the aircraft industry, the proportion of workers who had no other way to get to their jobs varied from seventy to more than ninety per cent. The average figure in heavily industrialized Michigan was seventy-five per cent. Similar results were obtained in surveys at other centers of war production. If the arsenal of democracy was to continue operating at top speed, the American motorist had to be saved from himself.

From the beginning universal gasoline rationing was seen as the only way to cut car use and preserve tires. This was sure to be an unpopular move politically, however, and the Roosevelt administration waffled on the issue for most of 1942. Finally, on December 1, nationwide gas rationing was instituted. As a further move to save tires, the national speed limit was cut to 35 mph. The rationing system administered by the OPA consisted of gas coupons and windshield stickers. The nonessential driver had to be content with an A sticker, entitling him to four (later three) gallons a week. War workers driving in car pools were typically awarded an extra-allotment B sticker. The high-allotment C sticker was for important officals, industrial executives, doctors, and the like. An X

sticker permitted unlimited car use; congressmen promptly voted themselves X stickers.

In *Don't You Know There's a War On?* Richard Lingeman defines the social stigma inherent in the system. "Obviously, if you were an A card holder," he writes, "you were a nobody — a nonessential who puttered about in his car on insignificant little errands while cars packed to the roof with joyriding war workers or large sedans driven by powerful men with mysterious connections blew carbon monoxide in your face." About half the car owners in the United States were important enough — or had connections enough — to rate B or C stickers from their local OPA boards. Primarily as a consequence of gas rationing, 2.4 million more cars were taken off the road in 1943 and 1944 (*Life* magazine printed detailed instructions for putting a car in dead storage), and car use dropped to sixty per cent of what it had been before Pearl Harbor.

Most of the nation experienced no problems in obtaining adequate gasoline within the rationing system. But in a few areas, notably the Northeast, there were times during 1943 when a driver clutching a handful of gas-ration coupons could find nowhere to use them. The continuing oil-tanker crisis left station pumps festooned with "Out of Gas" signs. It became a common sight to see tanker trucks being tailed on their delivery rounds by caravans of gas-starved drivers. In

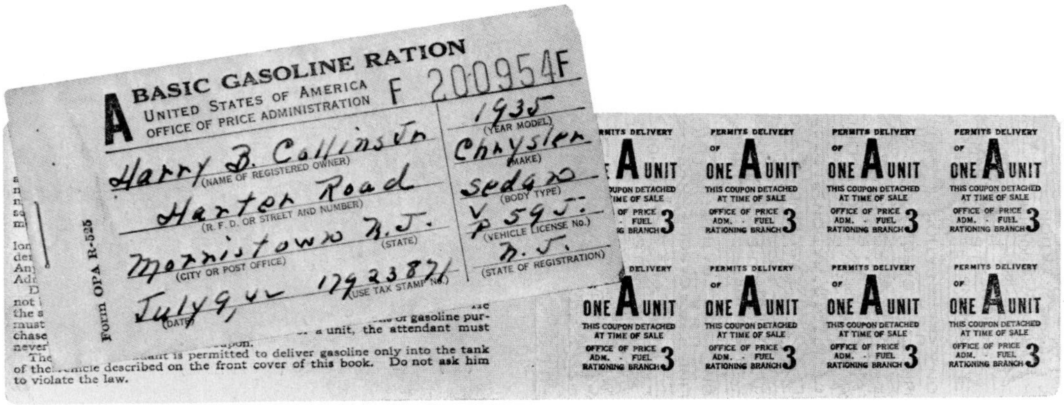
A
BASIC GASOLINE RATION
UNITED STATES OF AMERICA
OFFICE OF PRICE ADMINISTRATION
F 200954F
Harry B. Collins Jr
(NAME OF REGISTERED OWNER)
Harter Road
(R. F. D. OR STREET AND NUMBER)
Morristown N. J.
(CITY OR POST OFFICE)
(STATE)
July 9, 42
1792387
(USE TAX STAMP No.)
(DATE)
1935
(YEAR MODEL)
Chrysler
(MAKE)
Sedan
(BODY TYPE)
V P 595.
(VEHICLE LICENSE No.)
N. J.
(STATE OF REGISTRATION)
Form OPA R-525
of gasoline pur-
a unit, the attendant must
The attendant is permitted to deliver gasoline only into the tank
of the vehicle described on the front cover of this book. Do not ask him
to violate the law.
PERMITS DELIVERY OF ONE A UNIT
THIS COUPON DETACHED AT TIME OF SALE
OFFICE OF PRICE ADM. - FUEL RATIONING BRANCH 3

BROWN BROTHERS

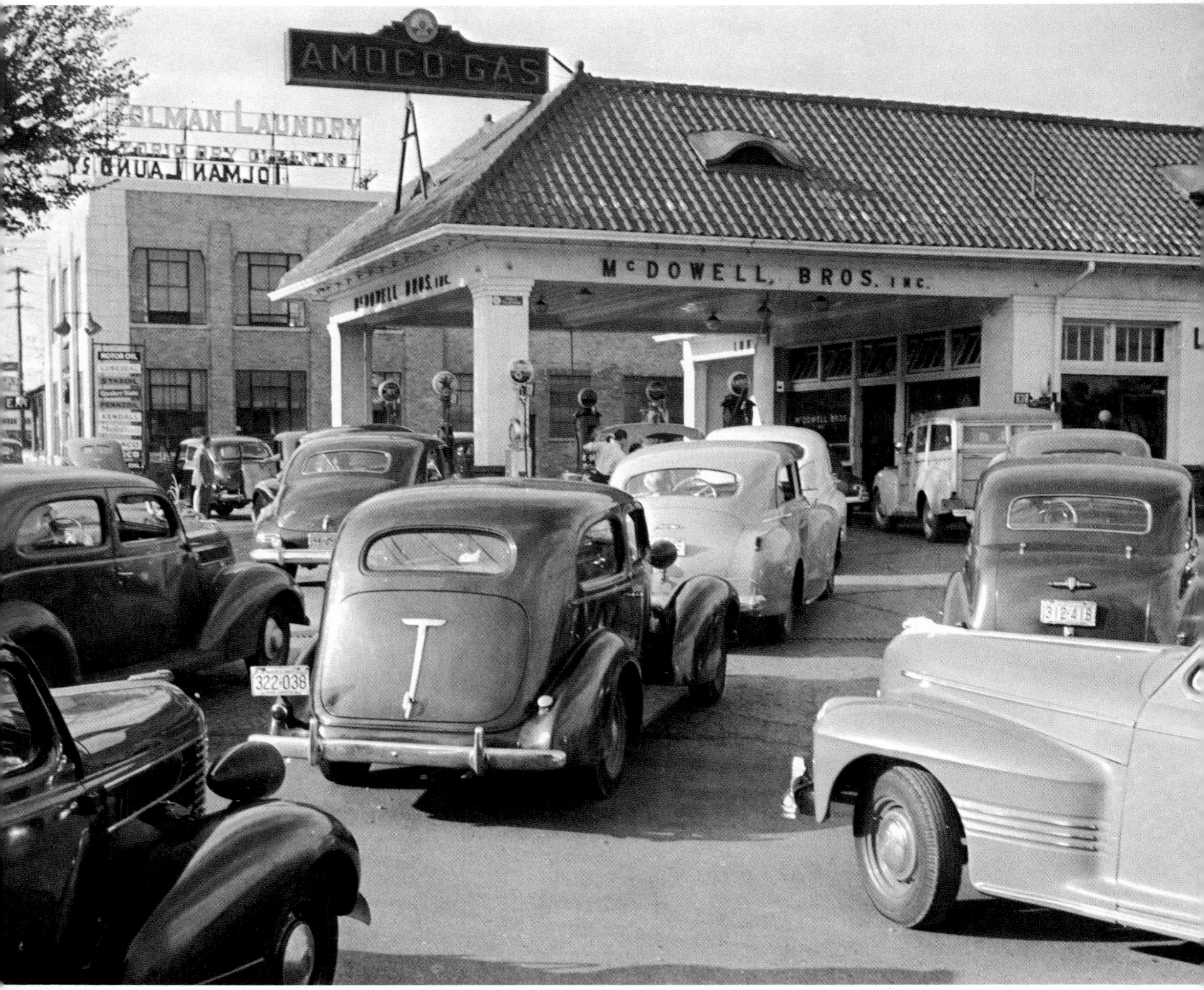
AMOCO GAS
OLMAN LAUNDRY
OLMAN LAUNDRY
McDOWELL BROS. INC.
McDOWELL, BROS. INC.
MOTOR OIL
322·038
312418

This picture was taken in the nation's capital in July, 1942, as motorists lined up to get their tanks filled on the day before local rationing began. Nationwide gasoline rationing went into effect the following December. The gas ration card and A coupons kept the 1935 Chrysler of Harry B. Collins, Jr., running—although slowly and not very far—during the war.

January, 1943, a total ban on pleasure driving was announced, and soon OPA inspectors were snooping around such places as the parking lots of race tracks, stadiums, and resort hotels trying to enforce it. They had little success, the plan came in for much justifiable criticism, and after nine months it was discontinued. Washington's bureaucrats had finally realized that a certain amount of recreation was a strong morale booster for war workers putting in long shifts and six-day weeks.

As a rule, people did not go far for their recreation or simply stayed at home. Many roadhouses and resorts closed for the duration. The national parks, which had counted more than 21 million visitors in 1941, had less than 7 million in 1943. Highways were all but empty. The Sunday drive was generally abandoned, as was driving at night in blackout areas. Courtship returned to the front parlor. To get where they were going people resorted to overburdened public transport, rode their old bicycles (new ones were rationed), or walked if they had to (shoes, too, were rationed).

The motorist's motto became "Make it do or do without." He patched and repatched his tires, drove slowly and carefully, and rejoiced when he was lucky enough to locate a used tire with some tread left on it. Sales of replacement parts soared—to $778 million in 1944—as old cars were cobbled together to last a few thousand more miles. Do-it-

yourselfers avidly turned to the Gus Wilson stories in *Popular Science* in hopes that the master mechanic and proprietor of the Model Garage would deal with one of the same problems plaguing them. Used-car dealers enjoyed a good war. Although used-car prices were regulated by the OPA, under-the-table dealing frequently raised the price of old clunkers to more than they had cost new. Home deliveries were heavily curtailed, and here and there milkmen resorted to horse-drawn wagons. A few old steamers were refurbished, if the kerosene could be found to run them, and once again little old ladies could be seen at the tiller of electrics, gliding silently past grounded A-card holders.

The majority of car owners, to repeat, accepted or were at least resigned to wartime restrictions on their accustomed way of life. But a minority did not, particularly during 1944 and 1945 when war weariness began to set in. Thefts of gasoline and tires became commonplace; young thieves once content to steal hubcaps from parked cars now stole tires from them. Those who had to park in the street often resorted to chains and padlocks to secure their precious tires. More typical was the flaunting of rationing and regulations by turning to the black market. Mr. Black also enjoyed a good war.

A black market was to be found in virtually every scarce or rationed commodity in wartime America, but probably none was more widespread than the one in gasoline. Collusion between the owner of the corner gas station and favored customers was common but fairly small scale—the occasional extra gallon, the occasional use of a friend's extra gas-ration coupon. More serious were the activities of professional criminals, both organized and free-lance. Counterfeiting C stickers and ration coupons was big business. OPA investigators estimated that fifteen per cent of all C stickers were forgeries, and that five per cent of all the gasoline purchased in the United States was done with counterfeit coupons. Outright thefts from OPA offices were frequent. One of the largest on record took place in a Washington OPA office, where coupons worth twenty million gallons of gasoline were stolen.

By 1945 the stuff of dreams for most people included a new car, a set of good tires, and a world without gas rationing. Like the young GI in the celebrated railroad advertisement "The Kid in Upper 4," they longed for "the feel of driving a roadster over a six-lane highway" in the world of tomorrow. And they had the money to make those dreams come true. Fat wartime payrolls had produced an unprecedented jump in personal income: $172 billion by 1945, an increase of sixty-eight per cent over the figure for 1939. When V-J Day came at last, on August 15, 1945, devotees of the car culture were primed for a tear.

7
AUTOMANIA

In the summer of 1945 the warfare in the Pacific reached fever pitch, but Detroit was looking ahead. "So nice to come home to!" exulted the headline of a Buick advertisement spotlighting a picture of a 1942 convertible. "No, the fighting isn't over," the copy admitted, but victory in Europe meant that the boys would soon be on the way home; "to many a fighting man, this will mean such pleasures as an open road, a glorious day—and a bright and lively Buick. The roads are here. The days come with each rising sun. And the bustle that now enlivens Buick's factories is the make-ready process for getting back into the production of cars. We aim to make those Buicks all that returning warriors have dreamed about —cars that from go-treadle to stop light will fit the stirring pattern of the lively, exciting, forward-moving new world so many millions have fought for. . . ."

Detroit may be excused for ranking its product alongside Mom and apple pie as worth fighting for. Auto makers confidently anticipated a postwar seller's market unmatched since the early days of automobiling. After fifteen years of economic deprivation and wartime austerity the car-buying public was in a splurging mood. This demand would trigger a national phenomenon deserving to be called *automania*.

At war's end there were 25.8 million cars registered in the United States, and *Fortune* reported that half of them were at least ten years old. Estimates of the number of clunkers overdue at the scrap yard ran as high as 8 to 10 million, and forecasters predicted a potential five-year new-car market of at least 20 million. (They were right on the mark; actual 1946–50 sales would be 21.4 million.) Orders piled up at dealers' showrooms faster than they could be counted. To be sure, Americans were short of a great many things on V-J Day—shoes, clothing, appliances, housing—but nothing was in greater demand than automobiles. The auto industry knew this, the United Automobile Workers knew this, and the Office of Price Administration knew this. As a consequence, the conversion to peacetime production had its chaotic moments.

Following Germany's defeat, Washington had authorized the building of 200,000 passenger cars during the remainder of 1945; with Japan's surrender it removed production ceilings entirely. To try to stem inflation, however, the OPA stipulated that car prices be held to 1942-model-year levels. Had the auto makers been able to resume full-scale production quickly this would have been a bearable hardship, but they could not. Detroit predicted a 1945 output of 500,000 cars; it built less than 70,000. The economies of scale disappeared. On a model whose price was pegged by the OPA at $728 Ford claimed it lost more than $300. Delays in re-establishing assembly lines and short-

CROISEMENT D'AUTOROUTES · LOS ANGELES, CALIFORNIE

DECOUVREZ UN NOUVEAU MONDE
VISITEZ LES ETATS-UNIS

The automobile-oriented postwar society traced distinctive patterns across America's landscape. Opposite is a factory parking lot outside Cincinnati. A Los Angeles freeway interchange locally celebrated as "The Stack" won ranking as a tourist attraction in a government travel-poster campaign directed toward foreign visitors.

ages of materials accounted for some of the production shortfall, but the primary difficulty was labor trouble.

Although their basic wages were frozen during wartime, auto workers had profited greatly from overtime pay, and the UAW was determined to hold those gains in the face of rising postwar prices. One walkout after another closed down key parts suppliers, and a bitter strike at General Motors in the winter of 1945–46 lasted 119 days. Auto production limped along in fits and starts. Not until the spring of 1946 was there a semblance of labor peace in Detroit, with the auto makers agreeing to a wage increase averaging about 15 per cent.

Those early postwar years saw the UAW grow to maturity. Between 1937 and 1941, it will be recalled, the UAW had won its war with the auto industry over the issue of union recognition, but unrest and confusion continued within its ranks. Now the union set its house in order. Under the vigorous leadership of Walter Reuther it purged itself of Communist elements and began speaking with a single voice, most notably by cracking down on wildcat walkouts that were in violation of contracts signed with the companies. In 1948–49 the UAW broke new ground in American labor relations by achieving wage packages tied to the cost-of-living index and worker productivity and by winning for its members company-financed pensions. Like the Ford

mass-production and the Sloan management revolutions that preceded it, this labor revolution of the late forties became a major force on the national scene. "Consciously or unconsciously," writes John B. Rae, "the American people had come to look on the automobile industry as the model for others to follow." The new look in labor relations came to be called "human engineering," a term originated by Walter Reuther and given currency by the new head of the Ford Motor Company, Henry Ford II.

There was symbolic significance in a Ford espousing the cause of human engineering; nowhere else had it been in shorter supply than at River Rouge. Intense interest was focused on this mightiest of industrial palaces and its new ruler.

Following Edsel Ford's death in 1943, the oldest of his three sons, twenty-six-year-old Henry II, was recalled from navy duty by government officials who feared the consequences of a war of succession at the nation's third largest defense contractor. Young Ford found himself set down in the middle of what *Life*'s Robert Coughlan would describe as "the Mad Hatter's tea party." Henry Ford, nearly eighty, slipping into senility, had resumed the company presidency upon Edsel's death, with the sinister Harry Bennett maneuvering at his side like a latter-day Rasputin. Bennett's first victim was his old rival, Charles Sorensen, whom he had

driven into exile by the end of the year. He then cast a suspicious, harassing eye on his new rival, the patriarch's grandson. "Nobody had any suggestions as to what I might do," recalled Henry II, "so I just moseyed around on my own, visited the plants, talked with fellows—trying to find out how things operated." He watched, learned, and waited.

Bennett's motives have never been fully stripped of the secretive cloak in which he wrapped them, but apparently he expected his failing patron to appoint him behind-the-scenes regent, where his iron grip on the Rouge would allow him to control any figurehead president. Bennett held a very strong poker hand, write Nevins and Hill, but "Henry II held all the aces—if he had the insight and nerve to play them." He had; and he had as well two powerful allies. His mother, Eleanor Ford, who now held forty-one per cent of the company stock, was an implacable foe of Bennett's. His grandmother, Clara Ford, was determined not to let her grandson be broken in a power struggle as her son Edsel had been. Young Henry played his aces, and the two Ford women devoted themselves to persuading old Henry to surrender the reins. At last, on December 21, 1945, it was done: twenty-eight-year-old Henry Ford II became president of the Ford Motor Company. His first official act was to fire Harry Bennett with the blunt rebuke, "I don't want you in my organization."

The strong sales of the all-new Ford designs for 1949–50 — in this publicity shot two stylishly turned out models admire a 1950 four-door — marked a major turnaround for the company, enabling it to recapture second ranking in the Big Three from Chrysler for the first time since the mid-Depression.

The elder Ford slipped quietly from public view. His once-sharp and inquiring eye was dimmed, his quicksilver mind dulled. He and Clara lived on tranquilly at his Dearborn estate, Fair Lane, and on April 7, 1947, his life flickered out. That day the flooding River Rouge had knocked out Fair Lane's power plant, and Henry Ford, the nineteenth-century man who had transformed the twentieth century, died in a room warmed by a wood fire and lighted by oil lanterns and candles. Uncounted eulogies and editorials attempted to assess the man and his works, but none was more incisive than the comment made by Will Rogers a dozen years before: "It will take a hundred years to tell whether he helped us or hurt us, but he certainly didn't leave us where he found us."

Despite a decade and more of neglect, the company Henry Ford II took over was by no means a foundering hulk. The crew might be demoralized and the navigation erratic, but as its overall excellent World War II production record demonstrated, the vessel was still seaworthy. It was in better condition, for example, than General Motors had been in 1920 when the Du Pont-Sloan regime displaced Billy Durant. Ford assets in 1945 totaled $815 million, and there was a massive cash balance of $697 million. The critical problem was future direction. While basically strong in production and sales, the company was woefully weak in design, engi-

neering, and financial management. After rooting out hundreds of Bennett's palace guards, Henry Ford set out on an executive talent hunt.

His biggest catch was Ernest R. Breech, who had come up through the General Motors ranks and was then head of Bendix Aviation. Although he was renowned as a trouble-shooter, Breech knew well Dearborn's reputation as a lion's den for executives and was reluctant to take a job there. Ford was persuasive, however, and his dispatch of Bennett and his cohorts had not gone unnoticed. "Well, here is a young man that is only one year older than our oldest son," Breech told his wife. "He needs help. This is a great challenge. . . . I hate to take on this job, but if I do not do it I will always regret that I did not accept the challenge." He took the post of executive vice president, Ford's right hand. Other key positions were filled and new management techniques set up in frank imitation of General Motors; G.M., Ford said simply, had "the outstanding automobile management." Ford also took on in a body ten bright young Harvard Business School-trained, ex-air force officers known collectively as the Whiz Kids, from whose ranks would eventually come six future Ford vice presidents and two presidents (Robert S. McNamara and Arjay Miller). The group leader, Charles B. "Tex" Thornton, would go on to found the huge Litton Industries conglomerate. Hiring the Whiz Kids was a prime ex-

ample of new-generation decision. Henry II's grandfather, who believed the only route to the top was the long climb up from the shop, would never have let them through the front door.

The next priority was a new design. Like the competition, Ford cars in the early postwar years were simply face-lifted 1942 models. Young Ford was determined to recapture the company's high ranking in the mass market with a fresh design. Normal model change lead-time was three years. Ford management believed it dare not wait that long. "We start from scratch," Breech announced. "We spend no time or money phoneying up the old Ford, because this organization will be judged by the market on the next car it produces, and it had better be a new one. So we'll have a crash program, as if in war time." The 1949 Ford was first shown to the public in New York's Waldorf Astoria Hotel in June, 1948. Except for the well-proven V-8 engine, it was all new virtually from the frame up, crisply styled, and for its era remarkably chrome-free. Here was the Ford of the new modern world, not just another disguised old prewar Ford that car buyers had been seeing for the last three years. It represented an investment of $118 million, and it had been produced in just nineteen months.

Such haste inevitably meant manufacturing slip-ups — one New England Ford dealer counted a consistent twenty-eight defects in the cars he was receiving, and a good deal of post-delivery repair and adjustment were required from dealers across the nation—yet for the first time in almost fifteen years there were smiles in Dearborn. The long slide was over. Sales of the new car were almost double those of the 1948 model, and in 1950 they topped one million, a figure not attained since Model A's heyday in 1930. Net income that year was $260 million, and the Ford Motor Company was back to stay in second place, ahead of Chrysler.

Ford's rejuvenation was the biggest news among the Big Three late in the forties. There was no comparable air of crisis in board rooms at General Motors or Chrysler. Well-organized and running smoothly, they could follow the comfortably conservative course of meeting the insatiable demand with warmed-over prewar models and not rushing fresh designs onto the assembly lines until demand slackened and car buyers had to be persuaded rather than simply lined up to accept gratefully anything the manufacturers wanted to offer them.

The biggest problem at both companies was restoring full production. At General Motors, for example, two months after settling the UAW strike in 1946 the company was still plagued by shutdowns at no fewer than 143 of its suppliers. "Repeatedly," writes economist Lawrence J. White, "the absence of items as seemingly trivial as seat cushion springs brought production lines to a halt." Despite such annoyances, these were good years financially. After strikes and reconversion tangles limited G.M.'s after-tax income to $87 million in 1946, profits began a steady upward march and topped $656 million in 1949. On the various scales used by economists to measure profitability, Chrysler did not lag far behind. In 1949 Chevrolet broke the one-million sales mark for the first time since 1927, and Plymouth sold more cars than it had ever sold before. And at long last, after twenty years, the industry as a whole exceeded its 1929 all-time record by producing more than 5.1 million cars.

The prewar Little Five became the Little Four in 1945 when Willys elected not to resume passenger-car production but to concentrate instead on a peacetime version of the Jeep as an off-the-road workhorse and recreational vehicle. Nash and Packard devoted most of their efforts to resolving production bottlenecks and taking profits in the seller's market, and they did not try to break any records in bringing out new designs. Hudson, however, chose to introduce an all-new car for 1948. Its "step-down" feature, the creation of designer Frank Spring, generated widespread comment. The floor was lowered flush with the bottom of the frame, enabling

---

One Man's Nash

The collective overriding postwar ambition of America, . . . once you got beneath the folderol about "building a better world" and "preserving lasting peace," . . . was a new automobile. The Gouldens' wish materialized one spring day in 1946, in the bulbous form of a maroon four-door Nash sedan, an off brand but the only car available.
. . .

Something about the Nash irritated father. The first day or so he spoke vaguely about its being "air-conditioned." . . . Summer came, but not the air-conditioning, no matter how Dad adjusted the dials. The Nash had a powerful fan out of sight under the dashboard, but the air didn't match the frigid, popcorn-scented gales that swept across the Saturday afternoon cowboy-double-feature crowds at the Lynn Theatre.
. . .

Later . . . I ran across an advertisement in a June 1946 issue of *Time* that supplied the missing ingredient to the story. The Nashes, the ad said, feature "the Nash *Eye* Conditioned Air System. . . ." Semantical flimflam, . . . and enough to beguile an East Texas appliance dealer who expected and *wanted* his postwar auto to have a modernistic feature, and was quietly mad when it did not.

—Joseph C. Goulden, *The Best Years: 1945–1950,* 1976

"Of course, the steering wheel costs $750, but we knock off fifty bucks for ex-soldiers." Cartoonist Bill Mauldin's GI anti-heroes Willie and Joe found it difficult to adjust to the harsh realities of the postwar auto market, particularly its used-car peddlers.

the roof to be lowered without loss of headroom. Long, sleekly aerodynamic with fenders fully integrated into the body, and low—it stood only five feet high—the step-down Hudson was a comfortable and roadworthy machine, and its sales of almost 144,000 were that marque's best since 1929.

One school of thought believed that the new Hudson presaged the automotive look of the future. Other commentators voted that distinction to the previous year's Studebaker. Automotive historian Maurice D. Hendry recalls that as a young man his first impression of the 1947 Studebaker Starlight "was that it must have flown in with Buck Rogers at the wheel." Although reflecting the influence of Studebaker's styling consultant, the celebrated industrial designer Raymond Loewy, the Starlight was principally the work of Virgil M. Exner. The great sweep of glass in the wraparound rear window gave the car the look of a greenhouse on wheels and inspired countless jokes about whether a Studebaker was coming or going; it was hoped that at least the driver knew. Exner's design was if nothing else an attention-getter—during its introduction in Chicago, police had to be called out to control the crowds—and sales were good. In 1948 Studebaker's share of the market exceeded a respectable four per cent and would remain above that mark through 1951.

Like Hudson, Studebaker was offering the American car-buying public a distinctive alternative to the products of the Big Three. This was the traditional credo of the independents, their *raison d'être,* and it seemed to be working. As a group, the independents captured eighteen per cent of the market in 1948 and fourteen per cent in the record-breaking year of 1949. These figures were well above their one-tenth market share in 1941. It was not known, however, how much of this sudden affluence was due to the special conditions of the seller's market, and the independents girded for the true test yet to come.

In any seller's market the buyer is less discriminating than he might otherwise be, and in the unique conditions of the late forties a car owner whose old machine was literally falling apart around him could not afford to be discriminating at all. He took whatever he could get. Demand far exceeded supply, and the response of many car dealers to this situation scarcely qualifies as their finest hour. The potential customer found a less effusive greeting at his local showroom than he had encountered in the prewar years when he last bought a car. In the first place, bargaining was out. The dealer took his full markup, offered little on a trade-in, and had nothing hopeful to say about quick delivery. Tawdry deals became commonplace. The buyer, for example, might have to take an array of unwanted accessories in order to get his car. Bribes

were freely solicited. An Oklahoma dealer was prepared to offer immediate delivery only on condition that customers also purchase his dog for $400; the dog "strayed" back to the showroom after each sale. Bribes were also freely offered. It is reported that one car-less customer grown desperate bet his local dealer $700 that he could hold his breath for three minutes; after pocketing the bet, the dealer suddenly discovered that he had a new car in stock after all. The end of OPA price regulations late in 1946 defused some of the more blatant abuses, but as late as 1948, Lawrence J. White reports, the "gray market"—in which new cars appeared on used-car lots—was still in vigorous operation, with a new Chevrolet, for instance, going for $700 above list price and a new Dodge for $500. Used-car dealers who had enjoyed a good war did as well or better in the first years of peace.

One further fact about a seller's market: it attracts new sellers. In 1945 and 1946 newspapers and the auto industry press were filled with announcements of the imminent birth of exciting new marques. There were prospectuses for full-size cars and mini-size cars, for three-wheeled cars and amphibious cars and flying cars with wings that unbolted and folded for storage in the back of the garage. Only three of these projects got much beyond the drawing board or prototype stage, and only one of them

A novel bit of Kaiser-Frazer promotion at
Willow Run. The bodies are entrained
for shipment to an assembly plant. In the
foreground are new Frazers. Kaiser-Frazer
turned out 838,000 cars in its decade
of life and lost $100 million in the process.

emerged as a serious challenger to the Detroit establishment.

The Crosley, a minicar in today's terminology, had actually been born in 1939, but the war intervened before it was properly launched. An offshoot of the Crosley Radio Corporation, Powell Crosley's little car was rather odd-looking but curiously appealing, and its hardy four-cylinder engine made it a snappy and economical performer. Crosley managed almost twenty-five thousand sales in 1948, but that was the peak. American car buyers were thinking big, not small. The marque expired in 1952, one more entry in the long list of right cars that appeared at the wrong time.

The Tucker Torpedo was a dream car personified. It was labeled the "Car of Tomorrow"—aerodynamic design, rear-mounted engine, independent suspension on all four wheels, disc brakes, doors extending into the roof for easy entry and exit, a third headlight that turned as the wheels turned, padded dashboard, pop-out windshield, and a host of other safety features—and all this to be delivered in 1948. A salesman par excellence, Preston Tucker aspired to create an automobile entirely free of what he considered Detroit's stodgy clichés. He leased the huge government-built plant in Chicago where Dodge had manufactured aircraft engines during World War II, raised money by selling dealer franchises and stock, launched a massive promotional ballyhoo, and produced a prototype and fifty demonstration models. Rumors that the car was nothing more than a glamorous pipe dream were laid to rest by Tom McCahill, a respected and often caustically critical automotive journalist. "The car is real dynamite!...," McCahill exclaimed. "I want to go on record right here and now as saying that it is the most amazing American car I have ever seen to date; its performance is out of this world. . . . It steers and handles better than any other American car I have driven. As to roadability, it's in a class by itself."

The Securities and Exchange Commission took a dimmer view of both the car and its creator. An SEC investigation resulted in charges against Tucker of thirty-one counts of fraud and theft in the promotion and financing of the Torpedo. A jury found him innocent, but not before newspaper headlines had tried and convicted him, and his dream was dead. "We were jobbed," he claimed, pointing accusing fingers at the Detroit establishment and at unjust government persecution. To be sure, Preston Tucker was a corner-cutter and not exactly a paragon of business virtue, but the evidence suggests that he deserved a better fate—or at least a better chance. The Tucker Torpedo became only a fascinating footnote in automotive history.

Henry J. Kaiser and Joseph W. Frazer in a combined effort came closer to winning a permanent place in the automobile line-up than either Powell Crosley or Preston Tucker. They made a strong run at it, and Richard M. Langworth has aptly titled his study of the Kaiser-Frazer phenomenon *The Last Onslaught on Detroit.*

Beyond a doubt, the two men began with strong credentials. Joe Frazer brought to the partnership a long and distinguished career in marketing that included tours of duty with Packard, General Motors, Pierce-Arrow, Chrysler, Willys, and Graham-Paige. Henry Kaiser was the most celebrated "get it done" industrialist of his day. He had built dams (Hoover, Bonneville, Grand Coulee), steel mills, cement plants, and during the war, ships in astonishing numbers. Kaiser had never built automobiles before—but then a few years earlier he had never built ships before, either. The partners acquired the Willow Run factory where Ford had turned out wartime Liberator bombers and in 1946 began turning out cars.

Their two lines—the Kaiser and the similar but more luxuriously appointed Frazer—did very well at first, and in 1947–48 K-F led all the independents in sales and earned a profit of almost $30 million. In 1949, however, the bloom began to fade from the seller's market, and car buyers took a more critical look at the two marques. What they saw were essentially conventional cars—albeit handsomely appointed and unusually comfortable—that were priced considerably higher than their competitors. Sales began to slip, losses mounted, and Joe Frazer left in exasperation over his partner's refusal to retrench. Kaiser plunged ahead, buying Willys, selling the Willow Run plant to G.M. and consolidating operations in the Willys factory in Toledo, and trying every imaginable innovation, but nothing seemed to work. The end came in 1955. Only the Willys Jeep survived the collapse.

The failure of Kaiser-Frazer is laced with irony. Good ideas were seeded in barren ground. Its cars were often distinguished in appearance — as Langworth writes, K-F "continued to astound observers with its persistent styling triumphs as it rode to oblivion" — but an era had begun in America when good taste did not sell. It stressed safety when car buyers had no interest in safety. K-F clung to its six-cylinder engine while the Big Three were promoting hot-performing V-8's. A pair of compact models, the Henry J and the Willys Aero, were introduced at a time when the bigger the car, the better it sold. In the last analysis, Kaiser-Frazer was unable to generate those two essentials for success in the auto business: buyer confidence and buyer loyalty. Americans entering the decade of the fifties were not inclined to try something new. Perhaps a Detroit automotive writer put it best when he viewed Kaiser's exceedingly handsome 1951 model and remarked, "If you'd slap a Buick nameplate on it, it'd sell like hotcakes."

In many respects the automania of the fifties bears comparison to the scene in the twenties. While there were two and a half times as many cars on the road in 1960 as in 1930, the problem of market saturation that Detroit had first encountered in the earlier decade returned to haunt it again. New car sales in 1960 (6.67 million) were only 9,000 greater than sales in 1950, and only once in the years between, in 1955, was a higher figure recorded. In this fiercely competitive no-growth marketplace the Big Three updated the same tactics developed late in the twenties — heavily promoted annual model changes, heavily merchandised appeals to what one observer called the car buyer's "dreams of sex, speed, power, and wealth." This costly competition made the decade another bad one for the independents.

As for the auto culture, the fifties generation embraced it with a fervor easily matching that of the twenties generation. There was the same enthusiastic acceptance of the automobile as an instrument of change — change in living patterns, in recreational habits, in social status. There was no pause in auto-fueled urban and industrial decentralization or in the rush to the suburbs. New shopping centers, new drive-in businesses, new highways, continued the alteration of the face of America to accommodate a nation of motorists.

In one important regard, the parallel between the twenties and the fif-

ties is not valid. By and large, the American motorcar of the 1920's represented honest value. At one end of the scale was the utterly practical and utilitarian Model T, at the other, the finely engineered and designed Olympian cars. Although styling assumed increasing importance toward the end of the decade, seldom was it indulged at the expense of engineering or safety improvements. In most cars of the 1950's, however, the honest-value quotient suffered a sharp decline.

In the highly competitive marketplace, the look of a car was deemed its most important sales feature. It would become fashionable among critics to condemn Detroit for following this line rather than the more "socially responsible" course of supplying car buyers with what was good for them — small, plain, economical, low-priced, practical transportation. With its enormous investment in the production and selling of cars, however, Detroit lived by an unwritten law: it followed the public's taste rather than taking the risk of being its arbiter. Motorists voted with their dollars, and just then they were electing size, weight, power, and ostentation. It did not escape the automobile industry's notice that in the mid-fifties big, gaudy, expensive Buick outsold little, plain, inexpensive Plymouth to move into third place in the sales race. In point of fact, the fifties was a period when the tasteless, the silly, and the excessive ruled supreme in

(continued on page 289)

Young car shoppers closely inspect a six-year-old Chevy on a Kansas used-car lot in 1958.

THE CAR CULT

Youthful fascination with the automobile dates back to the beginning of the auto era at the turn of the century, but in the period following World War II that fascination blossomed into a full-fledged cult activity. More youths drove, and more owned their own cars, than ever before. Some of what they did, where they went, and what the car cult meant to them is pictured here.

Scenes from the typical mobile daily lives of teen-age Americans. At the left is a drive-in restaurant favored as a fifties hangout in Bethesda, Maryland. Below left, Californians in a Model A demonstrated how to play hands-off-the-wheel "chicken" for photographer Ralph Crane. A park in Ann Arbor, Michigan, was the site of Robert Frank's view of alfresco romance. OVERLEAF: Frank's picture of a drive-in movie "passion pit" was taken in Detroit.

285

the United States. It should come as no surprise that a decade which spawned the hula hoop, pink flamingo lawn ornaments, rigged television quiz shows, painting by numbers, collegiate panty raids, 3-D movies, and the sack dress would also witness the salability of many exceedingly fatuous and impractical car designs. "A guy comes in and he looks at the shape, and that's all," a dealer observed. "Nobody wants to know how it's made or why it runs, or even if it runs." It is entirely appropriate that the automotive symbol of the age was an appendage known as the tail fin.

According to Alfred P. Sloan, the inspiration for the tail fin can be traced to World War II, when G.M. chief stylist Harley Earl was smitten by the look of the Lockheed P-38 fighter plane. The P-38 had twin engines, twin fuselages, and—what caught Earl's eye—twin tail fins. The 1948 Cadillac gave birth to the first groundborne tail fins, modest bumps atop the rear fenders housing the taillights. Within a decade or so the fins matured to enormous proportions (the 1959 Cadillac surely caused the marque's founding father, purist Henry M. Leland, to spin in his grave), marched downward through the G.M. divisions, and spread like a contagion to the other car companies. Tail fins stood bolt upright, canted over at odd angles, lay flat.

When Soviet Premier Nikita Khrushchev toured the United States in 1959, he stopped one day to point to a Cadillac tail fin and asked with malicious innocence, "What does this thing do?" It did nothing, of course, and it had stylistic parallels throughout the auto industry—great swatches of chromium and stainless steel that swept along fenders, around trunks, across front ends, and over roofs; fake louvres and vents and ducts; huge bumper "bullets" called Dagmars in honor of a buxom show-business starlet of the era; massively toothed and barred and ridged grillwork. The fifties was Detroit's age of the baroque.

What began as basically clean-lined designs, such as the 1949 Ford or the 1949 Oldsmobile, soon put on weight and chrome gewgaws. Virgil Exner, the creator of the novel 1947 Studebaker and a one-time denigrator of "massive Hollywood concepts" in auto design, moved over to the Chrysler Corporation and initiated "Flight-Sweep Styling," replete with multi-toned gaudery and fins and flairs of every description. The crisply designed mid-fifties Chevrolet degenerated into a 1959 model with grotesque spread-eagled rear fenders. Lithe 1955–57 Ford Thunderbirds (the "Early Birds") were displaced by Birds of a different and far bulkier feather. The purest design of the decade, Lincoln's Continental Mark II, lasted but two model years.

Engineering was made subservient to styling and directed at endowing these "insolent chariots" (as social critic Lewis Mumford christened them in 1957) with greater acceleration and top speed and more driver conveniences. Engines such as the landmark high-compression, overhead-valve V-8's pioneered by Cadillac and Oldsmobile in 1949 were reworked not to increase operational economy but to produce the doubling of horsepower needed to move unwieldy late-fifties models. The perfection of power steering, power brakes, and automatic transmissions materially reduced driving effort, but it was rare for comparable engineering resources to be devoted to improving such things as roadability, stopping power, and safety devices. On its 1956 models Ford promoted a number of standard and optional safety features—special door latches, a "deep-dish" steering wheel, seat belts, and padded seat backs, sun visors, and dashboards—under the rubric "Lifeguard Design," but detected no surge of public response. During 1955 Ford had sold only sixty-five thousand fewer cars than Chevrolet; in 1956 it sold a quarter million fewer. Factors other than the advertised emphasis on safety probably accounted for the decline, but the campaign was abandoned in rueful agreement with a saying making the rounds in Detroit: "Ford is selling safety, but Chevy is selling cars." Ford rejoined the crowd in putting its money on what sold, which was conspicuous consumption run riot.

289

The stylist held the upper hand in Detroit during the late forties and the fifties. This sampling of design elements, some of them fondly remembered, some notorious, recalls that era when a car's appearance, rather than its engineering features, was its primary selling point. At top is a view of Chrysler's well-wooded Town and Country, whose 1946–50 models the company proudly designated yachts on wheels; and the portholed 1957 Thunderbird, one of Ford's popular little two-seater personal cars known as "Early Birds." In the center row (left to right) are the soaring tail fin that adorned the 1959 Cadillac; the famous horse-collar grille of the infamous Edsel; the stone-guarded headlamp marking the first Fiberglass Flyer, Chevrolet's Corvette sports car; and the spare-wheel treatment of the 1956–57 Lincoln Continental Mark II, which harked back to the original prewar Continental design. At the bottom is the wraparound rear window "greenhouse" of the Studebaker Starlight coupe, a stylistic element that created a sensation when it appeared in 1947; and the massive saber-toothed grille that was a design characteristic of postwar Buicks until the late fifties.

ALL: FRANKLIN WILSON © 1976, 1977, PHOTO RESEARCHERS, EXCEPT EDSEL AND LINCOLN (HENRY FORD MUSEUM)

No other company put out more ostentatious designs in the fifties than General Motors—and none sold more cars or approached General Motors in profitability. Its 1955 after-tax profit topped $1 billion, which no doubt influenced *Time*'s choice of G.M. president Harlow Curtice as its "Man of the Year." In *Chrome Dreams* Paul C. Wilson suggests that the secret of G.M.'s success was its discovery of how to satisfy the "emotional needs" of average car-buyer Smith. "The naive designer of an automobile body," he writes, "imagines its future owner standing in his driveway admiring its sweeping lines, as he would admire a piece of sculpture. Certainly this relationship will exist some of the time, but a moment later the separation of car from owner vanishes as he takes the wheel. In an instant, the car is no longer a separate object but rather an extension of the owner, and in this transformation, the standards of appearance by which he judges the car change drastically. Purity of line, symmetry and balance are no longer as important as the symbolic features of the car. . . . Like an aborigine donning a horned and lurid ceremonial mask, the henpecked husband of suburbia happily climbed behind the wheel of his new 1950 Buick and set out to terrorize the populace. Few cars have had a more fearsome physiognomy: under a thick chromium lip its enormous mouth seems to stretch the metal skin above it in an effort to gape wider. Inside the

291

In his inimitable style, Norman Rockwell captured the vicissitudes of a summer's day auto trip to the lake in *The Outing,* a 1947 *Saturday Evening Post* cover painting. Grandma made the round trip stoically.

mouth is a row of gleaming, carnivorous-looking fangs. Transformed from insignificance, the driver of such a car luxuriates in his disguise."

Whether the Walter and Wanda Mittys of America truly satisfied their deepest emotional cravings by buying a toothed and bechromed Buick or other make of car may be argued, but there is no doubt that their love affair with the automobile was reaching a passionate peak. The kind of car one drove was more than ever an index to one's social standing. The announcement of new models was an annual event of moment. Detroit's traveling displays of fantasy-laden dream-car prototypes attracted audiences totaling in the millions. Critics might wax vitriolic on the subject of fifties autos—"overblown, overpriced monstrosities built by oafs for thieves to sell to mental defectives," was how John Keats phrased it—but their unrepentent owners drove happily on. If these vehicles were generally short on honest value compared to previous decades, still they worked well enough and they pampered driver and passengers with an array of conveniences and comforts previously unimagined. "Cars became mobile living rooms," writes Chip Lord in *Automerica,* "and Americans moved right in."

Vacationing by car (the method favored by four out of five families), for example, entered a new era. All the luggage and gear of average family Smith fitted easily into the capacious trunk, and the whole family fitted comfortably on the wide, soft seats. Rouse the big 200-horse-power-plus engine to life, put the automatic transmission in DRIVE, turn on the radio and the air conditioner, and soon the miles were clicking by effortlessly. Cornering might be mushy on the soft suspension, and the brakes might be slow in stopping two tons of machinery, but this was a vacation trip, not a road race. Gas mileage might be poor, but that too was of little concern. Gasoline was plentiful and cheap, and there was no suggestion that it might ever be otherwise. Roadside America offered everything from root-beer stands to candlelight restaurants, and motels and tourist courts could be found in growing numbers. The Smiths, in short, were hooked on automania. They loved their car, loved what it could do for them, loved the way it got them where they wanted to go; it was to them an unmatched bargain in mobility, privacy, convenience, and comfort.

The consequences of automania extended in every direction. The Smith family and its like descended on national parks in unprecedented numbers, the volume of visitors more than doubling, to 72 million, during the fifties. (The figure would double once again in the sixties.) All kinds of vacationing and outdoor recreation underwent a comparable increase, with the proportion of those who arrived at the various sites by automobile ranging from 83 to 93 per cent. This tourist boom produced more than simply enhanced personal enjoyment for millions of Americans. A major dividend was an acceleration of the trend to set aside and preserve additional wilderness and recreational areas at both the federal and state levels—the states motivated by a desire to enrich their economies with tourist dollars as well as by altruism. On the negative side, the hordes of recreation seekers created (and still create) problems of littering, defacement, and overcrowding at such popular parks as Yellowstone and the Great Smokies. There were proposals to ban all auto access to certain wilderness areas to preserve them unspoiled—and unvisited. Generally, however, recreation management rejected this elitist attitude in favor of the proposition that the land and its wonders belong to all, and that education, enforcement, and a certain amount of regulation are more democratic means of preserving the nation's natural heritage than banning the auto and stifling a primary benefit of the auto culture.

The business of accommodating these millions of auto tourists took on new dimensions. The tourist home that had housed a generation of prewar auto travelers was fading from the American highway scene in the 1950's, especially along heavily traveled routes. The old-fashioned tourist cabins, too, began to lose the through-traffic overnight trade; those

that managed to remain in business turned increasingly to rapid-turnover local trade that had little interest in a good night's sleep. Pushing them into obsolescence was the multi-unit motel. Until early in the fifties the typical motel was a small ten-to-fifteen-unit "Ma and Pa" establishment that differed from the tourist cabins it superseded only by being more modern and under one roof. "It was easy to become a motel keeper," writes Edwin B. Dean in a study of the motel phenomenon. "Virtually all you needed was a few thousand dollars, a tract of farmland on the outskirts of town; and since operating overhead could be kept low by Pa acting as room clerk, cashier, and general handyman, while Ma was the maid of all work, in many respects running a motel was better than working at a job." More ambitious entrepreneurs, however, were beginning to eye the motel business—notably Memphis real-estate man Charles Kemmons Wilson.

In 1951 Wilson returned from a family auto vacation determined "to build a motel that had all the things we missed"—telephones, television sets, a swimming pool. Seeing the movie *Holiday Inn* gave him the inspiration for the name of what he was beginning to envision as a national chain. Soon Wilson had four motels, built to a standardized design, in operation on the main routes entering Memphis and was franchising locations in other parts of the country. He had dis-

Tollway authorities and the Interstate System imposed limitations on billboards and other outdoor advertising, appreciably reducing highway clutter of the sort that confronted motorists traveling along New York's Route 17 in the mid-fifties.

covered a gold mine. By the end of the decade there were 160 Holiday Inns, with Travelodge and Howard Johnson ranking second and third as the big three of franchised motel chains. Growing apace with the chains were so-called cooperative motel systems (Best Western, Quality Courts), in which independently managed units cooperated in joint advertising, reservations, and setting operating standards. By 1958 there was one multi-unit motel or motor court for every thirteen hundred registered cars in the United States, and the motel business was about to enter the billion-dollar class.

What set Holiday Inns or Quality Courts apart was uniformity. After patronizing his first Holiday Inn a motorist knew exactly what to expect when he drove up to his second one, be it thirty miles or three thousand miles away. A similar uniformity began appearing in roadside America's fast-food eateries.

The genesis of that revolution dates back to 1940 and a drive-in hamburger stand operated in San Bernardino, California, by the brothers Richard and Maurice McDonald. After the war the McDonald brothers went to self-service, undertook a modest expansion in southern

California, and began the highly visible architectural practice of supporting their signs and the roofs of their drive-ins with tall gold-painted arches. Their large business volume caught the attention of fifty-year-old Ray A. Kroc, a businessman who was supplying them with special milk-shake-mixing machines. At the first McDonald's he visited, Kroc recalled, "I saw more people waiting in line than I had ever seen at any drive-in." In 1954, under a franchising agreement, he started building a chain of McDonald's drive-ins in cities and high-traffic suburban areas across the nation, and two years later he bought out the McDonald brothers. Ray Kroc has been called the Henry Ford of the fast-food business—before anyone else thought of it, he began serving up a precisely standardized product with the speed and efficiency of assembly-line mass production—and like Ford he quickly attracted imitators. (He also attracted a great deal of money—an estimated $300 million.) The fast-food drive-in became as ubiquitous a part of the car culture as the corner gas station.

By the mid-fifties a kind of universalized highway community could be found from coast to coast and border to border. It was born, as we have seen, in the twenties and reached puberty in the thirties; now it attained full growth. Part of this community catered directly to the automobile—gas stations, garages and other repair establishments, car washes, show-

rooms, used-car lots, auto junk yards. Part of it existed only to serve the motorist—drive-in eating places, tourist accommodations, parking lots. And part of it consisted of traditional businesses and services undergoing modification for the convenience of the motoring public. Before many years passed, Americans could (among other things) cash a check, meet a bill, pay a traffic fine, see a movie, return a library book, go to church, donate clothes, collect laundry, marry, or even pay their respects to the dear departed at a funeral parlor equipped with a drive-up window for displaying the deceased—all without leaving their cars.

In many instances these roadside communities degenerated into ribbons of visual pollution of the most garish sort, what journalist Bil Gilbert calls Highway Gothic, circa 1955: "If anyone is inclined to establish a monument to the highway culture of America," he writes, "he should buy up a few miles of [Route] 40 in northeastern Maryland and preserve it, just as it stands. All the components are there: greasy food, venal mechanics, blackened foliage, tourist-court rooms smelling of space heaters and linoleum; the sense of power, speed, danger; double-clutching rigs, eight-cylinder beasts snarling with excess energy, pacing along hour after hour, day after day." Such scenes, it should be said, were by no means universal. Cities and towns with the foresight to enact strong zoning laws and build-

ing codes—and with a citizenry determined to enforce them—accommodated themselves to the burgeoning car culture without damage to the appearance and values of the community. Others—too many others—surrendered to tawdry commercial exploitation without a fight.

Among the denizens of these roadside communities were members of a youthful generation swept up in an enthusiasm for the automobile that approached fanaticism. They cruised endlessly in their customized and personalized cars, haunted drive-in restaurants, engaged in drag racing at the drop of a challenge. Novelist Harry Crews recalled his membership in this automotive subculture in an article for *Esquire* in 1975: "I owned a 1953 Mercury with three-inch lowering blocks, fender skirts, twin aerials, and custom upholstering made of rolled Naugahyde. Staring into the bathroom mirror for long periods of time I practiced expressions to drive it with. It was that kind of car. It looked mean, and it was mean. Consequently, it had to be handled with a certain style. One-handing it through a ninety-degree turn on city streets in a power slide . . . , you were obligated to have your left arm hanging half out the window and a very *bored* expression on your face. . . ."

A large after-market in speed equipment and customizing accessories sprang up to feed this youthful component of automania. Enthusi-

asts' magazines such as *Hot Rod, Rod and Custom, Car and Driver, Road and Track,* and *Motor Trend* gained widespread popularity. The craze for drag racing was legitimized into sanctioned contests on abandoned airport runways and then on specially built drag-racing strips. It has become big business, today attracting far more participants than any other form of motor sport. Highly specialized and immensely powerful machines—racing driver Denise McCluggage describes them as "chopped, blued, channeled, filed, ported, russetted, relieved, fluted, chromed, gilded"—now reach speeds of well over 200 mph in a quarter mile from a standing start. There was a comparable enthusiasm for auto racing of every stripe. The leading event for full-blooded American racing machines, the Indianapolis 500, attracted crowds rivaling those that had turned out for the Vanderbilt Cup contests early in the century. Stock-car racing, born in the Barney Oldfield days of dirt-track barnstorming, underwent a spectacular growth of its own, particularly in the southeastern states. Imported European sports cars came into vogue, triggering a renewed interest in road racing.

Still another important demonstration of the car culture's impact on postwar America was to be found in suburbia. The growth of the nation's suburbs was explosive—a 49 per cent population increase during the

1950's alone—generating a way of living wholly dependent on the automobile. No other auto-related symbol of this lifestyle was more highly visible than the shopping center. As John B. Rae has written, the shopping center was "a logical response to the outward trend of urban population and to the flexibility of movement afforded by the automobile. It also illustrates how a response can become a stimulus. Dispersal made the shopping center possible; the shopping center in turn encourages further dispersal because it diminishes the need to have access to a downtown shopping district." In 1946 there were 8 shopping centers in the United States; in 1960 there were 3,841, doing an annual business of $35 billion.

These centers were founded on the principle of one-stop shopping, rather like the old general store multiplied manyfold and supplied with ample parking. Excepting such items as gasoline or new cars, large shopping centers stocked virtually every retail item a suburbanite could want. Their dominant pattern was established early: a large nucleus store—department-store branch, supermarket, an outlet of a national merchandising chain such as Sears, Roebuck—ringed by satellite specialty shops and stores, the whole surrounded by parking space. Access to public transportation was very seldom of concern to shopping-center planners, whereas highway acces-

sibility was of overriding importance. Not only did almost every one of their customers arrive by private car, but almost all their varied stock was delivered by truck.

The flight to suburbia was and is the subject of much hand-wringing—the critics, Rae writes, "are numerous, articulate, and frequently distinguished"—particularly because of its generally deleterious effect on the central cities. However, the suburb, at least early in the postwar years, was part and parcel of the American dream: a private place, with space, in the sun. Middle-class Americans in their wisdom voted with their dollars for an autoborne suburban lifestyle, just as they voted with their dollars for those insolent fifties chariots, and today suburbia contains half of America's population. It followed logically that suburbanites would become Detroit's best customers. The 1960 census revealed that not only did four out of five American households own a car, but that one out of five owned at least two cars, with nearly all these multi-car families living in the suburbs. Highway policy at all levels, federal, state, and local, reflected these realities.

The end of World War II unleashed a flood of highway construction. The most immediate need was to rejuvenate road systems that had fallen to pieces during the war. The California highway department, for example, estimated that $629 million would be required just to patch

up existing roads. Simply holding the line, however, was patently inadequate. The stark realities of car ownership and car use—the number of automobiles on the road would double to 52 million between 1945 and 1955—made it imperative that something be done about the urban-suburban traffic crisis and about finally constructing a comprehensive interstate arterial highway network. John Loudon McAdam's nineteenth-century dictum that "roads must be built to accommodate the traffic, not the traffic regulated to preserve the roads" was still being obeyed.

The nation's fast-growing metropolitan regions were transformed by an array of freeways and expressways and parkways and beltways and arterial ways and other coinages from the new highway lexicon that can be collectively called "urbanways." Their purposes were as varied as their names. Some were radial routes, devoted to delivering car and bus commuters from the suburbs to jobs in the central cities; some were lateral, expediting the movement of car and truck traffic within sprawling metropolitan areas; some were bypasses, diverting through traffic away from congested urban centers entirely.

Results varied with the skills and foresight of the planners. Generally most successful was the diversion of through traffic to bypass routes around city centers. Driving time, convenience, and safety were enhanced dramatically within the con-

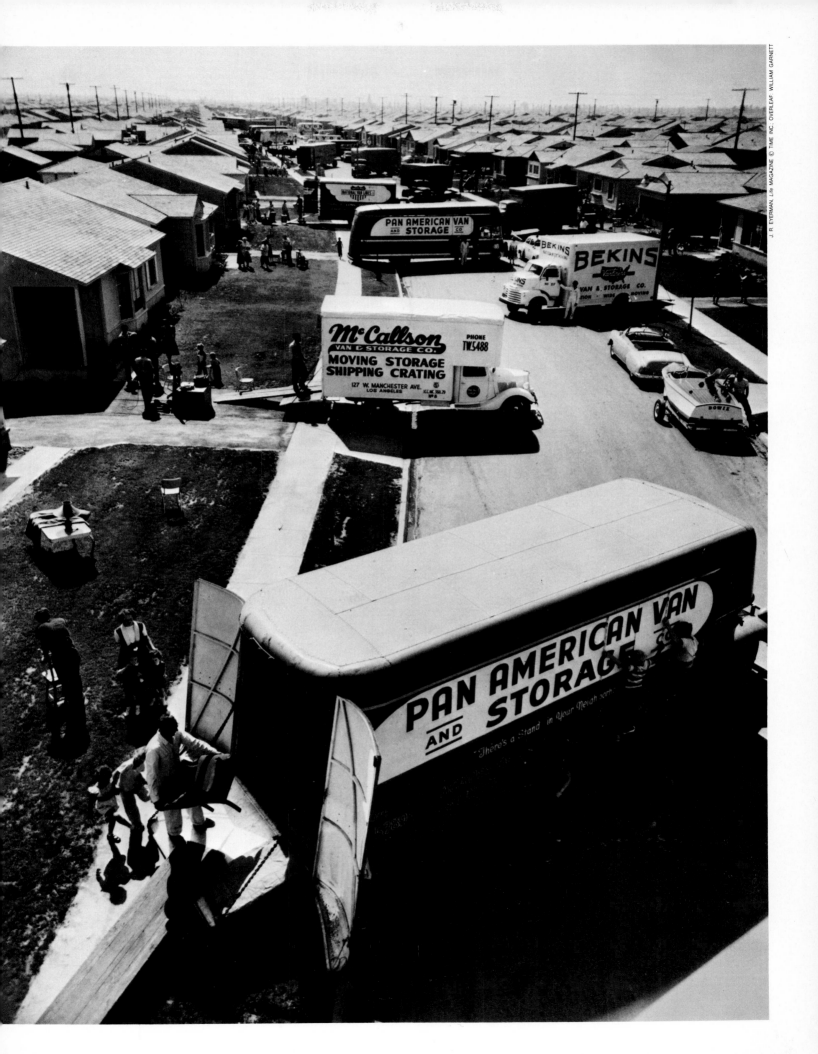

fines of many of the larger metropolitan areas. Least successful were misguided attempts to carry car commuters directly into central cities that had inadequate street and parking facilities to cope with them, and misplaced routes that mixed local with through traffic to create horrendous tie-ups. There were also examples of "bulldozer mentality" among highway administrators who gave little thought to what urban planner Lawrence Halprin has called "the fine grain of older sections of our cities." Ghetto and working-class neighborhoods were the most frequent victims; "unfortunately," Halprin writes, "neighborhoods are easily disrupted and destroyed by ploughing through them, particularly if they are occupied by groups with no great ability to bring pressure on City Hall."

Whatever their diversity of purpose and result, these urbanways had one thing in common: high costs. California's first urban freeway, the Arroyo Seco, had cost about $1.4 million per mile when it was built just before the war. The Hollywood Freeway, completed in the fifties, cost $5.5 million per mile. Construction costs in higher-density areas ran as high as $22.5 million per mile for New York's Cross-Bronx Expressway and $41.7 million for Boston's Central Artery.

California witnessed the most spectacular burst of highway construction. Los Angeles's election of a horizontal, decentralized pattern of growth—and a consequent dispersal of jobs—during the twenties was paralleled by an automobile consciousness unmatched anywhere. In 1947 the state legislature enacted a master plan of express highways, focused on San Francisco as well as Los Angeles, that within a decade constituted ten per cent of the state's road system and carried forty per cent of its traffic. California rejected the tollway concept in favor of the freeway, to be financed primarily through the gasoline tax and other vehicle-use taxes and fees. This was regarded as an equitable method of financing, for because of the state's size and configuration the vast majority of freeway users would be Californians on intrastate journeys; there would be comparatively few out-of-state motorists getting a free ride. (By contrast, in New York's tristate metropolitan area, where much of the traffic is interstate in character, much urbanway construction was financed by tolls.) Not lost on the California planners was the nightmare prospect of the traffic jams that would be created by the installation of numerous toll booths on the most heavily traveled highway system in the world. In 1959 the master plan of freeways was greatly expanded, with a new goal of constructing more than twelve thousand freeway miles by 1980. California's auto population was growing even faster than its human population—and faster than freeways could be built to nourish it.

Executed simultaneously with the urbanway boom was a massive program of interstate highway building. Its first phase was in direct emulation of the Pennsylvania Turnpike, which had begun highly successful operation before Pearl Harbor. By 1959 twenty-one states were operating more than 3,200 miles of limited-access tollways. The largest share of these miles was located in the heavily traveled northeastern quadrant of the nation, east of the Mississippi and north of the Mason-Dixon line. Less than 450 miles were west of the Mississippi. Because of the interstate nature of much long-distance expressway traffic, the states turned to the toll financing method so as not to put an unfair burden on their taxpayers. In 1956 motorists could boast of driving 840 miles from New York to Chicago without stopping for a single traffic light.

The second phase of expressway building was initiated by the federal government. It was an undertaking massive enough to be adjudged worthy of capitalization—the Interstate System. It was launched in comparatively modest fashion by the Federal-Aid Highway Act of 1944, which outlined a modern nationwide arterial system designed to serve (among other things) national defense needs. Funding was traditional, with fifty-fifty matching grants offered to the states. Many states, however, shied away, resorting instead to the more financially attractive tollway concept. This

"The American has sacrificed his life as a whole to the motorcar, like someone who, demented with passion, wrecks his home in order to lavish his income on a capricious mistress who promises delights he can only occasionally enjoy," Lewis Mumford wrote in 1958. Photographer Robert Frank found a Californian who lavished at least tender loving care on his motorcar mistress.

reluctance evaporated with the passage of the Federal-Aid Highway Act of 1956. This time Congress authorized the construction of a toll-free 41,000-mile Interstate System—12 per cent of it urbanway, the rest limited-access expressways crisscrossing the nation—with the key proviso that 90 per cent of the funding would come from the national treasury. The money, raised through new federal fuel and use taxes and imposts on the purchase of tires, trucks, trailers, and buses, would be doled out from a special Highway Trust Fund. The scheme was scheduled to be completed in fifteen years at a cost of $27 billion, and its sponsors labeled it "the largest single public-works project in the history of the world." It proved to be all of that.

States immediately dropped future planning for additional tollways and turned to welcome the influx of federal Interstate money. A galaxy of powerful interests—the construction industry, the oil industry, the auto industry, the trucking industry, the tire industry, vested-interest politicians, highway-user groups of every description—rallied behind the program. Late in 1956 the first stretch of Interstate, eight miles of I-70 outside Topeka, Kansas, was opened to traffic. Twenty years later some thirty-eight thousand miles had been opened, at a cost of $62 billion, all the routes toll-free except for segments of already completed tollway that were incorporated into the network. If the

balance of the system is ever completed, which is problematical, it will cost from $20 to $40 billion more. (The cost escalations over the past two decades have made forecasters chary.) "The impact of the Interstate System on the national life has been immeasurable," writes the New York Times's William K. Stevens. "It has extended the practical horizons of the everyday citizen by leagues, and become the ultimate agent of his liberation from the bonds of geography. . . . The superhighways have, indeed, become the centerpiece of a transportation system based overwhelmingly on motor vehicles. . . ."

The decentralization of industry already well begun under the influence of the postwar highway boom was given fresh impetus by the arrival of the Interstates. The new expressway arteries nourished an expanding outer ring of suburbia called exurbia. Distances once measured in miles were now measured in hours, bringing recreational areas of all kinds within easy reach. Motorists long familiar with the "wide-spot-in-the-road" community discovered uncounted new examples of the breed: the wide spot in the road was now an Interstate interchange, the new community an array of Holiday Inns and McDonald's drive-ins and other such enterprises devoted to the care and feeding of travelers. The rate of highway deaths and injuries was slashed. The volume of interstate freight delivered by truck rose during the fifties

from one sixth to almost one quarter of the national total, with the speed and cost of delivery cut dramatically. Interstates spawned millions of payrolls, both directly and indirectly. The Interstate System, in short, brought to reality the dream of a national road network articulated by the Lincoln Highway's Carl Fisher half a century earlier when the automobile was young. In the process, however, it generated an internal momentum that began to alarm concerned citizens. With so many powerful interests dependent on the continued munificence of the Highway Trust Fund, a variation of Parkinson's Law (the automatic proliferation of bureaucracy) appeared. Here was an automatic proliferation of highway projects not always based on demonstrated need but on the ready availability of money. "Our experience with the Highway Trust Fund," writes critic Helen Leavitt, "shows that 'planning' is guided by funding, not the other way around." The strongest protests were directed at the practice of thrusting Interstates into the hearts of cities without consideration of the city dwellers they were displacing and the urban values they were destroying. "As neighborhoods are sliced in two and cemeteries are relocated," the New York Times editorialized, "neither the quick nor the dead are safe."

The first stirrings of protest against Interstate excesses appeared in the late fifties and early sixties, probably the first time in American history that a significant segment of the population rose up to question the benefits of highways. This was one sign that the euphoria of automania was beginning to wear off. The majority of Americans were not yet changing their minds about what they considered the generally unalloyed benefits of the car culture, but they were beginning to question certain manifestations of it. In 1957, for example, they had a unique opportunity to cast their votes on the insolent chariots themselves, which they had previously been buying without complaint.

In coping with the tight competitive market of the fifties, Detroit's auto makers eagerly seized on the slightest advantage. At the lowest level was simple observation. Anything that attracted buyers to a competitor's showroom, be it tail fins or a pillarless hardtop model, was imitated in copycat fashion as fast as retooling permitted. On a different, more scientific plane was motivational research, which the auto industry indulged in less for guidance in styling—the man in the street had a hard time articulating how he wanted his car to look—than for pitching advertising toward specific segments of the market. When surveys suggested that in the public mind automobiles possessed distinct personalities, there was a rush to enhance (or change) those images. Research conducted for Ford by the Columbia University Bureau of Applied Social Research in 1955,

for instance, concluded that the popular image of a Ford was fast, masculine, and blue collar; a Chevrolet, by contrast, projected a more conservative, middle-class image, and a Buick was personified as a silver-haired lady from the country-club set.

The Columbia survey was part of a campaign by Ford to develop a personality for an entirely new car being readied for launch. Planning for the marque—as yet unnamed—had begun in 1948. Henry Ford II and his freshly minted management team decided that the company needed a second entry in the middle-priced field. Buyers of Fords were not "stepping up" to Mercury as expected but instead shifting to Pontiac or Buick or Oldsmobile. "We have been growing customers for General Motors," a Ford executive complained. The project was shelved during the Korean War in the early fifties when material shortages forced Detroit to retrench, but by 1955 stylist Roy A. Brown had designed, and the Ford management approved for production, a new car "unique in the sense that it would be readily recognizable." The description would return to haunt Brown and his colleagues.

Motivational research helped assign a personality to the new marque —"the smart car for the younger executive or professional family on its way up." Selecting this market strategy proved less of a problem than selecting a name for the car. As many as six thousand names were collected,

The highway spectacular has become almost
a commonplace in California. Above is
a toll plaza on San Francisco's Bay Bridge,
at right a new interchange that links
the San Diego and Santa Monica freeways.

cross-indexed, tested, and vigorously debated. The poet Marianne Moore enthusiastically entered the contest at Ford's request, submitting such exotic coinages as Resilient Bullet, Mongoose Civique, Turcotinga, Pastelogram, and Utopian Turtletop. The final decision, presided over by board chairman Ernest R. Breech, was rendered in the spring of 1956. "I don't like the goddamned things," Breech said of the final list of names presented for selection. Pointing to the "fall-back" choice honoring Edsel Ford, he said, "How about we call it Edsel."

So the Edsel began its march to automotive oblivion. When the car was unveiled to the world in September, 1957, with a fanfare not seen in Detroit since Henry Ford had introduced his Model A thirty years before, its break-even was budgeted at 200,000 sales in the first year. As John Brooks remarks, "There may be an aborigine somewhere in a remote rain forest who hasn't yet heard that things failed to turn out that way." Two years later, when the marque was quietly interred, some 110,000 had been sold. Contemporary estimates placed Ford's losses in the neighborhood of $350 million, but a careful analysis by economist Lawrence J. White puts the figure closer to $100 million. Whatever the loss, the Edsel was the largest fiasco in automotive history.

Many reasons have been advanced to explain the flop, beginning with the name itself. Indeed, *Edsel* scarcely evokes the "visceral feeling of elegance, fleetness, and advanced features and design" that the company had sought from Miss Moore and others, yet there is little evidence that it was an important factor in the public's rejection. No doubt the car's styling, especially its infamous horse-collar grille and its curious gull-winged rear end, disappointed many —although some of the styling criticism was Monday-morning quarterbacking. Unquestionably harmful was the Edsel's mixed press reception. Although *Motor Trend* said that "the Edsel performs fine, rides well, and handles good," it was condemned by *Consumer Reports* as "more uselessly overpowered. . . , more gadget bedecked, more hung with expensive accessories than any car in its price class." An excessively high percentage of lemons in the initial production run was particularly painful. "Within a few weeks after the Edsel was introduced," Brooks writes, "its pratfalls were the talk of the land. Edsels were delivered with oil leaks, sticking hoods, trunks that wouldn't open, and push buttons that . . . couldn't be budged with a hammer."

In the final analysis, however, the fatal blow to the Edsel was mistiming. Designed in 1955, it was the quintessential 1955 car—flashy, powerful, gadgety. The motivational research that shaped its marketplace personality was probably as accurate a reflection of mid-fifties America as any such research could be. But between

The annual model change was accompanied by heavy expenditures for advertising and promotion, but even more elaborate efforts were undertaken by Detroit when bringing out an entirely new model. A film crew is pictured here at work on the promotional packaging of Ford's compact Falcon in 1959.

1955 design and 1957 production the automotive world turned topsy-turvy. Just two months before the Edsel's introduction, the nation was plummeted into a sharp economic recession that adversely affected sales of all cars. A month after it appeared, the Soviets put their first sputnik in orbit, causing shocked Americans to cast a disgusted eye on what their own vaunted technology had been doing lately: producing excesses such as the Edsel. Sobering up after their long insolent-chariot binge, car buyers were beginning to purchase smaller, more rational vehicles. In an obituary written on the occasion of the Edsel's death in 1959, the *Wall Street Journal* took the opportunity to dismiss the charge that American auto makers "rig markets or force consumers to take what they want them to take." The fate of the Edsel, the *Journal* concluded, demonstrated that "when it comes to dictating, the consumer is the dictator without peer."

The Edsel was not the only marque to suffer a thumbs-down vote from consumers in the fifties. It was, in fact, the least noteworthy of the victims. Hudson, Nash, and Packard, three of the proud names in American automotive history, all expired; and a fourth, Studebaker, contracted its final illness. (Even the long-standing Big Three line-up was not immune. Chrysler had to excise its once-popular De Soto in 1960.) The cause of death in every case was a loss of consumer confidence.

George W. Mason of Nash was the first independent to recognize the unvarnished truth about modern automobile making. To remain alive in the world of the Big Three, Mason said in 1946, the Little Four must combine. With a full line of cars, ample plant capacity and capital resources, and an extensive dealer network, the merged independents might well attain full stature alongside their large rivals. Remain separate, he warned, and they would be trampled one after another in the competitive warfare between the giants—trampled unintentionally, to be sure, for the giants were very conscious of the antitrust laws, but they would be dead just the same. Ostensibly practical difficulties sabotaged Mason's merger scheme, but the deeper problem was myopia on the part of his fellow independents. Looking ahead no farther than the seller's market they knew would follow the war, they failed to appreciate that a day might come when the "plenty of room for all" situation no longer existed. That day came with the end of the Korean War in 1953. "Fundamentally," writes Lawrence J. White, "the Independents had been saddled with the status of 'off-brands': brands that were less well advertised, carried a connotation of 'inferior' in the eyes of many consumers, and were expected to sell for less than the 'major' brands." It was a dilemma that had been killing independents since the 1920's.

The wisdom of corporate merger finally dawned on the independents early in the fifties, but it was carried out in half-a-loaf fashion. Within the space of five months in 1954 the Little Four became the Little Two—the Studebaker-Packard Corporation and the American Motors Corporation (Hudson and Nash). Hudson, which was failing fast and had lost $10 million in 1953, was the first of the four marques to go. The last true Hudson came off the assembly line just six months after the merger with Nash. A.M.C. kept the Hudson name plate alive for another three years by affixing it to Nashes—"Hashes" in the Detroit vernacular. Nineteen fifty-seven was the last year for the Nash name plate as well.

Packard was the next to go, in 1958. The administration of Studebaker-Packard president James J. Nance spent large sums of scarce capital trying to graft a "new look" onto the Packard image, with negligible results. (In a symbolic move to erase all traces of the old Packard image the company's rich historical archives that dated back to 1899 were wantonly destroyed, an act that Packard aficionados compare to the sacking of the Alexandrian library in ancient times.) In Nance's post-mortem judgment, the company's attempt, begun in the Depression, to invade the medium-priced field resulted in "bleeding the Packard name white." Be that as it may, Packard lost the indefinable aura that had once marked it as

(continued on page 313)

Allan D'Arcangelo's *U.S. Highway 1* (1963) suggests the motorist's tunnel vision.

HIGHWAY LANDSCAPE

The Pop Art movement of the sixties, utilizing what critic Lawrence Alloway described as "popular art sources" to comment on the realities of contemporary civilization, found rich pickings among the visual clichés of roadside America. Pop artists' views of the commonplace, all-encompassing landscape spawned by the car culture were cool, ironic, sometimes wryly humorous — and sharply observant.

Edward Ruscha's starkly composed oil, *Standard Station, Amarillo, Texas* (right), painted in 1963, is an interpretation of the modern highway landscape that is reminiscent of Charles Sheeler's view of the industrial landscape of the thirties. George Segal's tableau assemblage (plaster and "mixed media") below, also dating from 1963 and titled simply *The Gas Station,* evokes the timelessness of a pre-eminent institution of the car culture.

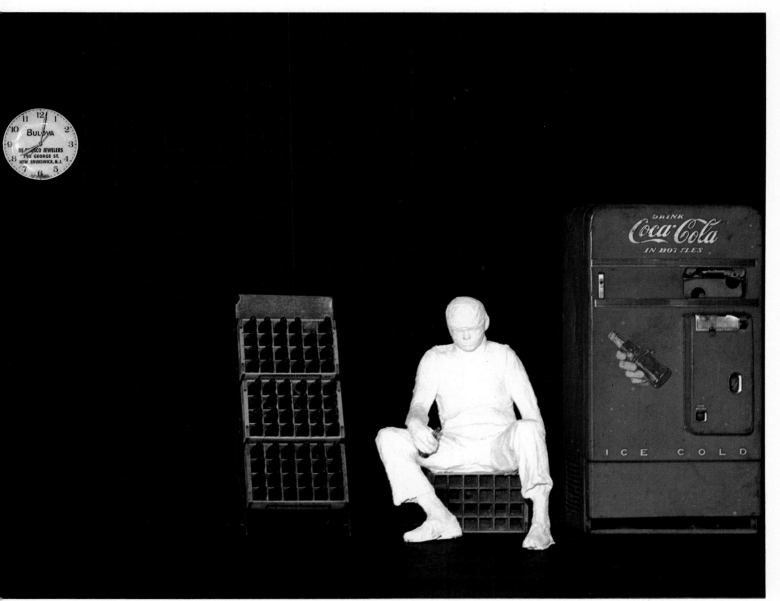

the best, and after 1949 it finished a poor second to Cadillac in the luxury field. The last, derisively named "Packardbakers" wrote a sad ending to the history of one of the original American grand marques.

Studebaker meanwhile limped on, producing some strikingly designed cars but not quite able to carve out a distinctive niche for itself in the marketplace and steadily losing what had once been one of its strongest attributes—customer loyalty. Five presidents took the reins at Studebaker-Packard in less than a decade, but none achieved more than fleeting success before the decline resumed. "It didn't seem to make any difference who was president," said a long-time Studebaker engineer. "Every time they came to a fork in the road they always took the wrong turn." The company lost ground steadily in the competition with the Big Three. The Studebaker cost too much to build, and its dealers were too few and far between. The car buyer's fear of being stuck with an orphan completed the vicious circle. In 1963 the last of the more than 4.5 million cars bearing the Studebaker badge was built in South Bend, where 111 years before the first Studebaker wagon had been built. The company continued production in its Canadian plant for three more years, then went out of auto making permanently.

Thanks to the foresight of Nash's George Mason, one company survived the general collapse of the independents. In 1950, recognizing the need to offer a distinct alternative to the product lines of the Big Three, he had dusted off a name that dated back to 1902 and introduced the compact Rambler. Following Mason's death four years later, the new head of American Motors, George K. Romney, took up the small-car crusade with all the fervor of a revivalist preacher. Dropping the Hudson and Nash full-size car lines permitted the company to devote all its energies to compacts. Romney played the role of Detroit's resident heretic with relish, inveighing against "wheeled juke-boxes" and "mechanized dinosaurs in the driveway" and insisting (in 1958) that "today, the showy car is becoming passé as the primary means of satisfying ego expression." American car buyers were beginning to listen to him. In 1958 American Motors sold more than 217,000 Ramblers, in 1960 more than 485,000, making it the third-best-selling car in the nation. The question facing American Motors—and still facing it—was whether it could hold its small-car-alternative position once the Big Three decided to enter that market. A General Motors executive observed of Romney, "He not only wants to make small cars, he wants everyone else to make small cars. He's just asking us to come and beat his head in, and it looks as if that's what we're going to do."

Despite initial doubts about the salability of small cars ("If G.M. has said it once," Fortune reported in 1957, "it's said it ten thousand times: 'a good used car is the answer to the American public's need for cheap transportation' "), the Big Three were keeping a wary eye on the Rambler and also on foreign imports, particularly that little German Beetle, Volkswagen. For the first time in more than half a century, imports were making a significant dent in the American market. Import sales in 1958 approached 380,000, the vast majority of them small economy models; adding in Rambler sales, this meant that the small car had seized a better than 12-per-cent share of the market. That share jumped to 18.4 per cent in 1959.

Whatever they might say in public, the Big Three now prepared to enter the small-car business. As usual, they were reacting to public taste rather than trying to mold it. In 1959 Ford introduced its compact Falcon, Chevrolet its Corvair, Chrysler its Valiant. The response to the new cars was good enough—first-year Falcon sales topped five hundred thousand—to repel the foreign invasion, at least temporarily. Before long there were compact editions of all the medium-priced marques as well, and for 1962 Ford came out with the new "intermediate-sized" Fairlane. Not only was the small car growing bigger, but Detroit was happily discovering that about two thirds of its customers ordered de luxe, accessory-laden versions. Americans were going for "economy at any cost," remarked *Time.*

Early in the sixties the worst excesses of the baroque age were gone, and automobile designs became cleaner, brisker, less glittering. There was also a bewildering number of them. The day was long gone when a car buyer visiting his Ford dealer, say, had only to decide between standard and de luxe models. Things became more complicated in the fifties when a prospective Studebaker customer, for instance, was confronted by a whole flight of Hawks: Sky, Power, Flight, Golden. By 1965, when average motorist Smith went window shopping for a Chevrolet (the nation's sales leader), he encountered Corvair, Chevy II, Chevelle, Impala and its sub-breeds Biscayne and Bel Air, Caprice, and Corvette name plates. If Smith decided to make a purchase, his choices were mind-boggling. According to Hal Higdon in the *New York Times Magazine,* "A Yale University physicist calculated that since Chevy offered 46 models, 32 engines, 20 transmissions, 21 colors (plus nine two-tone combinations), and more than 400 accessories and options, the number of different cars that a Chevrolet customer conceivably could order was greater than the number of atoms in the universe. This seemingly put General Motors one notch higher than God in the chain of command." Highly complex computerized plan-

ning enabled the auto makers to mix and match a limited number of basic standardized subassemblies (such as body shells) with an astonishing number of specialized components and options to produce, right on assembly-line schedule, a vehicle personalized exactly as the customer specified. Compared to the look of nearly perfect uniformity on the old Model T lines at Highland Park, the modern assembly line was a crazy quilt of models, colors, and even marques.

The proliferation of models in the sixties added dimension to the old Durant-Sloan tenet of a car for every purse and purpose. It also proved to be Detroit's solution to market saturation. Although auto sales fluctuated from year to year, in contrast to the fifties the general trend was upward, hitting a 9.3 million peak in 1965. This market growth consisted of increased purchases by government and business (particularly car-rental companies); first-car purchases that mirrored population growth; and, most welcomed by Detroit, the acquisition by suburbanites of second, third, and even fourth cars. There might be a sporty car for Dad, a station wagon for Mom, a compact for Sis. It was among these multi-car families that the array of new specialized models found their largest market, and no new model performed better in the sixties marketplace than Ford's Mustang. In Detroit's view, the Mustang was the car of the decade, pioneering a major trend toward the sporty "pony car."

The Mustang did much to remove the tarnish of the Edsel fiasco from Ford's reputation. If the timing of the Edsel was disastrous, that of the Mustang was perfect. Ford correctly read the trend toward smaller personalized cars, and when the new marque was introduced in April, 1964, it was an immediate smash hit. Advertisements promised a low-cost psychic renewal for buyers ("Desmond was afraid to let the cat out—until he got his Mustang"; "Life was just one diaper after another—until Sarah got her Mustang"), and the orders poured in at a rate that taxed production capacity. The 1965 sales exceeded half a million. By combining a distinctive and jaunty new body design—long hood, short rear deck—with standard components from its compact Falcon and intermediate Fairlane lines, Ford was able to keep development costs to a comparatively modest $40 million. Within two years the Mustang and its pony-car imitators held almost eleven per cent of the auto market.

Nineteen sixty-five would be remembered as a watershed year for Detroit. For a decade criticism of the auto industry and the car culture had been slowly building. There were attacks on the bechromed aberrations of the fifties, on the venal hucksterism of car salesmen, on the visual and literal pollution being spawned by the car culture, on the excesses and unrestrained boosterism of highway plan-

ners, on the rising number of deaths and injuries in automobile accidents. Then, in 1965, there appeared a bestseller titled *Unsafe at Any Speed: The Designed-in Dangers of the American Automobile,* by a Connecticut lawyer named Ralph Nader. His goal, Nader vowed, was to bring the auto industry "to justice" for "not introducing safety features as standard equipment unless there is a compulsion or threat of legislation or regulation." *Newsweek* described him as a "Jimmy Stewart hero in a Frank Capra movie."

Nader's polemic took as its prime target the Corvair, Chevrolet's entry in the compact field. In the hands of an expert, knowledgeable driver, the low-priced, air-cooled, rear-engined Corvair was Detroit's innovative and refreshing answer to European imports. However, mass-production compromises had made it something less than its designers envisioned, and with an average driver at the wheel, used to the undemanding qualities of most American cars, it could be unforgiving. *Car and Driver* would call it "one of the nastiest-handling cars ever built." By the time Nader's book appeared, the Corvair's handling problems had been corrected, but the damage was done. General Motors then foolishly cast itself in a sinister role by hiring private detectives to "get something somewhere" on Nader to "shut him up." By the time the unsavory episode was over, G.M. president James M. Roche

had publicly apologized for the corporate indiscretion before a Senate committee, and Nader had collected $425,000 in a settlement of his invasion-of-privacy suit against the corporation. Corvair sales fell off drastically, and in 1969 the marque would be dropped from the G.M. line. Detroit was hardly guilty of every charge in Nader's blanket indictment, but a climate had been created for continued sharp questioning of many basic premises of the car culture—especially questioning from Washington.

Until the mid-sixties Detroit's relationship with Washington had been a generally comfortable one. The major exception came during the New Deal years, when the auto workers were nourished from the White House and the Capitol in their fight for recognition, but eventually Detroit learned how to live with the United Automobile Workers—and how to pass on its increased labor costs to the consumer. Other transportation businesses—railroads and airlines—were regarded as public carriers and subject to often-minute governmental regulation, but the auto makers had escaped such restrictions on their operations entirely: indeed, Detroit could hardly have asked for anything more beneficial to its fortunes than the government-financed Interstate System. Now, however, all this was about to change. Under the impress of the national government, both the auto industry and the auto culture would be embarked on a new course.

8
A NEW REALITY

The crusade for safer cars, which Ralph Nader first articulated loudly enough to capture attention in 1965, was only one of many issues that began to press on the nation's automotive consciousness in the 1960's. What economist John Kenneth Galbraith called the consumership of the fifties, orchestrated from Detroit, became the consumerism of the sixties and seventies, masterminded from Washington. By the mid-seventies this revolution was well launched, promising a profound effect on Detroit and the way Detroit's products were viewed by the American people.

A major facet of the revolution can be traced back to the immediate postwar years. In 1948 Dutch-born Arie Jan Haagen-Smit, a chemist at the California Institute of Technology, began an investigation of the increasing prevalence of noxious smog overlaying the Los Angeles basin. (*Smog* was a coinage invented to describe the combination of smoke and fog that plagued London.) More than a decade before Nader charged that the American car was unsafe at any speed, Haagen-Smit reached the conclusion that it was unsafe in its effects on the public health and welfare.

Smog was first noted in southern California during World War II. By 1946 the Los Angeles *Times* was reporting, "Like a dirty gray blanket floating across the sky, a dense eye-stinging layer of smog dimmed the sun here yesterday. The fumes hung unmoving in the still air, raising tears and sniffles in thousands of Angelenos." Meteorologists spoke of "atmospheric inversion": prevailing winds caused a layer of cool air to rest atop this warmer layer of pollution, trapping it within the geographic bowl containing greater Los Angeles. Initially, industrial pollutants were blamed for the miasma, but Haagen-Smit's studies convinced him that the primary culprit was the automobile.

By early in the fifties both the incidence and the density of Los Angeles's smog had increased measurably, and it had taken on a brownish cast. Haagen-Smit's analysis of the contaminants included the same elements identified in auto emissions. These emissions fell into four categories: unburned hydrocarbons that escaped in engine exhaust or as combustion fumes from crankcase venting or as raw gasoline evaporating from the carburetor and gas tank; and three combustion products issuing from the exhaust pipe—carbon monoxide, lead compounds from anti-knock gasoline, and nitrogen oxides. The latter triggered a photochemical reaction with hydrocarbons and sunlight to produce the brown-tinted smog. The rising tide of smog in southern California—and in other metropolitan areas as well—

A modern urbanway at rush hour, such as Houston's Southwest Freeway (opposite), confirms the Old Testament prediction of the prophet Nahum: "The chariots shall rage in the streets, they shall justle one against another in the broad ways: they shall seem like torches, they shall run like the lightnings." Ever denser traffic produced a new public health menace, the Smog Alert. Here is the scene during an alert in downtown Los Angeles in 1958.

was attributed not only to the growing auto population but to the fact that high-compression engines introduced late in the forties operated at higher temperatures than previous low-compression power plants and so produced more nitrogen oxides.

While no conclusive clear and present danger to public health could be proven yet, the evidence suggested that smog could be a contributing factor in heart and lung disease. What *was* immediately self-evident on smoggy days was the toxic irritation of eyes and respiratory tracts, the blighting effects on foliage, the unpleasant smell, and the filth, all of which were enough to raise a public outcry for action. In 1953 California officials appealed to Detroit. The auto companies formed a joint committee, agreed to royalty-free cross-licensing of any anti-pollution devices to insure that no company gained a competitive edge, and undertook low-priority research that produced little more than assorted technical papers.

The industry's slow response to the pollution issue was due to the very real complexity of the problem and its solutions, but it was due as well to a reluctance to acknowledge implied blame for the problem itself. Pollution controls were not regarded as salable items; indeed, that they were needed at all might suggest to the buying public that Detroit's rendition of the American dream was flawed. Impatient with the delay and

well aware of the leverage granted them by the fact that their state made up the largest single slice of the domestic auto market, California's legislators passed the first of a series of emissions-control laws in 1959. The initial fruit of this action was the equipping of all 1963 model cars with devices to recycle crankcase fumes in the engine for more complete combustion. California maintained the pressure by passing ever-more-stringent laws, and Detroit continued to comply reluctantly.

In 1965 Congress took the highly significant step of passing the Vehicle Air Pollution and Control Act. For the first time Washington was mandating improvements (or at least changes) in the auto makers' products. Congress followed California's lead, generally adopting that state's existing pollution standards and making them mandatory nationwide on 1968 models. Relying primarily on modifications in engine operation, Detroit managed to stay abreast of the pollution regulations fairly comfortably until 1970, when Congress dropped a bombshell on it in the form of the Clean Air Act.

The mandated goal of the legislation was a reduction of ninety per cent in auto emission pollutants within six years. In reply to Detroit's vigorous protests that the technology did not exist for such a radical step, Senator Edmund S. Muskie, the bill's primary sponsor, said that he was out to "force technology."

Generally, the end results of the anti-pollution campaign were positive, although the time limit was extended and certain doubts were raised about the means used. Engine improvements, unleaded gasoline, and the catalytic converter—in which platinum and palladium catalysts break down hydrocarbons and carbon monoxide in the engine exhaust —produced often dramatic improvements in air quality. By 1974 the level of carbon monoxide in air samples taken in Los Angeles County was down fifty-two per cent from the 1966 level, and hydrocarbon pollution was down sixty-five per cent—this despite a sixteen per cent increase in the number of cars registered in the county. The reduction in nitrogen oxides was only three per cent, however, pointing up one of the contradictions in early emissions-control efforts: improving the combustion efficiency of automobile engines reduced only two of the three primary pollutants. (As will be seen, the demand for improved gasoline mileage has introduced a second contradiction into the equation.) The catalytic converter may prove to be only a stopgap in the pollution fight. It is expensive, it relies on scarce resources, and research suggests that it introduces dangerous sulfuric acid mist into the atmosphere. In any event, reports from Los Angeles indicated that by the residents' rough rule of thumb—the ability to see Catalina Island on a clear day—the smog

On the magazine cover: Aug 12 1972 — THE NEW YORKER — Price 50 cents — KOREN — COVER DRAWING BY KOREN. © 1972 THE NEW YORKER MAGAZINE INC.

Edward B. Koren's 1972 *New Yorker* **cover of the imprint of modern America on an older America—suggesting what has been lost in the process—is titled** *Pollution.*

situation was improving. "We'll never get back to the air the Indians had," a county pollution official remarked in 1975, "but come the nineteen-eighties when we get the pre-1974 cars off the road, the air here should be quite palatable."

Whatever short-term compromises and trade-offs may be nesessary, in the longer perspective it appears that technology for the control of auto emissions is within the auto industry's grasp, or will be within a reasonable period. As Henry Ford II pointed out, "It's not going to be necessary to get rid of cars in order to get rid of automotive air pollution." The miasma in our air, once regarded as perhaps the severest problem facing the modern-day car culture, may well turn out to be more easily resolved than some other problems.

Having gotten its feet wet in the matter of regulating Detroit's products through anti-pollution legislation in 1965, Congress plunged into the safety debate in 1966 by passing the National Traffic and Motor Vehicle Safety Act. The attitude of the auto makers toward safety made federal intervention almost inevitable. Its reading of the public mind led Detroit to conclude that stressing safety would deter sales. It was feared, writes economist Lawrence J. White, that once the customer "somehow comes to believe that the car is 'unsafe' (and that is why the safety device is being offered), he may well shy away from buying it in the first

place." Safety advocates such as Ralph Nader insisted that the bulk of the industry's investment in car styling be devoted instead to protecting car occupants. General Motors board chairman Frederic G. Donner countered with the industry's concern about the climate of public acceptance. "If we were to force on people things they are not prepared to buy," he told a Senate committee in 1965, "we would face a consumer revolt, and we want to stay in business."

Detroit's overall record on safety was not as black as it was sometimes painted—the devices Ford had offered on its 1956 "Lifeguard Design" models, for example, were not removed after the company concluded that safety did not sell and were subsequently adopted by other manufacturers; and the handling problems of the early Chevrolet Corvair were not typical of conventional front-engine cars—but G.M.'s assignment of private detectives to harass Nader severely damaged industry credibility on the issue. By failing to take more vigorous leadership on the safety question, just as they had failed to initiate anti-pollution efforts, the auto makers left themselves wide open to federal regulation. Congress's action mandated improvements in passenger protection, driver visibility, and braking systems and required public announcement of any recall of cars to correct safety defects.

The auto safety campaign produced mixed consequences. Although by 1974 the cost of meeting Department of Transportation safety standards had raised the price of the average car $300, the marketplace revolt G.M.'s Donner feared did not occur. No "horde of sans-culotte consumers, waving red flags," the *Medical Tribune* tartly observed, "attacked the castles of General Motors dealers, determined to rip seat belts, dual-braking systems, left-hand mirrors, safety tires, padded dashboards, etc., out of every car or die in the attempt." Nor was the recall of 52 million cars and trucks to correct safety defects during the first decade of federal regulation an appreciable deterrent to sales. The 11.4 million cars produced in 1973 set an all-time record. Discovering that safety sold after all, Detroit voluntarily began to devote increasing attention to such matters as braking, handling, and collision worthiness.

Safety advocates demonstrated a preoccupation with technology that sometimes bordered on the myopic. Federal grants of $7.8 million produced prototype cars crashworthy enough to protect occupants in almost any imaginable circumstance, such as rolling over at 70 mph, but they weighed nearly three tons, handled with the agility of a tank, achieved miniscule gasoline mileage, and stood no chance of ever seeing an assembly line. The so-called Bumper Law, first applied to 1973 models, was intended to preserve the "safety integrity" of lighting, steering, and braking systems in low-speed mishaps of the sort that commonly occur in shopping-center parking lots—and also to reduce subsequent repair costs. The primary result of the Bumper Law was to put a drain on the average car-owner's pocketbook. Compliance with the regulations increased car prices, accident damage to the complex energy-absorbing bumpers proved very costly to repair, and insurance premiums rose accordingly. In this instance, however praiseworthy the intentions, the forcing of technology was probably too hurried.

The motoring public's toleration for being legislated into doing what was good for it proved to have certain limits. A case in point was the federally mandated installation on 1974 cars of a seat-belt interlock that prevented the engine being started unless the front seat belts were fastened. The interlock system was both unwieldy and potentially dangerous in emergency situations, and public protests forced its repeal. Similar concerns caused repeated postponement of the Department of Transportation's efforts to make air bags mandatory, first proposed for 1972 model cars. The air bag, designed to inflate instantly to cushion motorists in the event of a collision, was challenged by Detroit on the grounds of cost and public acceptance, and by other critics on the grounds of effectiveness and the immutability of Murphy's Law ("Anything that can go wrong will go

321

wrong"). Both DOT aides and industry lawyers," writes journalist John Jerome, "shudder over the vision of an unfortunate car owner nudging a fence railing in a parking lot and thereupon being blinded by splinters from his own rimless spectacles." To avoid the fate of the seat-belt interlock, the air bag was subjected to further testing and evaluation.

One consequence of assigning the automobile the role of safety scapegoat was to divert attention from the driver, the real culprit in the vast majority of highway mishaps. No safety study undertaken since the issue first received serious attention in the 1920's had indicted mechanical faults for more than a small fraction of accidents. Even when worn brakes or bald tires were adjudged guilty, it was the car owner, not the car, that was at fault. Excessive speed, carelessness and incompetence, and alcohol abuse (involved in about one half of all accident fatalities) remain the primary highway killers. To be sure, the campaign for safer cars has reduced collision deaths and injuries, yet even more vital is the prevention of the collisions in the first place. Dramatic results have been achieved through improved highway design, particularly evident in the Interstate System, and in speed regulation. The imposition of a nationwide 55-mph speed limit in 1974 is credited with saving at least 9,000 lives annually for three years running, representing a drop of more than 16 per cent. Only

once before—during World War II, when a 35-mph limit was in effect—has this decrease in the absolute number of auto fatalities been exceeded. The 1976 rate of highway deaths (3.4 per 100 million vehicle miles) was the lowest since 1923, when such records were first kept. However effective the various automotive safety devices may prove to be, it is apparent that the long-range attainment of highway safety requires ruling off the road the incompetent driver, the speeding driver, and especially the drunken driver.

The third federal invasion of Detroit's sacred preserves promised to be the most far-reaching. Pleading a national crisis, Washington set about legislating out of existence the big car, the long-time centerpiece of the car culture.

So long as consumers expressed a willingness to buy large cars, Detroit was more than willing to build them, for the simple reason that they maximized profits. In terms of investment in plant and machinery, in labor, and in advertising, building a small car costs about the same as building a large one, assuming that the economies of scale apply in both cases; only in the cost of raw materials is there an appreciable difference—in the sixties perhaps $500. But since the list price of a full-size car is one or two thousand dollars more than what can be charged for a compact, the profit differential is substantial indeed. Thus it was with some trepida-

tion that the Big Three introduced their first compacts in the 1960 model year. Not only would unit profits be lower, but there was concern that compacts would cut into sales of larger cars. As it turned out, while there was some trading down, the compacts scored most heavily against imports, whose market share was halved between 1959 and 1962. Furthermore, compact buyers loaded up their purchases with high-profit options and accessories. Detroit breathed a sigh of relief.

Throughout the sixties, however, large and intermediate-size cars continued to be the industry's bread and butter, particularly at General Motors, and in 1969 they held a better than seventy-two per cent share of the market. But the import tide was on the rise. Led by Volkswagen, foreign cars captured more than one tenth of all domestic sales in 1968. Their compacts having steadily grown in size and price, Detroit's auto makers concluded that once again there was room for them to enter the bottom end of the market. A decade after they had first repelled the foreign invasion, they brought forth a new generation of small cars. And these were small indeed, with wheelbases shorter even than the old Model T's. The Ford Pinto, the General Motors Vega, and the American Motors Gremlin, all introduced in 1970, were christened subcompacts.

The Pinto did well in the marketplace, and the Gremlin helped keep

The highly automated manufacture of the subcompact Chevrolet Vega included these robot Unimate welders, which, General Motors claimed, performed ninety-five per cent of the body welds. The Vega's teaser ad promised an auto that would do everything well; it did not, at least for some time.

the wolf away from A.M.C.'s door, but the Vega created as much of a public-relations and credibility problem for General Motors, and by extension for the auto industry as a whole, as the Corvair had earlier. The giant seemed to have trouble fitting small cars into its corporate mold. Beginning in the Alfred Sloan era, General Motors had consistently compiled not only the highest corporate profits in the industry but the highest unit profits on individual products as well, and it was determined to maintain this pattern with the Vega. The goal was to slash labor costs by as much as $50 a car, which would effect savings of $20 million a year if the car sold as anticipated. A Chevrolet plant at Lordstown, Ohio, was revamped into a highly computerized and automated mode for Vega assembly. It was to be to innovative auto making in the seventies what Ford's Highland Park plant had been in the teens. Sophisticated robot welding machines called Unimates welded Vega bodies with relentless mechanical precision. (In her study of the Lordstown phenomenon Emma Rothschild compared the "blind and clutching" Unimates to the automated feeding machines in Chaplin's *Modern Times*.) The final-assembly line was tuned to spew out more than one hundred Vegas an hour; previous assembly of full-size Chevrolets at Lordstown had produced sixty an hour. Cost control, production economies, and worker discipline were put under the direction of the General Motors Assembly Division, an elite subdivision within the G.M. family famous—or notorious—for getting the work out. GMAD, said Lordstown's workers, stood for Gotta Make Another Dollar.

GMAD took command at Lordstown late in 1971. Less than six months later the workers were out on strike, not for higher wages or fringe benefits but to protest working conditions. They claimed that G.M. regarded them as robots, little different from the Unimates. They told of harsh discipline, of job insecurity, of speed-ups achieved not by increasing the pace of the assembly line but by requiring more labor of each worker by laying off fellow workers. Echoing the plaints of the 1937 sit-down strikers in Flint, Lordstown's workers sought recognition as human beings. "They don't want to tell the company what to do," a UAW official explained, "but simply have something to say about what *they're* going to do. They just want to be treated with dignity. That's not asking a hell of a lot."

Before it was settled by the relaxation of GMAD rigors, the Lordstown labor revolt received widespread publicity, none of it favorable to General Motors. Instead of an industrial Utopia, the *Wall Street Journal* remarked, Lordstown exemplified

---

The Love Affair: A Status Report

[The energy crisis] has once again cast a spotlight on the firm hold that the automobile has on the American psyche. . . . What really seems to have happened is that the ardor has cooled. The car may no longer be the object of romantic attention she once was. But she is slimming down and shedding some of her over-dressed and demanding ways. . . .

The American complains about traffic jams and mechanical failures. He rails against mechanics, dealers and auto companies he suspects of cheating or manipulating him. He winces at the high cost of the car and its operation. He looks at the auto makers' profits and turns red.

But with his neighbors he continues to buy new cars at the rate of more than 10 million a year. It can be argued that the highway lobby has rigged things so that he has no choice. . . .

Still, millions of Americans not only accept the way of life that the automobile allows, but eagerly embrace it—especially working people. . . . Not to them, they say, is a car in itself a measure of status or an agent of self-esteem. Necessary to the good life, yes. But a love object as such, no.
—William K. Stevens, in the New York *Times*, May 15, 1977

YOUR MONEY OR YOUR WAY OF LIFE!

I'M THINKING IT OVER

ARAB OIL

The dependence of a nation of motorists on costly imported petroleum reminded the Memphis *Commercial Appeal*'s Draper Hill of Jack Benny's famous dilemma. In Benny's shoes is Secretary of State Henry Kissinger.

Paradise Lost. It was pointed out that in many respects the "Fordist" nature of auto work had not changed in half a century. The pay might be high and the benefits extensive, but the basic nature of assembly-line work, which comprises about a quarter of Detroit's blue-collar labor force, retained many of the robotlike characteristics first revealed at Highland Park. Auto plants, Walter Reuther had said in 1964, were "gold plated sweat shops." In the opinion of most commentators, there seemed little reason to modify that view.

As if the unfavorable Lordstown publicity were not enough, an embarassingly large number of Vegas turned out to be lemons. The car suffered from design faults that required three major safety recalls, and from corner-cutting production errors that many buyers felt made a mockery of advertisements for "The little car that does everything well. Everything? Everything. . . ." The most persistent sources of complaint were the trouble-prone aluminum engine and the erratic brakes. G.M. president Edward N. Cole fathered the Vega, as he had fathered the Corvair when he headed the Chevrolet division a decade earlier; no doubt he wondered at the gulf between design expectations and production realities at this largest of car makers.

The Vega's troubles posed no real threat to the viability of the G.M. giant. On the larger stage of public opinion, however, the trials of the little car

served to aggravate the credibility problem plaguing Detroit. Critics were rising on every side to condemn American cars as unsafe, unreliable, uneconomical. It was said that the man in the street's love affair with the automobile was fading. General Motors's James M. Roche disagreed. "America's romance with the automobile is not over," he explained to the *Wall Street Journal*; "instead, it has blossomed into a marriage." In that event, it was a marriage increasingly marked by ups and downs.

The year 1973 will be remembered as the beginning of the end for the big car in America. Although domestic small cars were selling well, due in part to overseas inflationary pressures and two devaluations of the dollar that drove up the prices of imported models, there remained enough "gas guzzlers" on the road to set a postwar low in fuel economy. The 1973 General Motors line of cars, for example, averaged less than twelve miles to the gallon, and the balance of the domestic line-up averaged very little more. The steady decline in fuel economy had steepened over the previous half-dozen years thanks to the growing popularity of such engine-driven accessories as air conditioners and the inhibiting effect of pollution controls on engine efficiency. During 1973's summer travel peak there were sporadic but ominous gasoline shortages. Then, in October, a threat to the car culture appeared from abroad.

The petroleum-exporting states of the Middle East resorted to "oil diplomacy" in their conflict with Israel, declaring an embargo on oil shipments to Israel's allies, most notably the United States. More than one tenth of the nation's petroleum came from the Middle East.

The Arab oil embargo dragged on for six months. A 55-mph speed limit was imposed to save fuel. Gasoline prices shot upward some thirty per cent, and in certain areas of the country, particularly the Northeast, service stations were clogged with long lines of motorists impatiently waiting hours for their dole of fuel. As historian James J. Flink points out, the embargo was actually something of a paper tiger, with as many as seven hundred thousand barrels of Arab oil a day "leaking" into the United States. It was also revealed, in the aftermath of the embargo, that at no point had the supply of gasoline available nationwide fallen more than a tiny fraction below what it had been a year earlier, and that in fact three weeks before the embargo was lifted —when uncounted drivers were still lining up at their local stations— gasoline stocks were five per cent *higher* than early 1973 levels. This revelation triggered much public resentment and charges of conspiracy on the part of the oil oligopoly to raise prices and drive independent operators out of business. Whatever the facts of the matter, the embargo threw Detroit into a tailspin.

Car sales plummeted, particularly of the large gas guzzlers. The nation staggered into a sharp recession, further depressing the auto market. By 1975 car sales were running thirty-eight per cent below 1973's record level, the largest drop since the Depression. More than a quarter million auto workers were jobless. Chrysler was driven to the wall, reporting a 1975 loss of $259.5 million, the worst in automotive history, and raising grave doubts about the future of the number-three auto maker.

Although the auto industry, including Chrysler, rebounded strongly in 1976, the Arab embargo forced the nation to confront the harsh fact that its car culture was expending energy resources at a prodigious rate. Some thirty per cent of the petroleum products consumed annually went to run passenger cars. A growing percentage of the nation's petroleum—more than forty per cent by 1976—was imported, much of it from the politically volatile Middle East. Annual motor vehicle mileage, which had passed the one-trillion-mile mark in 1968, continued to rise each year. There were 106 million cars on the road in 1975, theoretically enabling the nation's entire population to go driving at any one time using only the front seats. The statistics went on and on, often chilling in their reality.

The auto industry's response to the emerging energy crisis suggested a new attitude toward social responsibility. Early in 1975 the heads of General Motors, Ford, Chrysler, and American Motors pledged a voluntary program to increase the fuel efficiency of their cars by forty per cent within five years. Had this initiative occurred a decade or so earlier, Detroit might have been hailed for its statesmanship. But the foot-dragging on the air pollution and safety issues was still fresh in many minds. The industry's credibility remained low. "We've become the whipping boys," Ford Washington lobbyist Rodney Markley told The New Yorker's Elizabeth Drew. "The industry is breaking its pick to get there, to build a more economical car—if we can, in light of the emission standards. Congress doesn't have to act, but it will. Our only hope is that in putting our feet to the fire it doesn't try to push us too fast."

Markley's forecast was accurate. The industry pledge was accepted, but to insure that it would be carried out it was enacted into law. The Energy Policy and Conservation Act specified that by the 1980 model year, in graduated steps, each auto maker must produce a line of cars capable of achieving an economy standard of 20 miles to the gallon on what was termed a "sales-weighted average." It was the most sweeping piece of legislation affecting the auto industry ever passed. Washington was inserting itself squarely not only into the process of designing cars, but into the marketing of them as well. For every five gas-guzzling 15-mile-per-gallon 1980 models a company sold, for example, to stay within the law it would also have to sell five economy models capable of achieving 25 miles to the gallon. For an auto maker such as General Motors, with its array of offerings of every shape and size, the marketing equation would be complex indeed. After 1980 the equation was scheduled to become even more complex. The mandated mileage requirement for 1985 models was set at 27.5 miles per gallon.

The irony of the situation was not lost on thoughtful observers. For years Detroit had suffered critics' charges that as an oligopoly it dictated consumer buying habits, that it forced impractical and wasteful cars on the American people. Whatever truth there once might have been in such assertions, the widening range of car types available in the seventies put the consumer in the driver's seat in the matter of choice, sometimes to Detroit's discomfort. During the Arab oil embargo, lobbyist Markley observed, "the industry built small cars as fast as it could—and guess what. The gasoline lines disappeared, and so did the public rush to buy small cars. We couldn't give them away." Now, to stay within the law and indeed to stay in business, Detroit had no choice but to dictate—or attempt to dictate—car-buying habits by limiting the range of choices. "We soon could be entering a period when we can build only what the government permits," an industry spokesman said in 1976. In order to minimize their risks under the sales-weighted average mileage formula, companies would have to make every car in their line as small and economical as possible. This foretold the eventual end of the traditional Detroit dreamboat—and the end of an era dating back to the close of World War II.

Undertaken in concert with the campaign to make the automobile safer, more economical in using energy, and less of a polluter were efforts to reduce automobile use. On trial were several deeply rooted traditions of the car culture.

One of the first traditions to be challenged was the long-accepted belief that the highway was an unmitigated social blessing. "Society has a disconcerting way of unexpectedly changing its standards of taste. . . ," writes Samuel C. Florman in his thoughtful study *The Existential Pleasures of Engineering*. "We have highways running all over creation because engineers never dreamed that one day people would decide that highways were ugly and unpleasantly noisy." This shift in viewpoint appeared first, as we have seen, in the nation's cities, where aroused citizens rose up to smite the highway lobby. No longer acceptable was the credo expressed in 1964 by New York's highway emperor, Robert Moses: "When you operate in an overbuilt metropolis you have to hack your way with a meat ax." San Fran-

ciscans halted construction of a massive freeway, known locally as the concrete monster, along the city's Embarcadero. A proposal to build (at an estimated cost of $100 million a mile) a ten-lane expressway across lower Manhattan was killed in 1969, the same year that plans to drive an Interstate route through New Orleans's historic French Quarter were blocked. Public debate forced similar cancellations, or at least modifications, of construction plans in many other cities. New procedures were adopted to grant the citizenry a larger voice in highway policy before, rather than after, routes were selected and planning well begun. The environmental impact of any new road project became a primary concern. In what was perhaps the most symbolic act of all, California's 1976 state highway budget called for a mere 77 miles of new freeway construction; the annual average for the previous eight years had been 280 miles.

However heretical the thought might seem to the highway lobby, by the mid-seventies, for the first time in three quarters of a century, the point was being made that the American road network was finally adequate to American needs. Most of the links in the Interstate System were in place, especially those needed to carry truck traffic, the lifeblood of the nation's economy. In recognition of that fact, the once-sacrosanct Highway Trust Fund was opened to the financing of other transportation needs in

1973. Instead of continuing to follow slavishly John Loudon McAdam's dictum of building roads to accommodate the traffic, it was suggested that the traffic be regulated to fit the existing roads.

Any effort to reduce car use was certain to be a thorny undertaking. The 1970 census revealed that three out of four working Americans used a car to get to their jobs. In California the figure was four out of five. The vast majority of car commuters (five out of six) drove to and from work alone. What was to be done about this enormous and growing mass of commuter automobiles—which passed the fifty-million mark in 1970—jamming the roadways of the nation twice a day, five days a week, was already of deep concern to municipal officials, urban planners, environmentalists, and the like well before the oil embargo of 1973. Subsequently, the car commuter became one of the primary issues in the national debate over energy conservation.

Of the multitude of roles the automobile plays in modern America, serving as transportation for the working population is by far the largest, accounting for some forty per cent of all auto travel. Any major shift in car use would have to begin there. It was generally agreed that a significant reduction in the number of commuter cars could be accomplished in only two ways—persuading people to shift to some form of public transportation

Segments of a typical American autoscape of the seventies, photographed in and around Denver by Robert Adams

or persuading them to leave their vehicles at home and form a car pool instead. Both efforts necessarily confronted certain psychological realities about car ownership.

The car as an expression of personal democracy is a thread that runs prominently through the course of automotive history. From the days of the Duryea brothers onward it has acted as a leveling social force, granting the average man a range of personal choices—where to travel, where to work, where to live, where to seek pleasure and recreation—once available only to the wealthy. Car ownership offered emancipation to the farmer, the urban laborer, the white-collar worker, even (to a lesser extent) the poor; the 1970 census recorded that better than two out of five of those classified as living below the poverty level possessed an automobile. Political democracy had a less obvious impact on the daily lives of millions of Americans than the personal democracy inherent in car ownership.

The substitution of mass transit for car commuting attracted intense interest and study. Transit advocates open any debate by pointing out the disparity in carrying capacity. A single track in a rapid-transit rail system, for example, can carry as many as sixty thousand passengers an hour (the figure attained at the peak rush hour in New York City), compared to a single freeway lane's capacity (assuming a predominance of one-car commuters) of about three thousand an hour. Since very few commuters would voluntarily elect the sardine-like quality of the New York subway at rush hour if any alternative was available, a more realistic comparison would match railroad or light-rail transit at its most attractive—no standees, modern and efficiently run equipment—against the highway. In this match-up rail still outcarries automobile by about ten to one. This is a very substantial advantage, particularly when energy use and environmental considerations are added into the calculations.

As indispensable as rail transit is in certain high-density urban situations, its long-range potential to reduce auto travel measurably has limitations. It can operate effectively only in regions where there are radial travel corridors well enough defined to justify the capital costs involved. These costs are considerable. America's newest urban rail system, Washington's Metro, had absorbed some $5.25 billion by 1977 and was still building. That figure was one twelfth the sum expended to date on the entire Interstate System. In 1976, for the third time in nine years, Los Angeles voters rejected a proposal to finance a $5.8 billion rail transit system to replace the region's once-extensive interurban network that had expired in the fifties, victim of the car culture and a highly devious scheme by General Motors to increase the market for its buses. Even where rail service already exists, the public

subsidies required to bring it up to par and maintain it as an attractive alternate to auto commuting are exceedingly high. The opening of the Highway Trust Fund in 1973 offered one solution to the transit dilemma. By rejecting Interstate highways scheduled for their communities, such cities as Boston, Philadelphia, Portland, Oregon, and Washington were able to funnel the allocated funds into mass-transit alternatives. Washington anticipated that the fund would eventually pay one fifth of the Metro's final cost.

The most widely favored mass-transit vehicle is the bus, primarily because if offers a realistic compromise between the two extremes of auto and rail commuting. In contrast to rail transit, buses offer route flexibility, represent far less of an initial investment, and operate on urbanways that are (in effect) already paid for through gasoline and use taxes and tolls. Carefully planned "bus only" expressway lanes are capable of matching the carrying capacity of rail transit at considerably less expense per passenger mile; costs vary from one fifth as much in high-passenger-demand areas to as little as one eighth as much in regions with lower passenger demand. To make an appreciable dent in current commuter patterns, however, not only requires buses that put a premium on passenger comfort, but a great many of them. It has been estimated that one hundred thousand new buses would be needed to double the share—to five per cent—of urban travelers carried by mass transit. Even that small an increase needs qualification: studies of mass-transit patterns suggest that improvements in rail service tend to draw patrons primarily from buses; upgraded bus service attracts former rail commuters. The urban car commuter—thus far at least—has resolutely stayed in his car.

Most authorities agree that the problem is mainly psychological. As Lawrence J. White observes, "A car perhaps represents one of the last bastions of privacy in modern America, where a man is away from his family and his boss and colleagues. He can sing, shout, scratch his ears, turn the radio on loud, and make threatening gestures and shout obscenities at other motorists, all without fear of social rebuke." The implied freedoms that have made the automobile so attractive to generations of Americans—the freedom to go when or where they like, with company of their own choosing or no company at all, without dependence on fixed routes or timetables—are no less attractive today. To those resolutely independent, even traffic jams are bearable, thanks to their stereo systems and the insularity their air conditioning gives them. Whether in bumper-to-bumper traffic or rolling free, writes urban planner Roger Starr, the car commuter regards himself as "master of his own destiny, captain of his own soul."

The quickest, most effective, most inexpensive route to reducing the number of car commuters is through car pools. Investigators in various communities find that the occupancy rate of rush-hour traffic averages between 1.2 and 1.5 per car. As Eric Hirst noted in a study for *Science* in 1976, "There is an enormous energy conservation potential in the empty seats in automobiles traveling during the daily peak hours." Theoretically, increasing a 1.2 occupancy rate by just 25 per cent would cut America's fuel bill by 440,000 barrels of oil a day, or about 6 per cent. Improved air quality and reduced traffic congestion would follow.

The nation's lone experience with the extensive use of car pools was during World War II, when they proved highly effective in reducing traffic volume. The practice was hardly voluntary, however: there was tire and gasoline rationing and an aura of wartime patriotism to encourage compliance. Also, the nation's living and working patterns were far less decentralized early in the forties than they are today. In Los Angeles in the seventies (to take an extreme case) only five per cent of the area's jobs are located in the downtown district. On any morning in a typical Los Angeles suburb, car commuters are likely to head off in half a dozen different directions to reach their work, making car pools difficult. Similar, if less extreme, patterns are found na-

Looking Forward

The individuality of automobile transportation is something that Americans, and others, are simply not going to give up except under a degree of compulsion completely unacceptable in a free society. Most of the plans for revised transportation policies recognize this fact and incorporate it realistically into their programs. . . .

The basic feature of change is that it continues. The transportation revolution of the past century is going to go on, and no one can predict accurately what new forms of mobility will appear in the future. . . . But unless there is a radical change in our social and economic structure, people will continue to want and use transportation that will give them maximum freedom to move about and to choose where they live, work, or locate their businesses. . . . For this purpose, there is no substitute in sight for the highway and the motorized vehicle, whether "motorized" means an internal combustion engine, steam, electricity, fuel cells, nuclear energy, or sorcery. This is the paramount mode of individual, flexible, door-to-door transportation of both people and goods. . . . Putting artificial restraints on highway transportation can yield only economic and social stagnation.

—John B. Rae, *The Road and the Car in American Life*, 1971

331

The brochure put out by the proprietors of
Honolulu's Ala Moana shopping center
describes the 155-store complex as "one of
the man-made wonders of the Pacific" and
"the best of all possible shopping worlds."
The multi-level parking area surrounding
the central mall can accommodate 7,800 cars.

WERNER STOY, CAMERA HAWAII

ALA◉MOANA
The world's most
interesting shopping center

Honolulu, Hawaii

tionwide. Nevertheless, through carrot-and-stick techniques, car pools are thought to have the potential for reducing car use in many areas at far less cost to the taxpayer than the expansion of mass transit. The carrot includes special urbanway lanes for car poolers, lower tolls, and various forms of subsidies. The stick involves making single-occupant car commuting both expensive and inconvenient through higher taxes and fees and restrictions on such things as downtown parking. The issue is finding an acceptable compromise between society's need to conserve energy and preserve the environment and the individual's rights and freedoms. At the heart of the matter is whether average commuter Smith can still view himself as "master of his own destiny" with a load of car-pool passengers.

One immutable fact about the car culture is that many of its elements will not or cannot be changed overnight. Dependence on the automobile is woven deeply into the American social fabric. As a New York *Times* editorial points out, to save gasoline "eighty million suburbanites who live miles from work, school and store can't be expected to abandon their homes." Mass transit is impractical outside metropolitan areas; as a congressman asked during an energy debate, "Did you ever hear of anybody catching a subway in Osceola, Arkansas, or a bus in Bugtussle, Oklahoma?" The decentralization of living and working patterns that began after World War II showed no sign of tapering off in the seventies; if anything, it was increasing. The Interstate System encouraged industrial dispersal, allowing the building of factories in the middle of nowhere yet easily accessible to both workers and truck transport. Demographers noted a lessening of the traditional dominant role of the central city in favor of self-sufficient suburban clusters and spoke of a "rural renaissance," a major migratory shift that since 1970 saw a million more people move away from population centers than into them. All these trends rested squarely on widespread car ownership.

A second reality about the car culture is its web of linkages to the national economy. As has been the case since early in the 1920's the Detroit auto establishment, whose financial health is highly visible to all, comprises only the tip of an economic iceberg. Auto making is the nation's largest industrial undertaking, drawing its machinery, raw materials, parts stocks, and accessories from every corner of the land. Beyond this is the enormous business of supplying and maintaining and financing the car culture in all its complexity, and the care and feeding of the motoring public in all its numbers. An estimated 14.7 million employees— one sixth of the nation's work force— depend for their livelihood on the automobile. Only government employs more people. Consequently, whatever is good economically for General Motors—and Ford and Chrysler and American Motors—is by extension good for a very sizable slice of the nation's population. Any alteration of the car culture requires the most careful planning and calculation if it is not to create an economic upheaval.

Detroit faces a challenge unlike any it has ever encountered. Within only a decade it went from one of the least government-regulated major industries to one of the most heavily regulated. The mandating of safety, emission, and fuel-economy standards insured radical future changes in the performance, appearance, and marketing of automobiles and perhaps evolutionary changes in the character of the car culture. The industry's credibility remained under attack. Critics were at its throat. Detroit faced "decline and possible extinction," warned Emma Rothschild in *Paradise Lost*. The Detroit-created phenomenon of automobility "was no longer a historically progressive force for change in American civilization," charged James J. Flink in *The Car Culture*. In the challenge, however, was opportunity, if the auto industry cared to grasp it—opportunity to restore the luster of its engineering eminence tarnished by the insolent chariots, to regain the reputation for producing vehicles of honest value, to reaffirm through innovation that the automobile is a valid and socially responsible vehicle of personal transport.

What the cars of 1980, 1985, and after will be like became the subject of the most intensive future-product programs ever undertaken in Detroit. General Motors and Ford announced budgeted investments between them of $23 billion for ten-year development plans. In certain repects the three qualities demanded of Detroit's products by Washington—safety, cleanliness, economy—are contradictory. Over the short term at least, not all may be achieved simultaneously.

Making today's standard cars fuel-stingy, for example, can be achieved by a variety of means. Among them are smaller and more efficiently running engines (such as the stratified-charge type), fewer power-sapping accessories, improved transmissions, and more aerodynamic design (about a quarter of an engine's output at cruising speed is devoted to overcoming air resistance). But by far the largest gain comes from reducing weight. Thus the full-size car of tomorrow: shorter wheelbase, less sheet-metal overhang front and rear, light aluminum and plastic components, slimmed-down engine and drive train, less elaborate interiors. Designer Syd Mead puts the adjustment required of car fanciers in historical perspective: "The pounding roar of hairy V-8's is certainly exciting, as, I suppose, was the slapping of canvas high on the masts of clipper ships

before the steam era." The six-passenger American car a decade hence will probably be the size of today's compact, weigh about a ton and a half, accelerate leisurely, and bear no resemblance at all to the land yachts of old. Such cars may be contrary to the safety mandate for crash-worthiness, however, suggesting the possibilities of enforced seat-belt use and the air bag.

There also promises to be a contradiction between fuel economy and emissions goals. The various means developed for improving combustion in gasoline engines achieve the happy pairing of increased mileage and reduced hydrocarbons and carbon-monoxide pollutants, but thus far they are less successful in coping with nitrogen oxides. Barring tighter control of the nitrogen pollutants, a trade-off between the energy and environmental advocates would be called for as the mandated standards become stricter. The case of the diesel engine dramatizes the trade-off situation. Before the energy crisis, the diesel for passenger-car use ran a poor second to the gasoline engine in many respects—noise, weight, cost, starting ease, acceleration, among others. Then the Arab embargo pointed up its one advantage, a twenty-five-per-cent edge in fuel economy, and spurred crash programs in diesel development. But the diesel's very high operating temperatures produce considerable quantities of nitrogen oxides, making it the bane of concerned environmentalists.

The mandated pressure for change sent automotive engineers hurrying to their drawing boards and to their shelves full of long-discarded ideas. One fifty-year-old scheme for shutting down several of the engine's cylinders once a car was moving well was updated by mating it with computer technology. In a six-cylinder engine, for example, a computerized sensor system automatically cuts off fuel to three of the cylinders for economical highway cruising, then cuts them back in as needed. A study by California's Jet Propulsion Laboratory in 1975 recommended a crash program to develop for mass production by the eighties the gas turbine, which Detroit had been experimenting with for two decades, and the Stirling-cycle engine, which had a pedigree dating back to 1816, when its design was patented by a Scottish parson and amateur inventor named Robert Stirling. In both, combustion takes place outside the "working area" of the engine, allowing effective pollution control. Superheated air does the work in the turbine, and expansive hydrogen gas acts on pistons in the Stirling. JPL estimated the two designs to be twenty to thirty-five per cent more fuel-efficient than conventional auto engines.

When they dusted off the internal-combustion engine's old rivals, steamers and electrics, the engineers confronted the same problems that had plagued those venerable power plants half a century earlier. The steamer was set aside as too fuel-inefficient and complicated for mass production. Investigators of the electric discovered that their modern versions ran about as well as the Bakers and Rauch and Langs their grandmothers had driven sedately about town. Speed and range were still restricted by the limitations of the lead-acid storage battery. Without a breakthrough in battery technology, the conventional electric appeared to have little utility except perhaps for limited urban use—a verdict first articulated as early as 1900.

A more esoteric electric proposal featured an energy-storing flywheel, made of very light, strong materials developed for the space program, operating in a semivacuum for minimum air friction loss. As Donald E. Carr describes the process in *Energy and the Earth Machine,* "One would simply spin up the flywheel (perhaps . . . to supersonic speeds of 12,000 or more revolutions per minute) with the motor running off an electric outlet; thus the flywheel would drive the car with the motor operating as a generator to supply power to smaller motors, one on each wheel." One recharge, according to Carr, would last six months or more. The flywheel electric is the sort of automotive alternative certain to be investigated in anticipation of the day when the oil runs dry.

"Someday, that's going to happen," writes Stephan Wilkinson in *Car and Driver.* "Perhaps not in your lifetime, maybe not even in your children's lifetime. But it will someday, and then we'll have to start feeding our internal-combustion engines plankton or powdered eggs or processed sawdust. Because there flat won't be any oil left." Estimating the date that the world's petroleum reserves will be depleted has preoccupied experts for decades and will continue to do so right up to the final day. The Carter administration's effort to establish a comprehensive national energy policy, initiated in the spring of 1977, looked toward that time, while seeking in the short term to stretch existing supplies and to reduce American dependence on imported oil. If the past history of the automobile in America is any guide, in the year 2001, or whenever, there will still be cars of some description, granting people the means to travel when and where they need or want to go. Perhaps by then Detroit will have relearned the responsibility of producing machines as honest in this new era as Model T was in its era. Perhaps the new reality of the seventies will persuade Americans that this most remarkable example of twentieth-century technology is (like all technology) the servant rather than the master it has sometimes become. For beyond everything else, the automobile represents freedom, and for three quarters of a century that freedom has been thought worth preserving.

A dashing Simplex attracts an admiring crowd at a California old car show.

THE COLLECTORS

The sober realities of today's car culture have triggered a growing interest in the individualistic cars of yesterday. At least 100,000 collectors and restorers are active in the United States. Attendance at auto shows, exhibits, and museums is in the millions. The motives of collectors are varied, but there is one that is common to all of them—an appreciation of fine machinery and good design. Here are examples.

Peerless's motto was "All that the name implies," and this restoration lives up to that claim. It is a 1910 Model 27 town car, one of the company's top-of-the-line offerings. At right is the car as it emerged from years in dead storage. Above is the four-cylinder engine renewed to factory-fresh condition. At top, restorer William E. Donze of Strongsville, Ohio, poses with the completed car during a 1962 rerunning of the famed Glidden Tour.

Where Peerless bespoke elegance and dignity, the 1932 V-12 Auburn Speedster pictured here was the epitome of dash and sportiness; E. L. Cord offered it to those, writes Ralph Stein, who "might dare drive it past Hoovervilles and breadlines." V-12 Auburns sold for well under $2,000, fully equipped. The Speedster's boattail configuration is seen at right, its finely restored cockpit above. At top is its owner, Joseph L. Percoco of New York, at an auto show.

The Auburn Speedster on page 339 was professionally restored at the workshop of William J. Gassaway in South Amboy, New Jersey, where the sequence of pictures at left was taken over a span of three years. The classic being reborn from the frame up is a 1934 Duesenberg SJ with coachwork by Walton, owned by Raymond L. Lutgert of Naples, Florida. At top is the cockpit as it looked before restoration; and a miscellany of original parts. The three pictures at center show the renewing of wood body framing; a display of rechromed parts; and the rebuilding of sheet-metal panels. The scenes at bottom detail the in-progress restoration of body and seats. Below, the nearly completed car is put on exhibit. Duesenbergs are regarded as American works of art, and priced as such; in 1977 a rare example brought $228,000.

These examples of American classic cars were photographed at an auto show held annually on California's Monterey Peninsula. At right is a Duesenberg Model S J, and above are two outstanding sports machines, a Mercer (left) and a Stutz.

BIBLIOGRAPHY

Anderson, Rudolph E. *The Story of the American Automobile*. Washington: Public Affairs Press, 1950.

Automobile Quarterly. Princeton: Automobile Quarterly, Inc., 1962 to date.

Editors of *Automobile Quarterly*. *The American Car Since 1775*. New York: Automobile Quarterly, Inc., 1971.

Boyd, T. A. *Professional Amateur: The Biography of Charles Franklin Kettering*. New York: E. P. Dutton, 1957.

Brooks, John. "The Fate of the Edsel," *Business Adventures*. New York: Weybright and Talley, 1969.

Carson, Richard Burns. *The Olympian Cars: The Great American Luxury Automobiles of the Twenties and Thirties*. New York: Alfred A. Knopf, 1976.

Chandler, Alfred D., Jr. *Giant Enterprise: Ford, General Motors, and the Automobile Industry*. New York: Harcourt, Brace & World, 1964.

Chandler, Alfred D., Jr. *Strategy and Structure: Chapters in the History of the American Industrial Enterprise*. Cambridge, Mass.: MIT Press, 1962.

Chandler, Alfred D., Jr., and Stephen Salsbury. *Pierre S. Du Pont and the Making of the Modern Corporation*. New York: Harper & Row, 1971.

Chrysler, Walter P., with Boyden Sparkes. *Life of an American Workman*. New York: Dodd, Mead, 1937.

Clymer, Floyd. *Henry's Wonderful Model T*. New York: McGraw-Hill, 1955.

Cohn, David L. *Combustion on Wheels: An Informal History of the Automobile Age*. Boston, Houghton Mifflin, 1944.

Crabb, Richard. *Birth of a Giant: The Men and Incidents That Gave America the Motorcar*. Philadelphia: Chilton Book Company, 1969.

Edwards, Charles E. *Dynamics of the Automobile Industry*. Columbia, S.C.: University of South Carolina Press, 1965.

Epstein, Ralph C. *The Automobile Industry: Its Economic and Commercial Development*. Chicago and New York: A. W. Shaw, 1928.

Fine, Sidney. *Sit-Down: The General Motors Strike of 1936–1937*. Ann Arbor: University of Michigan Press, 1969.

Flink, James J. *America Adopts the Automobile, 1895–1910*. Cambridge, Mass.: MIT Press, 1970.

Flink, James J. *The Car Culture*. Cambridge, Mass.: MIT Press, 1975.

Florman, Samuel C. *The Existential Pleasures of Engineering*. New York: St. Martin's Press, 1976.

Glasscock, C. B. *The Gasoline Age*. Indianapolis and New York: Bobbs-Merrill, 1937.

Greenleaf, William. *Monopoly on Wheels: Henry Ford and the Selden Automobile Patent*. Detroit: Wayne State University Press, 1961.

Gustin, Lawrence R. *Billy Durant: Creator of General Motors*. Grand Rapids: William B. Eerdmans, 1973.

Jardim, Anne. *The First Henry Ford: A Study in Personality and Business Leadership*. Cambridge, Mass.: MIT Press, 1970.

Jerome, John. *The Death of the Automobile: The Fatal Effect of the Golden Era, 1955–1970*. New York: W. W. Norton, 1972.

Keats, John. *The Insolent Chariots*. Philadelphia: J. B. Lippincott, 1958.

Kennedy, E. D. *The Automobile Industry: The Coming of Age of Capitalism's Favorite Child*. New York: Reynal & Hitchcock, 1941.

Kettering, Charles F., and Allen Orth. *The New Necessity*. Baltimore: Williams & Wilkins, 1932.

Langworth, Richard M. *Kaiser-Frazer: The Last Onslaught on Detroit*. Princeton: Automobile Quarterly, Inc., 1975.

Leavitt, Helen. *Superhighway—Superhoax*. New York: Doubleday, 1970.

Leland, Mrs. Wilfred C., with Minnie Dubbs Millbrook. *Master of Precision: Henry M. Leland*. Detroit: Wayne State University Press, 1966.

Lewis, David L. *The Public Image of Henry Ford: An American Folk Hero and His Company*. Detroit: Wayne State University Press, 1976.

Lingeman, Richard R. *Don't You Know There's a War On? The American Home Front, 1941–1945*. New York: G. P. Putnam's Sons, 1970.

Lord, Chip. *Automerica: A Trip down U.S. Highways from World War II to the Future*. New York: E. P. Dutton, 1976.

Lynd, Robert S., and Helen Merrell Lynd. *Middletown: A Study in Contemporary American Culture*. New York: Harcourt Brace, 1929.

Lynd, Robert S., and Helen Merrell Lynd. *Middletown in Transition: A Study in Cultural Conflicts*. New York: Harcourt, Brace, 1937.

MacManus, Theodore F., and Norman Beasley. *Men, Money, and Motors: The Drama of the Automobile*. New York: Harper & Brothers, 1929.

Marquart, Frank. *An Auto Worker's Journal: The UAW from Crusade to One-Party Union*. University Park, Pa.: Pennsylvania State University Press, 1975.

Maxim, Hiram Percy. *Horseless Carriage Days*. New York: Harper & Brothers, 1936, 1937.

May, George S. *A Most Unique Machine: The Michigan Origins of the American Automobile Industry*. Grand Rapids: William B. Eerdmans, 1975.

Lord Montagu of Beaulieu and Anthony Bird. *History of Steam Cars, 1770–1970*. New York: St. Martin's Press, 1971.

Musselman, M. M. *Get a Horse! The Story of the Automobile in America*. Philadelphia: J. B. Lippincott, 1950.

Nader, Ralph. *Unsafe at Any Speed: The Designed-in Dangers of the American Automobile*. New York: Grossman, 1965.

Nevins, Allan, and Frank Ernest Hill. *Ford: The Times, the Man, the Company*. New York: Charles Scribner's Sons, 1954.

Nevins, Allan, and Frank Ernest Hill. *Ford: Expansion and Challenge, 1915–1933*. New York: Charles Scribner's Sons, 1957.

Nevins, Allan, and Frank Ernest Hill. *Ford: Decline and Rebirth, 1933–1962*. New York: Charles Scribner's Sons, 1962, 1963.

Niemeyer, Glenn A. *The Automotive Career of Ransom E. Olds*. East Lansing, Mich.: Michigan State University Business Studies, 1963.

O'Connell, Jeffrey, and Arthur Myers. *Safety Last: An Indictment of the Auto Industry*. New York: Random House, 1965.

Olson, Sidney. *Young Henry Ford: A Picture History of the First Forty Years*. Detroit: Wayne State University Press, 1963.

Partridge, Bellamy. *Fill 'er Up! The Story of Fifty Years of Motoring*. New York: McGraw-Hill, 1952.

Pearson, Charles T. *The Indomitable Tin Goose: The True Story of Preston Tucker and His Car*. New York: Abelard-Schuman, 1960.

Pound, Arthur. *The Turning Wheel: The Story of General Motors Through Twenty-Five Years, 1908–1933*. Garden City, N.J.: Doubleday, Doran, 1934.

President's Research Committee on Social Trends. *Recent Social Trends in the United States*. New York: McGraw-Hill, 1933.

Rae, John B. *The American Automobile: A Brief History*. Chicago: University of Chicago Press, 1965.

Rae, John B. *American Automobile Manufacturers: The First Forty Years*.

Philadelphia: Chilton Book Company, 1959.

Rae, John B. *The Road and the Car in American Life.* Cambridge, Mass.: MIT Press, 1971.

Reuther, Victor G. *The Brothers Reuther and the Story of the UAW.* Boston: Houghton Mifflin, 1976.

Rothschild, Emma. *Paradise Lost: The Decline of the Auto-Industrial Age.* New York: Random House, 1973.

Seltzer, Lawrence H. *A Financial History of the American Automobile Industry.* Boston: Houghton Mifflin, 1928.

Sloan, Alfred P., Jr., with Boyden Sparkes. *Adventures of a White-Collar Man.* New York: Doubleday, Doran, 1941.

Sloan, Alfred P., Jr. *My Years with General Motors.* New York: Doubleday, 1963.

Sorensen, Charles E., with Samuel T. Williamson. *My Forty Years with Ford.* New York: W. W. Norton, 1956.

Stein, Ralph. *The American Automobile.* New York: Random House, 1975.

Stern, Philip Van Doren. *Tin Lizzie: The Story of the Fabulous Model T Ford.* New York: Simon and Schuster, 1955.

White, Lawrence J. *The Automobile Industry Since 1945.* Cambridge, Mass.: Harvard University Press, 1971.

White, Lee Strout (E. B. White, with Richard L. Strout). *Farewell to Model T.* New York: G. P. Putnam's Sons, 1936.

Widick, B, J., ed. *Auto Work and Its Discontents.* Baltimore: Johns Hopkins University Press, 1976.

Wik, Reynold M. *Henry Ford and Grass-Roots America.* Ann Arbor, Mich.: University of Michigan Press, 1972.

Wilson, Paul C. *Chrome Dreams: Automobile Styling Since 1893.* Radnor, Pa.: Chilton Book Company, 1976.

ACKNOWLEDGMENTS

We are greatly indebted to the following individuals and institutions for making available pictorial materials in their collections and for generously supplying research information:

Robert Adams, Longmont, Calif.
Automobile Club of Southern California, Los Angeles—Lura Dymond
Automobile Quarterly, Princeton, N.J.—L. Scott Bailey, Beverly Rae Kimes, Ian C. Bowers
The Bettmann Archive, New York, N.Y.
Black Star Publishing Co., New York, N.Y.—Yukiko Launois
Brown Brothers, Sterling, Pa.—Harry Collins
Mr. & Mrs. Frank B. Bushey, Bloomfield, Conn.
Mrs. William Cahn, New Haven, Conn.
California Department of Highways, San Francisco—Bob Halligan
Chicago Historical Society—John Tris
Cincinnati Historical Society—Edward P. Malloy
Frederick C. Crawford Auto Museum, Western Reserve Historical Society, Cleveland—Kathy Louie
Culver Pictures, New York, N.Y.—Bob Jackson
Curtis Publishing Co., Indianapolis—Linda S. Stillabower, Helen Wenley
Allan D'Arcangelo, Kenoza Lake, N.Y.
Wesley Day, San Francisco
Detroit Institute of Arts—Rosalind Ellis
Detroit Public Library, National Automotive History Collection—James J. Bradley
Dodge Division, Chrysler Corporation, Detroit—John G. McCandless
Dr. and Mrs. William E. Donze, Strongsville, Ohio
Fairleigh Dickinson University, Harry A. Chesler Collection, Madison, N.J.—Ursula Sommer
Gertrudis Feliu, Paris

Ford Archives, Henry Ford Museum, Dearborn, Mich.—Henry E. Edmunds, David R. Crippen, Winthrop Sears, Jr.
Robert Frank, Mabou, Nova Scotia
Free Library of Philadelphia, Automobile Reference Collection—Mary M. Cattie, Louis G. Helverson
Robert J. Gassaway, South Amboy, N.J.
General Motors Corporation, Detroit and New York—Nettie Seabrooks, Bill Adams, Bill Winters, Maureen Gage
George Hall, San Francisco
Gilman Paper Company, New York, N.Y.—Pierre Aproxine
Shirley Green, Bethesda, Md.
Mrs. John Held, Jr., Clinton, Conn.
Indiana Historical Society Library, Indianapolis—Tom Rumer
Frank H. Johnson, New York, N.Y.
Rosemary Klein, London
Paul M. Levy, Cambridge, Mass.
Library of Congress, Washington, D.C.—Jerry Kearns
Long Island Automotive Museum, Glen Cove and Southampton, N.Y.—Henry Austin Clark, Jr.
Los Angeles County Museum of Natural History—John M. Cahoon
Raymond L. Lutgert, Naples, Fla.
Magnum Photos, New York, N.Y.
Edward P. Manning, Highland Park, Mich.
Marlborough Gallery, New York, N.Y.—Paul Katz, Loretta Baum
Minnesota Historical Society, St. Paul—Bonnie Wilson
Motor Vehicle Manufacturers Association, Detroit—Bernice Huffman, Charles Witze
Museum of Modern Art, New York, N.Y.—Sharon Mechling
National Archives, Washington, D.C.
National Gallery of Canada, Ottawa—Alice Armstrong

National Park Service, Department of the Interior, Washington, D.C.—Lynn Parks, Dick Russell
Nebraska State Historical Society, Lincoln—Ann Reinert
The New Yorker, New York, N.Y.—Ruth C. Rogin
Brenda K. and Paul L. Pascal, Bethesda, Md.
Joseph L. Percoco, New York, N.Y.
Photo Researchers, New York, N.Y.—Bob Zentmeir, Van Bucher
Edward Ruscha, Hollywood, Calif.
Julius Rutin, New York, N.Y.
San Francisco *Chronicle*—Dianne Levy
George Segal, North Brunswick, N.J.
Sidney Janis Gallery, New York, N.Y.—Nicholas Brown
Smithsonian Institution, Department of Transportation, Washington, D.C.—Donald H. Berkebile
State Historical Society of Wisconsin, Madison—George Talbot
Time-Life Picture Agency, New York, N.Y.—Hannah Bruce, Jean Reynolds
Underwood & Underwood, New York, N.Y.—Milton Davidson
University of Louisville Photographic Archives, Louisville, Ky.—James C. Anderson
University of Oklahoma, Western History Collections, Norman—June Witt
University of Texas, Humanities Research Center, Austin—Joe Coltharp
United Press International, New York, N.Y.—Stan Friedman
Wide World Photos, New York, N.Y.—Fred Canty
Whitney Museum of American Art, New York, N.Y.—Anita Duquette
Worcester Art Museum, Worcester, Mass.—Lynn M. Bajema

Numbers in boldface type refer to illustrations.

Los Angeles: **298–99;** air pollution, 317, **317,** 318–19; Arroyo Seco Parkway (Pasadena Freeway), 265, 300; car ownership and use, 216, 226, 331; freeways, **275,** 300; rapid transit rejected, 216, 330; Westwood suburb, **227**
Los Angeles *Examiner,* 159
Los Angeles *Times,* 317
Louisiana Purchase Exposition (St. Louis, 1904), **34,** 74, 76
Lozier (company and car), 39, 62, 64
Lozier, Henry A., 39
Lunkenheimer, 85
Lutgert, Raymond L., 341
Luverne, 85, 129
Luxor, 85
Lynd, Helen: *Middletown,* 209, 212; *Middletown in Transition,* 254
Lynd, Robert: *Middletown,* 209, 212; *Middletown in Transition,* 254

McAdam, John Loudon, 185, 296, 327
McCahill, Tom, 281
Macauley, Alvan, 213, 238
McCay, Windsor: drawing by, **187**
McCluggage, Denise, 295
McCormick, Cyrus, 103
McCutcheon, John T.: cartoon by, **97**
McDonald, Maurice, 294
McDonald, Richard, 294
McDonald's, 294, 302
McDuffee, Joe, 57
Macerone, Francis: steam carriage, **12**
Machine tools, 37, 39, 103, 135, 190, 240, 246; World War II, 266, 267–68
McIntyre (car), **118**
McIntyre, W. H., **118**
Mackaye, Benton, 264
McManus, Theodore F., 205
McNamara, Robert S., 277
MacPhee, Rudy, 10
Macy & Company, R. H.: Benz car in Chicago *Times-Herald* race, 22, 23, **24–25**
Magee, Carl C., 254
Malcomson, Alexander Y., 45, 46, 158
Manchester *Union,* 80
Mangum (Okla.), **80–81**
Manijklisjski, Woljeck, 111
Markham, Edwin F., 9, 10
Markley, Rodney, 326
Marmon (company and car), 64, 66, 237; V-16, 238
Marmon, Howard C., 40
Marquette, 233
Marquis, Samuel S.: *Henry Ford: An Interpretation,* 139
Marriott, Fred, 61
Mason, George W., 308, 313
Mass transit: as substitute for car commuting, 216, 327, 330–31, 333; *see also* Buses; Interurban lines; Rail transit; Trolleys
Matheson, **89**
Mauldin, Bill: cartoon by, **279**
Maxim, Hiram Percy, 39, 46, 54; *Horseless Carriage Days,* 20, **22**
Maxwell (car), 73, 80, 86, **91,** 115, 119, 120, 169
Maxwell, Jonathan D., 39, 76, 80
Maxwell Motor Company, 81, 113, 114, 119, 120, 164, 169; Maxwell, 73, 80, 86, **91,** 115, 119, 120, 169
May, George S., 32, 134
Maybach, Wilhelm, 19
Mead, Syl, 334–35
Medical Tribune, 321
Meek, Donald, **208**
Meighan, Thomas, **170**
Mercer, **63, 75, 342;** Raceabout, 213
Merciless (car), 85
Mercury (cyclecar), **118**
Mercury, 253, **288,** 303
Merkel, Una, 208

Merritt Parkway, 264–65
Merz, Charles, 141
Metz, 81, 115
Metzger, William E., 119
Michener, Harry, 62
Midgley, Thomas H., Jr., 176, 193
Miller, Arjay, 277
Miller, L. A., 231–32
Mills, D. Ogden, 57
Mitchell Motors Company, **79,** 115, 192
Mobile (Stanley), 28, 57, **58**
Mobile homes and trailers, **151, 199,** 302, **334**
Model T, **2–3,** 46, 82, 97–98, **98,** 98–99, **99, 100, 101,** 102, 103, 104, **106–9,** 110, 113, 114, 116, 117, 119, 128, 129, 134, **137, 138,** 139, **140,** 141, 143, **144–45,** 146–48, 149, **149–55,** 153, 156, 159, 160, **161,** 162, 164, 169, 178, 179, 180–81, 183, 185, 193, 196, 207, **207, 210–11,** 211, 212, 214, 215, 236, **258,** 282, 336; accessories and add-ons, 143, **144–45,** 147–48, **152–53,** 156; adaptations of, **137,** 149, **150–55,** 156; colors, 100, 148, 176, 180; folklore and humor about, 141, **141,** 143, 146, 147; market change and need for replacement, 179, 180–81, 183
Modern Times (movie), 324
Montagu, Lord, 134
Montgomery Ward Company, 83
Moon, 115, 170, 237
Moore, Marianne, 306
Morey, Samuel, 16
Morgan & Company, 114, 119, 160
Morgan, J. P.: 265; in cartoons, **97, 114**
Morrill, George H., Jr., 26
Morris, Henry G.: electric car, **22;** Electrobat II, 22–23
Morris, Lloyd: *Not So Long Ago,* 263
Morrison, William: electric vehicle, 14, 23
Moses, Robert, 327
Motels, 202, 293, 294, 302; *see also* Accommodations
Motocycle, 56, **57**
Motocycle (term), 20, 26, 32, 56
Moto-Cycle Manufacturing Company, 14
Motor, 39, 231, 232
Motor Age, 49, 54, 56, 57, 64
Motor Horse (car), 85
Motor Trend, 295, 306
Motor World, 57, 87
Movies: automobiles and automobile culture in, 83, 207–8, **208,** 208–9, **210–11,** 263, **264;** automobiles owned by stars, 214, **214–15;** drive-in theaters, 254, **264,** 286–87, 295
Mueller, Oscar B., 22, 23
Muir, John S., 83
Mulford, Ralph, 62
Mumford, Lewis, 264, 289, 301
Murphy: custom coachwork, 213
Murphy, Frank, 252
Murray, Charlie, **210**
Music and song, the automobile in, 82, **83,** 85, 207
Muskie, Edmund S., 318
Musselman, M. M.: *Get a Horse!,* 186
Mustang, 314–15

N

Nader, Ralph, 315, 317, 321; *Unsafe at Any Speed,* 314, 315
Nadig, Henry, 19
Nance, James J., 308
Napier, 74, 80
Nash (company and car), 128, 163, 169, 179, 238, 240, 278, 309
Nash, Charles W., 116, 117, 128, 163, **163, 178,** 238, 253
The Nation, 17
National Association of Automobile Manufacturers, 61
National Automobile Chamber of Commerce: banquet, **178–79**
National Cash Register Company, 131
National Industrial Recovery Act (NIRA), 247, 248
National Labor Relations Board, 248, 249, 253
National Petroleum News, 193

National Traffic and Motor Vehicle Safety Act, 319
Nelson, Donald M., 266
Nervous Wreck (play), 207
Neskov-Mumperow (car), 85
Nevins, Allan, 52; on Ford and Ford Motor Company, 98, 102, 110, 135–36, 139, 148, 253, 276
New Orleans, 327
Newport (R.I.): auto fete, 54, **55**
New York *American and Journal,* 82
New York Automobile Show: (1900), 56–57, **58–59;** (1903), 37; (1924), 169
New York City: Crystal Palace exhibition (1857), 16; expressways, 300, 327; rail commuting, 216; traffic, **228;** tunnels, 264
The New Yorker, 99, 102, 326; cartoons and drawings, **203, 212, 319**
New York *Evening Post,* 180
New York *Herald,* 62
New York State: highways, 264, **294–95,** 300
New York *Sun,* 73, 111
New York *Times,* 56, 57, 139, 302, 324, 333
New York Times Magazine, 314
New York to Paris race (1908), 73–74, **74**
New York to St. Louis race (1904), **34,** 74, 76
New York *Tribune,* 36, 136
New York *World,* 52, 57, 83, 181
New York World's Fair (1939): General Motors "Futurama" exhibit, 265, **267**
Niemeyer, Glenn A., 117
999 (Ford), 61
Noise pollution, 51–52
North American Review, 212
Northern, 115, 119

O

Oakland, 115, 128, 176, 233; *see also* Pontiac
O'Connor, Jerry, 23
Odell, Allan, 204
Odell, Clinton, 204
Odell, Leonard, 204
Oelrichs, Mrs. Herman, 54
Office of Price Administration, 271, 273, 275, 279
Office of Production Management, 266
Office of Road Inquiry, 52, 185, 187
Ohio (company): electric car, **44**
Ohio Turnpike, 300
Oldfield, Barney, 62, **63,** 82
Oldsmobile (P. E. Olds & Son; Olds Motor Vehicle Company; Olds Motor Works), **32,** 32–33, **33,** 36, 37, 39, 40, 45, 46, 66, 73, 76, 82, 84, 104, 114, 115, 120, 128, 207, 231, 233, **257,** 289, 303; advertising and publicity, 33, 36, 56, 66, **67, 71,** 82, 86; General Motors acquisition, 114, **114;** Limited, **71;** Model Z, **67;** *Pirate,* 61
Olds, Ransom E., 26, 32, 56, **113,** 134, **179,** 253; Olds companies and Oldsmobile, 26, 32–33, 36, 37, 39, 40, 45, 46, 102, 104, 114; Reo Motor Car Company and Reo, 40, 76, 80, 102, 113, 114, 237
Olympian cars. *See* Classic cars
Opel: General Motors purchase of, 160
Ormond Beach (Fla.) speed trial, 61
Orth, Allen: *The New Necessity,* 185
Oshkosh (steam vehicle), 13
Otto, Nicolaus, 9, 17, **18,** 19
Outing, 52, 88, 196
Outings. *See* Recreation
Overland (company and car), 39, **102, 103,** 120, 238; *see also* Willys-Overland (company and car)
Overland Wind Wagon, **128**
Owen-Magnetic, 115
Owens, Bill: photographs by, **335–36**

P

Pacific Historical Review, 216
Packard (company and car), 40, 57, **71,** 73, **132–33,** 169, 179, 213, 214, **214–15,** 229, 237, 238, 247, 269, 278,

Library of Congress Cataloging in Publication Data

Sears, Stephen W
The American Heritage history of the automobile in America.

Bibliography: p.
Includes index.
1. Automobiles—United States—History. I. Title.
II. Title: History of the automobile in America.
TL15.S425   629.22'22'0973   77-23047
ISBN 0-8281-0200-7
ISBN 0-8281-0201-5 de luxe